Better To Reign In Hell
Serial Killers, Media Panics and the FBI

by Stephen Milligen

headpress

...war on crime...

A Headpress Book
Published in 2006

Headpress
Suite 306, The Colourworks
2a Abbot Street
London
E8 3DP
United Kingdom

[tel] 0845 330 1844
[email] hell@headpress.com
[web] www.headpress.com

BETTER TO REIGN IN HELL
Serial Killers, Moral Panics and the FBI
Text copyright © Stephen Milligen
This volume copyright © 2006 Headpress
Covers & art throughout © Ashley Thorpe
Design & layout: David Kerekes & Hannah Bennison
Editorial Assistants: Temple Drake & Ian Smith
World Rights Reserved

British Library Cataloguing in Publication Data
A catalogue record for this book is available from the British Library

ISBN 1-900486-53-9
EAN 9781900486538

headpress.com

Contents

Acknowledgements

IN ONE OF HIS PUBLICATIONS, AMERICAN SOCIALIST OSCAR Ameringer noted his intention that, "If I were a professional historian I would try to show how little truth I could tell in twelve volumes. But being only an amateur, I endeavor to put the greatest number of facts into the smallest possible space. I don't know all about history. But to my best belief and knowledge the things I tell are true and I'm willing to take an affidavit to that effect. This is a darned sight more than most historians will risk." This is the ideal that sums up the aim of this book, and I hope this work will add something to existing ideas about politics and criminal justice.

In researching *Better To Reign In Hell* many people assisted to varying degrees. I am grateful to all of them, and they all deserve credit. At the outset of my research, Marino Underwood and Frank Bone of the City of Eugene Department of Public Safety (Oregon) provided me with information about their own experiences as police officers in a serial murder investigation, and their colleague Jan Powers helped me to contact the late Pierce Brooks. When I spoke to Brooks he was open and generous with his knowledge, providing several ideas of how my research could progress, and he provided me with introductions to other law enforcement officers. Special thanks should go to Robert Keppel, Chief Investigator for the Washington State Attorney, for the time he gave up in his busy schedule to be interviewed, and for the frankness of his comments.

FBI agents Gordon V Compton (Portland), Arthur P Meister (VICAP, Quantico), Patrick W Kelley (Deputy General Counsel), and Rex S Tomb and Neal Schiff (Fugitive Publicity and Internet Media Services Unit) all took time to answer my questions and provided otherwise unavailable information and opinions. During my research Douglas Honig allowed me access to the ACLU (Seattle) archive, and Barbara Mickey and Audrey Sienkiewicz (Council For Prostitution Alternatives, Portland) gave up their time for an interview not evident in this book but which put much of the unreported violence against prostitutes, who constitute a large number of serial sex killer victims, into perspective.

I thank the Department of Education for Northern Ireland (DENI) for providing funding which allowed me to undertake this research and the secretarial staff of the Humanities faculty at the University of Ulster (Jordanstown) for putting up with me. Debbie Mitchell and Rob Walker regularly saved me from the tenth ring of Dante's Inferno (the one that Dante would have written about had he foreseen computers), without whom numerous technical problems would have driven me insane, and without whom this book would never have been completed. The library staff at Portland State University,

University of Oregon, the Bodleian library in Oxford, and the University of Ulster library (Jordanstown) all provided direction and assistance, especially Jenny Allen and the inter-library loans staff whom I plagued for years with odd requests. A number of people, among them Hamilton and Jennifer Mays, Damian Magee, Matt McKee and Gary McMurray, Larry Harman of *Genetic Disorder*, David Torrans and Laurence Besnard-Scott (No Alibis bookstore), Julia Riches, and Rick Hall all provided help in one way or another collecting information.

The enigmatic 'Der Todesking' helped me to collect information but, more importantly, he supplied his own irreplaceable perspective and wit, which helped to highlight some of the absurdities involved in this work. The irreplaceable esoteric trivia and leads he provided reflected his own unique lifetime of delinquency, not mine, and who also taught me a lot about redemption. I casually wrote David Nolte, in Australia, because of his personal knowledge of several serial sex killers, but his generosity surpassed any hopes I had when he sent me copies of some of his personal correspondence with John Wayne Gacy, thus adding an extra dimension to some of my ideas. John Backderf also shared some of his personal high school reminiscences of Jeffrey Dahmer, which added to my understanding of the killer. One unusual source of information, but nonetheless valuable, was Lawrence Bittaker who provided a view of the criminal justice system and media coverage of a serial sex crime case from the perspective of the accused.

Dr Richard Gid Powers (City University of New York), expert on most things related to the FBI, took the time to share some of his expertise, as did Dr Kathleen McCracken who offered her advice and encouragement for this project. And finally I thank Dr Bill Riches for having the faith to let me start this, the patience to let me continue, and the determination to make sure I finished. He will never be the same again.

For he shall have judgement without
mercy, that hath shewed no mercy; and
mercy rejoiceth against judgement.
(James 2:13)

Note: Whenever the phrase serial sex killer appears, assume that the word serial is in quotation marks; "serial" sex killer.

5

Introduction
Evil is a Medieval Superstition

IN THE 1980S THE SERIAL SEX KILLER EMERGED AS A DOMINANT figure in American popular culture. Credited with superhuman intellect and abilities, the serial killer was accused of attacking the traditional values underpinning American society in a decade marked by conservative politics and resurgent fundamental Protestantism. To patriots, the American way of life is considered especially sacred, a superior social structure in a country imbued with the belief that its origin and destiny has been made manifest by God. In the opinion of one author: "As the first 'democratic' society, the United States occupied a unique moral position and came to regard itself as the spokesman for all mankind."[1] At the beginning of the decade, Ronald Reagan was elected President of America, the most powerful political office in the world. While in office he was reported to have remarked to his friend Jerry Falwell, "I sometimes believe that we're heading very fast for armageddon right now."[2] It is this idea that shaped many of his policies, and of which the serial sex killer proved a suitable symbolic harbinger.

Reagan, however, had been preaching his apocalyptic political rhetoric for decades before becoming President, manipulating public fear of violent crime for his own political gain. In more recent years, the threat of the serial killer has been brought to the public's attention by the Federal Bureau of Investigation (FBI). Serial killers are usually, but falsely, depicted as highly mobile sexually motivated killers who select their 'innocent' victims at random, and they will continue their careers in crime until they are caught or killed. The emergence of serial killers as a 'new' phenomenon, with the offenders usually aged between twenty and thirty-five, subtly identified the 'new' killers as a product of the social changes brought about by Lyndon Johnson's Great Society programs and the liberalization of social values in the 1960s, which Reagan and other conservatives zealously opposed. The moral relativism associated with the change in social values was accused of undermining family values, personal morals and religious ethics. The consequences of the moral relativism and social changes were embodied by serial sex killers who were usually portrayed as products of dysfunctional families and linked with drug and alcohol abuse, sexual promiscuity and deviant religious practices, most commonly Satanism.

According to the FBI, serial killers constituted an attack on the moral fabric of American society, similar to many of the previous panics to which they had alerted the public. Cultural theorists refer to such threats as 'moral panics' that undermine the security and standards of a society as a whole, and they can come from a person, a group, or a particular condition. When "a condition, episode, person or group of persons emerges to become defined as a threat to societal values and interests," barricades are manned by moralists and experts who present their solutions, which are then transmitted by the mass media in a "stylized and stereotypical" fashion.[3] Moral panic is a heavily descriptive term identifying the process in individual cases of moral enterprise and political opportunism. As Richard Sparks has suggested, "It sensitizes us to the fact that a moment of heightened moral anxiety occurs but does not in and of itself illuminate what is substantively at stake in the rhetorics that encircle a given issue nor why that issue should attract a particular kind of attention at some particular time."[4]

A wide audience was familiar with the characteristics of the serial sex killer, and had been so for nearly a century, but the origin of the term serial sex killer is credited to the FBI in the early 1980s and coincided with the rise to power of the New Right of the Republican party. The FBI's long involvement in the investigation of sexual deviance was skillfully hidden behind the traditional myth of the dynamic G-Man fighting a perpetual war on crime to defend traditional American values. The formation of the Bureau's Behavioral Sciences Unit (BSU), however, marked the FBI's first overt involvement in investigating sex crimes. Joel Achenbach remarked that, "The imaginary serial killer is a powerful creation, brilliant at his craft, an implacable death machine. He's like a shark, driven not by mindless hunger but by a malevolence—evil if you will."[5] A concise description of the conventional representation of serial sex killers during the 1980s. Importantly, Achenbach does acknowledge that the serial sex killer is imaginary, but he does not enlighten his readers as to who is doing the imagining.

Crime is an important political issue, especially for the New Right, and a subject to which large amounts of space in magazines and newspapers, and airtime on television is devoted, magnifying public fear. The more

Introduction

shocking and sensational a crime is, the greater the amount of reporting and discussion there will be, and the greater the fear generated. The criminal justice system is not neutral, it is "run by men and institutions, many men, many institutions, often for their own ends."[6] Crime myths divert attention, and the ability to create crime panics and identify the threats faced by society carries a considerable amount of power.

The purpose of this book is to examine the emergence of serial sex killers in the 1980s. Why and from where did serial sex killers suddenly emerge? What did they symbolize? What was their social and political significance? The political significance of serial sex killers in the 1980s crime debate and the ideological relationship between the FBI, who defined the term, and the New Right of the Republican party who exploited crime issues as a means to justify extreme crime policies has largely been ignored. The symbolic crime panics in the 1980s were all clearly identifiable as being, according to the ideology of Reagan, the New Right and the FBI, products of 1960s liberalism and its departure from 'traditional' Christian family values. Other panics focused disproportionate attention on child abductions by strangers, 'satanic' cult crimes, and the detrimental effect of rap and rock music on American youth. Reagan's use of frightening figures as a primary means of social control is reflected in Steven Donziger's observation that it is not crime itself, but the public's fear of crime that drives American government policy.[7] Significantly Reagan's manner and political rhetoric was steeped in Old Testament zeal and imagery.

Crime rhetoric in the twentieth century has always been dominated by conservative spokesmen and has often reverted to superstitious language about 'evil' men and their deeds reflecting nostalgia for a pre-scientific era when Satan was used as an explanation for transgression and deviance; simple explanations appealed to superstitious fear rather than reason or understanding of complicated and confusing technological and legal terms. Mainstream political and social debate was irretrievably linked to the Puritan theology of John Calvin: individual predestination, either as eternal damnation or salvation, was beyond the control of anyone except God. Such theological explanations bypassed the need for effective policies to treat the systematic social causes of crime.

American politicians have produced some desperate scapegoats, whose credibility was derived more from public hysteria than considered judgment. However, the short-term political gains make this tactic appear effective. Walter Lippman observed that,

> Without a tyrant to attack an immature democracy is always somewhat bewildered. Yet we have to face the fact in America that what thwarts the growth of our civilization is not the uncanny, malicious contrivance of the plutocracy, but the faltering method of the distracted soul, and the murky vision of what we call grandiloquently the will of the people.[8]

With this statement Lippman summed up much of the political history of the

Better To Reign In Hell

United States. Politicians desperately seek an aggressor who plots to undermine the values and security of the state, but the real threat is posed by the citizens of the nation. In his famous 1933 inauguration speech Franklin Roosevelt identified the power of fear when he said, "Let me assert my firm belief that the only thing we have to fear is fear itself—nameless, unreasoning, unjustified terror which paralyzes needed efforts to convert threat into advance."[9] During the twentieth century numerous crime panics, often based on an ethnic or physical characteristic, made the deviant group instantly identifiable to the majority of the population. Emile Durkheim observed, "crime brings together upright consciences and concentrates them."[10] This creates a moral cohesion, and the focus of the panic shows the individuals which roles should be avoided and which ones emulated in the 'gallery of types' erected by society.[11] Crimes have to be brought to the public's attention before their consciences can be focused, and the manner in which crime myths are "created and dispersed throughout society has important implications for understanding how class interests become articulated in cultural forms."[12]

A resurgence in the belief in 'evil' as a cause of crime in the 1960s replaced an understanding of mental illness, and in that mode of thinking the death penalty became a ritual exorcism. Several writers have noted that in previous centuries mass and serial murder were explained by demonology, or a belief in external forces controlling events in human lives. Once convinced that the killers possess superhuman powers and are controlled by demonic forces, the public must resort to faith, hoping for a miraculous event to end the murders.[13] Caryl Chessman, who became a scapegoat for the Los Angeles Police Department (LAPD) in 1960, observed from his own experience that criminals become monsters *because* they kill, they do not kill because they are monsters. However, once they are misrepresented in such a way it is an outrage to the public to accord criminals the due process of law, especially in cases of serial sex murder.[14]

The return to apocalyptic religious explanations for many social and political issues in the 1980s reflected changes in how the American public perceived themselves and their place in the world. In *True Believer* (1951), Eric Hoffer wrote that, "Faith in a holy cause is to a considerable extent a substitute for the lost faith in ourselves." Hoffer's thesis was acted out in the US in the 1970s due to defeat in Vietnam, economic decline and liberal challenges to traditional values. Hoffer also noted that all mass movements "breed fanaticism, enthusiasm, fervent hope, hatred and intolerance... all of them demand blind faith and singlehearted allegiance."[15] This is an accurate description of the Republican New Right and the New Christian Right, "America's new old-fashioned zealots,"[16] who emerged from the 1970s economic *malaise*. Following his demonization of student dissidents during his time as Governor of California in the 1960s, Reagan's creation of bogeymen reached its symbolic apex in the 1980s with the identification of the serial sex killer, who selects numerous random victims and continues his criminal career for many years, as a major threat to American society. The FBI predicted nationwide increases in violent crime throughout the 1980s and into the 1990s,[17] a suitably

Introduction

apocalyptic estimation in light of the crime rhetoric of the era and a predictable continuation of J Edgar Hoover's annual pronouncements forecasting an ever increasing tide of crime. In this climate of exaggerated fear of crime, police agencies were called to do their duty, to 'protect and serve,' and politicians were less concerned with the social and economic forces which promote the likelihood of crime. All of these factors created a political atmosphere more heavily reliant on police control.[18] In the perceived crisis it was possible for the government to extend police powers or pass legislation which would normally meet with public disapproval, but in more desperate times and amid public calls for more action, mainly from victims rights advocates, extreme legislation seemed appropriate.

Relying on religious symbolism and language to justify the New Right policies Reagan and his supporters credited themselves as being part of a cosmic struggle, a holy war between good and evil. Richard Hofstadter described this as the "Paranoid Style of American Politics," a "way of seeing the world and expressing oneself." In this view of the world, "a feeling of persecution is central, and it is indeed systematized in grandiose theories of conspiracy... directed against a nation, a culture, a way of life whose fate affects not himself [the paranoid believer] alone but millions of others."[19] Hofstadter's 'paranoid style' is reflected in the rhetoric of J Edgar Hoover, Ronald Reagan and many other conservative figures seeking to draw attention to a particular issue or problem which serves their political purpose. During the Reagan era domestic crime panics became more apparent.

Better To Reign In Hell

A crime panic like that of the serial sex killer, because of the random nature of the crimes, affects everyone and everything and, therefore, inevitably it shapes how people perceive society, and how they live within that society. Hofstadter's observation that once unleashed the central idea of the panic sprawls out to become "a vast and sinister conspiracy, a gigantic and yet subtle machinery of influence set in motion to undermine and destroy a way of life,"[20] was clearly identifiable as a consequence of Reagan's rhetoric. In his book *Jeffrey Dahmer* (1992), Dr Joel Norris, one of many psychiatrists to involve themselves in writing 'true crime' books about sensational murders, claimed that serial killers such as Dahmer "represent an attack on the entire moral structure of a community."[21]

Dr James Brussel, the inspiration for the FBI's psychological profilers, describes paranoia as a "chronic disorder of insidious development characterized by persistent, unalterable, systematized, logically constructed delusion." He further adds that even when presented with information contradicting their delusions the paranoiac holds firm as the "world's champion grudge holder,"[22] an observation which provides an interesting insight into the ideologies of J Edgar Hoover and the New Right. The delusion is a way for the paranoiac to avoid admitting his own weakness by using others as a scapegoat. Brussel lists several possible expressions for the paranoiac, a "pathologically self-centered" or "narcissistic" individual, one of which is joining "oddball" political groups.[23] 'Paranoid' is an accurate description of the apocalyptic zeal of J Edgar Hoover and the New Right as well as the conservative world view of many serial sex killers.

The typical profile of a serial sex killer is a symbol of social degeneracy, the opposite of the conservative social values which had been promoted heavily by Richard Nixon, and which were making a strong comeback during Ronald Reagan's administration. These include family values, Christian morals, more subtle racial boundaries, and a heterosexual lifestyle. In contrast, the serial sex killer was what Harold Schechter described as a "savage force roaming in the dark, as the nuclear family huddles terrified inside the home."[24] However, some commentators have noted that in analyzing American values,

> We have resorted so often to violence that we have long since become a 'trigger happy' people. Violence is ostensibly rejected by us as a part of the American value system, but so great has been our involvement with both negative and positive violence over the long sweep of our history that violence has truly become part of our unacknowledged (or underground) value structure.[25]

Elliot Leyton, notable for his attempt to examine the social origins of mass murder, writes that, "No single quality of American culture is so distinctive as its continued assertion of the nobility and beauty of violence—a notion and a mythology propagated with excitement and craft in all popular cultural forms, including films, television, and print."[26] Elayne Rapping puts it more bluntly saying, "We, as a society, love violence, sanction violence, thrive on violence

Introduction

as the very basis of our social stability, our ideological belief system."[27] This 'love' of violence underpins much of the New Right's ideology, which condones dynamic militaristic conflict to provide a cathartic spectacle for the public rather than engage in mundane long-term policies to prevent crime and other social problems. 'Crime' is generally synonymous with 'violent crime' and is a powerful political weapon in elections, giving virtually all crime a political . significance.

After more than two decades of crime hysteria, conservative politicians, the FBI and the prison industrial complex got the Hell they wanted to reign in for their own professional and financial gain. The myths of crime that feed the political debate are a misrepresentation of the social reality that causes crime, and political denial makes the situation worse. The identification of the supercriminal as a threat to society requires police officers of superior talents to combat them, a conflict that has defined the image of the FBI G-Man since the 1930s, and adequate resources to wage a 'War on Crime.' For almost the entire of their history the FBI have fulfilled this role pursuing symbolic criminals to maintain the *status quo*.

Fidelity, Bravery and Integrity
The Rise and Fall of the FBI Myth

IN THE FIELD OF LAW ENFORCEMENT THE FEDERAL BUREAU of Investigation is popularly seen as an elite force with the most prestigious reputation of any agency in the United States: the moral guardians of society. The organization was headed by J Edgar Hoover who, in the tradition of Hofstadter's 'paranoid style' of politics, saw virtually any deviance as part of the insidious menace undermining every aspect of American society and its values. From the middle of the 1930s until the late 1950s, the Bureau presented an image through news media and popular cultural representations of a heroic crime fighter, the valiant G-Man who would protect the stability of American society against all who would try to subvert it. It was, quite simply, a battle of 'good' against 'evil.'

The image of a 'moral mission' was created and maintained by careful public relations and political ambitions, creating a fear, and providing a solution to a series of 'crime problems.' Eventually, publicity generated by the Bureau allowed it to become regarded, by the public and politicians, as the world's most efficient law enforcement agency, without necessarily fulfilling the role. In the chaos of Prohibition and the Depression, the Bureau assured an uncertain population that they could return to a previous era, a safer time: all that was required was to unleash the forces of law and order against the criminal and radical elements in society. In part this was achieved through a series of panics such as the Yellow Peril, White Slavery, Nazi Saboteurs and the Red Scare, all of which, it was alleged, threatened to overthrow the American way of life. During this time the FBI maintained a high prestige, becoming the "quintessential example of the crime-control establishment in American life."[1]

Rather than becoming the most efficient agency, the Bureau's power came from its ability to shape attitudes towards crime and crime control. Having a high media profile, the Bureau featured in numerous *Gangbusters* radio dramas, the *Crime Does Not Pay* and *Persons In Hiding* film series, and later *G-Men* and *The FBI* television shows, as well as conducting its own highly publicized investigations. It was born into, and has remained a part of, the American media circus. The Bureau's early role needs to be explored if its part in the creation of the serial sex killer panic is to be fully appreciated.

Theodore Roosevelt directed his Attorney General, Charles J Bonaparte to create an investigative service within the Department of Justice that would not be subject to control by any other government department or bureau; it would only report to the Attorney General. Before this, the Justice Department and other government departments had exploited the practice of borrowing Secret Service agents from the Treasury Department when necessary, but while on loan the agents would still report to the chief of the Secret Service. Borrowing agents was stopped by an amendment to the Sundry Civil Appropriation Act on May 27, 1908, with which Congress prohibited the Department of Justice and other executive departments from borrowing Secret Service agents to avoid congressional oversight. Creating a new agency was the easiest way to solve the investigative problem and the Special Agent Force (SAF) was established. Congress denied the initial request for a SAF on the grounds that it was anti-democratic, and likened to the secret police of Tsarist Russia. Bonaparte waited until the legislature went into recess and proceeded to illegally establish his 'secret police,' ignoring protests.[2]

Since its foundation in a "blaze of publicity,"[3] on July 26, 1908, the SAF was allegedly to fight the greed of big businesses that were, in conjunction with some US senators, ignoring government anti-trust laws. The agency was the sign that the federal government was fighting back against crime.[4] In a similar way, Roosevelt's reputation as a reformer was exploited in his anti-trust prosecutions, which had "little bite." Instead of real reform, Roosevelt used the weapon of publicity and his newly formed Bureau of Corporations to reassure the public that he shared their concern,[5] albeit symbolically more than practically.

The SAF caused enough positive public response that, under President Taft, it officially became the Bureau of Investigation on March 16, 1909, as an attempt by progressive legislators to expand federal jurisdiction over crime at the expense of local and state police agencies that had traditionally carried the responsibility. Before the formation of the Bureau, there was no real sense of national crime. Even acts such as assassinations were seen as a local issue, a challenge to local authority and order, and not set in a national context. Since

1830 crime reporting had been a staple of American journalism, but "local readers were interested in local crime." In the 1890s, thanks to the Pulitzer-Hearst press wars, "crime news gathered from police blotters everywhere and shared by papers all over the country was creating the impression in the local reader that crime was everywhere and that, no matter how far away, it concerned him."[6]

Editors of newspapers were faced with the problem of making a distant crime seem significant to their local readers. This problem was overcome by "treating crimes as facts not significant in themselves but significant as proving the existence of a much more important situation, a crime wave." Reporting of crime would change the public perception in the early years of the twentieth century, causing people to see a national crime problem, and demanding the federal government do something about it.[7] Once the idea of a crime problem is established in the media, "For the spectators of the political scene every act contributes to a pattern of ongoing events that spells threat or reassurance."[8] The SAF allowed Theodore Roosevelt to have a platform to publicly pose as a symbol of law and order to combat the problem, and the Bureau has continued to serve subsequent presidents in the same way.

The hero-making attempts of official FBI historians such as Don Whitehead were exercises in propaganda. In the opinion of former agent William Turner, "Whitehead's critical faculties remained suspended during the critical process. He omits or glosses over Bureau blunders, paints a glowing picture of unmitigated FBI successes, and never points an admonishing finger at the director or his charges."[9] The Bureau's function was the promotion of "mass quiescence by fighting crime in whatever symbolic form the popular mind might imagine it." Sustained by offering a convenient means for a succession of public officials to appear to exhibit concern for any issues, which might "disturb the tranquility of the public imagination,"[10] the FBI influence grew.

From its initial design, expansion of the Bureau's jurisdiction came with the White Slavery Traffic Act in 1910 (also known as the Mann Act), which was aimed at preventing the interstate transportation of, or foreign commerce in, women and girls for immoral purposes. The image of sexual slavery captured the public imagination by combining moral outrage and lurid sensationalism in headlines reporting white women descending to their ruin. The notion of prostitution as forced slavery was easier for the public and investigators to accept than the idea that some women preferred the oldest profession to avoid menial occupations, and in the panic it was commonly accepted that any woman not locked behind closed doors was at risk from the slavers.

The Mann Act raised prostitution from a local issue to a national concern allowing the Bureau to take the first steps towards becoming a national crime-fighting organization.[11] The Act itself did little to address an incoherent and exaggerated fear, but it did allow the government to avoid having to grapple with the source of the problem, because it was not in the government's power to do anything about it.[12] The 'White Slavery' Traffic Act allowed the government to show (symbolically) that it shared the general public's fear that traditional sexual morality and ideas of the sanctity of the family and

The Rise And Fall Of The FBI Myth

home were under attack.

David J Langum described the Mann Act as "an absurd law,"[13] and "a splendid example of the failure of American democracy and the federal government, at least as far as the politicization of morality is concerned."[14] In retrospect, he acknowledges, it was a "significant factor in the growth of the FBI,"[15] and adds, the "evils" of the Mann Act "far outweigh any benefits of combating the largely mythical white slavery."[16] The Bureau then became a police force to punish deviations from conservative values and sexual morality.

When faced with complaints that his Bureau would be duplicating work which local and state police agencies were already performing, Stanley Finch, the Bureau of Investigation's first director, responded in a manner which would be repeated by the Bureau many times through the following decades. He stated it was a job that only the Bureau of Investigation could do satisfactorily, and supported his claim with accusations of lax local and state investigations as well as corruption. Congress voted the requested funds to the Bureau, and Finch set in motion his plans that would act as the forerunners of the nationwide dragnet methods, which would prove so useful to the Bureau in the years that followed.[17] But Finch's Bureau became as politicized and corrupt as any other government agency.

Within a few years Bureau power was again expanded, at the expense of the Bill of Rights. With the outbreak of WWI, President Woodrow Wilson created the Committee on Public Information (CPI), the purpose of which was to win the "hearts and minds" of the American people. Headed by a journalist, George Creel, the CPI was a massive exercise in manipulating public opinion. In the absence of radio and television, newspapers were the main source of news for the general public and all newspapers printed CPI approved news, and even schools taught with CPI approved materials. Creel sent speakers to men's and women's clubs to lecture audiences on how they could win the war for America. The CPI also produced poems, blessings and prayers, and drew cartoons all with the single aim of making the war seem like an endeavor worth dying for.[18] This was done by planting the seeds of conformity and intolerance.

Anyone who dissented from President Wilson and the CPI was labeled a 'radical' and the term came to cover a wide variety of people, all of whom wanted to change the system. In this climate the Bureau was given responsibility for espionage, sabotage, sedition and draft violations, and an increase in its budget. Upon the signing of the armistice in 1918, the Bureau's funding was cut back to peacetime levels, but public attention and a higher budget were restored when the Bureau revealed the existence of a new menace, peacetime radicalism, which was "the gravest menace to the country today."[19] Returning veterans, four million of them, along with nine million domestic workers, had to find new jobs but there were few to be found. The America they returned to was different: "During the war Americans had been trained to the scapegoat theory. If something is wrong, don't try to solve it, but find someone to blame." With the war over the new enemy threatening the fabric of American life was seen to be Bolshevism, and everyone went hunting for Bolsheviks.[20]

Better To Reign In Hell

The anti-radical division (General Intelligence Division [GID]) was created in August 1919, with J Edgar Hoover assuming the position as its first chief, and along with the ambitious Attorney General Mitchell Palmer, who aspired to be president, they set about putting down 'Bolshevik' radical groups. Even before ascending to direct the Bureau of Investigation, Hoover already displayed Hofstadter's 'paranoid style' of politics, identifying a systematic conspiracy directed at the American way of life, and therefore affecting millions of people. Hoover set up a card file system to collect the names of suspected radicals, their organizations, and publications, and from these files Hoover estimated that there were 60,000 dangerous radicals. Since ninety per cent of them were alien immigrants, Palmer used the 1918 Immigration (Deportation) Act to rid the country of the radicals. Hoover told his agents that their investigations should be particularly directed towards "persons not citizens of the United States, with a view of obtaining deportation cases." Dragnet raids on suspected radical groups helped the Bureau to further expand their dossiers with membership lists and papers of radical groups. Soon deportation boats became known as "Soviet Arks," and Hoover promised more "Arks," as many as were necessary.[21]

Throughout the rest of his life Hoover would continue as he had started, hunting progressives and radicals, whom conservatives claimed were grave threats to American society.[22] 'Red Scare' raids reached their peak on January 2, 1920, with what became known as the Night Of Terror, when 4,000 radicals were arrested in thirty-three cities across the United States. Meetinghouses and private homes were searched and citizens were arrested without warrants. Ridiculously high bails were set on radicals, the normal sum of $500 was inflated to $10,000, far beyond the reach of common laborers, men whom Louis Post, the Assistant Secretary for Labor, described as mostly honest laborers and good citizens.[23]

The public wanted to believe that the raids were to protect them. The *Washington Post* described the raids' methods as "hair splitting," and comments by Hoover showed his lack of regard for the arrested men. In his view, giving aliens access to legal advice "defeated the ends of justice." But the Night Of Terror had gone too far. The public began to question Palmer's activities; the shock of the raids had prompted a return to common sense and decency. Of the 4,000 arrests in the Night Of Terror, 1,300 were released because the Justice Department lacked evidence against them, prompting questions to be raised about the Department's methods. But even if all the arrested men had been dangerous radicals, the Hoover and Palmer raids had managed to arrest less than one per cent of Hoover's own estimated total. "By any standards it was a poor showing." Red Scare raids, it was claimed, led to a "marked cessation of revolutionary activities in the United States." Palmer boasted of halting "Red Radicalism," but did not point out the terrible treatment of the prisoners, to the extent that some of them died of pneumonia in prison before they were charged. He also did not mention that in the course of the raids the First, Fourth, Fifth and Eighth Amendment rights of those arrested were violated. A report by the National Civil Liberties Bureau and

The Rise And Fall Of The FBI Myth

the National Popular Government League described the Justice Department abuses under Hoover and Palmer, and their propaganda as "an advertising campaign in favor of repression."[24] This was not, however, to be interpreted as an end to the threat and Palmer warned that Congress must not economize where the Bureau was concerned, further arguing that the Bureau's wartime rate of expenditure had to be maintained in order to safeguard the United States.[25]

After the war, passage of the National Motor Theft Act (Dyer Act) in 1919 broadened Bureau jurisdiction to include the interstate theft of cars. Even though boasts were made concerning the effectiveness of Bureau enforcement of the Dyer Act, no substantial decrease in the theft of automobiles was seen in Hoover's first twenty-six years in charge. It was only after Hoover's death that a decrease in motor theft was announced.[26]

On August 22, 1921, J Edgar Hoover was transferred from his civil service post as special assistant to the Attorney General to the post of the Assistant Director of the Bureau of Investigation. Shortly after this, in 1922, William J Burns, then Bureau chief, and his assistant Hoover, testified that the interstate commercial operations in vice had, for the most part, been smashed. Selective enforcement of the Mann Act enhanced the Bureau's statistics and prestige while adding to a panic in society that 'juvenile delinquents' were undermining accepted values. The Bureau had read more into the Act than was originally envisioned and was also arresting many persons who crossed state lines for non-commercial immorality. By 1930 Congressman Dyer of Missouri, the man responsible for the National Motor Theft Act, objected that the Act was being used against young people who had taken cars for "joy rides" without any intention of committing a crime such as those envisioned by the Act which he authored. Application of this Act by the Bureau had brought many juveniles into federal courts, and into the prison system. Between 1946 and 1950, enforcement of the Dyer Act by the Bureau was responsible for more than half of the juvenile delinquents in the federal prison system. This Act was to be a major building block for the future expansion of Bureau activity. Fears were already growing over the policy and actions of the Bureau, and resulted in demands that the Department of Justice should be investigated. In 1922 three Republican senators tried to introduce a bill to this effect, but their effort was unsuccessful and only ensured that their names were added to a list of suspects to be kept under surveillance by the Bureau.[27] Further accusations of improper conduct came in 1924 and 1931, but the Bureau always survived, and surveillance lists got longer.

On May 10, 1924, Hoover was appointed as director of the Bureau of Investigation by the new Attorney General Harlan Stone, and took control with explicit instructions to professionalize the Bureau. Before accepting the assignment, Hoover ensured that all appointments within the Bureau should be divorced from outside interference, and that he himself should have sole control over promotions. It was ironic that the architect of the 'Palmer Raids' was selected to reorganize and clean up the Bureau. Prior to that time criticism of the Bureau had grown from important, influential sources until Stone's appointment, when the anti-radical programs were temporarily halted and their methods of investigation altered.

Endorsing an ideology of 'scientific management,' Hoover took on the mantle of punishing lawbreakers, while at the same time enforcing a public conservative morality. The Bureau expanded its dossier collection as distressed citizens all across the country volunteered "all kinds of information about the travels of strangers, acquaintances, relatives, or even themselves."[28] Attempting to rationalize the Bureau's administration, Hoover sought the most efficient method of operation, and his background in law and bureaucracy prepared him well for the efficient management of information, no matter how irrelevant. Files were packed with miscellaneous trivia, which someday could be important in an investigation. While limited in their jurisdiction and power to act independently of local police, the Bureau functioned to gather information and co-ordinate interstate investigations. In the early 1930s this changed, and with it the nature of law enforcement.

Restricted by their lack of authority to carry guns and make arrests, the Bureau's agents had to be accompanied by local police officers. Under these circumstances they remained an obscure governmental agency during the Prohibition years.[29] This would remain true throughout the 1920s and into the 1930s, until Attorney General Homer S Cummings' anti-crime crusade and the opportunism of Hoover (with a few timely cases) further expanded the jurisdiction of the Bureau of Investigation, and began a legend. After Hoover assumed control of the Bureau emphasis shifted from publicly enforcing conservative sexual morality with the Mann and Dyer Acts, although information on sexual impropriety filled Hoover's files, to hunting for 'Public Enemies,' radicals and communists.

Historian Samuel Hopkins Adams believes that when Hoover took control of the FBI, the public's perception of government through newspaper reports was one of widespread political corruption and something had to be done to assure them that the government was able to cope with the crisis. The Department of Justice had reached its "lowest ebb in morale, morals and efficiency."[30] Using a diverse public relations campaign, numerous avenues of dissemination were used by the Bureau: magazines, books, newspapers, television, public speeches, radio broadcasts, leaks, and the FBI tour at the National Academy all spread the word as Hoover and his public relations advisors would have it heard. In the course of his career, at least 178 articles were attributed to Hoover, over a hundred of which were published in major magazines. Others appeared in *Christianity Today*, *Catholic Action*, *Disabled American Veterans* magazine, and *The Elks* magazine, among others, all of which found a conservative religious audience. Throughout his career Hoover was consistently successful in getting his (ghostwritten) manuscripts published. Distinctive for its longevity and success over five decades, the campaign was a "benchmark governmental publicity drive."[31]

Hoover's management of the Bureau is popularly thought to have been efficient and effective, but this is a retrospective judgment not based on fact. When Franklin Roosevelt assumed the presidency, Hoover's position as Bureau chief came under threat because of doubts about Hoover's effectiveness. Only when his prospective replacement, Senator Thomas J Walsh, died was Hoover reprieved, but the experience was one that he had taken seriously. Walsh had proposed many changes in personnel in the Justice Department, and after his near dismissal Hoover maintained a close alliance with President Roosevelt, Attorney General Cummings, and their inner circle of advisors.[32] Roosevelt and Cummings had ambitious plans for the Bureau, intending to exploit public interest in sensational crimes to advance specific legislative objectives.

New criminals who had emerged from the prohibition era were portrayed in newspapers as mobile and opportunistic. Villains identified by Hoover were, thanks to technology and public relations, much more vivid than earlier criminals, and therefore better known to the public. They were said to exploit the jurisdictional boundaries which existed between police agencies, by "fleeing across county lines after robbing... banks and trains,"[33] similar claims were made about serial killers in the 1980s. It was necessary to put an end to all of their immoral criminal careers. The criminal's mobility in the 1920s was itself a justification for the Bureau's involvement in these new investigations: as soon as the criminal crossed a state line special agents would join the investigation, and they 'always got their man.'

After creating an image of the criminals, Hoover created an image of the agents, dictating that they "should act like young businessmen."[34] Hoover conceded that, "our Special Agents, in a broad sense, are really salesmen."[35] Appearances, were, and are, everything to the Bureau. An agent's image was a metaphor for his, and the Bureau's, deeds, and the image was intended to show them as "a cross-section of American life."[36] The cardinal sin was to make an error that would embarrass the Bureau.[37]

Trained in law, science, engineering or accounting, agents were supposed to be versatile, and adaptability was as important to the Bureau as academic achievement. The image of dark suits, tidy haircuts, and an always clean-shaven appearance was transmitted into popular culture by gangster movies of the mid 1930s.

It was said that by stressing the careful selection of highly qualified candidates and their strong moral character, an agent cadre of unusually high quality would be built. This image was aimed to contrast with that of government investigators of the previous decade who had been found ineffective and susceptible to bribery.[38] A former Bureau agent believed that what Hoover really sought in a candidate was "a good white Anglo-Saxon, preferably an Irishman with conservative values," and that Hoover would see candidates who met these criteria got the job, no matter what their qualifications.[39] What Hoover was primarily interested in was the way that his agents thought. Applications from candidates with liberal views were passed over in favor of recruits who were more conservative and, according to former agent Jack Levine, they were "heavily indoctrinated in radical right wing propaganda."[40] Hoover's image building gave a structure to the Bureau but the agents were still anonymous to the general public, vaguely called 'feds,' but without notoriety. Later critics would call into question the ability of Hoover's "college boys," with their six months of criminology training, to crack the criminal underworld.[41]

Reportedly agents possessed a team spirit similar to that of the US Marines and showed a very low turnover. In the early years of the Bureau this was true because job security and benefits provided by the civil service were strong enticements, so much so that it was claimed that turnover of agents was only one half of one per cent in 1955, according to the FBI.[42] From their first day at the Bureau, agents were presented with the lure of retirement benefits, and once they had set their sights on that they were unlikely to do anything that might jeopardize it. The ideology of the Bureau was extremely conservative, as was the conduct it required. Secretaries were not allowed to smoke on the job, there were no coffee breaks, and agents were transferred for being overweight and reprimanded for reading *Playboy*. The bureaucratic structure, dominated by one man, bred sycophancy, with promotion going to those agents who pandered to Hoover.[43]

Problems became apparent in 1961 when Hoover issued a directive that prospective agents were to sign an agreement stating they would remain with the Bureau for at least three years. Too many new agents, after completing their training, would only remain with the Bureau for a brief service and then resign. Recruitment had suffered, and "the promise of an FBI career no longer cast a magic spell over young law graduates." New agent classes at the National Academy in Fall 1960 had to be postponed because new recruits were in short supply. There was only one solution to the problem: the lowering of admission standards for prospective agents. Directives claimed this was only a temporary measure and it was not to be publicized, but the 'temporary' relaxation was permanent. Enticements were made to lure retired agents back and to encourage those who were eligible to retire to stay on. The Bureau claimed that recruiting problems were due to the high requirements placed upon the agents, others believed that morale was at an all-time low because of Hoover's cult of personality and Neolithic personnel policies.[44]

By controlling the figures for its personnel the Bureau could manipulate the public impression of the situation, and since the Bureau was answerable to virtually no one it had a greater amount of freedom to paint the picture chosen. To support the good team image the Bureau relied on an orthodox and conservative structure in bureaucracy, with a strict procedure for every eventuality. Unfortunately, emphasis on teamwork may be more consistent with the bureaucratic process, but it "may not be the best way to solve crimes."[45] It has been noted by former Bureau agents that to advance in the Bureau an aptitude for bureaucracy, rather than detection, was required.

Inside the Bureau the myth caused an ambivalent attitude. Agents realized the benefit of the strong image that Hoover had built, resulting in the prestige felt by each agent, as well as the pay scales and retirement benefits for Bureau agents, which were unparalleled in government. But "they are also aware of a darker side: of the martinet whose system is a masterpiece of quibbling, the supreme leader consumed by megalomania, the insecure celebrity infuriated by specks of dust on his trophies."[46] It was not until after the Bureau's reputation had been long established, using statistics, the media and public relations, that Hoover's cult of personality became apparent.

Apart from Hoover's personality and public relations other factors increased the influence of the FBI. In 1927 the International Association of the Chiefs of Police (IACP) formed a Committee on Uniform Crime Reports (UCR) with responsibility to "develop a nation-wide system of uniform police statistics that would not only serve law enforcement administrators but would provide a measure of criminal activity throughout the country."[47] The Committee published its handbook in November 1929, and this still provides the definitive framework for the reporting of crime to the FBI. In turn, the collected statistics provide the basis for the Bureau's annual budget appropriations claim that goes before Congress.[48]

Uniform Crime Reporting began on September 1, 1930, as a specialized guide for law enforcement, but in the following half century the UCR statistics were a widely quoted research source for sociologists, legislators, municipal planners, scholars, the press, citizens and criminal justice planners.[49] American criminologists have long been skeptical of the accuracy of official crime statistics but they are "the only game in town,"[50] and with no real alternative they have reluctantly used them as the major source of data. Overestimation or underestimation of crime totals was quickly observed as a possibility, but it would be virtually impossible to tell which was the case. The statistics were compiled from thousands of local police jurisdictions, but different jurisdictions would not necessarily record crime accurately, or even in the same way: "Even the renowned FBI Uniform Crime Reports are dependent on the whims of many tiny police jurisdictions, who may file their reports if and when they choose."[51] Such was the state of affairs that even the FBI refused to vouch for their accuracy. Local police had an obvious stake in the representation of crime levels. If a local crime rate was seen to be decreasing (no matter what the reason for the decrease might be), local police could win public confidence and support for their perceived efficiency. If the crime rate were seen to increase then the police would have grounds to demand increases in their budgets for the fight against crime.[52]

To ensure their ability to solve crimes, Hoover is credited with pioneering the use of scientific laboratory techniques and the accurate reporting and filing of information. Hoover idolized science. According to Hoover, agents not only had to be right at all times, they also had to give the appearance of being right,[53] and science was presented as the definitive weapon for the future of law enforcement. The Identification Division, housing a centralized fingerprint file, was opened in 1925, followed by the crime laboratory in 1932, and the National Police Academy in 1935. Under Hoover the Bureau's fingerprint archive became the largest in the world, and he hoped one day to have everyone's fingerprints on file, not just the guilty. He could not understand why anyone would object, unless they had something to hide.

In 1933 Hoover wrote an article about the enforcement of the Mann Act, focusing on commercial prostitution, which did more to promote the Bureau fingerprint index and argued that "the extension of its use to vice cases is of extreme importance."[54] Pointing out that he thought it "strange" that some police departments would send the fingerprints of anyone arrested to the Bureau, except for those of prostitutes (who, he acknowledges, are usually arrested for disorderly conduct or vagrancy rather than prostitution), he noted that without fingerprints it is difficult to trace the whereabouts of such women because they frequently change their names.[55] Emphasizing the Bureau's economic utility Hoover alleges that "it is possible to cover the entire of the United States and the entire field of activity [white slavery] with but a comparatively small group of men."[56]

Hoover's method of building his archive was a departure from previous detective agencies, which would only retain prints of the guilty, or of those whose guilt or innocence, had still to be proved. Work associations through to women's sewing circles, believing it was their patriotic duty, would provide their prints, however unlikely the volunteer might be as a potential criminal, and the Bureau accepted them. Scientific police work was publicized as though it were a Bureau invention. While some of the discoveries were known to have been imported from Europe, such as fingerprinting, the model for the Bureau was the Chicago Crime Detection Laboratory, pioneered by Colonel Calvin Goddard. Bureau agents enrolled in Goddard's classes, replicated his equipment, copied his techniques, and then publicized themselves as the scientific authorities without giving credit to Goddard, much to his annoyance.[57]

Along with their scientific police work, popular myth would have the public believe that Bureau agents spent their time chasing dangerous criminals, Public Enemies, such as John Dillinger and Charles 'Pretty Boy' Floyd. When identified in the 1980s, serial killers were the contemporary equivalent of the 'Public Enemy.' This was certainly the perception presented in popular cinema. *G-Men* (William Keighley, 1935) established the G-Man as a man of action, dynamic and resolute, in the shape of James Cagney, who had, ironically, helped establish the image of the gangster in popular culture. Weapons training in the Bureau featured prominently in newspaper reports, and in early cinema, establishing the image of the 'action detective'; this satisfied the public fantasy about the war on crime. Later movies, especially *The FBI Story* (Mervyn LeRoy, 1959), established the Bureau's history as Hoover wanted it to be remembered with James Stewart playing an idealistic young lawyer who joins Hoover's new organization. As Stewart's character progresses his career becomes a rendition of the FBI's greatest cases from the Dillinger shootout to the hunt for communist agents, the narrative taking place against a traditional conservative values background. Stewart's family suffers from the stress of the Bureau's work but he always overcomes adversity, ending with a monologue praising the glorious history of the United States. William Turner, a former Bureau agent, commented that the movie was "mawkish and overripe," and it made him want to hide under his seat.[58]

In reality the Bureau spent much of its time with lesser crimes. Recovering stolen cars and other menial tasks such as apprehending military deserters and tracking corrupt minor government officials for petty theft were more commonplace applications of Bureau manpower. One of the main aims was simply to gather statistics. While these mundane tasks would not make much of a story to capture a cinema audience's imagination, other serious threats to society such as public corruption, white-collar crime, and terrorism were not explored by the Bureau investigators or exploited by the scriptwriters.[59] In Hoover's statistics, the arrest of a Mafia kingpin meant as much as the arrest of a car thief.

By 1964, all possible media had been tapped and, "[n]ever before, on any level of government, have the American people been subjected to such brainwashing on behalf of any agency."[60] Jack Alexander of the *New Yorker* concluded that, "All of this [public relations] was hailed as a masterpiece in the creation of a wholesome attitude towards crime."[61] The campaign to shape public opinion was maintained at great public expense, and according to one critic, Senator George Norris, Hoover was "the greatest publicity hound on the American continent today."[62] Every speech made by Hoover was transcribed and a copy sent to virtually every newspaper in the United States. In this way Hoover was "defining reality" for a general audience, and also for policemen, legislators and bureaucrats.[63]

Over the decades since its organization the Bureau faced numerous panics that, it has been claimed, threatened the integrity of the nation—panics whose threat was exaggerated far beyond reality and placed, by conservatives, as part of an overarching conspiracy against their 'democratic' ideals. Thanks to the public relations skills of J Edgar Hoover, the Bureau had been seen to be doing its job fighting the enemies of America. This reflected Hoover's aptitude for bureaucracy, his technique for running the Bureau and keeping it closely subject to his will by "ingenious networks of rules, regulations, reports and inspections," creating "an independent power base in the government and the public that was almost irresistible—required intelligence, dedication, sacrifice, and a sophisticated sense of public relations."[64]

It was events in the early 1930s that ensured the Bureau's sudden rise to prominence. Newspapers and radio bulletins were full of crime reports. Stories such as the Lindbergh case (March 1932), the Kansas City Massacre (June 17, 1933), the kidnapping of Charles Urschel, an Oklahoma City oilman by George 'Machine Gun' Kelly (July 23, 1933), and the exploits of John Dillinger and his gang, fed the public appetite for crime stories, and created demands for a cathartic response from the national government. Events culminated in the passing of laws that allowed the FBI to carry guns, make arrests, and place all interstate kidnapping under FBI jurisdiction.

Of all the kidnap cases the 1932 Lindbergh case, dubbed the Crime of the Century by columnist Walter Winchell, who, throughout his career, served as a media outlet for Hoover's propaganda, received a disproportionate amount of publicity. He remained front-page news for more than four years, and gave an unrealistic view of the efficiency of law enforcement. The Lindbergh baby was kidnapped and after payment of a ransom the baby's body was found a few miles away from its home in a shallow grave. In 1931 a total of 285 kidnappings were reported, but it was in 1932 and 1933 that the wave of kidnappings reported by Attorney General Cummings began. Newspaper editors were very sensitive to the "news value of the crime," but they reported no more than twenty-five kidnappings,[65] raising doubts about the Attorney General's allegations of a crime wave.

While the Bureau took credit for solving the Lindbergh case, it was Treasury Department investigators who had insisted on marking the ransom money, which was traced to Bruno Hauptmannn in the Bronx after two and a half years. Subsequently Hauptmann was found guilty and executed in the electric chair on April 3, 1936.[66] Other cases were appropriated by Hoover in this way to add to the prestige of his Bureau. Harry Brunette, a bank robber, was captured by the Bureau when their agents jumped in ahead of the New Jersey and New York City Police Departments,[67] and the now legendary shootout in Chicago with John Dillinger was also appropriated from local law agencies.

Kidnapping is considered to be one of the easier major crimes to solve since the kidnappers must contact the victim's family. According to one critic, "the life of a kidnap 'gang' has never been shown to be more than one kidnapping." This implies that there must either be many kidnap gangs who will commit only one crime, or that the number of crimes had been exaggerated, and "If there was no kidnapping wave, and there was none, the Bureau of Investigation can scarcely be indicted for failing to suppress it."[68] By the time any analysis of statistics could be done the Bureau could claim that it was the extension of their jurisdiction that had persuaded potential kidnappers not to commit the crime.

The Lindbergh kidnapping led to the passing of what was popularly known as the Lindbergh Law (1933), which began to enlarge the list of federal crimes, that the Bureau was empowered to investigate and prosecute. The Lindbergh Law also made a federal offence of sending kidnap notes in the mail and to cross state lines in a kidnap case. National-bank robbery; racketeering in interstate trade; crossing state lines to avoid prosecution or giving testimony; interstate transportation of stolen goods; and resisting arrest by a federal officer were all added the following year to the growing list of crimes coming under jurisdiction for the Bureau to investigate. As the panics over a series of crime waves grew, so did the expansion of the Bureau's opportunity to intervene in local police jurisdictions.

There were three conditions that favored the argument for expanding Bureau jurisdiction. Prohibition was alleged to have caused the development of gangs of interstate criminals, and it was also claimed that the increased availability of telephones and cars gave the criminals access to a new mobility with which local police were not equipped to deal. In addition to the advances made by criminals, those who argued in the Bureau's favor also accused the local police of providing protection to certain civilians, while their prosecution of criminals was incompetent, or corrupt, or both. When combined, these three conditions had created "a national crime wave of unprecedented proportions."[69] Only the Bureau, operating under new laws to develop a wider role for themselves, could defend society.

The anti-kidnapping, bank robbery, and racketeering laws of the 1930s were seen as revolutionary, because "[t]hey put the federal government for the first time into the business of punishing crimes of violence."[70] But, at the same time, the government was resisting making itself responsible for preventing the crimes it was punishing. Prevention of crime is much more difficult and expensive than catching criminals, and it is difficult to generate good publicity for preventative policies.

To effectively punish crimes it was necessary for Franklin Roosevelt to expand the Bureau into a 'super police force.' Offices in principal cities were enlarged, and the budget was increased from $2,880,000 to $4,380,000. The number of Bureau agents was doubled to 600,[71] and the old military prison on Alactraz Island was announced as a new secure federal prison to house the worst convicts in the drive against gangsterism. James A Johnston, then chief appraiser of the Federal Home Loan Bank Corporation, was selected in 1934 to be the first Warden of Alcatraz. Johnston was a logical choice because of his pioneering reforms in Folsom Prison and San Quentin. With the opening of Alcatraz, a message was being sent to the underworld by Cummings that they should take heed of the government's determination and "the grim facts that a criminal career leads inevitably to prison." Alcatraz was to be a showcase of the worst criminal offenders with such notable inmates as Al Capone and Robert Stroud, famously (mis)named "The Birdman of Alcatraz." The prison was never fully populated but Warden "Saltwater" Johnston initiated a merciless regime over his charges, and Hoover attached great importance to building up the reputation of the prison despite it costing taxpayers twice as much to keep a convict on Alcatraz than in any other federal prison.[72]

Another step in enlarging the Bureau's resources and developing recognition came with the case of "Machine Gun" Kelly, whose capture helped shape the myth of the Bureau by introducing the name "G-Man," slang for 'government man,' into the country's popular vocabulary. Kelly allegedly used the term to refer to his Bureau captors, thus giving an identity to formerly faceless agents—a case of rewriting history to fit wishful thinking. The term G-Man was not present in any of the initial news reports; instead, it was popularized in later news reports by Rex Collier, of the *Washington Star*. The arrest of Kelly was made by a Memphis police sergeant W J Raney, not by Bureau agents, who, in 1932, still could not carry guns or make arrests. When ordered by Raney to drop his gun Kelly is reported to have replied, "I've been waiting all night for you." He then dropped his gun and surrendered. This version of the story is more in keeping with Kelly's character as a minor and non-violent criminal,[73] than with the more grandiose version of the story told by the Bureau that featured a dangerous, violent and desperate criminal. The myth of the G-Man made a lasting impression on the public perception of crime and law enforcement for decades, giving the Bureau a recognizable public identity while the covert side of their activities remained hidden.

Hoover saw the FBI's role for what it was: to maintain the idea of law and order, and to fight crime symbolically. Once he had acquired complete control over crime statistics, allowing him to alter the public perception of crime, he then had to keep the federal government from extending FBI responsibility into the prevention of crime, instead limiting their jurisdiction to the 'crime problem.' Hoover realized that, "The public is stirred by the individual, highly dramatic offence that seems meaningful because it seems to be a symbol of all crimes." Once a 'crime problem' was identified, a single criminal who was seen to represent the 'crime problem' could be labeled and hunted. This transformed crime from being an unmanageable chaos with many faceless villains "into the sensational deeds of a few dramatic public enemies who could be dealt with according to a set of popular conventions featuring detection, chase, shootout and capture or death." Either capture or death provided symbolic catharsis and a reinforcement of the traditional social order. "What is being attacked by the law is an idea or a form of behavior, and individuals are accused not for their actions but because they have become symbols of proscribed ideas or behavior."[74]

Individuals themselves have little control over whether or not they become symbols—that will be decided by groups such as politicians, police, and the news media—and if they do, they have no part in defining what their symbolic meaning will be. The existence of a symbol, especially one which was threateningly deviant, was amplified by exaggerated political and media attention. When identified as criminals deviants become scapegoats, representations of dangerous cultural tendencies, and the people who create the definitions are empowered to hunt the offenders. The creation of the Public Enemy, an icon of crime, combined with the Ten Most Wanted lists of the 1950s, provided a gauge of how dangerous a criminal was to the public. The accolade of Public Enemy was attributed by the Bureau in cases that were close to resolution, the label being awarded just before the capture or death of the criminal. The timing of the labeling made Hoover seem more effective,[75] rather than highlighting the Bureau's opportunism. The Public Enemies were well known figures because of the media attention paid to their crimes, and the information published concerning their activities usually came from the Bureau's Crime Records Division.

During the 1930s, "Movie theatres, newspapers, popular magazines, and radio were full of real and fictional exploits of bad men [and women] who had somehow become folk heroes." Criminals in the midwest became best known to the public, replacing the empire-building urban mobsters of the previous decade. John Dillinger, Kate 'Ma' Barker, and Charles 'Pretty Boy' Floyd became the new trophies of the Bureau. Hunted down one by one, they were often killed rather than captured.[76]

Serialized newspaper strips turned to crime stories featuring two-fisted detective heroes, continuing trends begun in the true detective magazines of the 1920s and 1930s of popularizing crime and criminals for public entertainment. Chester Gould's *Dick Tracy* was an early strip portraying police procedural work and it introduced gunplay, brutality and torture into the storylines. The strip's grotesque violence was as much of an attraction for its audience as the detective's heroics. At the time *Dick Tracy* appeared audiences flocked to cinemas to see the latest Hollywood gangster movies, when the likes of *Little Ceasar* (Mervyn LeRoy, 1930) and *Public Enemy* (William Wellman, 1931) graced the screens. In 1931 alone there were forty crime movies released. Dick

The Rise And Fall Of The FBI Myth

Tracy was an antidote to what Gould saw as the glorification of gangsters and the maudlin sympathy they stirred in audiences. In his investigations Tracy was "deadly serious and thoroughly efficient,"[77] and in the growing anti-crime climate Gould's creation found a large audience.

Eventually Tracy, in the daily strip, was called to Washington and became a G-Man. One serious flaw in Gould's strip was that his research was drawn exclusively from newspaper reports, which were sensational, and not entirely impartial, which reflected in the strip. Part of the Bureau Crime Records Division's role was to feed crime stories to newspapers, magazines, and pulp magazines that would then disseminate the 'official' versions of the stories to their readership. Some stories became scripts for radio plays while others were illustrated in comic books such as *Crime Patrol, Crime Does Not Pay, War Against Crime* or *War On Crime*.

Building the Bureau's reputation as an elite force was central to Hoover and the agency stressed "vividness over authenticity"[78] in its own reporting of cases. Inevitably this vividness was intensified for printed and cinematic thrills. John Dillinger's media representation was an example of creating a vivid threat to that public, and is often cited as the greatest case in FBI history. It may not have been their greatest investigation, but it was the public relations department's finest hour. Dillinger became more than a criminal, he became a symbol of "diabolical evil in human form,"[79] everything the Bureau sought to protect society from.

Hoover became obsessed with Dillinger after he carried out a series of bank robberies and dramatic jailbreaks. Local police and newspapers built up his criminal exploits, hoping to gain more credit when he was eventually hunted down,[80] but this helped Dillinger capture the public imagination as no other criminal had been able to since Jesse James.[81] Dillinger's case came under federal jurisdiction when he crossed the Illinois state line in a stolen car, thereby violating the Dyer Act. Interstate transportation of a stolen car was the only offence Dillinger committed over which the Bureau could claim jurisdiction. His bank robberies, despite being of federal reserve banks, remained local or state crimes because the new laws making them federal offences could not be applied in retrospect. This single Dyer violation was enough to prompt Attorney General Homer Cummings to order Bureau agents to 'shoot to kill,' a doctrine that was later applied with deadly results many times with wide public approval. Assistant Attorney General Joseph Keenan explained the reasoning behind Cummings' doctrine when he said, "I hope we get him [Dillinger] under such circumstances that the government will not have to stand the expense of a trial."[82] After escaping a siege in Wisconsin on April 30, 1934, due to Bureau mishandling of the operation, Dillinger was declared Public Enemy Number One. In the aftermath there was even talk in Washington of demoting Hoover.[83]

Attorney General Cummings used the bank robber's escapes to push through Congress his twelve point anti-crime program, which expanded federal jurisdiction to include interstate racketeering, thefts from banks belonging to the Federal Reserve System and the murder of federal officers. This reinforced the earlier Lindbergh laws and increased the power of federal prosecutors, but undermined state authority. It was the "supercharged anti-crime climate" which enabled the legislative package to be accepted.[84] Reports of a crime wave had whipped the public into a frenzy and allowed the passage of legislation that would normally have been considered draconian. Six bills proposed by Cummings were passed in May 1934, and a further three in June gave the Bureau more practical powers. As a result they were granted the authority to carry any kind of firearm, and full authority to make their own arrests. These were of minor importance compared to the expansion of jurisdiction that the Bureau received. The Fugitive Felon Act, the National Firearms Act, and Anti-Racketeering Act brought new areas under the supervision of the Bureau, while the Stolen Property Act expanded the earlier Dyer Act, and the Lindbergh law was amended to allow the Bureau to intervene in kidnapping cases after seven days. The new laws, which added to federal jurisdiction, were tailored to "box office" crimes, those that were easiest to solve, such as kidnapping, especially after local authorities had been pressured into using Bureau facilities to "coordinate" their efforts. Interpretation of the vague new federal codes meant that whether crime was judged as a federal violation, or not, depended on whether or not a crime lent itself to a satisfactory conclusion.[85] To reinforce the serious nature of the crimes that the Bureau dealt with, harsher penalties were prescribed for any criminal violating the federal laws than under most local or state laws. Federal prosecutors were also directed to assume control of specific cases at their own discretion.[86] The public needed a target to channel its fear and "[b]eneath the enthusiasm for the war on crime lay, after four years of national panic, the public's desperate need for a bogeyman."[87] Now the particular bogeyman was the criminal, and one particular criminal was singled out, John Dillinger, Public Enemy Number One.

Only a few months later, on September 22, 1934, a Bureau ambush in Chicago ended Dillinger's career in crime permanently. Allegations that Dillinger had undergone plastic surgery and removed his fingerprints with acid to avoid detection made identifying the body difficult, cast doubt on the validity of any definitive judgment,[88] and freed law enforcement from positive identification of the body. There were irregularities in the identification of the body: Dillinger was known to have had blue eyes, but those of the corpse were brown. The corpse, supposed to have been that of Dillinger under his alias of 'Jimmy Lawrence,' had a chronic heart condition since childhood from which Dillinger had not suffered. 'Lawrence' was shorter and heavier than Dillinger and did not carry any of the scars or birthmarks of the man he was alleged to be. The existence of a body proved the Bureau's efficiency, and a dead body avoided the need for a trial. It has also been alleged that Hoover was too embarrassed to admit that the dead man 'Jimmy Lawrence' was a small-time hoodlum who had been set up and Dillinger had made a quiet getaway to another state.[89] Cummings described the death of Dillinger as "extremely gratifying."[90] As soon as Dillinger was killed all of the crimes with which he was credited were cleared up and files closed, a common practice for police who "automatically consider crimes closed when the man credited with them is killed or dies by his own hand."[91]

Cummings' New Deal crime control program also launched an ambitious public relations campaign at the suggestion of his friend Fulton Oursler, the editor of *Liberty Magazine*, an anti-New Deal journal. Other newspapermen participated in the "plan to publicize and make the G-Men heroes."[92] Henry Suydam, the Washington Correspondent for the *Brooklyn Eagle*, was hired in 1933 as a special assistant to the Attorney General assigned to embellish the Bureau's image. Suydam was well paid for his work with a salary of $10,000, almost four times the entry-level salary for agents. When he left the FBI in 1937, President Roosevelt personally thanked him for services rendered. Hoover quickly and enthusiastically accepted the role as the symbol of the New Deal anti-crime crusade and, once he had learned to get publicity, Suydam was no longer needed. With Roosevelt's support, Hoover focused his attention on public opinion and molding public relations. Courtney Ryley Cooper, a journalist, initially saw the possibility of a wealth of saleable stories in the Bureau's files, and was later hired by the Bureau to assist Suydam's public relations efforts.[93] Cooper wrote twenty-four stories, three books and four screenplays about the Bureau, the majority of his work crediting Hoover as the author.[94] His magazine stories, all but one of which were published in American magazines, glamorized the FBI's machine-gun toting 'war on crime.'[95] Cooper's stories were revised and published under his own name as *Ten Thousand Public Enemies* in early 1935, with an introduction by Hoover. It was the first (and still stands as the most important) book written about Hoover and the FBI.[96]

Many journalists and magazine writers were interested in the 'authentic' source material in the Bureau's files and their desire for access allowed Hoover to become friendly with prominent Washington newspapermen. Newspaper friends, with access to big magazine and newspaper distribution, would provide favors for Hoover in return for his 'true crime' file material. The Bureau version of events glorifying the G-Men would be reported in newspapers, which benefited from improved circulation.[97] This symbiotic relationship produced numerous pro-FBI articles.

Shortly after the shooting of Dillinger, a telegram was sent from Will Hays of the Motion Picture Producers Association (MPPA) to censor Joseph Breen stating that making a movie of Dillinger's story could be "detrimental to the best public interest."[98] For eleven years the Dillinger story remained off limits to Hollywood. In 1945, director Max Nosseck made a film of the story that grossed $4 million worldwide, but was banned in Chicago.[99]

In December 1934 a National Crime Conference raised the question of police professionalism and proposed to increase training, especially for the small police departments, to counter the threat posed by gangs such as 'Ma' Barker's and that of Alvin 'Old Creepy' Karpis. Hoover suggested the development of an FBI police training school in Washington DC. This proposal was endorsed, but a counter proposal, vigorously opposed by Hoover, advocated a national police force with Hoover as its chief. Hoover's reason for opposing the formation of a national police force was his belief that, "Law enforcement is essentially a local problem and all the Federal Government can or will be able to do is endeavor to aid or guide in such training through methods of scientific criminal detection and other law enforcement activities."[100] Perhaps it is more truthful to say that Hoover sought the prestige without the responsibility. Whatever the reasoning behind Hoover's beliefs, they shaped the Bureau's operations for the continuation of his reign and beyond.

On July 1, 1935 the Federal Bureau of Investigation (FBI) came into existence after lobbying by Hoover. By adding 'Federal' to its name, the old Bureau gave the impression that it was the only federal investigative agency, which increased the amount of tension and rivalry with the Treasury Department investigators. Hoover antagonized them further by ordering new letterheads with 'Federal Bureau of Investigation' printed in a type size nearly twice that of the US Department of Justice.

July 1935 also saw the opening of the National Police Training School. Hoover promised that this training school would be responsive to changing needs of law enforcement and would raise the professionalism of officers who could pass along the training to their own departments. In 1938 Fiorello LaGuardia, Mayor of New York City, stated at the thirteenth graduation from the training school that it should develop into a West Point for police officers.[101] The following year senior Bureau officials helped to organize, or participated in, over seventy conventions of state or local law enforcement officials. A reflection of the Bureau's growing importance was the increase in the size of its budget. Congress approved $6,025,000 in 1936, which was more than double the amount it received when Roosevelt took office in 1933.[102]

The war on crime, however, was not the only matter to engage the Bureau's resources. In August 1936, when the image of the G-Man had been established in popular culture, Franklin D Roosevelt directed Hoover to investigate the alleged growing challenge to democracy by systematically collecting information on subversive activities in the United States, particularly fascist and communist groups. This was to be done without subverting the democratic and constitutional process. Hoover's confirmation pledge as FBI director in 1924 swore him to abstain from various secret police practices such as counter-subversion and surveillance, which made it impossible for him to grant the President's request, unless it was an issue of national security. Cordell Hull, Secretary of State, issued such a request and "an ominous precedent" was begun.[103] It quickly became apparent that Hoover had little idea of the difference between political dissent and subversion.

Whatever genuine fears there may have been, the 'Red Hunt,' as pursued by Hoover, Richard Nixon, Senator Joseph McCarthy and the neo-conservatives, could not be explained on any rational level. It did, however, provide a ready scapegoat for any social problem that arose. The Bureau's role in maintaining a conservative social order was noted by *The Nation* in 1941, which reported ominously that the FBI was a "stronghold of anti-New Deal elements which may yet play a sinister role in American history, that the Attorney General has no real control over it, that it runs true to the familiar rightist pattern of secret police agencies everywhere."[104] Fred Cook, in his book *The FBI Nobody*

The Rise And Fall Of The FBI Myth

Knows (1964), concluded that Hoover's persistent overestimation of the threat posed by communism was a major factor in establishing "a national mood of hysteria and unreason."[105] In that environment American society became "sheeplike and conformist."[106]

While the FBI focused on capturing radicals and public enemies, and manipulating news media, they played no part in investigating the crimes of sex killers whom they would identify decades later in their serial killer stereotype. At the height of the hunt for Public Enemies, a child killer named Albert Fish became the oldest man ever to be executed at Sing Sing prison. Fish's story, a tale of sexual deviance, cannibalism and murder, made sensational reading, which attracted the attention of Dr Fredric Wertham. In his somewhat sensational reporting of Fish, Wertham compiled a list of perversions that his patient practiced, some of which had no clinical name. Insanity was perhaps Fish's only possible defense at his trial, but the state of New York was desperate to execute him—so desperate that the prosecutor claimed that his acts of coprophagia (eating excrement) was a "common sort of thing," and the people who indulged in such acts were "socially perfectly alright," not mentally sick. By the conclusion of the trial, it was Fish's rambling and obscene confessions that finally convinced the jury that he was sane, and that the murder of Grace Budd had been premeditated.[107] James Dempsey, Fish's attorney, ended his appeal of the conviction fervently claiming that, "Albert H Fish's insanity was disregarded by the jury, undoubtedly through passion and prejudice. His conviction proves merely that we still burn witches in America."[108] Fish was only convicted of one murder, but he confessed to several others and hundreds of sexual assaults.

A few years before Fish, Carl Panzram was executed at Leavenworth. Panzram was described as "one of the most hardened criminals in America,"[109] and his life story was a brutal indictment of the American prison system. He confessed to twenty-one murders on three different continents, hundreds of rapes (of men), and burglaries. Despite the international nature of his crimes, the FBI was not involved in Panzram's case either. He was arrested for a minor housebreaking charge, and not connected to any other crimes until he confessed in prison. Although the Bureau played no part in Panzram's capture or prosecution, Hoover kept the black hood from Panzram's execution and a length of the rope used to hang him in his anteroom museum of crime, alongside mementos of John Dillinger, Clyde Barrow and other Bureau cases. Despite the mythical status of the Bureau as an investigative agency and their habit of participating in cases with considerable media involvement, and pertaining to sex crimes, they played little part in the most famous sex crime case of the 1940s.

In January 1947, the body of a young woman was found horribly mutilated in Los Angeles, and the case later became known as the 'Black Dahlia' murder, the name by which the victim was better known. Numerous men and women confessed to the murder, but those individuals only limited the chances of solving the case by wasting police time. The Bureau's only involvement in the case was to identify the fingerprints of the corpse as matching those of

Elizabeth Short, who had been arrested at one time for juvenile delinquency. Some of the commentators pointed to other bizarre sex murders which occurred in the following months, but the case was never solved and the mystery grew over time in the same way that the Jack The Ripper murders achieved their legendary status.

While the Mann and Dyer Acts enabled the FBI to symbolically enforce a conservative sexual morality the Bureau were still not involved in the investigation of sex crimes. In a circular to law enforcement officials on September 1, 1957 Hoover emphasized the danger of failing to report minor sex offenses, stating that prompt reporting was of "vital importance" to prevent potential "sex fiend[s]" from continuing and escalating their careers.[110] According to Hoover, "Sex mad magazines are creating criminals faster than jails can be built, and the circulation of periodicals containing salacious material plays an important part in the development of crime among the youth of our nation...," an opinion with which Senator Estes Kefauver and Francis Cardinal Spellman concurred.[111] Contemporary scandal magazines echoed Hoover's warning with sensational headlines. The June 1957 edition of *Pose* focused on "Sex Crimes USA" and a one-off *USA Inside Report* special in 1961 examined the "Menace of the Sex Deviate."

In his 1960 New Years' greeting to law enforcement officials in the *FBI Law Enforcement Bulletin* Hoover ominously reported that in 1958 there was a "forcible rape" every thirty-six minutes, and, "This truly shocking and shameful state of affairs is made even more deplorable by the knowledge that sex crimes and obscene and vulgar literature often go hand in hand."[112] Advancing frightening statistics to demonstrate the connection between the rapid increase in sex crimes and the prevalence of pornography in America, the FBI reported that in 1953 there were 38.5 sex offenses (excluding rape) per 100,000 of the population, escalating to 47.5 in 1956. However, during this time homosexuality was illegal and accounted for many sex offense reports. UCR statistics also found a 101 per cent increase in crime between 1939 and 1958, and estimated that less than half of all rape cases were reported to the police, implying thousands of sex criminals were still at large, unreported and unpunished.[113] Members of the legislature and law enforcement officials voiced particular concern for the effect pornography could have on juvenile minds,[114] paving the way for later explanations of moral degeneracy and criminality, especially that of serial sex killers in the 1980s.

"As a law officer I have no doubt in my mind that the most sensible and most effective place to attack is through those who produce and distribute pornography," Hoover reported. He continued, "Yet it is not easy to stop the peddler. It is appalling that an entire community can work itself into an hysteria of outrage against the sex criminal himself, yet tends to regard the man who helped trigger the criminal as only a contemptible human being, better ignored than punished."[115] However, investigation of pornography was not a high priority for the Bureau. The Federal Interstate Transportation of Obscene Matter (ITOM) law of June 1955 made transportation of obscene materials across state lines illegal, and two or more pornographic items was considered

The Rise And Fall Of The FBI Myth

evidence of intent to distribute, giving the Bureau jurisdiction. Statements from FBI spokesmen claimed that it would be easy for an FBI agent to identify items that were obscene and prosecutable. Linking pornographic films with the earlier white slave traffic, on which the Bureau had built their reputation, the Bureau received most of its information from informants. Using their alleged scientific expertise, the FBI examined confiscated films for fingerprints, subjected them to lab tests, searched for serial numbers and analyzed film-processing techniques. At the Justice Department, Marshall Golding reinforced the claims made by Hoover and other conservative moralists, saying, "There is a danger to society in obscene speech... but the moral fabric can stand one or two books of this kind. But it can't stand a flood... You can't measure the moral fabric of society the way you can measure a bolt of silk."[116] FBI priorities were more interested in a purge of radicals than a crusade against porn.

The FBI image and reality were markedly different. From its earliest days under , the Bureau had collected information on political figures that Roosevelt stored in a private ledger to gain political advantage. In reality the Bureau was "acting privately to preserve discipline among the elite leadership of the nation, and acting publicly to impress the masses with the government's importance as the nation's protector against the enemies of the people."[117] Beginning in the 1920s during President Harding's administration, the Bureau became "a private secret service for corrupt forces within the government."[118] Hoover continued this policy to preserve his own power, and he made it known to members of Congress and Presidents that his Bureau was aware of their philandering and various other indiscretions. Stopping short of blackmail, his message was understood, and "no-one dared to question whether the director had outlived his usefulness." Political figures were not the only targets of the Bureau's information gathering. They kept files on many popular writers and movie stars such as Charlie Chaplin, Ernest Hemingway and Henry Miller. A long list of others were subjects of the Bureau's attention, with their comments and activities being collected on file for future reference.[119] Meanwhile, the FBI virtually ignored organized crime, white-collar crime, and terrorism because Hoover feared investigations into these areas might lead to controversy and embarrass the Bureau. Undercover operations were also shied away from, because such investigations were seen as time consuming and resulted in few arrests.[120]

FBI policies, which had become progressively more autonomous in the 1950s, increased in their independence in the mid 1960s, when the FBI expanded its domestic surveillance programs to investigate and disrupt civil rights groups and the anti-war movement. Domestic counter intelligence programs (COINTELPROs) were begun in 1964 and aimed at civil rights groups in the southern states that were neither supported by foreign governments or influenced by communist or fascist ideologies. After 1964, Hoover initiated further COINTELPRO activity affecting an even wider range of people and groups.[121] In most cases these groups had committed no crimes and they only sought to exercise their constitutional rights.

The Bureau's record in defending civil rights protesters using information

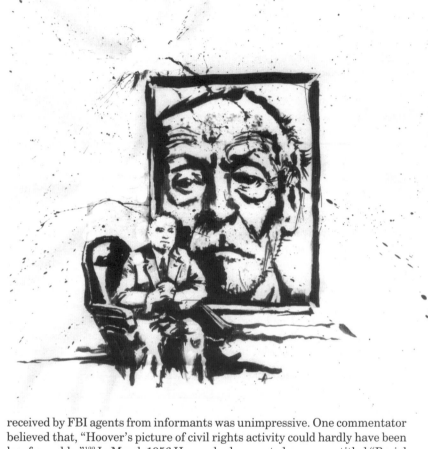

received by FBI agents from informants was unimpressive. One commentator believed that, "Hoover's picture of civil rights activity could hardly have been less favorable."[122] In March 1956 Hoover had presented a paper entitled "Racial Tensions and Civil Rights" to President Eisenhower and Attorney General Herbert Brownell, and in the paper he attacked the press for a "lack of objectivity" and "intermeddling" on the issue of civil rights. Hoover asserted that there was bound to be a "clash of culture when the protection of racial purity is a rule of life ingrained deeply as the basic truth." He defended the South's "paternalistic instincts" and claimed that the "Negro" need would be met, but that the South "does not yet consider that mixed education is the best means whereby the races can best be served." As an additional remark Hoover pointed out that "behind this stalks the specter of interracial marriages,"[123] playing on traditional ideas concerning sexual taboos and interracial sex as a moral deviance. To reflect rising social unrest in the 1960s the National Academy curriculum was expanded to include classes instructing agents in mob and riot control.[124] Also during this era, because of the changes in recruiting requirements, many Vietnam veterans enrolled in the academy. Among them were Robert Ressler and Roy Hazelwood, who would later rise to prominence in the Behavioural Science Unit (BSU).

Antiwar demonstrators, civil rights activists, and the hippie movement offended Hoover's conservative values. During protests against the Vietnam War, Paul Mavrides, a student radical, learned an abrupt lesson about Hoover's idea of American citizenship. The message was simple: "Exercising your Constitutional rights made you an enemy of the state."[125] Hoover made numerous fierce attacks on dissent during the 1960s, allowing him to become a symbol and spokesman for those who resented attacks on the racial status quo. He aggressively promoted the credo of God, country and family, and his reactionary ideology interpreted the *Escobedo* (1964) and *Miranda* (1966) decisions as attacks on the police by the liberal Supreme Court. In the social turbulence, he saw it as law enforcement's role to restore discipline to the nation and to reassert traditional values.[126]

Despite the excesses of Hoover and the Bureau, they still retained their status in American society.[127] Conservative society believed in the Bureau because to question it would be to question their own sense of security. The 1950s had been a period of unprecedented growth and affluence for the American economy. Never had Americans lived so well, or felt so threatened. As the civil rights movement and the antiwar protests gathered momentum in the 1960s, it seemed as though the 'dream' of the fifties had been destroyed.

Academics in the early 1960s argued that a crime scare was being created by federal agencies. Questionable conclusions were being drawn from unreliable statistics, giving the impression that a serious rise in crime had occurred. Although the academics agreed publicly that the rise was overblown, they did not attribute the blame to any one person or group. One reason for the apparent sudden rise in crime was the 1958 overhaul of the FBI statistical system. The pre-1958 figures were no longer considered compatible with the post-1958 figures, so they were sliced off the graph. In doing this the FBI achieved a 'skyrocketing' effect, showing a huge increase in crime. The crime rate in the 1960s always appeared to be increasing, and in their five annual reports, the Bureau invariably declared that crime was rising at a terrifying rate. In 1966 Attorney General Nicholas Katzenbach is reported to have commented, "It's bad enough to lose the war on crime, but to lose it five times a year is too much."[128]

The President's Commission on Law Enforcement and the Administration of Justice, appointed by President Johnson, recommended crime could be reduced through expanding the knowledge, experience, and instruction of policemen. In response, Katzenbach announced a $10 million increase in the FBI budget in May 1965 to expand training. In response the Bureau extended their curriculum to concentrate on academic learning, focusing on administrative skills, new management sciences, education, communication, and behavioral science courses. The President's Commission also suggested that all policemen should have at least a baccalaureate degree. One consequence was that special agent instructors at the Academy sought advanced degrees to support the new curriculum, culminating in 1971 with the affiliation of the FBI and the

University of Virginia as partners in the academic education of policemen.[129]

From the early days of the Bureau, it had been common to focus a crime problem on one person, or on a group such as communists or 'white slavers,' or to highlight Public Enemies such as John Dillinger and Al Capone. The Ten Most Wanted list had turned "a lot of seedy drifters into headline material."[130] Throughout the 1960s Hoover still preached his apocalyptic doctrine of a criminal onslaught on society. On his 'crime clocks' he reported that five offences were being recorded every minute. "There is a vicious crime of violence," he warned, "a murder, forcible rape or assault to kill—every two and a half minutes; a robbery every five minutes; a burglary every twenty-eight seconds; and fifty-two automobiles are stolen every hour."[131] 'Crime clocks' lend themselves to sensational conclusions that in reality mean virtually nothing. By interpreting crime in this way, a fear of strangers was justified. Crime was depersonalized, moving away from the individual suffering as a victim and instead focusing on the crime. Images of a rising national crime rate were translated into a personal threat in the minds of most Americans. In the 1959 edition of the Uniform Crime Reports Hoover declared "[t]he professional law enforcement officer is convinced from experience that the hardened criminal has been deterred from killing based on the prospect of the death penalty."[132]

Television coverage of a few spectacular crimes, such as the murder sprees of Richard Speck and Charles Whitman, the crimes of the 'Boston Strangler,' or of the urban unrest in Watts in 1965, created a sense of fear, particularly a fear of strangers, and a sense of crisis emerged. Debate on the quantity of violent crime in America flourished. Thornstein Sellin, dean of American criminal statisticians, was quoted in *Life* magazine as saying that the United States had the worst crime measurement statistics in any major country in the western world.[133] Lloyd Ohlin of Harvard went further, saying that the FBI crime index was "almost worthless,"[134] and other prominent academics agreed. These critics were expressing much harsher opinions publicly than were usually found in academic articles. Perhaps the most embarrassing statement of all came in 1968 when Attorney General Ramsey Clark declared, "there is no crime wave in this country."[135]

Dr Karl Menninger believed that there was less violent crime in the 1960s, than there had been in the 1860s but, with greater press dissemination and improved communications systems, crime was reported more widely than before. Because of improvements in police and ambulance response times, and improved medical techniques, criminal homicide had decreased by seventy per cent between 1933 and 1968, but increased coverage made the public more sensitive to violent crime. Americans were conditioned to believe that their chances of escaping violent crime were quickly diminishing.[136] One commentator skeptically remarked, "We shall be fortunate if we can even slow the rate of increase in crime; we shall be impossibly blessed if we can actually reduce the level of crime."[137]

Certain similarities were obvious between the various groups that Hoover persecuted, or at least he saw a connection. Radicals, communists, civil

The Rise And Fall Of The FBI Myth

rights advocates, students, and antiwar protesters were all identified by him as being sexual degenerates of some sort. They threatened the "integrity of the body and kinship ties" within America. Any left wing thought was "intellectual debauchery," and student radicals had a "depraved nature and moral looseness." Dating back to his enforcement of the Mann Act, Hoover had ignored the 'interstate commerce' section of the law and instead persecuted people who crossed state lines for "erotic purposes."[138] Hoover's notorious and formidable source of political power was his immense collection of scandalous material that he held on politicians and public figures.

The perceived moral decline of America was reinforced when the President's Commission on Obscenity and Pornography, which had been set up by Lyndon Johnson, reported its findings in September 1970. The report surprised many of its readers, especially conservatives such as Hoover, when it asserted that there was little evidence to support the contention that pornography was harmful. Interest groups such as Citizens for Decent Literature had, like Hoover, alleged for many years that there was a direct link between pornography and violent crime, especially sex crimes such as rape. The report urged government restraint in its attempts to "interfere with the rights of adults who wish to do so to read, obtain or view explicit sexual materials." President Nixon declared the report to be "morally bankrupt," and added that, "So long as I am in the White House, there will be no relaxation of the national effort to control and eliminate smut from our national life."[139]

Demoralized within and attacked from outside, the Bureau maintained prestige thanks to Hoover, but his death in 1972 brought the end of an era. The days of the G-Man were gone, and Hoover's Bureau died when he did.[140] It was popularly accepted that, "the FBI held the prestige and admiration that it did because of him [Hoover]. He had almost single handedly built the agency into what it was, and he was tireless in his fights for budget increases and pay rises."[141] The Bureau was still perceived by the majority of the public as being virtually free of corruption. To some critics, the Bureau's reputation for accurate and honest reporting of facts and its ability to handle complex investigations was well deserved, and contrasted with the tarnished reputation of the police who were seen to engage in brutality and sometimes fabricate evidence. Hoover's death brought an end to this kind of flattering journalism. At the time of his death, the FBI was plagued by allegations of civil rights violations and reluctance to protect civil rights marchers in the South, and worse was in store.

After his death many influential figures in the New Right voiced praise for Hoover, turning him into an icon of their ideology. Ronald Reagan, then governor of California, said "No twentieth century man has meant more to this country than Hoover."[142] To Chief Justice Burger, Hoover was "a man who epitomized the American dream of patriotism, dedication to duty and successful attainment."[143]

Those not on the New Right were not so flattering. Dr Benjamin Spock, an antiwar activist, claimed Hoover's death was a "great relief," and he hoped that the next FBI director would understand democratic institutions and the

American process better, a plea that was echoed by the American Civil Liberties Union (ACLU).[144] The general secretary of the Communist Party USA, Gus Hall, condemned Hoover as a "servant of racism, reaction and repression," adding that he had been a "political pervert whose masochistic passion drove him to savage assaults upon the Bill of Rights."[145]

The Bureau could no longer rely on the public relations abilities and behind the scenes manipulations of 'Public Hero Number One.' During his life, "He was the moral arbiter of the country, the czar of a national thought police,"[146] however, the Bureau that Hoover had created died with him. As a consequence the FBI "no longer displayed a firm conviction of what the nation should be and the evils it needed protection from... it retreated to a value-neutral, noncommittal stance on the great issues of the day." While Hoover's views seemed insulated from change, he also seemed to have distanced himself from his own Bureau. After his death people in the Bureau wondered what would happen next, and what effect his death would have on the agents and staff. There was no emotion over the loss of Hoover.[147]

After Hoover's death, Clyde Tolson took charge of the Bureau, but he was not to be Hoover's successor. Serious thought was given to the ways in which the Bureau needed to be changed with a meeting being called immediately by Attorney General Kleindeinst. It was agreed that Hoover's successor should be considered under two main areas; first, what Hoover's successor would do to the FBI, and second what he would do in relation to the Nixon administration. Whoever was to assume the role of the director would have to face questions concerning the Bureau's surveillance practices, its relationship with the Attorney General, its purpose in an era of radical politics, and the distribution of power within the Bureau.[148] L Patrick Gray III was chosen for the job.

On June 17, 1972, a group of men called 'The Plumbers' were arrested leaving the Watergate complex which housed the Democratic party headquarters. Initially, the architects of the Watergate cover-up were grateful that Gray had been chosen, for he was "abnormally receptive to guidance from above," and it was obvious that under him Nixon's administration did have control of the FBI.[149] After Watergate, the whole government establishment was in disrepute, and as the most aggressive and the best-known federal agency, the FBI had to absorb a large share of the punishment.[150] It was obvious that the reputation of the Bureau was already tarnished and in need of repair, but the worst was still to come. Acting director of the FBI Gray, who was being appointed the day after Hoover's death, had proven himself unworthy of the position, even to Nixon. His impartiality in the Watergate investigation was doubted when he made speeches supporting Nixon during his presidential campaign. During his confirmation hearings in March 1973, Democrats on the Judiciary Committee forced him to reveal that John Dean had sat in on all of the FBI interviews with White House personnel into Watergate, and had been given access to FBI reports.[151] Gray was forced to resign in disgrace in April 1973, after he admitted destroying cables which Howard Hunt, a Watergate conspirator, had fabricated in order to implicate John F Kennedy in the assassination of the Vietnamese leader Diem.

The Rise And Fall Of The FBI Myth

Misuse of the Bureau by Nixon was revealed in the Church Committee hearings (1975), and the FBI would find itself restricted by new guidelines to limit its investigations into criminal conduct, and its repression of dissident political beliefs. As well as tarnishing the present Bureau's reputation, the Watergate revelations showed that Hoover had operated independently of, and often in conflict with, his superiors.[152] Further, it was also clear that the FBI had lost its traditional immunity from outside supervision.[153] Misuse of the FBI in the Watergate cover-up was cited as the second article of impeachment by the House Judiciary Committee that led to Nixon's resignation. It was important to quickly find an acting director for the Bureau to restore its credibility.

William D Ruckelshaus was appointed as interim director of the FBI after he had established a reputation for independence and integrity as head of the Environmental Protection Agency, and he was respected by both Republicans and Democrats alike. Ruckelshaus only served for seventy days before being replaced by Clarence Kelley, a Kansas city police chief and former FBI agent. With a new Director appointed, the running of the Bureau should have returned to some sort of normality, but the worst was yet to come.

During the 1960s and into the 1970s, the FBI had seen its image and reputation repeatedly tarnished with revelations in the media about its civil rights abuses. Evidence was provided of the FBI spying on United States citizens during the COINTELPRO operations, of its attacks on the American Indian Movement (AIM) and the Black Panther Party (BPP), and of its involvement in the political espionage of Watergate. In December 1973, NBC reporter Carl Stern announced that documents from an FBI domestic surveillance program had come into his possession. In March 1974, further documents were publicized by Stern. Illegal break-ins to homes and businesses, unauthorized wiretapping, collecting derogatory information for political advantage and leaking information to damage political opponents, most notably Martin Luther King Jr, became publicized as the covert side of Bureau operations. Worst of all, the accusations were credible. The post-Watergate disclosures concerning Bureau investigative conduct showed the dangers of giving the FBI unlimited authority. "One after another, new allegations of misconduct kept national attention focused on what had happened years earlier."[154] Hoover's smear tactics repulsed the public, and in some areas feeling towards the Bureau became noticeably hostile.

Attorney General Edward H Levi established guidelines in 1976 to prevent the continuation of Bureau abuses. Friends and critics alike recognized the need for an FBI Charter to be established.[155] Allegations of misconduct increased. Senator Edmund Muskie alleged that the Bureau had conducted widespread surveillance on the Earth Day anti-pollution rallies in 1970. Representative Hale Boggs announced that he believed the FBI had tapped the phones of members of Congress.[156] As director, Kelley said, "I have been compelled to ... reconstruct and then explain activities that... were clearly wrong and quite indefensible."[157] The new approach sought to 'clean house' and show that the abuses of power had come to an end with Watergate and the Vietnam war. After Hoover's death, William Webster asserted that: "The days when the FBI used derogatory information to combat advocates of unpopular causes have long since passed. We are out of the business forever."[158] Even Hoover himself came under personal attack, with allegations being made about his private life, his contacts with criminal figures, and the possibility of a homosexual relationship with Clyde Tolson. It was noted that considering their conservative morality it was unusual that neither man had married, they worked together, socialized together, and spent most of their leisure time together, including vacations. If Hoover heard that anyone referred to him as "queer" he would send agents to harass and question the offender.[159] This sensitivity was ironic: as one commentator observed, "Hoover's whole life was one of haunting and hounding people over their sexuality, brutalizing them one way or another because of it."[160]

Issues raised after Hoover's death needed to be seriously considered. The Bureau's responsiveness to the Attorney General and the President needed immediate attention, as did the agency's role in a time of radical politics. The wisdom of combining criminal investigations and security surveillance was challenged, and the need to improve the relationship between the FBI and local police agencies was highlighted. Two further issues were pointed up: a need to oversee Bureau financing, but most importantly for the future, the need to control the dissemination of information stored on computer.[161]

After Kelley assumed the responsibility of directing the Bureau in July 1973, FBI agents and employees examined themselves and found it necessary to shed their old methodologies, especially their "almost obsessive concern with subversion."[162] Kelley put an end to the fixation with statistics and started the recruitment of females and minorities. Career boards were instituted to make the selection and promotion of personnel more objective. This 'liberalizing' of the Bureau continued under the direction of former federal judge William Webster. The retirement age was lowered to fifty-five, which dropped the average age from forty-five to thirty-eight, and a more relaxed atmosphere was sensed in the administration. Creation of an environment for change was important, but it was still limited by Hoover's legacy. After moving into the Director's office, Webster had a portrait and bust of Hoover removed, another sign of change.[163] While Webster's approach may have been more liberal, it was still staunchly conservative. Agents who engaged in premarital or extramarital affairs would no longer be dismissed, but homosexuals were still banned from Bureau jobs. Aiming to "build in more due process and put more emphasis on honesty and integrity than private lifestyles," Webster sought to discourage conduct that would make agents ineffective. In the best Bureau tradition, Webster did call for the latest "scientific data" on homosexuals, to see if the ban could be relaxed.[164] Attempts to rebuild a public image for the Bureau were still being undermined. In 1979 a former FBI agent, M Wesley Swearingen, attacked the Bureau's unwillingness to adopt real and meaningful reforms. He cited instances of abuse of position by Bureau agents, corruption and cover-ups that he knew to have taken place during his twenty-five years as an agent.[165]

Instead of domestic surveillance, the Bureau focused on important cases of white collar crime and political corruption and sought out information on criminal conduct. Some things did not change: the Bureau still guarded its image very carefully and despite the damage that had been done it still retained its mythic power.

Carter's vice-president, Walter Mondale, announced in 1977 that a program was being drafted to tighten guidelines governing FBI behavior,[166] but it was another two years before the draft charter was presented for public scrutiny. After three years of discussion by two administrations, a fifty-one page proposal for an FBI Charter Act was sent to Congress in July 1979. President Carter said that the public had to be assured that the Bureau was acting within the Constitution and that a balance between investigative demands and civil rights had been struck. Senator Edward Kennedy, who played a considerable role in preparing the Charter, asserted that the FBI had learned from its mistakes, and that the Charter would ensure that the past was not repeated.[167]

The Charter had three broad fundamental objectives; to enumerate the Bureau's jurisdictions, functions, and powers; to strike a balance between law enforcement and civil rights; and to limit the investigating powers to "the detection, prevention and prosecution of federal crimes." It stated that the aim of the limitation was to restrict the Bureau's accumulation of information. The Charter authorized two types of criminal investigations: criminal enterprise that involved racketeering, and criminal acts which violated federal laws. An investigation could only start if facts and circumstances indicated a suitable violation had occurred. Mainly functioning to codify current practices, the Act expanded two areas of FBI jurisdiction. Essential to the investigation of white collar crime was the ability to access financial records with "investigative demands," comparable to subpoenas. Secondly, "The FBI could investigate patterns of terrorist acts that involve[d] violations of state criminal laws even without federal violations, following the model of current racketeering statutes." Existing requirements for accountability and procedural controls were maintained, along with new restrictions on the use of informants.[168]

Conservatives wanted fewer restrictions on the Bureau and saw the Charter as too liberal. On the other hand civil rights groups, such as the American Civil Liberties Union (ACLU), opposed numerous provisions in the draft. Jerry Berman of the ACLU said his organization supported the idea of an FBI Charter, but that the draft proposals required a great deal of change. Specific problems arose because the Charter did not provide sufficient congressional oversight, rules for "investigative authority" were too permissive, and the FBI was left to regulate its own activities. No provisions were made to provide a resolution of any civil suits brought against Bureau agents by private citizens, and the Charter permitted the FBI to destroy files recording their past misconduct.[169]

National priorities were also established for the Bureau. There was to be less use of statistics as a measure of success, as even the FBI admitted that they did not really measure anything. Hoover's approach to crime as a case of 'quantity over quality' was seen as having inhibited the efficiency of the Bureau, possibly to the extent that during his reign the FBI may only have operated at half of its potential efficiency.[170]

It was acknowledged by the Bureau that mistakes were made under Hoover, and that there would always be mistakes, but the 'new' FBI administrator stated that in future errors would be admitted to and learned from. Despite cleaning up its image negative press reports still emerged. Stories of Bureau corruption appeared, as well as reports of attacks on dissident political groups, fabricated forensic evidence, and agents lying about money being paid to informers.[171] A Justice Department report in 1981 acknowledged that the FBI had discriminated in its hiring practices towards female agents,[172] and the trial of Patrick Gray and two of his aides once more raised questions concerning domestic intelligence gathering.[173] In 1981 FBI background checks carried out on Raymond Donovan before he could be confirmed by the senate as Labor Secretary were questioned, along with the inconclusive investigation into 'Briefgate,' where Reagan's campaign aides acquired Jimmy Carter's briefing papers for the presidential debates. These examples raised doubts about the Bureau's impartiality in political investigations. Despite improving its public image the FBI was still operating privately in the same way it had always done.

Within the law enforcement profession, the FBI was still promoting itself as the leader in its field. Between 1938 and 1985, over 700 police officers from sixty-six nations had attended the National Academy. Within the United States, National Academy graduates exert "considerable professional influence" as leaders in organizations such as the International Association of Chiefs of Police, the National Sheriff's Association, and the National Association of Black Law Enforcement Officers. Webster saw academic training as an investment in the future. He continued to support existing facilities as well as expanding the scope of the National Academy programs. Ominously, it was noted in the *FBI Law Enforcement Bulletin* that "the National Academy continues to carry its mission of the past into the future."[174] The mission of the National Academy was to train law enforcement professionals, with the training syllabus being set by the Bureau. But, in the words of one former agent, the Bureau was "over managed and underled."[175] Since the Mann Act of 1910, the focus of FBI activity has been on supporting a conservative social order by exaggerating threats to that order and punishing the deviants, and to enforce a conservative sexual morality.

In the years after WWII, the US became more politically conservative due to many social changes. The emergence of the liberal 'New Left' was matched by a 'New Right' in the Republican party, which shifted the parameters of political debate sharply to the right by the late 1960s. The right turn in American politics continued into the next decade, and was strengthened by events in the late 1970s when several prominent murder cases focused attention on a 'new' kind of deviant, which the FBI claimed to have discovered—the serial sex killer. They quickly sought to establish their qualifications in the hunt for these sensational sex killers who attacked the heart of the American family. And it was the notion of 'family values' that was central to the politics of the New Right.

Contagious, But Fortunately Not Hereditary
Origins of the New Right

THE NEW RIGHT EMERGED IN AMERICAN POLITICS AS A
conservative reaction against New Deal social welfare policies. Family
breakdown, a decline in religious values, and growing social unrest combined
in the 1950s to produce a backlash against economic and social policies.
Domestic crime rates became the focus of public attention. A shift in
criminological theory which later saw serial sex killers as compulsive and
'predatory' suited the Social Darwinist rhetoric of conservative anti-crime
policy. These new attitudes, which represented a reversal of the earlier liberal
view of criminals as misunderstood 'psychiatric anomalies', to conservatives
undermined everything that was desirable in society. The New Right realised
that symbolism was important, and throughout Ronald Reagan's career he
"played to the romantic past of small-town America, invoking the cultural
icons that were so important to Barry Goldwater's supporters, and later the
followers of George Wallace."[1] The symbols he adopted were the same as
the those upon which the FBI G-Man myth was grounded, the myth of the

American dream. But for people, everywhere, the "American experiment in symbolic politics has not been a happy event."[2]

The shift to the conservatism of the New Right had begun in the late 1930s when "politicians outside government used the red scare to harass a reform administration ultimately forcing it to abandon its left-wing allies."[3] The consensus politics which epitomised the New Deal were replaced by an anti-communist accord, and by the 1950s the dissenting conservative influence became an important part of a new consensus which permitted, and even legitimised, the New Right as an 'ideology'.

The turning point for New Right conservatives was President Lyndon Johnson's Great Society. Johnson began his political career in Roosevelt's New Deal administration, and when he found himself president after John Kennedy's assassination he initiated his Great Society programs. At that point, elements of the Republican party began distancing themselves from the "grandiose nonsense" of the 1960s and Johnson's version of liberalism.[4] In reality, the New Right were political reactionaries, but in favour of 'liberal' economic policies which would deregulate the economy, creating a predatory business environment. They believed this revival of 'trickle down' economics would boost the economy and, as modern-day pioneers they had no use for a welfare state.

New Right commentators noted that "the great expansion of their [liberals'] social programs coincides with the dramatic rise of most every index of social breakdown—divorce, illegitimacy, violence, crime, drug abuse, suicide, [and] untreated mental illness (disguised as homelessness)."[5] The welfare state was identified as the primary cause of the decline of society's institutions of social cohesion. Voluntary associations, local government, church and above all the traditional family structure had all suffered.[6] Never did they contemplate that the New Deal and Great Society might not have gone far enough with its social programs, nor did they credit either politically liberal endeavour with the successes they had achieved.

For the New Right, as it was for J Edgar Hoover, the only solution to the moral decay of liberalism was to reaffirm traditional values, religion, family, and the law. The same type of populism later advocated by Goldwater, Nixon, and Reagan, was aimed at a white middle class of American society who felt exploited by the 'Establishment', and appealed to highly symbolic issues.

Support for Reagan as President was composed of an "uneasy coalition" which generally consisted of long-time conservatives who had been attracted to Goldwater during his campaign in 1964. The 'Southern Strategy' courted southerners and midwesterners who had deserted the Democratic party and voted for George Wallace, and the economic libertarians who supported the free market policies of Milton Friedman. All disagreed on a number of fundamental issues, but were united in opposition to political (rather than economic) liberalism and Democratic social policies.[7] Their discontent stemmed from a moral self-righteousness. For the millions who voted for Goldwater and Reagan in the 1960s, "The virtues they have and practice are, in their eyes, conspicuously absent from society as a whole."[8] It was ironic that these values

Origins of the New Right

were also absent from the politicians chosen to represent them.

California in the 1960s was a cultural centre, superficially tolerant of unorthodox lifestyles, which strongly influenced the attitudes of the rest of the nation. It was also the 'home' of New Right politics. Millions of Americans had moved west to the promised land from the 1930s through to the 1950s, identifying California as being "to America what America used to be to the world."[9] It was the personification of the American dream. Even in California, the single most important concern to middle class Americans was the "decay of values," evidence of which, they believed, had been seen in the civil unrest of the sixties. "Crime on the streets" was also a major issue, as was juvenile delinquency, and "public lewdness."[10] Public awareness of these crimes was raised by the FBI's Uniform Crime Reports, and their ever-increasing crime rates.

Many in California had prospered with the military and industrial expenditures which began during WWII and persisted during the Cold War. After WWII, the Department of Defence spent more money in California than in any other state, and the prosperity of the state became inextricably linked to the dogma of anti-communism, communism often being equated with any type of radical movement. In such a climate, where party loyalty was "insignificant," the main factor of electoral success was how well the candidate's 'image' as a person was communicated to the public.[11] California's political culture was not, however, unique. Throughout the southwest, in Arizona and Texas, there was a similar pattern of politics.[12] Richard Nixon, a product of the Californian legal and political system, ran for the United States presidency in 1960 against John F Kennedy, and narrowly lost. At that time Nixon was a centrist. He had been a nationally recognised figure for over a decade thanks to his active anti-communism, and the prosecution of Alger Hiss, but he had not yet adopted the New Right ideology.

Nixon thought that the "frightening weakness" of the Republican party all across America had been the major problem with his campaign.[13] However, during Nixon's campaign the power of television became apparent in the new presidential debates, and this provided lessons for future political campaigns. But the conservatives were still not in a position to attack the sacred creed of the New Deal, as Barry Goldwater learned four years later. Nixon failed in 1960 against Kennedy, ironically, because he was seen as being soft on communism. The press found Nixon to be self-righteous, and he blamed his 1960 defeat on a media backlash, along with Kennedy's dirty tricks. His defeat in running for governor in California in 1962 made Nixon question his political future, and he told the "liberal media" that they would not have him to "kick around" anymore. Again in 1962, he accused the media of distortion and lack of professionalism in their reporting of his campaign.[14] Further reflection encouraged him to shift to the emerging New Right, ensuring he would not be seen as 'soft' on anything ever again.

Barry Goldwater, a "surreal anticandidate"[15] in the 1964 presidential election, had first promoted the same conservative rhetoric later adopted by Nixon, Wallace, and Reagan. They all identified a "rot and decay" in American "moral fibre." Goldwater's campaign appealed to a religious middle class, and called for a return to a "higher morality." The issue of moral decay was tied to urban disorder, race riots, juvenile delinquency and escalating crime rates.

Despite his politically disastrous electoral failure, Goldwater's nomination resulted in the consolidation and expansion of conservative influence in the Republican party. His nomination was seen by his supporters as a "mortal wound" to the liberal Republicanism of Nelson Rockefeller, who was shouted down during the 1964 party convention, and in its place the conservative wing of the party was dominant.[16] The material prosperity of the United States was attributed by Goldwater to the free market economic system, as it was later under Reagan. However, the nation's ills, "The deterioration of the home, the family, and the community, of law and order, of good morals and good manners is the result of thirty years of an unhealthy social climate."[17] The choice of candidate, not the philosophy, was pinpointed as the reason for failure in 1964. Henry Salvatori, a key financial backer to both Goldwater and later Reagan, said that Goldwater's "philosophy was sound, but he didn't articulate it moderately."[18] It would have been more truthful to blame Goldwater's failure on his inability to develop any issues in depth; the public saw him as a threat to peace, and his grossly inept campaign offered no acceptable solutions to the problems he identified. Goldwater's attack on New Deal liberalism won few supporters in 1964. Despite the attempts by New Right spokesmen to salvage what they could from his defeat, the reality was hard to deny. Receiving thirty-nine per cent of the votes, he polled 7.5 million votes less than Nixon had done four years previously in his failed Presidential bid. "It must be remembered," comments Richard Hofstadter, "that under our party system even Jack the Ripper, with a major party label on him could hope to get close to forty per cent of the votes." Goldwater asserted, as Reagan would later, that politics was not a place for special interests; rather, it was a sphere for fundamental moral values. Goldwater, Nixon and Reagan were all backed by their own private 'special interest' groups of wealthy California businessmen who encouraged their economic liberalism. What had become known as the "Goldwater Cult" attracted mainly non-political people, especially those in business, who had only recently become involved in politics.[19]

Lyndon Johnson won the 1964 election by a record breaking margin and the Democrats took control of Congress and the Senate with a huge majority. During the 1964 election, Barry Goldwater's rhetoric established 'crime' as a national issue. His attempt to politicize crime on that particular occaision failed, the voters choosing a "War on Poverty," along with increased spending on education and employment, civil rights, and social reform, over Goldwater's harsher sentencing proposals and expanded police powers. Subsequent elections saw a complete policy reversal. Recognizing the political value of crime as an issue, Lyndon Johnson created a blue ribbon panel in 1965 to examine the problem "fully and deeply." This led to the passage of the Law Enforcement Assistance Act (1965), which increased FBI funding for training.[20]

The Great Society, which New Right supporters objected to, was unveiled by Johnson in his first message to the 89th Congress by January 1965. In

Origins of the New Right

the legislation which followed, the federal government role was expanded. Rights and entitlements promised in the Constitution were enforced by federal legislation for groups of citizens who had previously been excluded. Johnson launched "a war on poverty and disease and secured a passage of legislative acts that constituted something close to a social revolution in America through installation of Medicare and Medicaid programs and aid to education, cities, and mass transit systems."[21] When the 89th Congress concluded its affairs at the end of 1966, it had one of the most constructive political records in American history. During the first two years of Johnson's administration more mental health facilities were established, more aid was given to arts and humanities, as well as a new fair immigration act, and additional legislation to tighten clean air provisions and water pollution controls were put in place. The franchise was also extended to African-Americans by the Voting Rights Act. At the end of the 1965–66 Congressional session, "the American economy had enjoyed six solid years of extraordinary economic expansion, pushing the annual gross national product almost to $740 billion, employment almost to seventy three million persons," all of which brought "record smashing prosperity."[22]

Johnson's administrative policies also adopted a broader and more progressive approach to crime. The report of the President's Commission on Law Enforcement and the Administration of Justice (1967) asserted that, "Warring on poverty, inadequate housing and unemployment, is warring on crime. A civil rights law is a law against crime. Money for schools is money against crime. Medical, psychiatric, and family counselling services are services against crime."[23] In rhetoric at least, the Great Society wanted to address the causes of crime in cities as well as controlling the symptoms. Conservatives accused Johnson of throwing money away on social problems because there were no immediate results. They did not believe that his policies would result in a long-term change in society. The result of urban deprivation had been seen graphically in 1965 in the Watts riots in Los Angeles, which brought home the reality of inner city life to both the state of California, and the nation. The law and order backlash to racial demonstrations and ghetto riots made crime as important as Vietnam as a political issue, promoting Hoover's usefulness to President Johnson.[24]

However, the 1965 riots were mostly in black neighbourhoods, located in decaying inner cities, well away from the upwardly mobile, middle class whites who had moved to newly constructed suburbs in the post-war years. After the white exodus, cities became "grim holding area[s] for the nation's superfluous people, its poor, its minorities, its elderly, its incompetent, its 'pathological'."[25] The suburbs of America's new rich are "like the sunbelt, unashamed of their gains, [and] unburdened by liberal conscience."[26] For Reagan and other New Right supporters, these suburban families were the "forgotten Americans." With the breadwinner working up to sixty hours a week to support his family, they were heavily taxed by the government and underrepresented by politicians.[27] With the middle- and upper-income population moving from urban areas, the tax base of many cities declined and housing crises worsened. But in the sunbelt from Atlanta, Georgia, to Los Angeles, California, metropolitan growth exploded because of disproportionately high federal government defence spending, NASA research, and highway construction. By 1960 almost three quarters of the US population lived in metropolitan areas, but during the previous decade seventy-five per cent of metropolitan growth had been in the suburbs. With rural Southern blacks settling in urban centres, American society was becoming increasingly segregated by race and class.[28] Between the Watts riots of August 1965 and July 1968, over a hundred cities across America experienced violent urban unrest.

Reagan sought to attract the votes of middle class whites who moved to the suburbs. Working long hours to provide for their families, security was an important issue to the suburbanites. Easily alarmed by threats to their lifestyle, they were prone to accept assertions by people such as J Edgar Hoover, or politicians who carried the authority of public office, that a particular type of crime or criminal threatened them. But Watts provided a justification for the beginning of a conservative backlash in California, evident in the 1966 gubernatorial election, with Ronald Reagan defeating the incumbent liberal Democrat Edmund "Pat" Brown. Hofstadter's 'paranoid' politics became a way of life.

Throughout his life Ronald Reagan liked to portray himself as a hero, participating in a struggle of good versus evil, retelling the traditional story of the white male hero. Reagan's childhood had been spent in small towns which he later idealised, saying it had left him with a sense of tradition and its associated values. When describing his origins he said, "It was a good life. I have never asked for anything more, then or now."[29] It was this set of values which Reagan was seen to embody thanks to his own determined efforts and the exertions of public relations experts who moulded his image as an actor and a politician.

Smashing the Money Ring (Terry Morse, 1939) starred Reagan as Brass Bancroft and was his first heroic acting role. Up to that point he had played obscure or supporting characters, but as Bancroft he became known as the "Errol Flynn of the B's." Warner Brothers released the Bancroft movies at the same time that Paramount released its series of films based on Hoover's *Persons in Hiding* (Louis King, 1939). While Reagan may not have actually portrayed a G-Man, his character status as a T-Man (Treasury Department Agent) gained him recognition as a federal officer and few members of the audience made any distinction between G-Men and T-Men.[30]

Several of his movies were propaganda aimed at reinforcing all-American ideals and motivating a fighting spirit against whoever or whatever might be considered an enemy of traditional values. Gary Wills noted that, on reflection, Reagan "specialized in uplifting, even devotional tales about young martyrs serving a perfect cause, tales that entered his permanent repertory, undislodgeable by others' disbelief or by evidence."[31] He injected his character into the movies, and adapted their stories into his own life, meshing fantasy and reality. The concept of a conspiracy was encouraged by his own personal sense of struggle against 'evil', which reflected the characters Reagan played in films.[32]

Origins of the New Right

Good propaganda provokes a reaction from its audience, and mobilises strong feelings. By identifying himself with all-American hero characters, Reagan personalised the wholesome message of the film. Any attack on him (or his character) was an attack on the values of American society. He was never an actor of great dramatic intensity but his clear voice, timing and skill with dialogue ensured him a measure of success as a "light romantic leading man." These basic strengths were of crucial importance throughout Reagan's life from his days as a radio commentator right through to the White House. Playing the same character and displaying the same attributes, "He always acted like Ronald Reagan, it was a heart-warming role."[33] The characters played by Reagan had a special appeal to new white suburbanites.

Before WWII, Reagan's name appeared on an FBI list compiled by a special agent in Hollywood, because the agent believed that Reagan might be of help to the Bureau. In 1947, during the anti-communist witch hunts, Reagan became an informer for the FBI (he was assigned the number T-10) supplying information to the Bureau which they used for character assassination.[34] Reagan secretly gave information to the FBI concerning 'suspect' people within the Screen Actors Guild (SAG) to prevent unwitting collaboration between the union and communist causes. Progressing from a fictional T-Man to a real one, Reagan was busy, in his own mind, saving America, and as a result his marriage and acting career suffered. But such consequences were dwarfed beside the threat of a communist conspiracy.

The opportunity to host a television show came when Reagan's film career was floundering, so his presentation of *General Electric Theatre* (1953-62) proved to be critical in allowing him to develop wider recognition. This "sudden and unexpected" good fortune initially paid Reagan $125,000 a year to host the show plus an additional fee for any show in which he took an acting role.[41] Reagan was selected to host the show because the public thought of him as being of "good moral character" due to his film roles playing all-American boys. He perpetuated those roles in *GE Theatre*, because the sponsors knew about his political beliefs.[35] At the peak of the McCarthy witchhunts, GE wanted an "ultraconservative" to promote their belief that excessive liberalism dominated the American government and threatened the stability of American society. Earl B Dunckel, the developer of *GE Theatre*, was a politically conservative former newspaperman who found liberal conspiracies everywhere, even within the conservative GE company. Beginning with public appearances on tours of the GE plants and progressing to delivering short speeches, Reagan took his first tentative steps toward a formal political career. Employing fables in his speeches to make his political points was common for Reagan and earned him a warm reception from his audience. It was no problem for him that often the stories he told bore no resemblance to any recorded history; they were "an apparent product of his fanciful world of pretend." At one impromptu speech, Dunckel "finally began to realise the breadth and depth of his [Reagan's] knowledgeability... everything that went into that mind stayed there." Within a year of the tours starting, Reagan had become a walking symbol of the company's interest in its employees and responsiveness to its customers. On subsequent tours Reagan adopted the image of the travelling ambassador, incorporating into his schedule speaking engagements with local groups, among them the American Legion, the Elks, and the Rotary club as well as GE factory workers. When he spoke he idealized America the beautiful and addressed subjects which were concerns for his audience, such as the need for Christian family values, taxes and economic problems, and juvenile delinquency.[36]

After a few years Reagan's speeches changed suddenly, refocussing on what was wrong in the US. Travelling with Dunckel, Reagan came to agree that the Democratic party which he had supported had "turned the corner and gone in a different direction." The party had deserted him and the people. By 1958 Reagan's speeches dealt mainly with political and business issues.[37] Reagan finally left the show when the company felt that he had become too conservative, even for their liking. Shortly after Kennedy's nomination as a presidential candidate in 1960, Reagan wrote to Nixon advising him not to try to "out-liberal" Kennedy, and warned him that some of the programs Kennedy proposed were Marxist. Reagan made speeches supporting Nixon even though he was still a registered Democrat.[38] The extent of Reagan's political realignment became obvious in 1961 when he spoke at a fundraiser to support the Congressional re-election campaign of John Rouselot of the John Birch Society.[39]

In 1962 Reagan changed his voting registration to Republican, to reflect his new political perspective, and he had also become actively involved in Republican politics. California Republicans at the time regarded Reagan as "unelectable," and believed he was "two degrees to the right of Barry Goldwater." While this was true, he still possessed a casual style and an ability to put complex problems into very simple language.[40] Agreeing to moderate his speeches, in order to have a chance of winning, Reagan cultivated his image as a citizen politician.[41] Boy-next-door film and television roles had given Reagan ready made political appeal: "The combination of the celebrity's fame, the wisecracking humor, and healthy suntanned good looks made him an instant hit." When speaking he reminded members of the audience of the Evangelist Billy Graham. Once he arrived at his New Right philosophy he clung to it with religious determination.[42] Adopting the role of the heroic everyman, a 'citizen politician' assured of his own righteousness, Reagan began to build his image as a credible political candidate, waiting for his chance in the spotlight. Mocking Reagan's 'citizen politician' campaign slogan, Governor Edmund 'Pat' Brown said, "This is your citizen pilot, I've never flown a plane before but don't worry. I've always had a deep interest in aviation."[43]

Serious unrest erupted at the Berkeley campus in late 1964 when Free Speech Movement demonstrations were broadcast on the evening news, and the scenes of the student 'radicals' holding police at bay angered and frightened ordinary citizens of California. At the time of the unrest Governor Brown, a liberal Democrat, did not respond as aggressively to the disturbances as the electorate demanded, but Reagan saw that the people of California felt emotionally involved in events because of pride in their state's university system. Reagan expressed his disgust, angrily denouncing what he saw as scandalous behaviour by students, and his statements were calculated to keep public indignation running high.[44] J Edgar Hoover was also obsessed by campus unrest, and both he and Reagan behaved as though the student protests justified stripping universities of their traditional function—exchanging different ideas and viewpoints.[45]

In this atmosphere, Reagan declared his candidacy for governor. Shortly afterwards, a student dance was held on the Berkeley campus. Police reports of the dance made their way to the Reagan campaign headquarters, probably through Edwin Meese who was then District Attorney of Alameda County. In response to the information, Reagan made claims that the party had been an orgy of sex and drugs, enabling him to take a stand as a staunch defender of family values and launch an attack on the youths. In this respect Reagan shared the same ideological worldview as J Edgar Hoover, who remarked, "The call of the future must be a rekindled American faith, based on our priceless heritage of freedom, and the religious spirit."[46] Radicals, beatniks, and advocates of filthy (free) speech were alleged to have brought shame to the university in the name of "academic freedom." All of Reagan's allegations were untrue, but he had nothing to lose from attacking militant teenagers. By identifying "academic freedom" as the culprit, Reagan could claim that the unrest had been caused by the indoctrination of students by professors on campus, which magnified the problem and justified tough action. Liberals defended the alleged radical academics and were added to a growing list of enemies.[47]

Reagan skilfully manipulated the 'campus war' issue in his 1966 gubernatorial campaign to highlight specific populist themes, those of morality, law and order, strong leadership and traditional values. His campaign provided a blueprint for the perfect populist campaign.

To his audience Reagan was "Mr Conservative, a True Believer."[48] The central point of Reagan's Social Darwinist conservatism was the responsibility of the individual for his/ her own actions, economic and moral. From this it followed that criminals were personally responsible for their crimes, and during his first gubernatorial election campaign Reagan made the death penalty a political issue. He claimed that incumbent Governor Edmund Brown had opposed the death penalty and that under his administration there had been no executions. Because of this alleged 'soft' approach by Brown's administration, Reagan claimed that an "urban renewal project" was needed on death row.[49] San Quentin's death row was overflowing its capacity and more cells had to be added, but Reagan wanted to speed up the executions and reduce the need for increasing the prison's capacity.

Contrary to Reagan's accusations, Brown had refused clemency on a number of occasions during his time as Governor and had signed execution warrants. Most notably Brown had given a temporary stay of execution to Caryl Chessman, who had been convicted as the "Red Light Bandit." The Bandit raided secluded roadways around Los Angeles, surprising young couples, robbing them, and orally raping some of the females. Chessman always denied the sex charges, which had shocked the public, and claimed to know who the 'Bandit' really was. The case attracted worldwide media coverage, and he drew support from many notable figures, among them Eleanor Roosevelt. During his twelve years on death row Chessman was given eight stays of execution. Governor Brown actually granted a ninth stay of execution on May 2, 1960, but his secretary dialed the wrong telephone number, and by the time she corrected the mistake Chessman's execution had already begun.

Some officers in the LAPD had failed to reveal to Chessman's defence attorney, even when specifically requested, original reports made by the Bandit's victims which indicated that the sex crimes had not taken place. Chief William Parker, head of the LAPD, told George Davis, Chessman's defence attorney, that "the files were closed not only to journalists but to Chessman's lawyer's as well." They refused to release information that was in the public interest. Parker's attitude was seen to typify the official attitude to Chessman, and the "unthinking determination that his death sentence would be carried out."[50] With his execution, Chessman became the first criminal to be executed in California for a crime other than murder. After his execution Milton Machlin and William Read Woodfield published *Ninth Life* (1961), which established that Chessman had not received a fair trial. After arrest the police reported that Chessman had confessed to the Red Light Bandit crimes. However he maintained that his confession was extracted after he had been beaten by police officers, a practice which was later prohibited by the *Escobedo* (1964) court ruling. Another application for clemency that Brown rejected was that of Aaron Mitchell. It would be left to Reagan to make the final decision concerning Mitchell's sentence.[51]

The mid-term elections in November 1966 shocked Democrats. The American public undermined their domination of the House, Senate and the governorships of the states. Reagan's election as Governor of California in 1966 saw "right-wing kingmakers" and money men turn to him.[52] This was a successful trial run for the New Right philosophy, an exercise which Reagan understood.[53] As a "conservative political neophyte" his victory over Brown was one of the most extraordinary Republican victories of the campaign. At the time it was said that "Seldom has a more inexperienced person stepped into a more difficult job."[54] Reagan's campaign had been based mainly on attacking the Brown administration's excessive 'interventionism' in various issues. His message was simple: "God, Home and Country—that's what Reagan believes in, and that is what he sells so well on television and before live audiences."[55]

When Reagan came to power in California, "In the cities the permanent layer of black unemployed was increasing in the ghettos, bringing with it more despair, alcoholism, drugs and violent crime."[56] But he offered little in the way of solutions. As a warning of what was to come, his 1967 budget was the most severe retrenchment of California state government since the depression era. Economic differences became increasingly obvious between the wealthy, who were able to enjoy the good life that California could offer them, and the poor, who could only observe. Modernising Roosevelt's 'fireside chat', Reagan turned away from the usual political pageantry and relied instead on television, just at the time when it came to dominate American culture. His election was the

Origins of the New Right

arrival of the long-prophesised era of the "manufactured candidate." Such politicians were made by public relations men and political strategists and they were able to discuss issues in simple terms for short news broadcasts.[57] In his speeches Reagan spoke as though society was being overrun by criminals. From his propaganda movies supporting the American way of life, through the conservative *GE Theatre*, and into his political career, Reagan consistently identified and exaggerated deviant groups, allowing his own ultra-conservative political views to appear moderate.

The prison system in California benefited from Reagan's New Right ideology and enthusiasm for law and order. The deputy Director of the Department of Corrections, L M Stutsman, boasted that the Department had a special relationship with the Reagan administration, stating, "We've got all we asked for since Reagan took office." California prison budgets soared between 1964 and 1973, increasing by more than thirty per cent, but the number of prisoners incarcerated declined from 26,600 to 20,500, meaning that the cost of keeping a prisoner had more than doubled. Jessica Mitford wryly noted that it cost more to keep a prisoner locked up in San Quentin than it did to send him to Harvard.[58]

At the same time that he was willing to spend vast sums of money sending prisoners to jail, Reagan was taking additional steps to ensure that less money was being spent on social welfare. His Welfare Reform Act of 1971 removed 350,000 claimants, whom Reagan portrayed as undeserving cheats, and saved taxpayers almost $2 billion according to the Governor's claims. The California legislature disagreed, putting their estimated savings at $40 million. They also pointed out that during Reagan's time as Governor, the number of recipients on welfare doubled (with costs tripling) whereas the state population growth was decreasing.[59] The increasing numbers of poor were subjected to the new, harsh law-and-order legislation of the administration.

Reagan made it clear that not only would he use the death penalty, but he also intended to weaken the rights of the accused. He believed that police officers should have fewer restraints in making arrests. Judges were appointed by Reagan who exercised "judicial restraints," a euphemism which meant they would refrain from limiting police powers in the way the Supreme Court had done in the *Miranda* decision. Shortly after being elected, he arranged a meeting with the Southern California branch of the American Civil Liberties Union (ACLU). There Reagan spelled out his position and, to justify his stance, recited a macabre murder story which involved graphic descriptions of sexual mutilation to the male victim.[60]

Flamboyant speeches by Reagan in support of capital punishment meant that he signed the execution order of Aaron Mitchell in 1967. His enthusiasm for the death penalty was put to the test as the day and hour of Mitchell's execution drew nearer; the issue ceased to be an abstraction, and the moral complications had to be faced. Pressure to go ahead with Mitchell's execution came from white middle class voters. Mitchell's case served as a sign that the new administration was taking a tougher attitude towards crime and while the execution went ahead, Reagan's conscience was troubled. As a consequence, the next death penalty case that came before him was granted clemency. In fact Mitchell was the only criminal to be executed during Reagan's time as Governor.[61]

Reagan had fewer doubts about a plan to phase out state mental hospitals in California, which was implemented during his administration. The policy had its origins in a passionate appeal which President John F Kennedy made in 1960 for the nation to pursue a "bold new approach" and adopt community based mental health facilities. Boosted by Congressional guidelines, a pledge of funds in 1963, and a belief that all mentally ill persons could be treated in the community, the 'community care' movement was spurred on by federal court rulings that mental patients should be treated "under the least possible restraint."[62] Deplorable conditions had led to some legal objections to institutionalisation, but such considerations were secondary to arguments stressing individual autonomy.[63]

Cuts in California's mental hygiene department budget were dramatic and added to Reagan's self-promoted image as a great economiser. State governments could save money by restricting the admissions to state-run psychiatric hospitals even after federal funds were cut, and states whose budgets funded civil and criminal commitments differently could economise by classifying some patients as 'dangerous' and relocating them into the criminal justice system. Courts adopted 'dangerousness' as a convenient legal guideline to replace clinical criteria for commitment, justifying their action by claiming it was the court's responsibility to protect the public not the patient.[64]

On July 1, 1969, the Community Mental Health Services law (CMHS) went into effect in California. This was a pioneering effort in establishing the principle of a single coordinated system for the care of the mentally ill and it received support from across the political spectrum. It was originally hailed as a "'Magna Carta' for the mentally ill,"[65] but the theory was more liberal than the implementation.

The report compiled as a background study for the benefit of the California state legislature, *The Dilemma of Mental Commitments in California*, effectively described the possibility that patients were being "railroaded" into state mental hospitals. However, it never mentioned that the general population of society may have a limited tolerance for the behaviour of mentally disordered individuals in their community: "If the entry of persons exhibiting mentally disordered behaviour into the mental health system of social control is impeded, community pressure will force them into the criminal justice system of social control."[66]

By 1973 three state mental hospitals were closed, one more was in the process of closing, and Reagan announced plans to close all fourteen hospitals by 1977, except for two which were to house criminal offenders.[67] Community based facilities which would provide care in the community were initially envisioned in Reagan's rhetoric, but the main aim was budget costcutting for short-term savings. Patients from the closed mental hospitals had three choices. Some could live with relatives, and others who could afford to pay $100 a day for private treatment did so. The remainder drifted to run-down boarding houses, in areas that would become known as "psychiatric ghettoes" in San Francisco, San Jose and Los Angeles. Of these ex-patients one rose to infamy, a young man called Herb Mullin.[68] He was obviously mentally ill, suffering from severe paranoid delusions, and posed a danger to others.

Mullin was a native of Santa Cruz, and for the early part of his life he was an all-American boy who achieved good grades in high school and was voted "most likely to succeed" by his class. It was alleged that the death of his friend Dean Richardson in 1965 catalysed Mullin's mental decline. Afterwards he turned his bedroom into a shrine to his dead friend and broke off his engagement to his girlfriend, saying he was homosexual. But, while attending San Jose State college, Mullin discovered acid (LSD) which resulted in him being placed in several different mental hospitals during the following few years. By 1972, he lived in San Francisco and began hearing voices which allegedly told him that a steady flow of deaths (a total of thirteen for some obscure Biblical reason) was required to prevent a cataclysmic earthquake. Mullin killed his thirteen victims before being captured. He was diagnosed paranoid schizophrenic but still legally competent to stand trial. He was convicted on two counts of first degree murder and eight counts of second-degree murder, but was not formally charged with the other three murders. By the time Mullin is eligible for parole, in 2025, he will be seventy-eight years old.

In an open letter to Governor Reagan and the California state legislature in late 1973, Ken Springer, the jury foreman in Mullin's murder trial, wrote, "None of this need ever have happened... Five times his [Mullin's] illness was diagnosed and at least twice it was determined that his illness could cause danger to the lives of human beings. Yet, in January and February of this year [1973] he was free to take the lives of ten Santa Cruz residents..."[69] Springer went on to question the consideration which the legislature and Governor had given to the future of the patients who were released from the hospitals. The California legislature responded by passing a bill prohibiting Reagan from closing any more state mental hospitals, a bill which Reagan vetoed. The legislature was able to override the veto and halt Reagan's program. Hospitals which had already been closed were not reopened, and the few hospitals and mental health facilities which remained open became overcrowded. Follow-up checks on discharged patients were difficult because of their transient lifestyles. When checks were possible they were often inadequate. This lack of follow-up treatment became an issue when Richard Chase was identified as the "Vampire of Sacramento" in 1978.

After a bizarre and apparently motiveless murder of a young woman in Sacramento, Russ Vorpagel, the Sacramento coordinator of the FBI's Behavioural Sciences Unit (BSU) contacted Robert Ressler at the National Academy to inform him of what had happened. Ressler saw it as an opportunity to try his 'psychological profiling' technique.[70] After a second attack, which was believed to have been carried out by the same criminal, Sheriff Duane Low called the murders "[t]he most bizarre, grotesque, and senseless killing I've seen in twenty-eight years."[71] The 'Vampire' killings shocked the public and caused hysteria: "doors were being double-locked, window shades pulled down; some people were even loading up their cars, station wagons, and small trucks and moving out."[72]

The police were led to Chase by a woman who knew him in high school and had seen him a few weeks before the killings. She was shocked by his emaciated appearance and believed that he was about to attack her. Ressler's profile correctly identified a white male loner with a history of drug abuse as the perpetrator of the crimes, and he referred to the killer as "disorganised" to reflect someone who had "full blown and serious mental illness."[73] Chase had been treated by several doctors, all of whom had diagnosed him as paranoid schizophrenic, and one believed him to be a danger to others. After several hospitalisations, Chase was released with prescribed medication but, as he did not have regular contact with any medical professional, no one knew his mother had weaned him off the drugs. Shortly after that he began killing humans instead of animals.

The Center for Study of Responsive Law (CSRL), a Ralph Nader organisation, published a report in 1972 which examined the implementation and effectiveness of community health programs. The report concluded that the community system had been "vastly oversold" and "quickly perverted" into an unresponsive bureaucracy. A few weeks before the CSRL report Dr Martin Birnbaum, a physician and lawyer from Brooklyn, filed a law suit to halt Medicare and Medicaid programs until they included the one million Americans who were annually treated in public mental health institutions. Both Kennedy and Nixon's plan for national medical health care specifically excluded the mentally ill. Birnbaum wanted federal funds to be paid to the hospitals not to the general funds of the state, and he believed until that happened the mentally ill would be unlikely to receive adequate treatment and care.[74] As the case of Richard Chase showed, Birnbaum's plea fell on deaf ears.

On June 29, 1972, the United States Supreme Court declared, in *Furman, vs., Georgia*, that the way in which capital punishment was applied was unconstitutional. Reagan was angry that it had been the Californian Justice Donald Wright who wrote the majority opinion to overturn the death penalty legislation. It was Reagan who had appointed Wright to the California Supreme Court but, unlike the liberal judges who opposed execution, Wright believed in capital punishment. In his opinion new legislation was needed to speed up the process, and there were not enough executions being carried out for his liking. Whatever the reasons expressed by individual judges, Reagan believed the decision made a mockery of the constitutional process.[75] Existing death sentences of many nationally known criminals, such as Richard Speck, who murdered eight nurses one night in 1966, were commuted to life, or in Speck's case 400 years. With no death sentence available, a series of Californian murderers were instead sentenced to multiple life sentences, ensuring they would be in prison until they died.

After Mullin came the capture and trial of Ed Kemper. Kemper had spent five years in Atascadero State Hospital for the Criminally Insane in California. He was released as 'cured' in 1969, but shortly after he began a "killing spree"[76] that went unnoticed by the police, and it was only after he killed his mother and her friend that he turned himself in. Once arrested the string of decapitation murders of young college girls over an eleven-month period provided fodder for sensational news stories nationwide. After his trial and conviction he was regularly referred to by the FBI during the 1980s in newspaper reports as a prime example of a serial killer. He also became one of their favourite subjects to interview. During his trial Kemper asked for death by torture as the penalty for his crimes but the court would not grant his request.

For some concerned citizens in California, Kemper's trial and conviction on eight counts of first-degree murder raised questions about who should be confined to mental hospitals. The previous two years had seen seventy murders committed in California by people who had at one time been confined in state mental hospitals. Department of Mental Hygiene figures show that between 1967 and 1973 Reagan's policy had closed three mental hospitals and released 15,000 patients into society. In the wake of Kemper's trial Earl Brian, California State Secretary of Health, Education and Welfare, and psychiatrist Bernard Diamond both stated that they believed, "[e]xperts are not able to predict violent behaviour in individuals."[77] Brian urged the creation of a $1.3 million centre for the prevention and (medical) detection of violence as a measure to avoid a repeat of the Kemper murders. The California legislature blocked the proposal when information was leaked to the press, and critics pointed out that the Centre for the Study and Reduction of Violence would conduct "questionable experimental brain surgery and behaviour control operations."[78] The Centre was originally proposed a few years earlier by Reagan. It was supposed to have been located in a former military base in a remote area of California with several facilities around the state developing treatment models, as well as implementing pilot studies and demonstration programs for the centre. One facility which had been proposed for use was Vacaville prison, well known as a CIA drug-testing site during the 1960s and 1970s,[79] and the place where sex killers such as Ed Kemper and Richard Chase were incarcerated.

In 1974 the American Psychiatric Association agreed that psychiatric expertise was not able to accurately predict the long-term behaviour of patients, but the Supreme Court rejected all protests, not wanting to believe that psychiatrists could not predict dangerousness over any timespan.[80] The issue of multiple murder was made more serious in California by statistics which showed Santa Cruz to have had the highest homicide rate per capita in the United States in 1972. This concern was increased by the trial in 1970, which captured the public's attention, of Charles Manson and the "Family" in Los Angeles for a series of murders in 1969. Also in 1970, John Lindley Frazier's killings of Dr Victor Ohta and four others in their own home almost started a civil war between conventional citizens and the hippies in Santa Cruz.

California was not the only state to embrace the "bold new approach" which Kennedy had called for but, along with New York, it had led the way. By the late 1970s serious doubts were being raised in both states. New York had released 65,000 patients between 1968 and 1979, but was unable to account for their whereabouts. Despite reducing the number of patients by over two-thirds, only thirteen per cent of the mental health budget was being spent on community based health care. In effect communities became dumping grounds, and a similar pattern was seen in Washington DC, Colorado and Massachusetts. Just before he resigned, James Dolby, the head of Colorado's Division of Mental Health, summed up the results of inadequate community health programs: "What we have done in the name of good mental health is to create a public tragedy... It is a sin and a crime."[81]

Robert D Miller reports a national study of the criminalization of the mentally ill which found ten per cent of all inmates in American jails were suffering from "serious mental disorders," concluding that those prisoners should have been sent to psychiatric facilities, not criminal justice institutions. The restrictive commitment criteria set by the courts meant that a patient's condition had to deteriorate to the extent that they had committed criminal offences before treatment would be provided. While many of the cases of mental patients committing crimes were scarcely reported beyond state-wide news, some were sensational enough to receive national coverage, and their prominence benefited the ideology of the New Right. After the failure of Goldwater, they learned from some of the mistakes which had been made and planned a second Presidential campaign in 1968.

After Goldwater, Nixon was the only acceptable national candidate on the right who had any chance of winning the presidency.[82] Accordingly, he was adopted by those people who had supported Goldwater and Reagan. Murray Chotiner, a lawyer and political publicist in California, taught Nixon a special campaign style which he had developed specifically for California. The system was based on Chotiner's belief that in elections people vote against a candidate, not for a candidate, and that "A candidate's chance for error, if he makes a statement on anything, are marvellously broad in California." In response to this, he advocated telling the public as little as possible about his own candidate's range of views, so that voters would have less to oppose and, at the same time, telling them as much as possible about a select portion of any opponent's views; selections that voters would resent and oppose. Chotiner obsessively refined this negative style of politics, which eventually became known as the "politics of resentment."[83]

By 1967 a broad swathe of American opinion had become more conservative. The race for the Republican party nomination was dominated by one issue, law and order. Each of the three candidates tried to outdo each other in their promises of "how many people they would arrest if they were elected, how many new jails they would build, how many armed cars and sniper rifles they would buy for the police." In the course of his campaign Nixon actively sought to polarise the country for political gain. The poor, the black community and the young were all targets for Nixon.[84]

Campaign pledges by Nixon to increase law and order budgets, whilst sincere, would ensure the police took on a paramilitary nature. He assured the party faithful continually that there would be no liberal Republican sharing the party ticket with him for the 1968 Presidential election.[85] He turned to old racial prejudices and fears in his campaign rhetoric, appealing to 'silent majorities' and their fear of 'street crime'. Civil rights marches, anti-war protests and racial violence across America had enraged the middle classes and made them fear for their safety. Nixon used this to his political advantage. The similarity between Nixon and J Edgar Hoover's use of crime issues was ironic since Nixon had applied to join the Bureau in the late 1930s. His application had been approved but "just before the notification was to be mailed their [the FBI's] appropriation request for the next year was cut; if it had come through, I might have had a career as a G-man for the FBI."[86] Budget cuts, which had prevented his FBI career, were the last thing Nixon intended; rather, he proposed massive new expenditure.

Despite the doubts of many, Richard Nixon won his coveted prize in 1968. Nixon's election signified the end of the New Deal, the end of progressive liberal legislation, and a retrenchment of extreme conservatism.

When leaving office Lyndon Johnson, in conversation with Nixon, referred to Hoover as "a pillar of strength in a city of weak men." He went on to say, "He's the only one you can put your complete trust in." Instead of civil rights legislation Nixon sought to find an Attorney General who would "observe the law," and a Chief Justice who would "interpret the law… not make it."[87] Nixon focused his attention on public fear of crime in the streets, as justification for his severe stance on crime and punishment. And late in 1969 an opportunity presented itself for Nixon to combine his attack on the counterculture and antiwar protesters with his moral political agenda, and to legitimise tough law and order measures. That opportunity was Charles Manson.

Manson was dubbed by the media as the "most evil man in the world" after being implicated in several brutal murders at the homes of Sharon Tate and later the La Bianca family in Los Angeles. Initially the LAPD did not see any connection between the crimes, but newspapers linked the two sets of murders. Coverage plunged LA into panic: "Sales of guns for home defense quadrupled, guard dogs were purchased, [and] human bodyguards were hired, as residents feared there were killers on the loose who were slaughtering not only showbusiness figures but ordinary people as well."[88]

Manson was alleged to be the leader of a disturbed hippy cult called "The Family" who indulged in drug taking, wild orgies, and murder. Much of the myth of Charles Manson and his Family appears now to have been created by Susan Atkins, attention-seeking murderess and Family member, and prosecuting attorney Vincent Bugliosi.[89] A few years before, in 1967, a media backlash against hippies had begun, resulting in a forceful social reaction against them.[90] The myth of The Family became part of this attack on the counterculture and was propagated in several books, such as Ed Sanders' *The Family* (1971), Vincent Bugliosi and Curt Gentry's *Helter Skelter* (1974), Atkins' *Child of Satan, Child of God* (1977), as well as the sensational news media reporting which surrounded the trial. The term "Manson Family" was even a creation of the media, coined in 1968 by a reporter covering the hippy culture at the time. The name stuck in the press and this was how the Spahn ranch group would be known to the world.[91]

Manson was seen to epitomise hippy and counterculture excesses and his 'cult' activities were taken as a direct attack on the traditional order of society. They were drop-outs and runaways, shirking their responsibility to society, violating accepted standards of sexual behaviour with their communal lifestyle. In her autobiography *Child of Satan, Child of God*, Susan Atkins repeatedly identifies worship of nature and drugs as the hippy lifestyle, with some group sex to bolster community spirit.[92] Richard Nixon condemned Manson as guilty, directly or indirectly, of eight murders before the jury had returned its verdict.[93] Nixon's comments were prominently displayed on newspaper headlines and Manson felt that the Presidential condemnation "pretty much made up the minds of the people."[94] Manson provided an ideal scapegoat for an uncertain America, and an opportunity to attack what was seen as a decadent and rebellious teen culture. "The Family" was not a name used by Manson in his memoirs: instead, he uses terms such as "circle" or "group." To conservative America, a term like 'family' has an almost sacred moral meaning, so that the immoral lifestyle of Manson's people when joined with a term like 'family' became an insult to middle class America and an attack on a conventional lifestyle. Manson himself was obviously not an authoritarian leader or a father figure; he was in a position of superiority probably because he was the eldest male, rather than because he exercised control. For conservatives, Manson's Family epitomised the degeneracy of the counterculture and the decline of society, a descending spiral of promiscuity, drugs, and violence. Manson, Susan Atkins, Patricia Krenwinkle and Leslie Van Houten were sentenced to death in March 1971.

The Supreme Court ruling on capital punishment declared in the *Furman vs. Georgia* (1972) verdict, that the way in which capital punishment was carried out was unconstitutional, and the ruling was a reasonable reflection of public opinion on the subject. A 1965 Harris poll showed that while thirty-eight per cent of Americans favoured capital punishment, forty-seven per cent opposed it.[95] Sentences were commuted from death to life in prison.

Less than a year later conservatives in states across the nation were drafting new legislation to have the death penalty reinstated; the issue became valuable in local politics, and invaluable in gubernatorial races.[96] The reassertion of authority and collective exacting of revenge symbolized by the death penalty was decried by crowds of protestors in the 1960s, but by the end of the Reagan presidency executions drew crowds of enthusiastic supporters.

Nixon played on the middle class fear of crime for his own political profit, and his rhetoric conveyed a hardline stance on crime but did little to enlighten the public or address the social issues which created crime, as Johnson had tried to do. Sending criminals to prison might have provided a short-term means to protect the public but the average felony conviction meant less than three years in prison, and prison was acknowledged as creating more criminal behaviour than it cured. Prisoners would be more dangerous to society upon release than they had been at the start of their incarceration. Crime was initially an escape from poverty for most convicts and "an ineffective and counterproductive prison system tends to keep them in that career."[97] Some opponents of the death penalty came from unusual backgrounds. Clinton

Origins of the New Right

P Duffy, a long-time warden of San Quentin who had carried out ninety executions, primarily opposed the legislation because he believed killing was wrong under any circumstances. He also added that capital punishment was "a privilege of the poor. I don't know of a wealthy person ever executed in the United States."[98] Duffy's comments were unfortunately accurate. At the time of capital punishment's temporary demise, the majority of death row prisoners were black and poor.

During the election campaign of 1972, Nixon was stalked by a gunman named Arthur Bremer, who had vowed to kill the President to prove his love to a high school girl with whom he was infatuated. Deciding that Nixon was too difficult because of the security which surrounded him, Bremer switched his focus to George Wallace. On 15 May, 1972, in Laurel, Maryland, Bremer shot Wallace and crippled him for life. It is notable that Bremer wrote in his diary, "The silent majority will be my biggest benefactor in the biggest hijack ever."[99] The shooting caused a panic in Nixon's White House and years later, in a secret session of the Watergate Hearings, Howard Hunt testified that, within an hour of the shooting, he received a telephone call from Charles Colson, an aide at the White House, asking him to go immediately to Bremer's apartment in Milwaukee and break in. The goal of Hunt's mission was to look for any materials which could link Bremer to an identifiable left-wing cause. As the Committee to Re-Elect the President (CREEP) had provided "excessive loose change" to fund numerous political dirty tricks, it was thought that Bremer had been one. The request was impossible, as Hunt could never have got to Bremer's apartment before the local police. Left-wing literature belonging to Bremer was found, as well as his diary, which made it clear that he was not a supporter of Nixon's.[100] The attempt on Wallace's life brought back memories of the assassinations of John and Robert Kennedy, and it was publicised that Bremer had read about their assassins. The state of Maryland put Bremer on trial, found him legally sane, and convicted and sentenced him to sixty-three years. A second trial was planned by the federal government, an action which William Shannon felt discredited the judicial system. The legal posturing added to the public's misunderstanding of mental illness.[101] Asking laymen to "arbitrate the professional disagreements of psychiatrists" was a surreal experience for the jury participants. The foreman from Bremer's state trial said, "They use so many big words. They couldn't agree. They were so evasive. You had to use horse sense." Confusion over the legal terms of 'sanity' and 'insanity' added to the lack of comprehension. The simple truth of 'horse sense' should have been apparent to the jury, but when the defence introduced Bremer's diary as evidence in the trial, to provide proof of his insanity, several jurors took the diary, a textbook example of paranoia, as evidence of Bremer's sanity. The incomprehension of Bremer's mental state reflected a lack of understanding of mental illness. While medical science had successfully wiped out many childhood illnesses, attempts at treating the mentally disturbed were sadly lacking. Public institutions were overcrowded and understaffed, and many of their children later turned up in the criminal justice system.[102]

Better To Reign In Hell

Less than two weeks before the attempt on Wallace's life came the death of J Edgar Hoover, which was hailed as the loss of a great American, but shortly after the nation suffered a much greater loss: the loss of belief in its institutions of government. None of Nixon's activities were without precedent, but the scale and organisation of political espionage was without equal.

The arrest of the 'plumbers' outside the Watergate complex was the beginning of a series of bizarre revelations about the conduct of the President and the country's security agencies. As the story unravelled, it became apparent that the FBI and CIA, at the highest levels, were involved in illegal political activities, giving advice and consent. J Edgar Hoover himself had advised Nixon that wire taps were the "only really effective" means of discovering where leaks were coming from in his administration. On that advice, Nixon gave his authorisation to Hoover to take any necessary steps to find the source of leaks.

In his eulogy to Hoover, Nixon identified increasing permissiveness in society as a threat to American heritage, and claimed that, thanks to the efforts of Hoover, and those like him, the dangerous trend was being reversed. He continued that, "American people today are tired of disorder, [and] disrespect for the law." Nixon contended his policies reflected public sentiment that, "America wants to come back to the law as a way of life."[103] After Hoover's death the appointment of Patrick Gray was an important political act and Nixon announced repeatedly that he had instructed the new director to operate the FBI in a totally non-political way. Gray claimed to be surprised at his selection but felt that he was "thoroughly qualified" to assume the position.[104] Many public statements testified to Nixon's friendship with Hoover, from his days as a Congressional freshman through to occasional visits to the race track and exchanging Christmas gifts, but it was made clear that Gray and Nixon's relationship would be professional. The resignation of Gray in 1973, following reports of how he had directed the Watergate investigation to Nixon's advantage, undermined any notions of professionalism.

Nixon's "true crime," according to Theodore White, was destroying "the myth that binds America together... that somewhere in American life there is at least one man who stands for law, the President." The irony of the situation was not lost on some of the spectators. The great law-and-order administration had subverted the Constitution, the supreme article of faith in the rule of law.[105] Nixon's successor would have to try to rebuild public faith.

Following Nixon's resignation, Gerald Ford assumed the presidency. Many considered that Ford was "too dumb to be president," and his nomination for vice-president (after Spiro Agnew's resignation over bribery charges made against him) had been a political move. Richard Rovere in the *New Yorker* asserted that to hold the office of vice-president all that was required was "a warm body and occasionally a nimble tongue."[106] Nixon could not afford a confrontation with Congress so Ford, the man who had no political enemies, was chosen. The knowledge that Ford, who was considered to be severely lacking in intelligence and initiative, was vice-president, and ready to assume the presidency, led some Republicans to believe that impeachment of Nixon

Origins of the New Right

would be less likely.[107]

After Nixon's resignation, Ford's public record concerning the Watergate investigators was "touching, a monument to loyalty or stupidity." Vietnam and Watergate had left an indelible mark on the American public and their perception of their government. This was Ford's inheritance. The first priority for Ford, identified by his transition team, was "restoration of the confidence and trust of the American people in their political leadership, institutions and processes." Once this was established, "firm and efficient" control of the administration was needed and a "national feeling of unification and reconciliation" generated by a strong Presidential style.[108]

After much apparent indecision, Ford pardoned Nixon and with that the public and media lost faith. Attempting to establish confidence in the administration was a lost cause and his short time in office was characterised by a domestic policy which was a case of damage control and crisis management. As Ford's Presidency came to its end, the Manson Family made a sudden return to prominence.

Family members and the Symbionese Liberation Army were reported to have plotted to help Manson escape from prison in 1974. Their plan was never put into effect but the threat generated considerable publicity. The following year Sandra Good, a Family member, sent a manifesto for the International People's Court of Retribution to the Associated Press. She alleged that her organisation was composed of thousands of people around the world, and that board members (and their families) of large corporations committing environmental crimes had been targeted for assassination. The two attempts on Ford's life, by Lynette "Squeaky" Fromme (September 5 in Sacramento), and Sarah Jane Moore (September 22 in San Francisco) made front-page news.[109] Fromme, as an associate of Sandra Good and Charles Manson, brought the Manson Family killings back into the headlines and reminded the public of the assassinations (or attempted assassinations) by Lee Harvey Oswald, Sirhan Sirhan and Arthur Bremer. Fromme and Moore became the first women in American history to be charged with attempted assassination of the President, and after being found competent to stand trial they were both sentenced to life in prison. Events left the nation feeling grateful that Ford's life had been spared, and gave credibility to conservative attacks on the counter culture. Despite this, Nixon's lawlessness, combined with the pardon, ensured Republican defeat in 1976 by the little known Democratic Governor of Georgia, Jimmy Carter.

After defeating Ford in 1976, Carter instituted his own reforms. His budgets made cuts in the FBI and his proposed FBI Charter Act made conservatives uncomfortable because they feared that the Bureau's investigative abilities would be undermined. During his presidency the death penalty was restored, and Carter himself supported capital punishment for criminals convicted for killing police officers.

The restoration of capital punishment in the United States after 1978 was contentious, and states used their discretion as to which inmates would face execution first. Anti-death penalty arguments reflected concern over the representation of the poor and minorities, who constituted a disproportionate number of death row inmates. On May 25, 1979, John Spenkelink was executed in Florida, marking the return of the death penalty to the United States. After Spenkelink's execution, "there was no great public outcry against the execution, any hopes of turning political pressure against the death penalty faded."[110] At the time of Spenkelink's execution, eighty-four per cent of death row prisoners were in eleven southern prisons. One of the major arguments to support the death penalty was the 'deterrent' debate, but no reliable data could prove any deterrent value. Despite that, a 1977 Harris poll showed that sixty-one per cent of people believed it had a deterrent value, and thirty-nine per cent of whites polled said they would support it even if it was not a deterrent.[111]

William Bowers and Glenn Pierce of North Eastern University report that blacks and whites may have been sentenced to death in more or less equal numbers in the years after *Furman vs. Georgia*, but it was not the race of the criminal which was the decisive factor in sentencing, it was the race of the victim.[112] Virtually all states enacting death penalty legislation chose to execute white prisoners who had been convicted of particularly unpleasant crimes as a way to maximise support for the death penalty.[113] According to Carol Palmer, of the NAACP Legal Defense Educational Fund, inflation influences the views of members of the middle class with economic interests to protect: "When times are tight, people think more about crime and they start looking for panaceas." She concluded that the motivation to enact capital punishment legislation always rises with inflation.[114]

The recession of the late 1970s appeared to validate New Right attacks on 'liberal' Democratic economic policies, with crime statistics contributing support to the retributionist law and order rhetoric of conservative Republicans. Perhaps it is not by chance, in light of American society's insecurity, that the serial killer panic occurred during the presidency of Ronald Reagan. His policies were not as popular with the American public as the media reported and, despite having the Cold War to justify military aggression, he needed an active and sensational domestic threat, a symbol upon which he could focus public attention and his law-and-order policies. Reagan's 'paranoid' world view connected a number of social problems together to target 'soft' liberalism as the cause of the decline in many aspects of American culture which, in turn, weakened the nation in the face of the Soviet 'evil empire'.

Walt Disney's Last Wish
The New Right and Ronald Reagan[1]

THE DEVELOPMENT OF THE NEW RIGHT 'IDEOLOGY' REACHED ITS peak with the election of Ronald Reagan in 1980. One flattering biographer previously described Reagan as a "Lone Crusader," the "White Knight of the Right," despite years of criticism for being too far outside the political mainstream.[2] Reagan's image was defined in terms of popular frontier mythology, emphasizing a steadfast dedication to his personal conservative ideology, even when it lost favor with the masses. Exploiting social insecurity, political dissatisfaction and an economic recession, as previous New Right candidates had done, Reagan campaigned to support a decidedly 'paranoid' conservative agenda.

Military strength along with domestic security were prominent issues, as they had been throughout his political career. Emphasizing violent crime, which contributed to the serial killer panic, Reagan used similar tactics to Hoover's "crime clocks" to distort the incidence of reported crime and increase public fear, asserting that crime was an American "epidemic" and rates were increasing regardless of the efforts which had been made. For Reagan, the problem was the way in which crime was dealt with by the legal system. In his opinion, "There has been a breakdown in the criminal justice system in America. It just plain isn't working. All too often, repeat offenders... are robbing, raping and beating with impunity and... quite literally getting away

The New Right and Ronald Reagan

with murder." A change was needed, according to Reagan, to win the war on crime. It was time to see crime as a moral problem requiring a spiritual solution. Describing murder as "objectively evil," he stated "right and wrong matters; individuals are responsible for their actions; [and] Retribution should be swift and sure for those who prey on the innocent."[3] Echoing his earlier rhetoric as well as that of Barry Goldwater, Richard Nixon and J Edgar Hoover, his speeches rang with Old Testament zeal.

Issues that concerned the New Right ranged from gay rights and women's liberation to the need for censorship in public schools and libraries. There was also a desire to reverse the general stance on civil rights taken by successive federal governments from the 1960s onwards.[4] True to Hofstadter's 'paranoid style' of politics, the religious conservatives saw attacks on Christian values coming from all directions; education, the media, the judiciary, the government, Catholic bishops, and even other Protestant denominations. It seemed to them that everyone was trying to undermine their values, and, more importantly, their right and authority to educate their children morally and in a Christian way.[5] Abortion, censorship, and school prayer became major issues for the religious right. "Never in history," one conservative commentator alleged, "have the purveyors of a degraded, almost uncensored, culture had direct, unmediated access to the minds of a society's young." Mainstream media was attacked for not just glorifying violence but trivializing, MTV was described as a "festival of misogyny," and primetime TV a "laboratory of 'alternative-lifestyles.'" The New Right brought their own puritanical moral judgments into the debate on deviancy, terming it a "cultural war" and believing it was necessary to complement their attempts to rein in the liberal welfare system.[6]

They began to organize politically and sought links with traditional conservative groups who also wanted a return to "ordered liberty." The New Right focus on welfare "corrupting the souls of its recipients" helped make welfare reform a major issue in the eyes of the religious conservatives. It facilitated a merger between the religious conservatives and New Right supporters, which was considered to be largely completed with Reagan's election in 1980.[7] In the 1980s the resurgence of Social Darwinism was mixed with an ultra-conservative fundamentalist Christian crusade of the self-proclaimed 'Moral Majority.' The consequence was that serial sex killers were seen not as human failures but as predatory examples of original sin, a result of the lax morality of the Great Society. By the end of the decade, Reagan's belief in Social Darwinist philosophy was the accepted theory in Washington. According to one skeptical commentator, Reagan saw that, "Inequality was a requisite result of sound economic growth and the wealth created by the rich would lift up the poor as well, by way of a 'trickle down.'"[8] Egalitarianism and a redistribution of wealth would, for the New Right, lead to adverse economic effects, creating a static or depressed economy. In Reagan's view, self-determination was a duty as well as a right.[9]

In November 1979, the *New York Times* reported a nine per cent increase in serious crime according to FBI statistics for the first six months of the year, an announcement made more worrying because it contradicted expert opinions that crime rates would fall. Coincidentally, the rise was most pronounced in small cities, towns and rural areas, where it exceeded population growth especially in the south and southwest—exactly the constituency to which Reagan was appealing. The increase was blamed on social and demographic changes, especially from what was described as a "surge of violence and defiance of the law" originating in the 1960s civil rights and antiwar protest movements. Further, an increasingly transient population, the break up of families, and the severing of ties to traditional institutions of church and family were also emphasized as contributing to the crime problem.[10]

Law and order were highlighted by the press and parties during the election campaign, when the Republican Party platform declared, "We will work for the appointment of judges... who respect traditional family values and the sanctity of human life."[11] Reagan was noted for his "no-nonsense toughness" during his governorship of California, but several of his own staff who worked closely with him in California during his time as Governor disputed his version of the facts. William Bagley said Reagan's account was an "absolute, total misrepresentation of the facts." Journalists also picked up on the discrepancies. Lou Cannon of the *Washington Post* commented tactfully that, "overall the real picture [of Reagan's governorship] is substantially different to the one Reagan paints for his audiences."[12]

It was claimed that Reagan, with his optimism, strength, enterprise and inventiveness, would help the country recapture what had allegedly been lost. He presented himself as "the political wizard whose spell made everyone feel good."[13] Reagan tapped into a longing for national pride that had been deadened by the Vietnam War and Watergate.[14] Throughout his presidency Reagan delivered the message that had been scripted for him. "Better days are ahead" and "America is back" were common statements in his campaign speeches. "Morning in America" was the regularly repeated slogan in the early days of his administration. Reagan's administration was "a presidency of pictures, symbols, and staging. Every public act of his presidency was planned by his media experts for its maximum impact through television."[15] Earl Dunckel, Reagan's companion from his GE days, was convinced that no matter how many speechwriters there were available at the White House the end product was Reagan's.[16]

Reagan's mandate for change, which he claimed after his 1980 election victory, was fragile. Only twenty-eight per cent of the eligible voters had chosen to support him.[17] Neither Reagan, nor Carter, had presented a campaign to excite the electorate, and many voters waited until the closing weeks to make up their minds which way they would vote. During the 1970s, public confidence in government institutions had fallen, due to the *Pentagon Papers*, Watergate, the Iranian hostages, and the oil crisis. By 1980, the level of faith in government and the credibility of the President had suffered, leaving the result of the election to be interpreted as a vote of no confidence in Carter rather than an endorsement of Reagan.[18]

To a worried and uncertain country, Reagan delivered a spectacle the

The New Right and Ronald Reagan

like of which had never been seen before. No longer the public event it had been, prices for tickets to the January 20 inauguration soared, ensuring it would be an "outpouring of wealth and privilege."[19] Traditional values were commonly recognized as those of white picket fence America, but also of "the freewheeling, backroom card-shark ethos of high-toned dining, flashy apparel, and drinks galore."[20] The event was the costliest and most opulent inauguration in American history, giving credence to critics who likened it to "a bacchanalia of the haves."[21] At later White House functions, Reagan invited his old Hollywood friends to mix with diplomats. Among his celebrity guests were politically conservative Hollywood stars such as Jimmy Stewart, Charlton Heston, Bob Hope, Ginger Rogers and Frank Sinatra.[22]

From the very day of Reagan's inauguration, it seemed like a change for the better had occurred. The release of fifty-two American hostages who had been held for over a year in Iran emphasized that the time for uncertainty was over. Hopeful but not convinced, the public suspended judgment on Reagan's leadership, praying that his promises would be realized.[23] From the beginning Reagan "emerged as a president whose indifference to factuality [was] matched only by his devotion to theatricality."[24] Enactment of his economic policies, it was believed, would "reduce inflation and interest rates, expand business, add three million jobs to the economy, sharply curtail bureaucratic red tape, and eliminate waste from social programs without in any way injuring the truly needy."[25] For the first year of his presidency, he was one of the least popular presidents since WWII, according to opinion polls. The media at this time was referring to him as the "Great Communicator" and tried to justify his low popularity in polls as a consequence of his policies, but rated his personal popularity highly. Even this was not a reflection of the reality. In 1982, Gallup reported that Reagan's personal popularity was not disproportionately greater than his predecessors. In fact the *Los Angeles Times* reported in August 1982 that one-third of those who had voted for Reagan in 1980 said they would not vote for him should he be nominated again.[26] After eight weeks in office, the *New York Times* reported that Reagan had won less public approval than any newly elected President in the previous twenty-eight years. Disapproval of Reagan's handling of the presidency was disproportionately larger than it had been at comparable times for other presidents, and it was growing rapidly.[27]

Not disillusioned, Reagan asserted that the American law-enforcement community and courts had a new mandate from the American people, a "new consensus on crime issues… a consensus that utterly rejects the counsels of leniency toward criminals and the philosophy that fostered it." In Reagan's opinion the 1960s and 1970s were "grim" years when crime more than tripled in the United States. The result was that by the 1980s crime was costing in excess of $10 billion in financial losses and affecting thirty per cent of American homes. The death toll was heavy too, estimated at almost 25,000 lives. Rising crime unsettled public faith in the criminal justice system, and its ability to protect citizens and punish criminals.[28]

During the 1980s, women's fear of crime in particular became a *cause celebre* for radical feminists and criminologists alike.[29] However, the initial response to Reagan's federal crime strategy was not positive, and the *New York Times* described it as relying "heavily on the jawbone." Despite strong rhetoric declaring "War on Crime" the Reagan administration cut back by one-third at the end of 1981 on FBI investigations into gambling, prostitution, pornography and gangland murders, along with other activities associated with organized crime. The man chosen to wage war on crime was William French Smith, an old friend of Reagan's, and his personal lawyer during his days as governor. Once in office, Attorney General Smith reorganized Justice Department priorities toward violent crime and changed the definition of white-collar crime to focus on fraud against the government. Dramatic staff reductions and a freeze on Bureau hiring coincided with an announcement that no new undercover operations would be authorized against white-collar or organized crime.[30] Senator Paul Laxalt, along with several other conservative Republicans, sought to undo the reforms of the intelligence agencies and proposed an alternative FBI charter that would eliminate many of the existing administrative controls.[31] Reagan proposed cuts in federal funding, increasing the economic burden on local and state agencies to deal with crime instead of financial commitments to improve the system. In effect he was "cheerleading for those on the front lines," but without pledging financial support the federal crime strategy was almost meaningless.[32] Reagan's tough stance on crime was uncomfortably reminiscent of Nixon's "War on Crime" in the late 1960s, and while his rhetoric might have provided some comfort to an uncertain public, legal experts and Reagan's own advisory group agreed that his policies would do little, if anything at all, to make the streets safer.[33] Ira Glasser, executive director of the ACLU, described Reagan's anti-crime policy proposals as a "fraud in being serious proposals to reduce crime."[34] The policies were attacked by Judge David Bazelon for threatening civil liberties, but an FBI agent in Washington noted that, "Nothing could have given Reagan's war on crime more legitimacy than an attack from Bazelon... The liberals, taking their lead from Bazelon, would follow suit, saying that Reagan was being too tough on crime. In fact Reagan had one of the softest attacks on crime we'd seen in years."[35] Clearly, Reagan's 'War' was a war of words.

Attorney General Smith quickly set up the Attorney General's Task Force on Violent Crime (1981) which was designed to produce recommendations on possible courses of action to curb the alleged increase in violent crime, and as part of the task force, the FBI was required to submit a report outlining how it could assist in the national effort to combat violent crime. The task force report raised public awareness about a variety of crimes, especially violent crime and the prevalence of drugs in American cities. Terms such as 'street crime' or 'violent crime' were used by the FBI to describe the types of crime committed by people with low economic status.[36] Attacking lawyers and "utopian" social thinkers for suggesting that poverty breeds crime, Reagan attacked the legal system itself, alleging that the public had lost confidence in the courts' ability to convict criminals.[37] Recommendations from the task force were used as a basis for Reagan's crime policy. Skirting proposals for major spending, Reagan called for a relaxation of legal rules against using illegally seized evidence and

The New Right and Ronald Reagan

tough mandatory sentencing for "gun crimes," although he ignored the task force recommendation for tighter gun control,[38] despite statistics showing the US rate of handgun murders was seventy-seven times that of Britain, Japan, Sweden, Australia, Israel and Canada combined.[39]

Reagan's opulent, but unimpressive, start to the Presidency was suddenly and almost fatally ended. On March 31, 1981, John W Hinckley Jr attempted to kill Reagan as he left a Washington hotel with his security agents. Standing in a group of people on the sidewalk Hinckley fired several shots, wounding the President, his press secretary James Brady, a Secret Service agent and a police officer, before being restrained. Hinckley was a social inadequate who had been given an ultimatum by his father, an oil executive, to find a job and support himself. It was widely reported that Hinkley's actions were spurred on by his belief that he loved actress Jodie Foster, who despite her career as a movie star, was attending Yale at the time.[40] To prove his love, he intended to kill the most famous person in the world.

Hinckley's attempt on Reagan's life invoked memories of a series of political assassinations, most obviously that of John F Kennedy. For the fourth time in less than twenty years an attempt had been made on the President's life, and within minutes the news had spread across the nation: "For hour after hour that day there was no way for Americans to escape the replaying of an old national horror."[41] Initial news reports had a great impact on the public and intensive radio, TV and newspaper coverage amplified the sense of crisis. As Reagan's life lay in the balance it was felt that for a generation, "violent acts had disrupted the political process, torn at the nation's leadership, [and] left citizens numbed by a cycle of terror."[42] In the wake of Reagan's speeches about increasing crime, the attempt on his life made the public more aware of the possibility of violent crime, reinforcing his own personal views and causing a shift in public opinion.

The attack took place nine weeks after Reagan's inauguration, and not since the assassination of Kennedy in 1963 had the American public been so riveted to their television sets. The assassination of a President in office is an event of great political significance, it "affects a large part of the population in a profound way because it strikes at the deepest political loyalties, commitments and fears of the masses of people." The result is a crisis of authority and the shocked population exhibits "unusual political behavior" which, after John F Kennedy's assassination, saw the deification of the dead President and public support rallying behind policies which were seen as being initiated by him. Samuel Patterson reported that in the few hours following President Garfield's assassination he was transformed from being a "colorless figure to a leader of towering stature."[43] The crucial difference between Garfield, John F Kennedy and Reagan is that Reagan did not die. Reagan's survival was seen as a change in American political fortunes and won him praise from journalists who were not necessarily sympathetic to his policies.

White House officials pushed Reagan's legislative program and public sympathy made it hard for Democrats to criticize him. It was almost an exact reproduction of the public response to the assassination of John F Kennedy when Lyndon Johnson used public sentiment to enact the social legislation which Reagan sought to undo. The long lasting effects of the attempt on Reagan's life were quickly seen. William R Hamilton, who took polls for many Congressional Democrats, told David Broder of the *Washington Post*, only hours after Reagan was shot, "I think he will remain popular throughout his term now, whether or not his program works."[44] A powerful national mythology was rekindled, enabling Reagan to begin to transform himself from a "politician of dubious credentials and public achievements" into a "mythic figure of American life."[45]

Once recovered from his injuries, Reagan returned to the White House to continue his crusade against 'street crime.' Republicans talked about a new emerging privileged class of repeat offenders and career criminals, people who had been created as a price for the "years of liberal leniency." This leniency came from the "misguided" belief that "it was society, not the individual, at fault when an act of violence or a crime was committed. Somehow, it wasn't the wrongdoer but all of us who were to blame." Johnson's "Great Society," or as Reagan referred to it, the "too great society,"[46] was attacked as the cause of many of society's problems. Reagan's remarks were intended to show that the years of "pseudo-intellectual apologies" for crime and the criminal were now over.[47] After the abuses of government power in the 1960s and 1970s, Reagan needed to reassure the public that the law and order programs which he proposed were directed at issues which menaced the general public. Focusing on crimes which fitted with its conservative social agenda, the administration legislated against violent crime and pornography, while treating white-collar crime leniently. By superficially redirecting FBI jurisdiction towards these threats, the administration could convince the public that the excesses of the previous decade had been corrected.

Conservative judges appointed by Nixon to the Supreme Court endorsed a reactionary view of the law throughout the 1970s and into the 1980s. There was growing political value in supporting strong law and order policies which outweighed public debate of the Constitution. After the death penalty's formal return in 1979, the pace of state executions steadily increased, and by the mid 1980s about 250 prisoners a year were being added to death row, ensuring that future execution rates would follow the rising trend. Henry Schwarzchild of the ACLU attributed the increase in death sentences and executions to widespread public concern about the increasing levels of violent crime and anger at the criminal justice system.[48]

Sandra Day O'Connor, one of Reagan's appointees to the Supreme Court, regularly sided with the prosecution in death penalty appeals and the conservative influence showed quickly in the Court's decisions. Between 1976 and 1983 eight prisoners were executed, but with the Court's ideological shift, that increased to forty between 1983 and 1985.[49] In June 1984 the Supreme Court, dominated by judges sympathetic to Reagan's ideology, ruled that "public safety" considerations could justify overriding the accused's right to have an attorney present when being interrogated by the police, overriding the rulings of three New York state courts and eroding rights protected

The New Right and Ronald Reagan

by the *Miranda* decision. Justice Thurgood Marshall dissented from the majority opinion, finding the ruling to be in direct conflict with the Fifth Amendment.

Early in 1984 Reagan proposed a package of anti-crime legislation to protect "innocent, law abiding people" from the criminals who prey on them. The legislation, which sought tougher sentences, would give judges the right to deny bail in some cases, permit the government to seize the profits of drug traffickers, and allowed evidence obtained in "good faith" to be used in court. The Senate passed the bill, but in the House of Representatives it met with opposition from Representative William J Hughes, who was then the chairman of the House Judiciary Committee's Subcommittee on Crime.[50] O'Connor voted for the 'Good Faith' ruling which relaxed earlier interpretations of the Fourth Amendment. Paul Vossler, a public defender from Florida, was angered by the ruling; in his opinion, "The Court is saying that even if a policeman violates the Fourth Amendment—which prohibits unreasonable search and seizure—it's all right if he didn't mean to be a bad cop."[51]

The public's awareness of crime and the alleged breakdown in the criminal justice system paved the way for retributionist judgments coming from the Supreme Court. Evidently, the conservative majority of justices were determined to shorten the appeals process for prisoners under death sentences, and were "reaching out for cases with which to convey that message." But there was increasingly bitter dissent from the minority opinion. The majority Justices of White, O'Connor, Powell, Burger and Rehnquist viewed the lower courts as being too willing to allow the appeals process to drag on, manipulated by creative lawyers who continually devised stalling tactics.[52] Judge Rehnquist exemplified the New Right attack on 'liberal' courts when he expressed his dissenting verdict in a 1981 case. He wrote, "I do not think that this court can continue to evade some responsibility for this mockery of our criminal justice system."[53]

Chief Justice Burger saw fit to denounce lawyers who submitted a plea for a stay of execution on behalf of their clients, when he alleged that they were turning the administration of justice into a "sporting contest." Attacking the lawyers undermined the entire premise of the legal adversary system which Burger (supposedly) represented. The lawyers were *not* playing any games. The steadily growing population on the nation's death rows increased the workloads of a relatively small number of lawyers. Of the condemned, a considerable number of prisoners lacked adequate legal counsel, and large numbers did not have any legal help at all. At trial, many were convicted and sentenced in botched trials where they were represented by inadequately prepared defense lawyers.[54]

Media coverage of crime as a political issue ensured that Ted Bundy was the best-known killer in America in 1986. Governor Bob Graham, his Attorney General Jim Smith, and Supreme Court Justice Lewis F Powell attacked the American justice system for being too permissive to death row lawyers in the way that they were allowed to use the appeals process. Powell urged for the right of habeas corpus, the cornerstone of the American justice system, to be

75

Better To Reign In Hell

restricted—in clear violation of the Constitution.[55] The New Right advocates believed that the slowness of the appeals process undermined public confidence in the justice system. Not all conservatives agreed with the extreme views of Graham, Powell, and Smith. Baya Harrison III, a conservative lawyer from Tallahassee, saw the problem resting with incompetent lawyers who acted more like businessmen than legal professionals. In his opinion the delays were not due to the justice system, but rather it was money-minded lawyers who wanted lucrative cases and would not volunteer their time to expedite the appeals.[56]

Ironically, while Reagan was demonizing dangerous criminals as a threat to the nation, violent crime declined. Between 1981 and 1984, probably due to a decrease in the numbers of young people in the population, there were 9.5 per cent fewer incidents of violent crime.[57] No long-term plans to lower crime rates were proposed outside of locking up greater numbers of offenders for longer periods of time. Of the $40 billion spent by all levels of government on criminal justice programs, only a small fraction was allotted to building community resources or education about crime. Most of the money was directed into a control system that focused on punishing working-class crime, employed a militarized police force, harsh sentences, and ran punitive prisons with minimal attempts at rehabilitation. Federal prison overcrowding was obvious in the 1970s when the number of inmates increased by thirty per cent, but by 1981 a National Institute of Justice study found that sixty per cent of state prisoners and seventy per cent of those held in jails were, because of the deregulation of health and safety standards, living in overcrowded conditions. Reagan continued, and even accelerated, the deregulation trend.[58] Coupled with his mandatory sentencing policies, more people were in prison and serving longer sentences than at any other time in US history,[59] while the conditions were progressively deteriorating.

As an alternative to rights of the accused, Reagan's administration promoted the rights of crime victims and since no one wanted to be seen to oppose such rights, victim's legislation was easily introduced. The victim's rights movement, which had its origins in the 1960s, changed in the 1970s and 1980s, becoming more conservative and retributionist, and reflecting public frustration at official reports of high crime rates. The Victim and Witness Protection Act (1982) and a Presidential Task Force sought to redress the balance. The Task Force recommended over 100 reforms for state and federal government and a follow-up report in 1986 found that seventy-five per cent of the reforms had been implemented. One such recommendation meant that by 1987, forty-eight States allowed victim participation in sentencing. Victim opinions which were reported often reflected conventional reactionary, uninformed and outdated views of the legal system, society and psychology which reinforced the self-righteous morality of the New Right and their focus on revenge rather than justice.[60] Dissenting voices were ignored. Reagan's rhetoric, attacking liberal 'coddling' of criminals and moral decay, was repeated almost endlessly, and his 'paranoid' vision of society was accepted by the mainstream as accurate.

The New Right and Ronald Reagan

In fighting the decay FBI director William Webster identified 'street crime' as the responsibility of local law enforcement, hence the Bureau claimed to focus on white-collar crime and political corruption. Satisfied with the 1979 guidelines for the FBI, Webster stated that he wanted, and foresaw, no change in FBI responsibilities under the Reagan administration. He believed that he shared the President's view that the FBI should be doing the work that local police could not do, or could not do as well.[61] The agents thus resumed the role of 'supercops' which they had performed for J Edgar Hoover for the benefit of the public. However, Meese encouraged the Bureau to turn their attention away from white-collar crime, despite complaints from members of Congress that it was being ignored.[62]

Whatever the Bureau's role was to be, Reagan obviously saw the organization as a priority, increasing its budget from $622 million in 1980 to more than $1.3 billion by 1987.[63] Upon taking office one of Reagan's first acts was to issue Executive Order 12333, which was based on recommendations from the right-wing Heritage Foundation, and effectively restored to the CIA and FBI most of the intelligence gathering powers stripped from them by the Church Committee hearings. Reagan expanded the FBI's authority to use wiretaps and surveillance, to procure the services of informants, and to contract with other (right-wing) private intelligence gathering sources if and when they saw necessary. Domestic security operations were not only expanded by the Executive Order, but the FBI was also given the authority to conduct such operations in secret.[64] The forty-six per cent increase in Justice Department funding ($1.2 billion) was used to file more cases against spies than at any other time in US history. All this at a time when the administration argued that cuts in social programs were needed.

A climate of fear was established through political rhetoric. High-profile media reporting of misleading but authoritative official statistics justified the need for law and order issues to be dealt with as an urgent priority. As described by Hofstadter's 'paranoid style' of politics, every panic was framed as a threat to the stability of the nation. Victims had to be identified, a group who could easily be perceived as threatened, whose vulnerability would outrage most of the public, and whose numbers could be counted. Part of the concern about victims resulted in national debate in the US about the number of children abducted annually. Following intense media coverage of three stories, the disappearance of Etan Patz,[65] the abduction and murder of Adam Walsh,[66] and the murders which became known as the "Atlanta Child Murders," public awareness was drawn to a problem which tied together in the public consciousness the idea of serial sex killers and child abduction. Statistics concerning the exact numbers of missing children were not presented clearly by the activists or the media and led to exaggerated public fear.

Advocates cited a 1983 Department of Health and Human Services report and claimed that there were 1.5 million missing children each year.[67] A report in the *New York Times* the same year cited an estimate that 1.8 million children disappeared each year. No analysis of the statistics was offered which, by being printed beside a picture of John Walsh, father of Adam Walsh, might lead the reader to assume that the figure represented children who were abducted and murdered by strangers.[68] Private organizations widely circulated the government statistics to promote their own interests. Representative Paul Simon cited, as a conservative estimate, that 50,000 children annually were abducted by strangers and not returned,[69] the sort of exaggerated figures and disproportionate publicity often associated with a moral panic. The public were being led to believe crimes were being committed by 'strangers' against children in such large numbers. When 'stranger' murders were subsequently used as a euphemism for serial sex murder, the panic expanded further.

Sex offenders and extortionists were identified as the 'strangers' abducting children, with ten per cent of the children being recovered alive, ten per cent found dead, and the remaining eighty per cent never being recovered by their parents.[70] Few people bothered to examine the statistics, and if they had they would have found that ninety-five per cent of the 'missing children' were runaways, many of whom would return home after only a few days, only to run away again, meaning that they could be counted multiple times and hence inflate statistics. Of the remaining five per cent, most were taken by estranged parents in custody battles with only a fraction being accounted for by genuine 'stranger' abductions.[71]

John Walsh became a national figurehead, a moral entrepreneur for the missing children activists, and went on to host the 'reality' television show *America's Most Wanted*. When executives considered candidates to host the show, a list of actors, actresses, politicians, journalists and crime authors were all judged by two criteria. The show needed "somebody who could not only speak clearly and follow cues, but also someone with credibility."[72] Walsh's credibility came from public recognition of his family's loss, and additionally because he looked like "J Edgar Hoover's dream of a G-Man."[73] The Walsh family story had been filmed as *Adam* (Michael Tuchner, 1983) and a sequel *Adam: His Song Continues* (Robert Markowitz, 1986) which brought widespread attention to that particular case and promoted a figure of 1.5 million missing children. In addition there was an HBO child safety film, and John Walsh's role in a legislative 'crusade' prompted hundreds of state laws and brought attention to the wider phenomenon. After winning numerous accolades and being photographed shaking hands with Ronald Reagan at the White House, Walsh was a well known public figure. Walsh was seen as an 'everyman' with whom a wide general public could identify, an "ordinary guy who had been hit hard by crime and that would be important to the audience."[74] While the audience could identify with the loss of the Walsh family, *Adam* and its sequel used their grief to endorse a retributive criminal justice system. After Adam's remains are found in the film, John Walsh says, "I want to see him [the killer] caught, punished, executed, killed. I want revenge." The effect of losing his son made him lose faith in the creed of 'God, country, family,' the mainstays of the American dream. For Walsh revenge, not justice would recover that faith.

Public service donations of airtime by television stations broadcasting "pathetically out-of-date" photographs of children, missing for years, provided another means for the fear to reverberate into suburban homes.[75] Initial insecurity about missing children became more pronounced when they were found murdered, creating a panic which paved the way for the later serial sex killer panic. Critics pointed out that the milk cartons and billboard campaigns failed to differentiate between stranger and parental abductions, again exacerbating the problem and increasing parental concerns about the safety of their children.[76] Skeptical of the hysteria, Dr Benjamin Spock, the famous pediatrician, believed that the emotionally charged educational programs were themselves a danger: "It's causing unnecessary fright in children, morbid fears." Stated simply, "It's wrong to scare children."[77]

In 1983 Ottis Elwood Toole, who would later be labeled a serial killer, confessed to the murder of Adam Walsh. At the time Toole was in jail awaiting trial on a fatal arson charge, and told police he wanted to talk about a child he had killed in Fort Lauderdale.[78] Toole later retracted his confession (along with a few dozen other confessions), and the police acknowledged that it was highly unlikely he had been the perpetrator. However, the link had been made in public perception connecting the idea of traveling sex killers to the missing children problem. Sociologist Michael Agopian believed "there are tens of thousands of additional Adams that are not so prominently reported by the media."[79] The link between child abductions and serial sex murderers was not officially made for more than a decade, until the "Serial Killers and Child Abductions" hearings in 1995. The other 'Adams' were not necessarily from middle-class families with the means to draw so much attention to their losses. John Walsh's claims were heard partly because he was a successful businessman with enough finance to back his campaign, but favorable press attention also enabled him to gather support and gain political influence.

As a white middle-class businessman, John Walsh successfully gained political influence for his crusade, but political influence was the one thing most black families of missing children lacked. However, when a public outcry developed in Atlanta in 1980 over the lack of police interest in the murders of young black children, a city with a sixty per cent black population, officials were forced to acknowledge the protest. But the Carter administration was reluctant to commit itself. After the death of Dean Corll in Texas in 1973, and the capture of Jeffrey Dahmer in Wisconsin in 1991, both of whom killed boys and young men, similar public outcry was heard when it was found that the police had made little effort to investigate the missing boys and men. In both of these cases, resolution was accidental and circumstantial evidence was overwhelming.

Camille Bell, the mother of one of the murdered children in Atlanta, was unhappy at the official response to the killings. She found that, "There seemed to be more concern for how the city would look or how people would react."[80] City Hall officials would not admit that there was a problem, a lack of response which Bell attributed, at least in part, to the city becoming more metropolitan. She felt that the city no longer knew how to care, that people were indifferent. In response to the perceived indifference, the mothers of victims set up the Committee to Stop Children's Murders (CSCM), and

Better To Reign In Hell

The New Right and Ronald Reagan

attended any public meeting or forums where they could be heard. They did not want their children locked up and living in terror.[81]

It was the threat of the loss of investment in the south's largest city which prompted police action. Beginning in the mid 1970s, Atlanta began to transform itself from a regional centre into an international city by attracting investment from abroad. Between 1976 and 1979, a dozen foreign banks chose the "city too busy to hate" as a location for their investments, and other business interests followed.[82] The murders threatened to halt the progress. Attention was shifted from the image the city wanted to project to the world to long-term social problems, such as unemployment and poverty, which Mayor Maynard Jackson acknowledged posed a "grave, persisting and escalating" problem if not confronted by coordinated and systematic efforts.[83]

Rarely was it reported that the Atlanta Chief of Homicide retired because his department was too understaffed to do its job, or that in 1979 Atlanta had the highest homicide rate among the largest thirty US cities.[84] In Atlanta, race was seen as a dead issue, both ideologically and in daily life, and in such a climate a racial motive for the murders was unthinkable.[85] The possibility of racially motivated abductions and murders of black children threatened to tarnish the city's reputation and undermine its economy. Tension grew in Atlanta with the black population's frustration at apparent police disinterest. By winter 1980–81, "Atlanta was a city under siege."[86]

In November 1980, William Webster had tried to calm public fears by saying that there was no racist conspiracy behind the Atlanta murders, which at the time had claimed eleven victims. To allay fears of racism and present an image of unity, considerable emphasis was placed on the searches by black and white citizens, and the "renewed sense of community" which resulted.[87] Rather than producing racial harmony and unity, the murders created fear and suspicion which spread beyond black communities, because the police had no leads or clues or motives for the murders.

There was considerable discussion among residents of black communities about the resurgence of violent Ku Klux Klan activity and paramilitary training in the south.[88] In response, a group of black military veterans called for similar paramilitary training for blacks so that they could defend themselves against white racists.[89] Coincidentally, the brutal murders of six black men in Buffalo, New York, added to fears of racial antagonism.[90] William Webster tried to calm concern over the murders in Buffalo, saying that they were not racially motivated either,[91] but Webster was proved wrong when Joseph Christopher, a white soldier stationed at Fort Benning, was arrested for the murders.

However, as the murders in Atlanta continued, the black community's fears persisted. As the body count increased in Atlanta, officials continually urged the population, and the nation as a whole, to believe that race was not the reason for the crimes. Contradicting the ideas of community activists, Mayor Jackson again advised residents to "lower their voices" when discussing the possibility that racism was the motivation for the children's murders.[92] Many reports talked about a single killer but Dr. Joseph Burton, medical examiner of DeKalb county, was not convinced at the beginning of the murders that there was a "single killer methodically snatching children" but, "if that man didn't exist, we have created him and he is killing now."[93] Other officials argued that the wide portrayal of the killings as probably being the work of one killer may have wasted police time and lost contacts who might have provided valuable information.[94]

Receiving increased publicity nationwide, the Atlanta case became a political issue for the New Right and was crucial in establishing the perception of efficiency and accuracy of the FBI profilers in their chosen field of expertise. Making no headway the police called Dorothy Allison, a psychic, to join the investigation. Police Chief George Napper acknowledged the decision was "unusual" but the usual methods had not produced any results. Allison left the investigation after two days.[95] Five "street smart" detectives from around the country joined the investigation in November 1980 for several weeks. All of them were well respected with long careers in homicide investigations and chosen for their extensive experience. One of them, a retired LAPD captain, Pierce Brooks, later joined with the FBI at the senate hearings on serial violent crime in 1983 to propose his Violent Criminal Apprehension Program (VICAP) to track criminals who were moving from one location to another. When the detectives left, the city's Public Safety Commissioner, Lee Brown, reported that their "mission" to give a second opinion was a success.[96]

Two FBI agents were sent to provide technical assistance and begin a preliminary investigation to see if the missing children were being held in violation of federal kidnapping laws. One of the agents was a behavioral scientist, the other was a specialist in organizing investigations. John Glover, who was notable for being the first black agent to head a FBI field office, explained that the behavioral specialist "develops a profile, a very general list of categories, of who might be a logical suspect in the case."[97] Major Maynard Jackson and Lee Brown both asked Carter for as much help as possible and criticized the Bureau for "unjustified" discrimination against the city of Atlanta. Attorney General Civiletti hoped that federal involvement would benefit the investigation and bring a speedy resolution to the "shocking" murders.[98] By that stage of the investigation there were still "no solid leads," and no evidence to conclusively identify the number of persons involved in the crimes, Lee Brown explained that "The investigation is being carried out as if we have fifteen separate cases."[99] An investigative assumption of a connection was also acknowledged,[100] and this would be a feature of the so-called serial slayings. However, that was only because the killings had taken place in a relatively short time. Police were "baffled," however, by the "varying circumstances" of the murders and abductions.[101]

People in Atlanta became cautious. Children especially displayed an "extremely high level of distrust of strangers"; their reaction ranged from a "detached awareness" to a "persistent worry about their vulnerability." Atlanta Board of Education psychological testing officials found significant and discouraging results in test performances, especially in the predominantly black low-income southeast section of the city where most of the victims had come from. Many children were found to become withdrawn and less verbal; other findings reflected that a significant number of the children had diminishing self-esteem and self-confidence. The fear evident in the children of Atlanta may well have been what Dr. Spock was warning about and criticizing in relation to the missing children crusade of John Walsh and its exaggerated media coverage. Recognizing that speculating on long-term effects was premature, the Atlanta psychologists still believed that the fear could stay with the children for years.[102]

A few days after his inauguration, Reagan told reporters that "civil rights" would be the only basis upon which the FBI could justify involvement in Atlanta,[103] and the FBI officially entered the investigation in February 1981 to offer assistance with other Justice Department agencies. The official death toll then stood at fifteen children dead and two missing. Vice-President George Bush announced that it was essential to end the "nightmare of slayings and disappearances,"[104] and indicated that the Bureau's role was to discuss with the Atlanta police their request for additional equipment and technical assistance.[105]

To show the federal government's concern about the situation, $1.5 million in federal funds was provided to bolster the investigation. The federal funds were a pathetic attempt to solve a crisis by throwing money at it, in the manner of many of Reagan's short-term solutions to problems, but no serious attempt was made to improve the area's substructure in the long term and make it safer for its inhabitants. Several White House aides acknowledged that the funds were a way of blunting criticism of Reagan's economic program for its obviously harsh effects on the poor, but the grant only caused confusion between the police agencies involved. Aides also commented on the administration's concern about setting a precedent for giving financial aid for local police matters.[106] FBI agent John Douglas asserted that, "crime is a moral problem. It can only be resolved on a moral level,"[107] emphasizing that crime was personal and not political. This effectively removed any necessity to deal with the social factors effecting crime, and evaded the dire need for long term social spending, both echoes of the political agenda of the New Right.

Money from the grant was earmarked for the families of victims attributed to the child killer, which caused problems because the law enforcement agencies were unsure about exactly which victims had been killed by the serial sex killer. Even the FBI profilers Douglas and Hazelwood did not believe that all of the murders were by the same killer, but the 'pattern' which they claimed to have found linking most of the victims made no sense. FBI allegations that the killings "[d]efinitely fit[ted] a sexual pattern" seemed to be wishful thinking in light of their acknowledgments that there was no clear evidence of molestation on any of the bodies.[108] But the bodies kept being found and "The List" kept growing.

To be entitled to a share of the federal grant, the family of a dead child who fitted the victim profile had to be added to what became known as "The List." Once their child's name was added to The List the family would be entitled to claim a share of the grant which could be as much as $100,000.[109] It became financially worthwhile for families of any murdered black child to try to have their child's name associated with the child murders, and to be placed on The List, thus increasing the number of crimes which were attributed to the serial sex killer and increasing the panic. Later in the investigation William Webster announced, very prematurely, that in several cases a child's killer had been a member of their own family. Atlanta officials were angry at Webster's comments. Mayor Jackson believed the statement would "undermine the public's confidence in our investigation and create a great deal of media speculation and invective."[110] Webster also stated that the Bureau was almost certain who had killed between twelve and sixteen of the twenty-three murdered children. Two or three such "casual press statements" were made by Webster, hinting at suspects and solutions to crimes, but none of which ever led to an arrest.[111] During his tenure J Edgar Hoover also prolonged police investigations by sidetracking manpower into checking up on leads which distracted attention away from apprehending a suspect.

Shortly after Bush's announcement, the Atlanta Task Force was restructured and the investigation shifted from tracking the children to finding the "killer or killers." Previous investigative leaders had been criticized for being too sensitive to the political concerns involved in the investigation, but the involvement of the Justice Department and the FBI was intended to end that. Numerous opinions were voiced by investigators in relation to the crimes. Some believed a 'copycat' killer was active, others said that some of the murders were cult-related, but all acknowledged that one killer was not responsible for all (or even most) of the murders.[112]

The murders in Atlanta occurred at a time when Reagan was trying to establish himself as a man of action, and the media attention surrounding the child murders meant they could not be ignored. A second group of detectives was brought in from around the nation on May 21 for a consultation with Atlanta Police Department officers. Among them were detectives from the most prominent sex murder cases of the 1970s, Lt Frank Braum (John Wayne Gacy case), Lt Joseph Borelli (Son of Sam), Lt Ed Henderson and Detective Phillip Sartuche (Hillside Stranglers), and Lt Frank Chase and Robert Keppel who had tracked the notorious Ted Bundy. All of these detectives, from their investigative experience, shared one assumption: they were looking for a serial sex killer. Keppel felt that, from the information presented to them, they should look for "exclusive" rather than "inclusive" characteristics. Therefore, cases which might have offered valuable leads were excluded from the investigation.[113]

The Bureau of Police Services had asked the FBI for assistance in March 1980, and the consulting detectives were eager to find out what "gems of wisdom" the Behavioral Science Unit had provided as they were self-proclaimed experts, despite never having investigated a single lead in a murder investigation. To the experienced detectives the FBI were "the kings of follow-up but couldn't solve a crime in progress." According to the profile provided by the BSU the killer was white, suggesting to Keppel that they had given in to community groups and accepted that the crimes were racially motivated.[114] In the years that followed, John Douglas of the FBI would assert

The New Right and Ronald Reagan

that their profile had *always* been for a black killer, ignoring the existence of an earlier profile for a white killer, but the profile of the black offender was only presented by Douglas *after* Wayne Williams, a young black man, was taken into custody. However, claiming credit for an accurate profile emphasized the accuracy of the Bureau, provided a satisfactory solution to the political unrest, and symbolically reinforced Reagan's crime policies.[115]

The turning point in the investigation occurred on May 22 at 3:00AM, when a surveillance team, headed by an FBI agent, on a bridge over the Chatahoochee River heard a splash which they believed was a body being dumped into the river. A car seen leaving the bridge was followed by the team. The driver, Wayne Williams, was stopped on the highway while his car was searched but no list of its contents were made at that time. Later police and FBI reports differed as to what the contents of the car were. Williams was released after being questioned for two hours at the roadside, but he was *not* put under surveillance for almost two days, during which time he reportedly removed several boxes of materials from his house. After the incident with Williams, the FBI agent in charge of the surveillance team did *not* inform the other task force investigators of what had happened until hours later,[116] a delay which angered investigators and could have wrecked the entire investigation.[117] As soon as Williams was identified, the consultants, who were in the middle of their consultation and had just finished their profile of a black sex killer, were thanked for their help and left the city almost immediately.[118] According to Robert Keppel, the FBI practice of producing a profile which reflects the investigator's "best suspect" is a trick the FBI became well known for: "They con you into structuring your interview into a way to find out what your best suspect is, and it begins to form an opinion about their profile, and so they give you this thing that matches what you're [already] looking for."[119] Effectively, the Bureau profilers told investigators what they wanted to hear.

Detained for twelve hours by law enforcement officers, Williams waived his *Miranda* rights and was "interrogated" intensively for two and a half hours as well as being given three lie-detector tests. Even at that time the FBI wanted to file charges, but Lee Brown and other local police authorities argued that stronger evidence was needed.[120] While Williams was in police custody, his house was searched and several bags of material were removed for forensic examination. The turn of events made William Webster more optimistic about the investigation, but Roger Young, an FBI spokesman, asserted that "nothing decisive has happened."[121]

Williams had not previously been identified by any of the investigations as a suspect, but with the FBI under "terrific pressure" to make an arrest and get their agents out of the city they pursued him as their prime suspect. Local law enforcement officers quipped that they could probably make a good case against Williams for lying, but there was insufficient 'hard evidence' for a murder charge. The fiber evidence which had been collected would strengthen a case based on physical evidence, but it was thought to be unable to produce a conviction on its own. Even the quality of the forensic evidence was in doubt. At Williams' trial the defense called Randall Bresee as an expert on clothing and textile fibers and in his opinion the prosecution should have conducted more in-depth tests before concluding that the victims had been in contact with Williams.[122] One forensic expert summed up by saying, "In terms of overall handling this is not a gold star case." Local officials held no illusions about the FBI's enthusiasm to make the arrest: "They don't worry so much about charging someone with a crime because they don't have to try the case."[123]

Media coverage of the child murders continued when Williams was interviewed and his house searched. Designated a public figure, his life was dissected even before his arrest on June 21. Four days after the Williams' arrest the FBI agents assigned to the task force were withdrawn. Spokesman Dave Divan explained that the need for investigative work was no longer so intense, even though Williams had only been charged with one murder and there were still at least twenty-seven more unsolved murders, but he pledged that the Bureau would "support fully" the continuing investigation.[124] Eventually Williams was charged with the murders of two young men, not children, and he was 'linked' to a dozen other murders with which he had not been, and never would be, charged. Lewis Slaton remarked, "There is not enough evidence to prosecute, but there is enough evidence to close out."[125] Even though John Douglas believed that the forensic and behavioral evidence pointed to Williams in certain cases, he acknowledged that there was no strong evidence linking him to all, or even most of the murders. Other murders, he suggests, were not fully investigated because there was neither the public will nor the evidence to seek indictments.[126] Local police and other investigators were not convinced that the task force had done its job, but it was ordered to close down because the "primary" killer had been caught, dashing defense attorney Al Binder's hopes that Williams would be exonerated in a continuing investigation which would solve the other murders.[127] During the trial Binder undermined the credibility of the two police rookies on the bridge stakeout, accusing them of drinking and sleeping on duty, and while large amounts of circumstantial evidence was amassed against Williams none of it was conclusive, and often it was contradictory. Even some of the victim's families sided with Williams and continued to hunt for the killer (or killers) of their children.[128] Once Williams was convicted, a message flashed across television screens in Atlanta—"Wayne Williams Guilty"—reassuring the population that the FBI and police had done their job. Camille Bell said the verdict only proved one thing "that there is no justice in America." In her opinion, during the trial, "The defense had to prove Wayne innocent. It's supposed to be the other way around."[129]

In the years after Williams' conviction, additional information emerged about the case, discovered by the defense attorneys. Late in 1985, while pursuing evidence, the attorneys discovered an FBI classified '8100' file containing information on covert Bureau investigations into the Georgia Klan. The FBI's informants reported that the Klan were killing children with suspicion falling on three brothers, Charles, Don and Ted Sanders. It was alleged that one of the Atlanta victims, Lubie Geter, had been threatened by Charles Sanders three weeks before being found strangled. It was also reported to the FBI in early 1981 that after killing twenty children the Klansmen boasted they would

The New Right and Ronald Reagan

begin killing black women.[130] Attention was drawn to the fact that twenty-seven black women were reported murdered in Atlanta during 1980–81, and a task force was organized in May 1982 to investigate the cases, just a few months after Williams' conviction, but the crimes were never solved.[131]

In 1987, in response to litigation and legal pressure, 5,328 pages of police files were made available. A transcript of the police interview with Bobby Toland, a key prosecution witness, was included in the files and cast doubt on his reliability as a witness and his motives for testifying. Described as a "reluctant witness," Toland only came forward in the middle of the trial, and Williams accused him of being a liar, adding that, "With the reward as high as it is, I'd probably get out and lie about it too."[132] Toland described himself as a bounty hunter and did not hide his dislike for Williams or his desire to get the reward money. His testimony, which was presented near the end of the trial, was seen as crucial because it provided the prosecution with a motive for the murders—Williams' hatred of lower-class blacks—which until that point they had been unable to establish.[133] Without Toland's testimony there was no motive. The Atlanta Child Murders established for the public the New Right's determination in the crusade against crime and the effectiveness of the Bureau's application of their scientific knowledge. The large number of children associated with the murders gave credibility to the developing missing children panic, and the identification of Williams as the sole offender set the scene for the subsequent serial murder panic.

In response to the perceived increase in child abductions, the Missing Children Act was signed on October 12, 1982, and under it the FBI were empowered to become involved in the "plight" of America's exploited, missing, and murdered children.[134] The bill was described by Reagan as an attempt to provide "peace of mind" for the distraught parents of children who had gone missing, and after signing the Act he said that it was "high time the legal system showed the honest citizen as much concern as it does the criminal."[135] At the same time Reagan also signed into law the Victim and Witness Protection Act to reinforce the existing legal statutes concerned with intimidation and victimization, giving judges in trials the power to order restitution by offenders or provide a reason why not. After the signing, Reagan met John Walsh, his wife Reve and their daughter Meghan, and a photograph of the meeting was published in every major American newspaper and televised on all three network evening broadcasts.[136] The intention was to show, symbolically, to the American public that the government was concerned about the security of its citizens and that it would listen to them when shaping its policies.

Collection and dissemination of information on unidentified deceased persons resulted in the creation of the Unidentified Person File (UPF) in the National Crime Information Centre (NCIC), designed to aid in the identification of unclaimed bodies by matching medical records and physical anomalies. Also at the request of a relative, legal guardian, or next of kin, the Act required the FBI to search the Missing Persons File (MPF) to ensure that the data had been entered, however, "[t]his aspect of the law enhanced the ability of agents to connect files on unidentified missing persons with cases that otherwise would remain open."[137] The Missing Children Act also permitted the FBI to begin a fingerprint file for the missing person. It did not actually expand FBI jurisdiction to investigating cases of missing children, but created a "national clearinghouse of computerized information."[138] A confirmed kidnapping was still the only way that the FBI could be drawn in. However, if the child had been kidnapped by a parent the Act specifically stated that the Bureau would not be involved (unless the parent was wanted on charges of a felony violation). After one year the MPF stored over 19,000 cases of missing juveniles.[139] The Missing Children's Assistance Act was passed in 1984 to provide funding for the National Centre for Missing and Exploited Children, reinforcing the government's public commitment to the issue. But the FBI has no responsibility in the investigations, nor does the federal government.

While the government legislation for missing children was being discussed in Washington DC, and in the wake of the publicity surrounding The Atlanta Child Murders, another serial sex killer case was being uncovered in Seattle. The Green River Killer, as the killer became known, selected prostitutes or sexually promiscuous young women as victims and after killing them, dumped their bodies in, or in the vicinity of, the Green River. Emphasizing the number of victims increased public insecurity, even though it was, predictably, prostitutes and low economic status women who were most vulnerable. As fear increased so did public demands for action.

In Reagan's view, "The liberal approach of coddling criminals didn't work and never will."[140] He wanted tougher measures to deal with those society labeled deviants, stern retribution for their actions, and punishment for their sins. If serial killers were presented as being created by social factors, as 'products of their environment,' they became less responsible for their actions, and responsibility would then fall upon the government to change the underlying conditions in society. Just as the New Right announced the decay of society in the early 1980s, there were numerous incidents of multiple murder prominently reported in newspapers and on television.

The news reports had begun earlier. In the 1970s Los Angeles was plagued by the Freeway Killer (which turned out to be at least three separate killers and possibly accounted for over a hundred victims), the Hillside Strangler (initially thought to be one killer, but the case concluded with the conviction of Kenny Bianchi and Angelo Buono) and Ted Bundy's case sprawled across the nation. In 1981 the Atlanta Child Murders captured the public's attention, and 1982 saw the beginning of what would be known as the Green River Killings. In 1983 Bobby Joe Long, the "Classified Ad Rapist" turned murderer was captured, as well as Henry Lee Lucas, Gerald Gallego, and the Sunset Strip Slayer Douglas D Clark. The following year Robert Hansen was arrested in Alaska. Numerous other states reported the capture of serial killers or evidence of their crimes.

In 1984 Christopher Wilder (a 'spree' killer by the FBI's definition but widely publicized as a serial killer) and his trail of crimes were reported as representing a serious threat to the public. In six weeks Wilder traveled from Tallahassee, Florida, to Los Angeles and back across America to New Hampshire where he was killed in a shootout with police. During the six

The New Right and Ronald Reagan

weeks, Wilder was thought to have abducted eleven women, subjecting them to rape and torture, and killing four of them. The FBI became involved after the kidnap victims were transported across state lines, and Wilder soon made the Ten Most Wanted list,[141] demonstrating the extreme mobility attributed to serial killers. Continuing the trend in the summer of 1985, the Night Stalker terrorized the LA suburbs and grabbed front-page news across the country.

The serial killer was often referred to as a 'new' type of criminal[142] by people such as John Douglas of the BSU, and identified specifically with the late twentieth century. However, contradicting himself, Douglas also suggested that folk stories about vampires and werewolves might be ancient explanations of serial crime.[143] True crime author Colin Wilson claims that serial crime began in the 1960s, but later in the same book he contradicts himself, pointing out that the modern atrocities of serial sex killers are paralleled by historical incidents.[144] It is alleged that the disproportionate number of males born in the baby boom was reflected in the increase in the number of serial killers,[145] people who came of age in the late 1960s and early 1970s. One author dated the emergence of serial sex killers exactly to 1972,[146] but avoided going into any detail to identify why he picked that specific year. The one thing that the BSU and crime writers agreed on was that the numbers of violent sex offenders had increased sharply.

The stereotype which has developed from interest groups, such as the BSU, to describe the personal history of serial sex killers contrasts starkly with Reagan's image of the traditional family. Conservative assertions that capitalism was a noble and selfless system were trumpeted by Reagan's advisors and their homilies on poverty preached hard work, family, and religious faith as the only dependable route out of poverty. In short, they repeated Andrew Carnegie's Gospel of Wealth. According to FBI research, "virtually all serial killers come from dysfunctional backgrounds or sexual or physical abuse or any of the related problems."[147] Serial sex killers were those who were unable or unwilling to improve their social position with hard work, and in their dysfunctional families they had replaced spiritual faith with sexual depravity. They were 'born bad.' Conventionally depicted as, "[b]rutalized in childhood, the serial killer grows up full of a murderous rage that is turned against all humanity. He can know pleasure only by administering pain. He can feel alive only when he is inflicting death,"[148] but this view owes more to fictional criminal masterminds than real criminal offenders and reflects much of the Freudian theory which the FBI exploited.

Usually the killers were reported as being white and male. They were illegitimate or born into unstable family environments, often with a female employed in prostitution heading the household. The female head of the family was usually considered to be domineering, smothering the child as it grew, and there was no male role model to emulate. In childhood, serial sex killers were said to exhibit three traits: bed wetting (enuresis), firesetting (arson), and the torture and killing of animals.[149] It is rarely noted that even if a child displays all three traits it does not mean that the person will become a serial killer.

Physical or sexual abuse was cited as often occurring in the kind of childhood which might result in a serial killer. Combined with alcohol abuse, and sometimes drug abuse, this was commonly reported in their family histories. As the child grows, a "mask of sanity" develops, allowing the developing killer to mingle with normal members of society. Because of poor family backgrounds, many of the serial killers have had an institutionalized upbringing, with periods spent in juvenile correction centers or mental hospitals, and later in state or federal prisons. But since many individuals passed through the juvenile system from childhood through to adulthood, suffering severe sexual and physical abuse, and living in dysfunctional environments, why were there not considerably more incidences of serial murders?

Far from being 'normal,' the would-be killer is said to develop an avid interest in pornography and become fascinated with police work. Ted Bundy provided much support for the idea that "pornography made me do it," but while on death row another inmate remembered that Bundy never sought pornographic magazines in prison: instead, he favored 'true crime' magazines.[150] Other killers' cases flatly contradict the influence of pornography. Henry Lee Lucas' favorite book was the Dr Seuss children's book *Horton Hears A Who*, Albert Fish found his perverse delights in the Bible, and Jeffrey Dahmer was a big fan of *Nancy Drew* mysteries.[151]

Despite being credited with above average intelligence, potential serial sex killers do poorly in school and often take unskilled jobs, working as security guards or in similar occupations. References to looking like the boy next door highlighted how anonymous these so-called 'new' killers were. But if your next-door neighbor looked like Henry Lee Lucas, Ottis Toole, or Ed Kemper, it was time to move house. From this kind of stereotyped history, it becomes easy to see that serial sex killers were usually victims who had become victimizers, and rehabilitation was not considered an option. By identifying white males as the culprits, the cultural representation of serial killers ensured that feminists and black groups, who were unlikely to praise any of Reagan's other policies, would support his extreme law and order stance, and the fears of white middle-class suburbanites were also increased. The constructed history of the killers was a reworking of the 'white trash' racial stereotype. To combat the threat of serial murder it was necessary to increase the funding to law agencies, specifically the FBI, who had identified themselves as experts on the subject.

A national clearinghouse was considered necessary to collect information which could be used to compare violent crimes across the United States. The cost of setting up the National Center for the Analysis of Violent Crime (NVAVC) was $1.5 million, with annual running costs estimated at $200,000 to 300,000.[152] This expenditure came in an era of heavy budget cuts,[153] but Reagan made a point of announcing plans for a "sophisticated detective program" as part of his weekly radio broadcast. He called for a return to traditional values in the same broadcast, in which he specifically identified the new program as a means for police to identify and capture serial killers who murdered women and children.[154]

Around the same time as the creation of the NCAVC and the expansion of the Investigative Support Information Systems (ISIS) and Missing Persons

The New Right and Ronald Reagan

File (MPF) through computer technology, Reagan's own re-election committee developed a computer system, the Political Information System (PINS), to test their campaign strategy.

Spending on computer equipment was found to be increasing at a faster pace within the FBI than in many other major government agencies, such as health and human services, and even defense. The Bureau's experimental new computer system "easily bested the agents in the speed, thoroughness, and accuracy with which it located the needed records." The decision to buy and operate the ISIS, costing between three and four million dollars a year to maintain, was an example of the Reagan administration's plans to "substantially increase the computerization of the Bureau's daily operations." Concerns had been raised in 1982 when Congress' Office of Technology reported that its research suggested "the mere existence of the FBI's computerized network threatened the strong decentralized nature of law enforcement in the United States and the long-term balance of power between local, state, and national governments." Representative Don Edwards, a Democrat from California, and even FBI director William Webster, warned that some aspects of computerization could have unanticipated harmful effects. But in the face of public concern over serial murder and missing children there was little public or legislative dissent. Webster even told the Senate Judiciary Subcommittee on Security and Terrorism that he opposed expanding the FBI's computerized file system to include information on people who were thought to be 'suspicious,' but who were not wanted for any crime.[155] While expanding domestic surveillance and information gathering, thanks to generous budget and jurisdictional increases, the Bureau still had some mundane jobs to carry out.

Focusing their attention on serial sex crime, the FBI publicly devoted their attention to promoting their own scientific and investigative abilities. Meanwhile the captured 'serial killers' continued to provide scapegoats for politicians. Ted Bundy was a recurring figure in political law and order rhetoric throughout the 1980s. Bundy's 1979 murder trial in Florida, among the first to be televised in Florida and featured nightly on public TV stations across the country, ensured state-wide recognition for the killer second only to that of the governor. Newspaper editors were so hungry for news on Bundy that the Associated Press transmitted hourly dispatches to meet the demand. On July 25, 1979, Bundy was found guilty of the murders of two women from the Chi-Omega sorority and given a death sentence for each. The following year another conviction, for the murder of a twelve-year-old girl, earned him a third death sentence. He became an archetype for serial sex killers, with his "enigmatic face... the face of evil, his undistinguished flesh the embodiment of America's spreading dread." A four hour NBC television film, *The Deliberate Stranger* (Marvin J Chomsky, 1986), ensured public recognition, especially because it was shown at primetime. After the film, five books and numerous newspaper and magazine articles were written about him. He became a symbol for American society and "the whole vast, chaotic enterprise of the death penalty boiled down in the public mind to a single man. Ted Bundy."[156]

Many opponents of capital punishment also believed Bundy deserved to be executed, but the time taken for the appeals process frustrated those in favor of the death sentence. One 'Moral Majority' leader, Cal Thomas, denounced serial murder as an example of spiritual evil, and for Thomas such evil rendered any possibility of reform or rehabilitation unrealistic.[157] Conservatives wanted to shorten the time between conviction and execution. As the years passed and Bundy remained alive on death row, "he became Exhibit A in the fulminations of politicians, editorial writers, talk show hosts, and ordinary citizens who railed against the tortuous appeals of death row inmates." It was popularly believed that Bundy (and all other convicted criminals) employed delaying tactics, exploiting the justice system. In Bundy's case this was totally wrong. The prosecution even acknowledged that the court had put his case on the "fast track" to execution, and the Florida state Supreme Court had "bent over backwards to affirm his convictions." By the time of the second serial murder hearings in 1986, the "Bundy express" was "running with a full head of steam." Despite his convictions coming from two complicated cases both had moved through the appeals process to the end in less than a year.[158]

Incumbent Florida Senator Paula Hawkins, who was closely identified with the missing children panic and had testified at the first serial murder hearings in 1983, received Reagan's support in her 1986 campaign. Ironically, she was defeated by former Florida governor Bob Graham who won primarily due to his stance on speeding up the execution process for those who had been sentenced to death. Under Graham's governorship in Florida, Ted Bundy had "leapfrogged" past forty or fifty other prisoners to get his execution date set. When Florida's new governor, Bob Martinez, was elected in 1987 he promised that "Florida's electricity bill will go up,"[159] and Bundy's case was the focus of his attention.

Finally, Bundy's appeals ran out, and the most notorious killer of the late twentieth century was put to death in 1989. His final gesture was to grant an interview to James Dobson, a member of the 1986 federal pornography commission, which was broadcast on television. In the interview Bundy cast himself as a victim, a good Christian boy corrupted by pornography. He also acknowledged that he deserved the most extreme punishment which society had to offer. His 'expert' testimony provided ammunition for conservative claims-makers lobbying for federal anti-pornography legislation, which became known as the "Bundy Bill."[160]

Network television turned the execution into a "media circus." Broadcasting the interview along with shots of the crowd which had gathered outside the prison in Starke, the media renewed Bundy's "nightmarish grip on the media's attention."[161] In the crowd were the parents of Susan Rancourt, one of Bundy's victims. Despite feeling a sense of relief, Rancourt's parents were not happy to see the triumphal display, the cheering, T-shirts, and bumper stickers seemed out of place to them: "A carnival atmosphere was not what we were feeling." A few opponents of capital punishment were lost in the crowd which cheered when Bundy's death was announced.[162] The sentiment of those celebrating reviled Bundy for his personal demeanor as well as his acts. His smug attitude during his trial, allegations of delaying tactics, and the well-publicized games he played with law enforcement officials presented the public with an unsympathetic picture of a brutal killer who thought he could get away with his crimes.[163]

Even after his execution Bundy caused problems for the legal system. In his final confessions he enabled police in various states to close the book on thirteen murders, provided information on fourteen more cases in five states, and "touched on" a further twenty murders dating back to 1969.[164] Bundy's attorney, Ms Weiner, said he wanted to confess to "scores" of other murders but his execution, motivated "purely out of political reasons," meant he ran out of time.[165] Whether the confessions were complete or not, the FBI called a meeting of law enforcement representatives from six states.

Politicians in other states recognized the value of using serial killers to promote new legislation. In the late 1980s, the state of Texas passed a 'serial murder law' which permitted a defendant to be tried for more than one murder at the same time, even though they were committed at different times and in separate locations. Previously each offence required its own trial. An anonymous tip led to the arrest of Daniel Lee Corwin for the attempted murder of a Texas University student and, pleading guilty, he was sentenced to ninety-nine years. Eventually he admitted to three further murders, and became the first person to be prosecuted under the new law in March 1990; he was convicted and sentenced to death.

In other states, extreme serial criminals encouraged judicial and popular support for the death penalty, especially if their crimes were against children. Westly Allan Dodd pleaded guilty to the rape and murder of several young boys and even wrote to the Supreme Court asking that his death sentence be carried out quickly. In his own highly-publicized words: "I must be executed before I have the chance to escape; because if I do escape, I promise you I will kill and rape again—and I will enjoy every minute of it."[166] His sentence was carried out in January 1993, and he became the first criminal to be executed in Washington State for thirty years.

The following year, one of America's most notorious serial sex murder cases reached its ultimate conclusion. On May 10, 1994, John Wayne Gacy, the "Killer Clown," credited with being the worst serial sex killer ever caught in America, was executed. The case attracted world wide news coverage and made a great impact on the American public because Gacy had been a very popular local businessman, until the bodies of twenty-seven young men were found under his suburban home, and another six recovered later from other sites. With the weight of evidence against him, even one of Gacy's lawyers described him as a poster child for the death penalty. Undeterred the ACLU argued that Gacy's life should be spared and opponents of capital punishment gathered outside Statesville penitentiary, outnumbered by families of the victims, death penalty advocates, and members of the "Guardian Angels" who demanded his execution.[167] Because of technical problems with the injections, it took eighteen minutes for Gacy to die, which supported the ACLU claim that the death penalty was a "cruel and unusual punishment," but few people outside the prison could sympathies with the suffering of the dead sex killer.

As appeals ran out another serial sex killer, William Bonin, made legal history in 1996. He was the first convict to be executed by lethal injection in California after the Supreme Court declared the gas chamber to be "cruel and unusual" punishment and suspended its use. Remembered for the "depth and breadth of the horror he sowed" from 1979 to 1980, he was seen as a "terrifying new apparition assaulting the national consciousness." The victims were often male hitchhikers who were tortured and sexually abused before being murdered and their bodies dumped on the highways of southern California. Hence the media titled the unknown perpetrator the "Freeway Killer."[168]

Bonin was convicted of the murders of fourteen young boys on the testimony of three former confederates, one of whom, Vernon Butts, committed suicide before trial. Bonin had a stereotypical dysfunctional upbringing in an abusive family, spent some time in an orphanage, and served in Vietnam. Returning to America, he was convicted of raping a young man and sent to a mental hospital and later prison. Shortly after his release from prison in October in 1978 the murders began. During his trial, Bonin's defense argued that Butts was the ringleader and that Bonin, Gregory Miley and James Munro had been his pawns. Appearing unrepentant, and even reveling in the suffering he had caused, Bonin was unsympathetic to the jury. Despite defense arguments, Bonin was convicted of crimes with which Butts had originally been charged, and Munro and Miley received lesser sentences for their parts in the crimes.

Carol Waxman, a victim's advocate in Orange County, worked with the families of Bonin's victims in the aftermath of the murders. She described them as 'emotionally devastated' with some virtually putting their lives on hold during his appeals process. Governor Pete Wilson remarked that Bonin's appeals had lasted longer than most of his victims' lives. Waxman added that, "I tell them there are some things we aren't able to forgive and we should let God do that."[169] In a parking lot a few miles away from the prison relatives of some of Bonin's victims celebrated his execution with champagne.

When Bonin's appeals finally ran out his execution was scheduled for February 23, 1996. Witnesses and reporters were prevented from observing the complete execution procedure by prison officials at San Quentin, who denied the public access to first-hand accounts of the process. Reporters and the public had to rely exclusively on prison officials for information, and they would only admit that there had been difficulties inserting intravenous injection but added little more. The ACLU branch in northern California obtained a preliminary injunction a month later on behalf of journalists, news organizations and First Amendment advocates to prevent prison officials from restricting observers from further executions. Kenneth Williams, the next criminal to receive the death penalty in San Quentin, was observed by non-prison persons.[170] However, by then the new method of execution had been introduced with public support, and any suffering by Bonin seemed minor when compared to his crimes. After a decade of Reagan's Old Testament retributive rhetoric and policies few complained.

The New Right and Ronald Reagan

New Right conservative politicians, loudly trumpeting tough law-and-order policies, were able to find a series of criminal threats to society to legitimize their policies. Their Social Darwinist philosophy not only justified their privileged position in society, but served to explain simplistically the nature of criminals as being born, not made. There was no possibility of rehabilitation for criminals, especially not serial sex killers,[171] and no need to change the social environment. Execution was a public exorcism of the 'evil,' but the social origins of crime were ignored and denied. While the FBI created the popular definition of the crime, the Reagan administration supported a crusade against the threat which the killers posed, and it was the media's need for sensational news stories which alerted the public *en masse* to the threat. The effect of the heightened public awareness to the crimes of serial sex killers persisted beyond Reagan and Bush. One critic noted that the "whole political establishment has followed the lead of the New Right in successfully staking out this terrain of insecurity and couching its repressive measures in a populist moralism."[172] Political and moral demagogues cloaked their conservative rhetoric in the same language of commonsense wisdom exploited by Reagan, offering "simple-minded panaceas" to a public prepared to concede democratic rights in exchange for an immediate solution to the problem of insecurity.[173] Once alerted, the public avidly followed the stories as they developed, and in the competition for ratings the reporting of grisly sex crimes became increasingly prominent in the news. While the media definition of serial murder was so imprecise as to render it relatively meaningless, it was based on the themes described by the FBI and on statistics provided by Justice Department sources.

Plague-Rats
Founding the Behavioral Sciences Unit

SERIAL SEX KILLERS ARE A POWERFUL IMAGE IN SOCIETY, AND presented politicians and claim-makers with an effective tool to incite public fear and generate support for tough crime legislation. The political rhetoric of Reagan's administration and the much-publicized "War on Crime" meant that the American public was excessively aware of the threat violent crime posed to them in their daily lives. However, in light of Reagan's budget cutbacks, psychological profiles were presented as a "cost effective" and "more efficient way to reduce... investigative man hours."[1] The sudden prominence of such criminals raises questions about the origins of the term serial killer.' How did the term gain widespread acceptance and how has the portrait of the murderer as a serial sex killer influenced popular culture?

The term serial sex killer was defined and popularized by the 'new' FBI, following a period of crisis and scandal that greatly undermined public faith in the 'old' Bureau, and in an era when increased executive control was evident. In the late 1960s in the midst of the antiwar and civil rights campaigns, in "the dawn of the space age, the director was still living in the long-faded days when the FBI legend was born."[2] After Hoover's death in 1972 the aura of invulnerability that surrounded the Bureau was gone, it had lost its power to command the public's obedience and fear.[3] The FBI had not changed with the times.

Founding the Behavioral Sciences Unit

By identifying the Bureau abuses of power with the deceased Hoover and the 'old' FBI, bureaucrats and politicians began to build the 'new' FBI. Since the old subversives were gone, and the FBI was publicly shamed, a new area of specialization was needed to justify the Bureau's budget and continued existence. Serial sex killers became symbolic 'plague-rats' for the New Right and the FBI, carrying a diseased morality into society in the same way that rats carried plague-bearing fleas into towns during the Middle Ages. Congressman Glenn English declared, "In these crimes, one person commits a long series of offenses, often striking over a period of months or years. Their innocent victims are selected at random, plucked from their homes, their neighborhoods, or local shopping centers."[4] The killers' activities undermined accepted values and their victims were publicized as being those who represented the hopes of future generations. To the New Right, this highlighted how the liberalism of the 1960s, and sexualization of society, had created murderous monsters by challenging the traditional values of society, although such killers did not originate in the 1960s and 1970s.

Lois Haight Herrington, the chairperson of the President's Task Force on Victims of Crime, described the climate created by the threat of violent crime as having "made victims of us all." She continued:

Awareness of its danger affects the way we think, where we live, where we go, what we buy, how we raise our children and the quality of our lives as we age... Every citizen of this country is more impoverished, less free, more fearful, and less safe because of the ever-present threat of the violent criminal.[5]

The raised awareness of the existence of violent crime led to questions being asked concerning police agencies' performance and their apparent lack of success in containing the problem and catching the culprits. This led to a call for more active measures to be taken to solve the problem.

Police showed high clearance rates in murder cases in the past, but the traditional homicide, committed by a friend, relative, or associate made it a relatively easy crime to investigate, with about sixty-six per cent of murderers being taken into custody within fourteen hours. Clearance rates for murder dropped from ninety-three per cent in 1962 to seventy-four per cent in 1982.[6] Police methods used to solve such cases have been exposed by the alleged increase of 'stranger' homicides because predictable motives are lost, but the majority of murders occurred between people who knew each other. In 1985, fifty-eight per cent of the 18,980 reported homicides in the US were carried out by relatives or acquaintances.[7] Like the FBI, writers such as Steven Egger, a former policeman and law-enforcement consultant, attributed this drop to the 'stranger' homicides, the work of traveling killers who roam the country looking for "self-selecting" victims. These victims are 'targets of opportunity,' with the killers allegedly picking the most vulnerable, and then moving on.[8]

The flaw in police strategy was partly due to the reactive nature of the investigation, which restricted detectives. Despite the alleged rise in 'stranger' homicide, law-enforcement agencies continued to investigate for one or perhaps two killers for each single murder. This was because most agencies had never investigated related crimes of this nature before, and so-called serial sex crimes are a very unusual occurrence for most law-enforcement agencies.[9] Old methods of looking for traces of contact between victim and criminal were not fruitful in such an investigation, and their use only frustrated many serial homicide investigations.[10] As traditional reactive methods were ineffective, Robert Keppel found serial cases were, "usually resolved by some serendipitous occurrence even though we law enforcement agencies had a sense of the killer's identity." It was claimed that outdated methods allowed the killers more time to increase their body counts, with serial sex killers like Ted Bundy, John Wayne Gacy and Jeffrey Dahmer only being arrested long after their careers in murder had begun.[11] Chance capture made 'true crime' writer Ann Rule speculate how many serial sex killers are not caught,[12] adding to public fear. In response, the 'new' FBI publicized proactive investigative techniques developed to re-establish their prestige and professionalism.

The staff of the FBI's Behavioral Sciences Unit (BSU) is credited with being world experts in serial murder and the originators of the term "serial killer," but their definition is unclear and imprecise. Established in 1972, the BSU's formation allegedly "signaled the Bureau's first—if tentative—move out of the J Edgar Hoover era."[13] Trying to cast off their 'old' tarnished image, the Bureau affiliated with the University of Virginia and produced an accredited course in the quest for 'police professionalization.' The FBI was able to rebuild credibility by encouraging their special agents to pursue higher academic qualifications. At Quantico, courses emphasizing the "vocational skills" of policing stopped: instead, the Bureau focused on behavioral science, law, forensic science, education and communication, and management science. Once achieved, the 'new' FBI once more presented an air of professionalism with the authority to assert itself, and its jurisdiction, and interfere with other police agencies. The Bureau's own publication, the FBI *Law Enforcement Bulletin*, which loudly boasted of advances made by the FBI, reached 200,000 people each month, making it the most widely read journal of its kind and a valuable public relations tool.[14]

The appellation serial sex killer is credited to FBI agent Robert Ressler of the BSU who originally used the term to define an episodic killer, because the behavior of these criminals supposedly reminded him of the movie-house serials he enjoyed as a child.[15] Others have claimed that they were the originators of the term, such as Richard Rappaport, a forensic psychiatrist who had worked on multiple murder cases with the FBI, who claims he was the first to use the term to describe the crimes of John Wayne Gacy in 1978.[16] While this may or may not be true, it was Ressler and the FBI who popularized the term through articles in professional, academic, and popular journals, government reports, newspaper articles and television interviews. Later, after the term had been established, authors of crime fiction, such as Thomas Harris, Mary Higgins Clark and Patricia Cornwell, sought Bureau assistance in researching for their novels, and Hollywood produced films based on the FBI definition.

Founding the Behavioral Sciences Unit

However, defining the term serial killer was not as simple as it might seem for such a well-publicized criminal type. The phrase is widely misunderstood by the news media and misrepresented in cinema. It is clear that despite a variety of professional groups seeking to define what a serial killer is, no universal definition emerged. Arguments appeared over the time-intervals between murders or the minimum mandatory body counts, but there are general similarities which the interested parties agree on: the killers are white and male, their attacks are sexual and random, and they are mobile. A further commonality between the professionals is that despite the differing opinions on details, they all shared a common interest in defining a particular type of crime at the same time. To all the authors there was a basic similarity in the perpetrators of the crimes, and the unknown killers are a threat to the population at large.

"Serial killer" officially became a public term in hearings on July 12, 1983, entitled, "Serial Murders: Patterns Of Murders Committed By One Person, In Large Numbers With No Apparent Rhyme, Reason, Or Motivation," where speakers spelt out the threat to American society of a 'new' type of criminal who posed a "major problem" for law enforcement.[17] In 1980, when Reagan challenged Jimmy Carter for the presidency, the New Right seized the initiative and attacked Carter's social and economic policy, and the hearings on serial murder preceded the impending 1984 presidential election campaign and foreshadowed the political debate which was dominated by anti-crime rhetoric. Crime panics in the first four years of Reagan's presidency identified child abduction and abuse, cult crime and sexual deviance, as epidemic, and identifiable as originating from 1960s liberalism. Media reporting of the crime panics and conservative analysis was superficial and distorted reported levels of violent crime and sexual abuse.

Serial killing, as defined by the FBI, was a 'new' form of violent crime and an attempt to bring "order out of chaos."[18] It accentuated specific characteristics, especially the random nature of the crimes, the killers being white and male, and the possibility of the series of offences spanning years with large numbers of victims. According to John Otto, FBI Assistant Director, "Their innocent victims are selected at random, plucked from their homes, their neighborhoods, or local shopping centers."[19] Making it clear that these killers attack the assumed security of society, and by using examples such as homes, neighborhoods and shopping malls, which are usually considered safe, the FBI definition shows the serial killer's lack of respect for traditional values—an anathema to society. Choosing a stranger for a victim "overtly threatens the preservation of social order."[20] Examples used are aimed at suggesting the threat is focused on a particular segment of society. The panic surrounding the serial sex murder was particularly aimed at suburban families who shopped in malls, whose young children played in their neighborhoods, who relied on the security of their homes for preservation of their nuclear families, and who sent their teenage children to college. In this way, a striking contrast was drawn between the image of the 'evil' killers and their innocent victims. Ted Bundy selected some of his victims at malls, others were college girls; John

Better To Reign In Hell

Wayne Gacy's victims came from his own neighborhood; the "Night Stalker" burgled and murdered in suburban homes he knew were occupied; Ed Kemper was also known for selecting college girls as his victims. Often it is noted that the killers are avid collectors of pornography, a practice that deviates from conservative social and religious values. In that respect Ted Bundy became a favorite case study for religious groups. The case of Leonard Lake and Charles Ng is often cited too, because they made their own extreme pornography in rape and torture home movies.

Writer Colin Wilson notes that it is doubtful if one layman in a hundred understands the difference between a serial killer and a multiple (mass) murderer,[21] and misuse by various writers and authors only confuses the issue further. Unlike multiple murders, which produce a number of victims, usually in one incident, Robert Ressler's notes that serial murders are involved in three or more events separated by an "emotional cooling-off period" between homicides. He adds that the crime is premeditated by the offender with every detail being planned, "with the possible exception of the specific victim,"[22] and the crimes would be committed at different locations. However, the BSU definition is vague, with no explanation of the "cooling off" period. Colin Wilson asserts that this period is a "unique emotional break in the murder cycle."[23] These criteria set the serial killer apart from other varieties of multiple murderer but no author defines exactly what "cooling off" period is or how long it lasts.

It is usually accepted that serial sex killers are mobile. In Steven Egger's opinion the killer "adroitly confounds law enforcement by his high degree of mobility within our society. He kills within a community and, when law enforcement draws close, he moves on."[24] The reason for this increase in 'stranger' homicides, according to FBI executive Roger Depue, a former Administrator of the National Center for the Analysis of Violent Crime (NCAVC), is that, "We've become a highly transient, stranger-to-stranger society. Criminals are going to take advantage of that."[25] Using the 'All-American' icon of the automobile, the killers are reported to spread their crimes over a number of states, as had the Prohibition gangs and kidnap gangs of previous crime panics.

At the first "Serial Murder" hearings (1983), Ann Rule asserted that it was not unusual to find serial sex killers traveling 150,000 to 200,000 miles in a year when ordinary people would only drive 15,000 to 20,000.[26] The BSU definition does not allow for the existence of a series of murders in a single location such as in the cases of John Wayne Gacy, Dean Corll, or the Jeffrey Dahmer case. The necessity of different locations exaggerated the killer's mobility at the expense of a better understanding of the variety of behavior of the murderers, but it did legitimize FBI claims that the Bureau was constrained by jurisdictional limitations and emphasizes the need for a national clearinghouse for information. Ted Bundy and Henry Lee Lucas are often cited as examples of the traveling killer, but some, if not most, serial killers operate in specific areas and few cases could be cited to support her claims. This is evident in the monikers they are given by popular newspapers

Founding the Behavioral Sciences Unit

such as "The Green River Killer" (Gary Leon Ridgway) or "The Genesee River Killer" (Arthur Shawcross), which reflect the localization of the crimes. Other convicted killers, such as David Berkowitz, John Wayne Gacy, Bobby Joe Long, and Wayne Williams all had specific 'hunting grounds' where they would find their victims.

It could be argued that the exaggeration of the serial killer's mobility serves purely as a justification for the FBI to involve itself, as it had done in the past, in murder cases that would normally be considered a matter for local law enforcement agencies. Bundy may have traveled across America, but that was to avoid the police who were closing in on him. The bodies of his victims were still found in small geographic areas. Confessions made by Lucas concerning his nationwide career of crime are very dubious, and no conclusive decision can be made about the crimes he claims to have committed. However, the Bureau became involved only insofar as to function as an agency to co-ordinate local investigations, overseeing task forces and lending their resources and expertise rather than conducting the investigation.

The FBI acknowledged that there had been isolated examples of serial killers in the past, but after a study of homicide reports spanning the past few decades, the Bureau asserted that history offers nothing to compare with the United States since the beginning of the 1970s.[27] An entire *Life* magazine article in August 1984 interviewed the BSU 'experts' and argued that serial killers are a particularly American phenomenon, as well as a great danger to American society. The authors reported that "In the last twenty years the rest of the world, with a population of about 4.5 billion has produced no more than forty serial killers. In the United States at least 120 have been captured or singled out by the police in the same period."[28] It is not clear what 'singled out' means, but the term's vagueness only makes the validity of the statistics more dubious, and it was not until the mid 1980s that the Soviet Union would acknowledge the existence of serial sex killers, which, like AIDS, were seen as a curse of decadent western society.[29] Ironically this added to the claims makers' credibility in the US. It may be that the bulk of serial killers are found in America but it does nothing to explain why it should be so. It has often been suggested that media attention paid to this type of crime results in disproportionate reporting and the over use of the term serial killer. After it was defined the media attributed it retrospectively to numerous killers ranging from Ted Bundy to Jack The Ripper, and even to criminals such as Charles Manson, who is most famous for the trial that convicted him of conspiracy to commit murder, but not actual murder.

The intelligence of the serial killer is commonly reported as higher than average, adding to the image of the supercriminal. The majority have been of at least normal intelligence, but "usually they are brilliant."[30] This may be true for some killers, allegedly Ted Bundy was well above average intelligence, but among the most prominent of the serial killer studies are Henry Lee Lucas and Otis Toole whose IQs were measured at eighty-five and seventy-five respectively—both *well* below average. Nonetheless, the serial killer is still portrayed as having no conscience—ruthless, manipulative, shrewd and cunning.

Perhaps one of the most telling aspects of the dominant FBI definition is found in the title of the collected findings of the prison interviews they conducted, *Sexual Homicide: Patterns and Motives* (1988), which reflects the BSU agents' selection of convicts specifically for sexual motives in their crimes. One of the academics working with the BSU, Ann Burgess, specialized in studies of rape crimes, becoming a prolific author on their psychological consequences, and Roy Hazelwood and John Douglas of the BSU also published articles on this subject. It is evident that the BSU definition is

heavily influenced by Robert Brittain's article "The Sadistic Murderer,"[31] and updated with contemporary case studies. The focus of Brittain's article, and the BSU's study, was a particular type of sex crime, crimes which strike at the heart of society, and its morality, updating Jack The Ripper for late twentieth century America. The FBI went looking for sexual criminals and, using Freudian interpretation, they found sexual criminals.

However, because Ressler and his fellow researchers were only investigating sexually motivated murders their sample could be atypical and the prominence given to the study may paint a distorted picture. But the BSU findings were

Founding the Behavioral Sciences Unit

the only published work that used original data from the convicted criminals as well as archival information, and became a source for academic study. Since the BSU used the same few case studies repeatedly, all involving sensational killers who had received considerable media coverage, it suggests a degree of audience manipulation. For example, the BSU estimate in their report that eighty per cent of sexual criminals use "violent pornography," a statistic which moral crusaders seized upon to bolster their anti-pornography arguments.[32] In contrast Levin and Fox, in *Mass Murder: America's Growing Menace* (1985), estimate that seventy-two per cent of multiple murders have *no* sexual component.[33]

The term 'predator' is commonly used in conjunction with serial sex killers, as a reference for a psychopath who behaves without conscience, guilt or remorse. According to John Otto, the Executive Assistant Director of the FBI, the serial killers are "human predators,"[34] seeking out their 'prey' so they can fulfill their fantasies. Their attacks are random, compulsive, and senseless. This means they have defied textbook solutions to homicide by killing without an apparent motive, and showing no sign of ceasing because of their compulsive nature. Unknown killers, in FBI jargon called 'unknown subjects' or UNSUBS, are alleged to have long careers, spanning years and claiming many victims. John Douglas emphasizes, "There is no burnout period for a serial killer."[35] Seen as compulsive killers, they are said to be driven by an inner urge rather than reacting to a situation and lashing out in anger, making it obvious that they will kill until caught, accentuating the need for the resources to track them, and the impossibility of rehabilitating them. The necessity of capture, or death, to prevent their trail of murder means a dramatic and satisfactory resolution will symbolically reassure the public of their security and the efficiency of police agencies. These people are anti-social, animalistic and 'monstrous,' but sane and therefore liable for legal prosecution.

After mobility and sexual motivation, one of the most prominent features of the killers was that they were claimed to be white and "invariably" male.[36] They looked normal. Previous 'bogeymen' had distinguishing features, often racially stereotypical, but always recognizable. Identifying the killers as white distorted the problem. African Americans were a sizable proportion of serial killers, judged to vary between thirteen and sixteen per cent depending on the author,[37] but portraying serial killers as white and serial murder as an intra-racial crime meant that only white sex offenders and victims would be the focus of serial crime.

It is *not* a distortion to say that the killers are all male. Several authors have examined the existence of female serial murderers, and concluded that they do exist and that they represent approximately the same proportion of women as are found in other types of murder in the United States, around fifteen per cent, but this observation confuses serial and 'multiple' murder. While Keeney and Heide did conclude that there may be more differences than similarities between female serial killers and their male counterparts,[38] they did not explicitly state that the women were *not* sex killers, they commit multiple homicides and tend to be poisoners. Less prominence is given to female 'multiple' murderers because the nature of their crimes is not as sensational as the well-known male serial sex killers. Because of the lack of clarity in the definition there was confusion about the existence of female serial killers even within the FBI. After the arrest of Aileen Wuornos in 1991, FBI spokeswoman Kelley Cibulas falsely claimed that she was the "first female textbook case of a serial killer."[39] In contrast Roy Hazelwood, after retiring from the BSU, announced to a homicide conference in March 1995 that, "There are *no* female serial killers."[40]

There is, however, a principal danger in accepting the assumption that the perpetrator's actions followed his intentions, and then imposing motivational patterns where none existed.[41] It is the imposition of the patterns that makes the 'series.' In interviews some killers, such as David Berkowitz, have acknowledged that some of their attacks did not go according to plan. Assuming that the action reflected the intention of the killer may cause misdefinition of his crimes; a rapist who meets with resistance from his victim may panic and commit murder although it may not have been his original intention. Furthermore, numerous accounts of serial crime are based on a willingness to believe convenient confessions. Albert DeSalvo, Henry Lee Lucas and Jeffrey Dahmer all made confessions which were supported by little or no physical evidence, and therefore it was impossible to verify their stories.[42]

Preying on the weak and innocent showed serial killers undermining accepted societal standards of morality and behavior. The notions of family values, which were promoted by the Reagan administration, reinforced a need for an increase in law enforcement activity. As one commentator noted, "American people could find nothing comfortable in the fact that between January 1980 and September 1984 they were being introduced to one new killer every eighteen months."[43] Repeated, sensational news reporting over an extended period of time, which focused on the most lurid sexual aspects of the crimes, undoubtedly affected the general attitude of the population towards issues concerning law enforcement. The media focus on sex is understandable considering the FBI was hunting for sexual deviants. In the midst of political claims and media generated hysteria suburban middle class families seemed to be the focus of the killer's attentions, and as taxpayers, they felt insecure and vocally questioned what the police were doing to protect them. They demanded action.[44]

The only reassuring feature about serial sex crime was that recidivism was not a serious problem since the offenders, once captured, receive lengthy sentences. David Berkowitz received over 400 years in prison, Richard Ramirez was sentenced to multiple death penalties, as were Ted Bundy and Aileen Wuornos. However, it should be remembered that the criminal justice system had failed to notice early on the tendencies of Ed Kemper, Arthur Shawcross, and Henry Lee Lucas when they were initially convicted of particularly unpleasant murders as teenagers or young adults, and after their sentences were served they were released into society to kill again. In an attempt to thwart that possibility NCAVC would retain a killer's *modus operandi* for future reference.[45]

Founding the Behavioral Sciences Unit

During the 1983 "Serial Murder" hearings, the FBI presented no clear estimate as to the size of the problem. Prior to the hearings Bruce Porter wrote an article for *Psychology Today* about the BSU citing Bureau estimates that twenty-five per cent of 'stranger' homicides, the type of crime committed by serial killers, may have been committed by people with psychological disorders and associated them with the 5,000 unidentified bodies that the Missing Persons Bureau (MPB) dealt with each year.[46] During the hearings a number of statistics were reported, confusing the issue. William Webster noted there were approximately 6,300 unsolved murders in the US each year,[47] and Paula Hawkins estimated 3,600 "random and senseless" murders in 1981, which she describes as an "epidemic."[48] She added, to increase the sense of threat, that "[f]or every Ted Bundy who has gained national notoriety, there are dozens of unknown killers who have been responsible for untold deaths."[49] On a similar noted Ann Rule pointed out that there were more than 5,000 unidentified bodies in morgues around America at any time, and that VICAP could help track the killers.[50]

Early in 1984 Robert O Heck was reported as claiming that serial murderers killed as many as 4,000 people each year, and at least half of the victims were under eighteen years old. Heck estimated that there were thirty-five active serial killers, and also referred to them as an "epidemic."[51] While the number of victims and killers was uncertain most commentators agreed that the number was rising and, writing in the *New York Times,* Robert Lindsay claimed that many officials believed the increase in serial murder was due to the "sweeping changes in attitudes regarding sexuality that have occurred in the past twenty years."[52]

John Walsh testified at the Congressional hearings in the Missing Children's Assistance Act (February–March 1984), and in his testimony Walsh claimed that the number of "random unsolved murders" of women and children in America rose from 600 in 1966 to 4,500 in 1981 without giving any source for his statistics. In Phillip Jenkins opinion Walsh was inflating the July 1983 estimate of 3,600 victims and claiming they were all women and children.[53] Later that year in an article for *Newsweek* (November 1984) Mark Starr reported that "law enforcement experts" estimated as many as two-thirds of the 5,000 homicides that went unsolved annually may be committed by serial killers.[54]

By 1984, twenty-six per cent of homicides in the United States were unsolved[55] and *Life* magazine did not idly speculate about the possible association between serial murder and rising crime rates. It asserted that, "[t]he FBI estimates—much too conservatively in the opinion of many criminologists—that in 1983 about 5,000 Americans were slaughtered by serial killers alone."[56] The official estimates of the numbers of serial killers was much smaller than the unofficial US Justice Department estimate, which was then thought to be as many as one hundred.[57] Other writers go further, claiming at least 300 working serial killers,[58] or even as many as five hundred.[59] Holmes and DeBurger's article "Multiple Murder" (1988) estimated that 3,500 to 5,000 people each year are killed by serial killers. Their figure is based on a series of unfounded assertions, and their statistical analysis is flawed because they assume that each killer will kill ten to twelve victims in a year rather than during their career in murder (which is said to be a number of years). This average victim count, when combined with their assumption of 3,500 to 5,000 victims, creates a staggering figure of 350 to 500 killers. One critic challenged Holmes and DeBurger to justify one-tenth of their estimate for any year of their choosing.[60]

Holmes and DeBurger also make unstated assumptions about the consistency and efficiency of police departments in their investigations, assumptions that are impossible to justify. Statistical misuse or misunderstanding is evident in many scholarly journals, and was common in discussions of serial murder. Readers may be misled by the superficial or the provocative, and the commentators "may not only be imprecise—sometimes they will simply be wrong."[61] One of the academics seeking to define the term, and an associate of the FBI, Dr Park Elliot Dietz, describes serial murder as a "low-rate phenomenon" despite evoking a high degree of publicity.[62] Ignoring the opinion of Dietz, the FBI continued to report on serial killers knowing the media attention it would attract. By 1986 further hearings on the "Federal Role In The Investigation Of Serial Violent Crime" reduced the number of homicides associated with serial killers to eighteen per cent of the 4,500 unsolved homicides,[63] but the FBI confirmed a decrease of five per cent in violent crime in 1983.[64] The most honest comment on the subject of the number of killers active came from Egger who stated, "we really don't know the extent and prevalence of the problem."[65]

Eventually a CNN documentary *Murder By Numbers* (1993) examined the official BSU summary of cases that claimed that from 1977 there were 331 serial killers, accounting for nearly 2,000 victims. CNN found that after adding in missing cases and removing duplicates they found 191 killers and 1,007 victims, almost half the number of victims the BSU claimed. The Bureau pointed out that their statistics were compiled partly from media reports as an explanation for such serious inaccuracies. Some time after the original FBI statistics were circulated Les Davis, an FBI spokesman, tried to explain the exaggerated figures saying that with "more experience and development we have in this area, you start to realize that you really don't know, and you can't throw numbers around like that."[66] However, the distorted original Justice Department claims established the scope of the problem and hence the need for an immediate and substantial response. By exaggerating the problem of serial murder the FBI created a bogeyman to haunt society.[67]

Growing fear justified a larger budget for the 'new' FBI in a time of spending cutbacks, and an increase in society's need to be protected. Since the killers were credited with almost superhuman abilities, it is obvious that law enforcement must respond to the changes in conditions of crime with their own 'supercops' and these men came from the FBI's Behavioral Sciences Unit (BSU), known to more skeptical law enforcement agents as the 'Bull Shit Unit.' The only solution that the FBI offered is the expansion of the BSU.[68]

None of the popular reports or attempts at definition point out that a rise or fall in the murder rate is not necessarily related in any way to a rise or fall

Founding the Behavioral Sciences Unit

in the multiple murder rate,[69] or that the "typologies generally fail to pick up interactions between the killer, the victim and the environment, and do not appear to be flexible enough to accommodate a killer who may have different motives for different victims or changing motives over time."[70]

In January 1983, before the congressional hearings took place, the FBI Director authorized the Behavioral Sciences Unit to explore the idea of a National Center for the Analysis of Violent Crime (NCAVC) which had been a topic for discussion at a series of meetings supported by four Justice Department agencies: the National Institute of Justice, the Office of Justice Department Programs, the Office of Juvenile Justice and Delinquency Prevention, and the FBI, through a 'cooperative agreement' with the Criminal Justice Center at Sam Houston State University, Texas.[71]

Robert Keppel described the FBI pitch for NCAVC and Violent Criminal Apprehension Program (VICAP) as a "sales job," adding that everyone knew the best place for it was in civilian police hands funded by the federal government. The FBI is jealous of the civilian police systems, which the local police are enthusiastic about, and the Bureau thinks they are trying to take away its federal funding. Keppel felt that VICAP should never have been placed in the FBI because the information flow is always one way with the Bureau. In contrast, Keppel's own HITS system contacts the local police departments who supply information every week to discuss cases, something that VICAP could never do.[72] However, as far as the FBI was concerned, the National Academy at Quantico was the natural choice of location for such a center. Response to the hearings on 'Serial Murder' in 1983 prompted the FBI director to formally establish the NCAVC on June 6, 1984, with funding from the National Institute of Justice (NIJ).

For Keppel the main problem with VICAP was where it was located. For him, it belonged anywhere but inside the FBI. Initially Pierce Brooks had argued that VICAP was to be based with the Colorado Police Department in Colorado Springs,[73] but with the FBI in charge this was not possible. They took control of the project arguing that some of the VICAP program already existed at the National Academy. Despite Keppel's feeling that VICAP needed to regionalize, he continued to be one of VICAP's most vocal supporters while he developed his own idea for a state system after discussions with his fellow detectives in Seattle.

The foundations for the NCAVC to become operational were laid by July 10, 1984, after a speech by Reagan at the National Sheriff's Association. At this conference he identified combating violent crime as a priority of his presidency, giving more attention to law and order issues than previous administrations. The NCAVC was part of the Reagan administration's 'War on Crime.' Its mission was not only to work with local police, but also to strengthen and broaden local police and state training by the FBI, which served to further expand the Bureau's responsibilities and influence. Presentation of the serial sex killer as a modern criminal allowed the Reagan administration a means to legitimize the increased 'new' FBI budget and to expand its data collecting activities as well as superficially to support its own Republican agenda on law and order issues. By responding to sensational crimes that had received considerable media attention, the Reagan administration did not have to tackle the social issues that contributed to the majority of violent crime.

The BSU imposed a deadline on themselves to begin to collect data from police departments on unknown, motiveless homicides for June 1, 1985.[74] In the first six months of the Violent Criminal Apprehension Program (VICAP) database's existence, one-third of the cases about which it held information were provided by Robert Keppel,[75] and the BSU met its deadline and became a functioning part of the NCAVC.[76]

Before the information collecting for the NCAVC had officially begun, newspapers had picked up on the term serial killer and published articles which recycled the official FBI definition, never questioning what it said, and applying the misunderstood term in retrospect to other crimes which could be associated with the 'new' menace.[77] The serial sex killer who seems to have an "unquenchable lust for blood" has the ability to exercise "a special grip on the public's imagination because his murders are so incomprehensible,"[78] wrote one journalist. This extended the myth of the serial sex killer into a reinvented past, where they were fewer, and added to the panic of the present. During their careers Ted Bundy, Albert Fish, Edmund Kemper and Ed Gein had never been referred to as serial killers. Instead 'mass murderers,' 'maniacs,' 'fiends' and 'psychos' were all used at one time or another to describe these killers and their deeds. Even in a 1980 article directly referring to Robert Ressler various descriptive terms were used but not serial killer.[79] As far as law enforcement at the time was concerned the term did not exist. After its definition the new crime required more specialized training for police so they could effectively identify and combat the problem. Hence the NCAVC came into existence.

The NCAVC was composed of four main programs, and according to Pierce Brooks, "is a law enforcement-orientated behavioral science and computerized resource center that consolidates research, training and operational support functions."[80] It has, since its formation, become the world's clearing house for the pursuit and capture of irrational, abnormal offenders,[81] showing that the FBI have, at least superficially, set themselves up as authorities in the field of investigating serial violent crime, giving their program more credibility. Arthur P Meister, a VICAP unit chief, added that "In a sense, VICAPs utility *precedes* the determination that a single offender is responsible for multiple offenses."[82]

The 'Research and Development' program that established the BSU's expertise on serial murder was organized to study violent criminals, their victims, and the crime scenes, for insights into the criminal's motivation. Beginning in 1979, thirty-six convicted 'sexual' murderers were selected by FBI agents as part of their study on sexual homicide crime scenes and patterns of criminal behavior, and the FBI reported that the criminals were cooperative during interviews.[83] The goal of the interviews of serial and 'exceptionally violent' criminals was to use the information gained to recommend innovative investigative techniques and potential solutions to resolve homicides.[84] It was claimed that the study subjects represented twenty-five serial murderers (the

Founding the Behavioral Sciences Unit

number of separate victims with time breaks between victims ranging from two days to weeks or months), and eleven sexual murderers who had committed either a single homicide, double homicide, or spree murder.[85] The choice of some of these convicts for interview is questionable and may in part explain why the FBI has never released a full list of those who participated as subjects. A handful of criminals who had been convicted of crimes that had received extensive media coverage were included, and the FBI perhaps hoped that the public would assume the study was as scientific and as thorough as it claimed to be. When testifying in serial murder trials, John Douglas cites the prison interviews as part of his expert credentials.[86]

The problem with the initial interviews is that few of them were with anyone who was a serial sex killer, or even necessarily 'exceptionally violent.' Among the interviewed subjects were Charles Manson, Sirhan Sirhan, Arthur Bremer, Sarah Jane Moore, Sandra Goode, and Lynette "Squeaky" Fromme, none of whom fitted the description of a serial killer. Ted Bundy, while being a serial killer, was manipulative in interviews, trying to delay his execution, so his truthfulness was always in doubt. The FBI claimed that the serial killers were cooperative during interviews,[87] but Bundy alleged that at least one of the other interview subjects, Ed Kemper, had lied to the FBI in his interview. Ironically, John Douglas believed that Ed Kemper was analyzing his own crimes and learning to perfect his technique[88] and Ressler felt that his interviews with Kemper were the most productive for the study.

Robert Keppel, who also interviewed Kemper, believed him to be a complete liar, constantly changing his story to please his audience.[89] Ressler boasted in his own books and interviews that when talking to serial killers he was manipulating them;[90] in reality it looks like he was being manipulated by his subjects. While believing that the interviews were a good idea Keppel did not think that the FBI studied the case files thoroughly so they were unable to refute what their subjects said.[91] Lucas went on a storytelling spree. Dahmer also lied. The killers obviously knew that generally the criminologists who interviewed them were not really interested in their cases, and in a letter John Wayne Gacy described criminologist Steve Egger as "about as phony as the day is long."[92]

The duration of the interviews also casts doubts on their usefulness. Associating the names of Moore, Fromme, and Goode with the program may have boosted it superficially, but all three women were interviewed in a single day, whereas David Berkowitz was interviewed on three separate occasions in 1979. Of the other interviews, one of the subjects was "uncommunicative," one was "docile and polite" but had nothing useful to say, and a third was described as a "prisoner of his own delusions."[93] This again calls into question the source material for the profiles. Were these killers telling the truth if it would jeopardize appeals which they may have had pending in the legal system? Did these 'predators' really suddenly develop a social conscience? Or was their cooperation a way of drawing attention to themselves? Whatever a killer's motives for cooperating, the FBI was eager to listen.

Another problem was that the majority of the subjects were white, reinforcing the FBI assertion that the killers are most likely to be white. The most famous serial sex killers are white, for example, Henry Lee Lucas, Ted Bundy, Ed Gein, Kemper, Albert DeSalvo and David Berkowitz, but black killers of a similar type such as Carlton Gary and Coral Eugene Watts were not mentioned. In 1993 alone there were three separate series of black victims in Detroit and another in Chicago.[94] Robert Keppel described George Russell, a black, educated, middle-class man who had grown up in a white neighborhood and killed white women, as being truly a serial killer of the nineties.[95] In 1997 Henry Louis Wallace, a confessed serial killer, was convicted of nine murders. He is black, and killed people he knew, not strangers. It was reported that by his *not* fitting the normal profile, the police were distracted into other avenues of investigation.[96]

Keppel was not the only person to notice this apparent change in the nature of serial crime. FBI agent Paul Lindsay believes: "Of all the plagues visited upon inner city ghettoes over the years, serial killers seemed to be the one thing they'd escaped. Now it's as if the triple plague of poverty, crack and AIDS is breeding a new specter, a new kind of grim reaper."[97] The new grim reaper is the serial killer. This shift in the perpetrators of serial crimes has not been generally acknowledged. Despite the existence of many serial killer films, few portray a killer who is not white, reinforcing the notion of intra-racial crime. This is reflected in the findings of the study, but the study's size and the sampling of criminals from a different generation, with a different social climate, leads to an out-of-date perception of the crime. The higher profile of white killers might reflect nothing more than their inefficiency and carelessness. For all their alleged cunning they make mistakes. It may be that white killers were found because the police were looking for a white killer in an era when black crime was confined to black areas.

In other cases media attention has made it politically expedient to find a single killer. The Son of Sam murders in the late 1970s were "whitewashed" by authorities to fulfill their wishes and restore calm in New York even when it became apparent that several killers were at work.[98] In the case of John Wayne Gacy, it was considered a "minor oversight" that some leads were not followed up. There is little doubt that Gacy was a principal offender, but Robert Ressler acknowledged that, "leads suggesting that other people might have been involved in luring young men to the house for sex, drug deals and torture—if not for murder—were not completely pursued."[99] Gacy himself, in a 1992 court appeal, named David Cram, Phillip Paske and Michael Rossi as suspects implicated in the crimes for which he had been convicted. Cram and Rossi became "coached" witnesses for the prosecution despite being implicated in some of the murders at the Gacy house. Gacy also alleged that in 1992 an FBI agent, Marie Dyson, was investigating Cram and Paske in connection with the 1980 murder of a seventeen year old boy, similar to ones for which Gacy was convicted.[100]

This method of investigation is similar to the G-Men 'shoot to kill' approach to solving crimes. Once the suspect is dead, all of the crimes they are associated with are considered cleared, allowing one Public Enemy to take credit for more crimes than they actually committed. Now politically directed investigations and the concept of 'linkage' allow a serial killer to acquire inflated body counts so police can improve their case clearance rate. The implications of this are obvious; if not all of the criminals are caught then they are free to continue their careers. Furthermore, if the FBI was interviewing prisoners for crimes they did not necessarily commit (as in the case of DeSalvo, Berkowitz and Lucas), or which they committed in conjunction with others who were not convicted (in the case of Gacy) and analyzed the crimes as the work of an individual serial sex killer, its results will be seriously distorted.

When serial killers are apprehended, it is usually by luck or by the mundane and tedious checking up of leads. David Berkowitz, the Son of Sam, was caught by local police checking up on all of the parking tickets issued in the vicinity of one of his killings. Henry Lee Lucas was arrested for violating his parole by carrying a gun, then while in jail Lucas began to confess to dozens of murders of which he had not been suspected, and his captor, W F Conway, was voted Sheriff of the Year for capturing such a prodigious killer.[101] Dean Corll was only discovered after he had been killed by Wayne Henley, an associate of his, who then began to relate the history of the pair's activities, and in the case of John Wayne Gacy, Chicago's Killer Clown, the 'missing persons' were only identified as having been killed by Gacy when their bodies were discovered under his house.[102] Apparently no one knew anything about the murders being committed by Leonard Lake and Charles Ng until Lake was detained after an incident of petty theft aroused police suspicion.

Stopping when one murder is attributed to a killer is not necessarily good enough for the FBI. Senior profiler John Douglas believes, "When you come across a subject who has been identified at thirty-five years of age, the first thing you say to yourself is this is not the first time this man has ever killed. Serial killers don't surface at thirty-five." The BSU advise law-enforcement agencies not to be satisfied with just 'your case.'[103] The 'your case' mentality arose from competition between law enforcement agencies at all levels, with the FBI being notorious for taking credit for locally solved crimes to boost their own statistical performance.[104]

Often the local and state police do not like the FBI; they feel that they do all the important, but mundane, groundwork in a case only to have the FBI take the information without providing any assistance.[105] By encouraging local and state police to examine for a potential career of murder, what was once a local or state crime could become a federal or even an international investigation giving FBI jurisdiction, and it is their technical skill that apparently results in the criminal's capture.

Initially, the number of murders committed by a killer is uncertain, and at this point an opportunity is presented to law enforcement agencies to clear unsolved murders. Robert Keppel, an experienced investigator, notes that "Unless incriminating physical evidence was overwhelming or they actually managed to catch the perpetrator in the act, detectives usually need the suspect to confess in order to get resolution to all murders in a series."[106] The most notorious example of this was the confessions of Henry Lee Lucas who, it was claimed, killed over 300 men, women and children in several states. Other estimates associate many more murders with Lucas, some reports are in excess of five hundred. However, claims made in a confession and verifying the suspect's actual involvement are two different matters.

Due to the nature of his alleged crimes a conference was held to allow law enforcement officers from around the United States the opportunity to examine Lucas. It was claimed that of Lucas's three hundred confessions, "[m]ore than 142 of these have reportedly been verified by the police."[107] But it should also be remembered that Lucas was diagnosed as being a pathological liar.[108] Eventually Lucas was only convicted of two of the murders and law enforcement agencies were humbled when their methods for extracting confessions became publicized. Overzealous detectives had been feeding Lucas information on crimes in an attempt to clear unsolved cases. Tom Whitlock, Lucas's lawyer in Texas acknowledged that, "Certainly there's a temptation for law-enforcement agencies to clear up their books this way. I'm getting too many calls from agencies who have a body and want someone to blame it on."[109] Robert Ressler believed that the police departments did need to close their difficult unsolved murder cases, but the fiasco was also partly due to "the boredom of local policemen, many of whom convinced their superiors that it was important for them to go to Texas on a sort of paid holiday in order to join the queue waiting to get in to interview Lucas."[110]

Wayne Williams was convicted of the Atlanta Child Murders, a total of thirty killings, but Williams could be *linked* with only twenty-three[111] and was eventually charged and convicted of only two of the murders. Even the number of cases 'cleared' when a serial killer is apprehended fluctuates. One article reports that twenty-nine killings were associated with the Atlanta murderer, and of these twenty-two were 'cleared by arrest' when Williams was convicted.[112] Ted Bundy finally confessed to eleven murders, but he was only found guilty of three. While on death row in Florida, Bundy was repeatedly visited by law enforcement officers in an attempt to extract information from him relating to other crimes in which they felt he may have been involved. Because of Bundy's methods of playing with the police to try to prolong his life, he has become associated with possibly a hundred or more murders. In the report of Bundy's execution in the *New York Times*, he was officially linked to "a dozen or more similar crimes" that had occurred while he was active.[113] How many murders he actually committed will never be established for certain.

After the arrest and conviction of Jeffrey Dahmer for the murders in Milwaukee, investigators explored his past and raised questions about five murders which had occurred in Germany while Dahmer had been stationed there. After the arrest of Ted Bundy in Florida and Henry Lee Lucas in Texas, law officers came from all over the United States to interview them about unsolved crimes. A criminal such as Manson, with a vastly inflated reputation as a mass murderer, may have been prepared to meet and discuss his life with the FBI once he was caught, convicted and jailed. The final program in the NCAVC would track violent crimes, hunt for active killers, and backtrack the possible careers of serial criminals, making it possible to clear many cases at one time by associating them with a captured killer.

A training program for federal, state and local law agencies as well as for selected behavioral scientists and others who deal with violent crime matters was offered by the BSU,[114] and by midsummer 1982 the need for training was obvious enough. There were still only a few homicide investigators in the United States who had encountered serial killers in their jurisdictions, but serial murders were alleged to be on the increase.[115] Yet the training is in a field that has still not proven its worth. The training was offered to law-enforcement agencies from all around the world. Between June 1985 and December 1986 over 3,500 hours of training were given to 40,000 people in over 400 locations in the United States, Canada, the Caribbean, Britain and Europe.[116] However Ressler's findings have been questioned for their applicability to a non-American population. The homicide rate in the United States is eight per 100,000 but in other countries, such as England and Wales, the rate is only 1.3 per 100,000.[117]

The results of the FBI interviews were recorded, statistically analyzed and applied to investigations in the form of psychological profiles. Profiles included estimates of the perpetrator's age, race, sex, socioeconomic and marital status, educational level, arrest history, location of residence in relation to the scene, and certain personality traits. In compiling the profile, "The profiler is searching for clues which indicate the *probable* personality configuration of the responsible individual."[118] According to Dr Park Elliot Dietz, "It's much more useful for the police to know a person's age, race, and marital status than read a precise diagnosis from the American Psychiatric Association's *Diagnostic and Statistical Manual of Mental Disorders*."[119] Identifying personality characteristics with a profile is useful in "directing consideration toward persons who possess characteristics of known offenders who have been responsible for similar crimes in the past."[120]

Roger Depue claimed the interviews produced the first research into the *way* serial sex killers commit their crimes rather than *why* they commit them,[121] emphasizing the FBI's lack of interest in social causes of crime. Once presented in a profile "[t]he data is admittedly uncontrolled, incomplete and missing specifics of the study group."[122] Despite shortcomings, this data was used to generate profiles for the second program, "Profiling and Consultation." At the first hearings on "Serial Murder" (1983), Ann Rule, included on the panel because she had worked with Ted Bundy, stated that killers will rarely vary their pattern of killing, a characteristic which would be very important in cases where bodies of victims were not found quickly and pathologists could not identify the cause of death.

According to the FBI, research results have "greatly expanded" the services offered by the NCAVC and helped to "sharpen" their profiles.[123] Patterns were said to have been found, thanks to the BSU questionnaires, which were "revealing and consistent."[124] Colin Campbell believes that, "Good profiles, it seems, are generally the work of detectives... psychologists and psychiatrists who work with the police eventually begin to think like the police, while the police, of course are now famous for thinking like criminals."[125]

Better To Reign In Hell

While studying for advanced degrees in social sciences, the BSU agents emphasized that they intentionally avoided using psychiatric terminology to describe suspects. John Douglas acknowledged the "dabbling" other police departments had done with individuals who have "very little training in profiling" and, because they are drawn primarily from psychiatry, psychology and "the area of rehabilitation," their profiles are "not good." The weakness of the civilian profilers, in Douglas' opinion, was their use of terms such as 'paranoid schizophrenia,' 'manic depressive psychosis,' and 'paranoia.' Such terms, he contends, mean nothing to law enforcement officials so he, along with Roy Hazelwood, another senior BSU agent, came up with very simple terminology of 'organized' and 'disorganized' criminals which reflects the condition of the crime scene rather than the criminal.[126]

Profilers claimed to get inside the minds of serial sex killers, but at the same time they declared a disinterest in what motivates the killers. Roy Hazelwood said, "We don't get hung up on why the [serial] killer does the things he does. What we're interested in is that he does it... What we're interested is that he does it in a way that leads us to him."[127] That attitude, like Reagan's New Right policies, refused to adopt any approach to crime which might actually lower the rate of criminal offending. If the generic serial killer history was predictable and common to all of the killers, would social policies in education, welfare and mental health not have been an effective means to decrease the numbers of serial killers? But those were exactly the policies which Reagan's administration were cutting back on.

In their study the FBI agents "did not find it helpful to perceive the victims as provoking the murder. Rather, the agents tried to be aware of how the offender thought and subsequently, how he would respond to key characteristics of a victim." A passive victim invited a particular image of the crime, the criminal and the individual victim. The crime becomes premeditated if the criminal was looking for a specific characteristic to respond to, and victims need to be protected if they were being attacked without provocation. No longer was murder an unplanned occurrence. In the FBI's opinion: "An organized murderer is one who appears to plan his murders and who displays control at the crime scene. The disorganized murderer is less apt to plan, and his crime scenes display haphazard behavior." This simple differentiation is *not* consistent, even by the FBI's own admission: "there are *no* situations where the organized and disorganized offenders are mutually exclusive."[128] Both types of murderers are capable of all types of behavior. The case of Danny Rolling, The Gainesville Slasher, makes a mockery of the FBI organized/disorganized distinctions, and of profiling which provided "absolutely nothing" to connect him to the murders he is currently convicted of committing.[129] In part, the differentiation was a way to make it easier for police officers who had not been trained in psychological profiling,[130] but the 'either/ or' approach which is publicly presented offers an unrealistically simple view of the serial sex killer. It is this simplistic view which is the basis for the FBI's "Profiling and Consultation" program, and the main weapon in the fight against elusive, predatory serial offenders.[131]

Founding the Behavioral Sciences Unit

John Douglas, one of the most prominent FBI profilers writes, "If you want to understand an artist then you have to look at the painting."[132] Similarly the profilers reviewed the handiwork of criminals before constructing their profiles. Robert Ressler's method was to lay out the available documents over the floor and then "absorb it like a sponge," he would just "sit and suck it up," adding that, "Having access to everything, looking at everything, and just getting perceptions is the way you develop profiles."[133] This meant that the method employed by the criminal in carrying out the crimes would have to be examined thoroughly and, "[f]or that reason" Park Elliot Dietz added, "a high premium is placed on observable attributes that could narrow the field of suspects under consideration and characteristics that suggest routes of investigation."[134] But without first-hand experience of the crime scene, the condition of the body and the site in which it was found it is difficult to see how profilers could check thoroughly for clues, unless they were only looking for what they expected to find. For Robert Keppel, visiting the crime scene to get a "geographic perspective" is crucially important, something which the FBI profilers do not understand because they have no investigative experience.[135] Absence of agents from the crime scene is in contrast to the timeless image of the hunter crouched down in the mud, examining the quarry's tracks.[136] It also contradicts the impression given by newspapers. The earliest report of the BSU profilers, in the Chicago *Tribune*, sought to emphasize the meticulous examination of the crime scene and evidence by agents in the hunt for the Vampire of Sacramento (Richard Chase). The bizarre nature of the crimes and the Bureau's claimed expertise in investigating them allowed the FBI the opportunity to involve itself in state murder investigations.

It is often pointed out that the FBI does not catch these serial criminals;[137] instead, agents assist local police in focusing their investigations, then suggest some 'proactive' techniques that might help draw a criminal out.[138] Profiles are used only as a guide for the investigators, and as a way to display the 'new' FBI technical superiority over local and state police. The FBI 'innovation' claimed to give new insights into the systematic nature of the criminal mind, and formed the framework for law-enforcement in the future.

'Psychological profiling' was by no means a new idea when the FBI took it up in the 1970s, and it had already had a "colorful history."[139] In the nineteenth century Edgar Allan Poe's C Auguste Dupin may have been the first behavioral profiler, and together with Arthur Conan Doyle's Sherlock Holmes, gave a high prominence to analytical investigation of crime scenes,[140] often being used as reference points for the BSU 'Mindhunters.' Park Elliot Dietz believes that historically anyone who has attempted to find a solution to criminal activity has always used a 'variant' of profiling.[141]

In 1956 Dr James A Brussel, a psychiatrist, worked with the New York City Police in the case of the Mad Bomber which had been ongoing for sixteen years. Brussel's profile of the bomber and the subsequent arrest of George Metesky is often cited as evidence of the accuracy of profiling, and its usefulness in police investigations. However, much of Brussel's Freudian interpretation of the evidence focused on Metesky's sexual abnormalities and had little to do with the case resolution. The most commonly repeated anecdote concerning Brussel is his prediction that the Mad Bomber would be wearing a double breasted suit, and it would be buttoned, a claim which Brussel later admitted was a case of him letting his imagination get the better of him. This fine detail may be of interest, and in retrospect it may be impressive, but did it actually help to catch the killer? It was clues from letters written to newspapers by the Mad Bomber and the diligent work of secretaries searching through the files of Consolidated Edison which led police to Metesky. Predictably Brussel was compared to the famous fictional detective Sherlock Holmes and referred to as the Twelfth Street Prophet and the Psychiatric Seer by journalists.[142] His notoriety began with his involvement in the Mad Bomber case in the 1950s, but until being invited to join the Boston Strangler task force Medical-Psychiatric Committee in April 1964 he had not worked on a case which involved two or more murders.

Brussel's profile of the Boston Strangler might be seen as an accurate description of Albert DeSalvo but none of the other psychiatrists, and none of the police agencies involved believed they were investigating a single killer. Susan Kelly's book *The Boston Stranglers* (1995) convincingly argues that DeSalvo's confessions were orchestrated primarily by his attorney F Lee Bailey to advance his own legal reputation rather than to advance the interests of his clients.[143] When studying the case files of the Boston Strangler murders Brussel, reflecting his training as a Freudian psychiatrist, looked for a pattern in the killings involving sex and violence while the police focused on similarities between victims or locations to narrow their investigation.[144] Brussel's unique theory was based on the observation that all of the victims were women and he emphasized the importance of the semen stains left at each crime scene. However the police saw many more fundamental differences between the *modus operandi* throughout the series of crimes. To explain the alleged change in the killer's *modus operandi* and the cessation of the murders Brussel said:

> What has happened to him [the Boston Strangler], in two words, is instant maturity. In this two year period he has suddenly grown, psychosexually from infancy to puberty to manhood… He had to commit these murders to achieve this growth. It was the only way he knew to solve his problems, find himself sexually, and become a grown man among men.[145]

Theoretically this enabled the Boston Strangler to make sexual progress, which normally takes years, in a matter of months, and explicitly states that the offender had "cured" himself of his sexual problems by raping and murdering.[146]

The Green Man sex offences for which DeSalvo was charged and the earlier Measuring Man sexual assaults for which he was convicted, could not accurately be described as 'rape' because in most cases the women acknowledged consenting to sex and there was no violence involved. By the time the Green Man trial began in January 1967 DeSalvo had already been named as the Boston Strangler and as a repeat sex-offender by Gerold Frank in his book *The Boston Strangler* (1966). During the Green Man trial Brussel testified for the defense that DeSalvo was not responsible for his actions, but the jury disagreed and convicted the accused.[147]

John Douglas describes Brussel as a "trailblazer in the field," but during Hoover's reign at the FBI, psychology and soft sciences were not attributed any great value. In fact, many in the FBI in the early 1970s, as well as law-enforcement officers in general, considered the application of psychology and behavioral science to criminology to be "worthless bullshit."[148] Despite this some FBI agents believed that there was a useful potential to behavioral sciences which should be used for the benefit of the "law enforcement profession."[149]

Following Brussel, "Pioneering work has been done by a succession of Supervisory Special Agents some of whom have since retired or moved on to positions elsewhere in the bureau, and others of whom continue to develop, apply and teach profiling."[150] But it would appear that no-one in the twenty years that followed Brussel's profile of the Mad Bomber could match the accuracy with which he was credited. Detectives in New York City talked with experts hundreds of times since Brussel's profiles but what a number of them recall about these consultations with psychiatrists is that they were "interesting" or "helpful in a general way" or, that they were "not very interesting" and "not very helpful."[151] Comments such as these are not encouraging.

Involvement in the Atlanta Child Murders investigation (1980–81) was crucial in establishing the BSU profilers' credibility. According to John Douglas: "The case was good for our program. We'd proven that a psychological profile can help convict a killer."[152] Whether the right man, Wayne Williams, was convicted is still being questioned. Investigation of the Atlanta Child Murders brought together many prominent members of the law enforcement community and academics and, from such an experienced group, quick results were expected.

At Williams' trial he was charged with two murders, but they were murders of adults, not of children, which he was linked to by forensic evidence. The most important feature of the trial was the judge's unprecedented action to allow the prosecution to use evidence against Williams arising from crimes he was *not* being charged with. The profile, provided by the FBI *after* Williams' identification, fitted the suspected killer and forensics tied him to the crime. Forensic evidence is often used to provide 'linkage' between crimes, and most of the case against Williams was based on the forensic fiber evidence collected by the FBI and analyzed by its crime laboratory. Forensic evidence can lead the jury astray and the FBI is not always forthcoming when its methodology is questioned, claiming 'privilege against self-criticism' in hearings which have challenged its testimony. The Bureau also opposes outside evaluation of its performance, assuming that no-one is qualified to evaluate the FBI.[153]

One former Atlanta policemen said that the forensics evidence used to convict Williams was flawed and that the case should be reopened,[154] and the case for Williams' innocence gained much more credibility after recent attacks on FBI forensic reliability. A Justice Department report in 1997 revealed that the FBI crime laboratory had tampered with evidence in some cases.[155] In light of such accusations, a conviction based on forensic evidence might not be as conclusive as is commonly thought. Whatever the reliability of the forensic evidence against Williams he was convicted and the FBI took the credit, adding prestige to its program and weight to the arguments in favor of its training program.

The guilty verdict against Williams was seen as a validation of the FBI-imposed notion of a black serial killer. Al Binder, Williams' attorney, recognized the importance of the trial but for a different reason from that of the BSU. Binder believed,

> This is a very noteworthy and controversial case because, for the first time, law enforcement tried to give fiber evidence the strength of fingerprint evidence, even though there is a great question whether fiber evidence can ever be established beyond reasonable doubt. Then the prosecution claimed there was a pattern in these murders of asphyxia and strangulation, yet one child had multiple knife wounds and had been strangled. Where's the pattern?[156]

The message sent out by the FBI's profile and Williams' arrest meant that there were no racially-motivated murders and that the law agencies had done their jobs effectively. The FBI-imposed notion of a black serial killer appears to be a case of wishful thinking, or the imposition of a politically acceptable solution to an awkward problem. Perceiving a racist element in the crimes would damage the business economy of the 'city too busy to hate,' undermining its regional pre-eminence. One journalist commented that no pattern existed to the crimes, but 'finding' a pattern that was specifically being looked for, and finding a serial killer was a quick and relatively painless way to pacify a restless and increasingly belligerent population.[157] At a time when the entire nation watched, even the White House, it was crucially important for the killer to be caught. John Douglas admitted that if the Bureau profile had been wrong the whole program would have died.[158] As it was, a killer was found and the FBI was seen as successfully leading the investigation.

If the Atlanta Child Murders case was seen as a boost for the FBI and the BSU, then the investigation into the Green River Killer served as a counterbalance. The Green River Task Force was operational from 1984 to 1989 and was not able to identify the killer, despite the aid of BSU profiling and onsite FBI investigative support. Experts even disagreed on whether it was a single killer or several independent killers. Despite the forty-nine murders which were associated with the killer, or killers, there was not enough information to construct a definitive profile of the murderer or murderers, due to the absence of a crime scene and the poor condition of the recovered corpses from the areas where they were disposed. When the task force was disbanded it was a major failure for the Bureau,[159] as well as costing an estimated 15 million dollars.[160]

BSU participation in the investigation of the explosion on the USS *Iowa*

Founding the Behavioral Sciences Unit

in March 1989 was intended to reinforce their reputation. Instead, the panel of experts stated that they felt that professional training was needed in order to carry out standardized interviews of subjects, and would also be required to interpret the data,[161] training that the BSU agents did not have. Without a standardized method of interview there is no systematic, scientific validity to the conclusions which may be drawn. According to Elliot Leyton, as a data source, interviews are a "profoundly flawed tool," with the subject having a long time after the event to prepare the story he wants you to hear.[162] The BSU are fitting new cases into parameters defined by existing case studies.

The FBI's ability to predict scientifically and accurately a criminal personality lost a great deal of prestige at the 1990 hearings on the USS *Iowa* explosion. The BSU had been asked to profile one of the crew members, but their analysis was thought to be questionable, so a team of independent experts was brought in. The 'Mindhunters' were promoted as being "exceptionally well trained to identify the nuances which suggest that one case might be related to another, and to advise investigators on special investigative techniques which may be beneficial."[163] But the expert witnesses called to the hearings challenged both the conclusions the FBI agents reached and the scope and methodology of their analysis. The experts felt that there was insufficient knowledge to interpret the information, and they saw "little synthesis; they viewed many of the items selected to support key points as suspect or selected without consideration of context." And they made no attempt to present both sides of the suspect Clayton Hartwig's character.[164]

As in most BSU cases, the investigators did not interview any of the individuals involved in the incident; instead, the interviews were carried out by agents of the Naval Investigative Service (NIS), and the FBI assumed that the interviews were unbiased. The interviews carried out by the NIS were part of a criminal investigation, not part of a study to gather clinical psychological data. This left one expert feeling, "concerned about the unreliability of interview data used, particularly selective bias of the interviewers." It was also pointed out that, in both quality and quantity, the evidence was not sufficient to support the conclusion reached by the BSU. Despite lack of information to back up their opinions the FBI agents believed their opinion was valid and claimed that their profiles were always "definitive in nature." The panel of experts judged the BSU opinion to be merely "informed speculation," *not* a scientific opinion.[165] The opinion of the experts did nothing to change the FBI's approach to their investigations or their methods for training future investigators.

On other occasions the profiles have been badly wrong, such as an early profile by police and psychiatrists in the case of the Skid Row Slasher in Los Angeles, claiming that the killer was white, with blonde hair. While the police were hunting for a white killer they arrested Vaughn Greenwood for two non-fatal slashing attacks. Greenwood was black. If the police had relied on the profile they would never have caught Greenwood. He was caught not because of the profile but because of a letter he dropped at a crime scene.[166] The Skid Row Slasher case did highlight the potential danger of profiles, in that the profile did seem to provoke reaction from the killer. A few hours after the details of the profile were reported on television, another vagrant on skid row was murdered by the slasher. After several years of producing inaccurate profiles, the BSU adopted the tactic of putting 'if' statements in their profiles, 'if this is true then that is true,' which does not give police confidence in their case from the direction of their investigation. 'Ifs' keep the FBI covered in case anything goes wrong because they have been criticized so much for previous profiles. They do not have an active feedback mechanism to say how many times they have been right.[167]

A few examples of where the profiles have been used are regularly cited, the Atlanta Child Killer, the Green River Killer and Jack The Ripper are the most commonly discussed, yet there is no statistical analysis of cases where profiles are actually responsible for identifying the perpetrator of a 'serial homicide.' In some cases credit is taken falsely by the BSU agents. Robert Ressler claimed that his profile of the Vampire of Sacramento fitted Richard Chase "precisely," and the case provided information for the BSU on how to evaluate characteristic signs left by murderers in future crime scenes.[168] Lt Ray Biondi, who investigated the Vampire of Sacramento murders, acknowledged the importance of Chase as classic case study material for law enforcement officers being trained in profiling, but he was livid about Ressler's claims[169] and he felt that, possibly due to excessive zeal, often "the facts are massaged or omitted to illustrate how the case was solved by the sole use of a psychological profile." While Biondi believes any new training which benefits the efficiency of law enforcement should be used, he sees the practical use of profiling as "very limited." In his opinion, "The danger in the belief of psychological profiling is that it may cause an investigation to focus away from the true killer." To try to correct misconceptions that complex cases are solved solely using profiles, Biondi published his own account of the Chase crimes in *The Dracula Killer* (1992).[170]

Profiles provided to law-enforcement agencies can have serious negative implications. Colin Campbell conceded that "It is conceivable, for instance, that the wrong man might be harassed, arrested and even convicted on no better grounds than his resemblance to a psychological profile."[171] At the trial of Wayne Williams, the case which established the value of profiles, the prosecution sought to show the jury another side of Williams, eventually provoking him into losing his temper. In an outburst Williams told the prosecution that he knew they had a profile of him and that they were trying to make him fit the profile.[172] But Williams was still convicted. Patrick Jewell was publicly investigated by the FBI and the media after the Atlanta Olympics bomb in 1996 solely because he fit the FBI lone bomber profile. A simple examination of the chronology of events should have told the FBI that Jewell could not have planted the bomb, but it took the Bureau eighty-eight days to announce that Jewell was not a suspect. In the meantime Jewell's civil rights were repeatedly violated by the FBI and media, the Bureau lied to Jewell's lawyers and leaked information to the press implicating him in their profile, before the Bureau was forced to acknowledge that he could not have planted the bomb.[173]

Founding the Behavioral Sciences Unit

It should always be remembered that the profiles are very general, and can offer multiple suspects where the police only want one person: "Averages do not predict the behavior of individuals."[174] When profiles are used in a serial sex murder investigation they seek to direct the police agencies to look for a suspect with specific characteristics. Yet when investigators look for these similarities, they will exclude the differences a suspect might exhibit. This leads police to find a suspect who fits the profile and not necessarily the crime. Paul Lindsay, who was one of the FBI's top investigators, is skeptical enough to ask, "how many serial killer cases have the FBI [profilers] solved—if any?"[175] In the 1970s Harvey Schlossberg, a psychologist with the New York City Police Department and Martin Reiser, a psychologist with the Los Angeles Police Department, were asked about the relevance of their profiles, and neither of them was willing or able to recount the details of a useful and accurate profile which they had constructed.[176] Since the profiles are so general they often fail to fit the offender, and "even if they do, the profile seldom if ever helps the detective initially identify the killer."[177] The suspect must be identified by good police work, not by a vague profile. Paul Lindsay believes that profiles can be terribly misleading. In the course of a normal investigation there is a process of elimination, a narrowing down of the field of suspects by age, blood type, anything that can be used to eliminate people—it is usually not about finding the right person, it is about eliminating everyone else. By looking for killers between twenty-five and thirty-two years of age, as the profilers direct investigators to do, investigators will find more killers in that age bracket, it is a self-fulfilling theory.[178] In effect, this serves to protect older and younger serial offenders by focusing the search elsewhere.

Colin Wilson points out that, "Even the most experienced of mental health consultants are liable to submit opposing views when jointly asked to profile some unknown, violent offender."[179] The influential New York psychiatrist Dr James Brussel also sought to emphasize that, "the personalities of multiple murderers did not fit any single type but varied widely, as widely as the personalities of normal people."[180] As far as Colin Campbell can see, "there is no clear evidence that psychologists are any better than bartenders at the remote diagnosis of killers."[181] Campbell quotes Russell Boxley, a psychologist at Boston University, as saying that the profilers are bastardizing their discipline, and that "to solve a notorious series of murders psychologically from no other clues than the results of demented passion, would be truly extraordinary, a victory of intellect over madness worthy of Edgar Allan Poe."[182] Lindsay acknowledges a profile can be useful, but he adds, "you better hope your guy is in the profile. Otherwise you're in a heap of shit."[183] Alongside the information gathered by the BSU prison interviews the FBI sought information on active cases from local police departments for the NCAVC databanks.

The Violent Criminal Apprehension Program (VICAP) was the idea of Pierce Brooks, a career detective, and conceived of as a nationwide repository of homicide information: "Sharing investigative information can supply more pieces of the puzzle necessary to strengthen the investigative process and expedite the identification and apprehension of the suspect."[184] According to

Ressler the services offered by the profilers are unique and "available to law enforcement on a twenty-four-hour basis, 365 days a year."[185] Availability of assistance of this sort is in theory ideal, but, "If VICAP provided that type of service to law-enforcement officers on a daily basis, their personnel would be overwhelmed with inquiries from thousands of investigators."[186] The cost of running such an operation would also require the FBI budget to be increased. Between 1981 and 1983 the 'new' FBI attempted to expand its databanks but met with serious challenges from both civil libertarians and other law-enforcement agencies. The missing children and serial sex killer crime panics helped overcome opposition and justify information collection which was gradually expanded.

During his career as a police officer, Pierce Brooks was frustrated by the lack of communication and cooperation he discovered between police departments. In 1967 the National Crime Information Center (NCIC) had been set up to allow local and state law agencies access to an FBI central index of wanted and missing persons and information on stolen property, yet "in a country that was sending rockets into space there existed no efficient system by which police could exchange information on cases of violent crime."[187] Until the founding of the NCAVC it remained true that a serial criminal could only be traced through newspaper reports.[188]

VICAP's declared aim was to be "exclusively a serial murder tracking program. Its only function was to compare an incoming murder case with the data base of serial homicides to determine if another murder was committed by the same person."[189] Yet since its official origin VICAP has been promoted as tracking other types of crime, such as rape, child abduction, and arson. The number of unsolved murders each year in the United States meant that VICAP staff could not concern themselves with routine murders; there were too many and, of course, too many questions about them. If all the unsolved murders would overload the systems capabilities then this means that VICAP can only deal with a limited number of requests no matter how many hours it may be open for business, and it can effectively function only as a database for 'stranger' homicides, not for all violent homicides. By 1986 the BSU could accept only the "toughest cases."[190] No criteria were given to explain exactly what the toughest cases were, instead it was left open to the public's imagination and its manipulation by media reports and cinematic representation. Cases which had gone unsolved for years seem to be the only stated criteria for the difficult cases that the FBI accepted. The Bureau constructs about 800 profiles a year, falling a long way short of the 7,688 unsolved murders. With profilers turning away 100–150 cases because of a shortage of staff,[191] weight is added to any claims that the BSU makes to increase their budget.

The VICAP computer system is not located in the National Academy with the rest of the NCAVC; instead it is held in the FBI headquarters in Washington DC, with information being exchanged between the two locations via secure telecommunications lines.[192] VICAP's purpose is to, "collect, collate, and relate all aspects of the investigations of similar pattern multiple murders throughout the nation regardless of location or the number of police

Founding the Behavioral Sciences Unit

agencies involved."[193] This would allow for pattern analysis which can reveal "multidimensional trends and profiles" and which, according to FBI analysts, have gone undetected in the past.[194] Special forms were put together by Pierce Brooks which initially came in three volumes consisting of sixty-eight pages of questions, in which he was careful to ask the right questions, and to ensure enough detail in the answers so that the form would demonstrate, changes in the *modus operandi* as well as a killer's 'signature' in the form of additional behavior from one case to the next. The information from the forms was fed into a profiler computer where more than a hundred *modus operandi* similarities were compared with all other cases in the VICAP database. This 'template matching' uses crime pattern recognition to detect and predict the behavior of violent criminals and provides the source that the NCAVC would rely on for its support and consultation services. A system that relied on multiple choice questions to gather information for 'definitive profiles' is hardly able to provide an in-depth analysis. Its reliance on previous criminal patterns may cause the system to overlook new patterns of crime, thus adding to the possible oversights of local police collecting crime scene information. The situation was not improved by the profiler's failure to take a first-hand look at the evidence.

The VICAP crime reports which Brooks had drawn up were seen as being too lengthy. It was quickly decided by VICAP that the reports had to be reduced in size in order to get the cooperation of local police agencies. Pierce Brooks would not even attend the meetings to discuss the reductions in the size of the VICAP form because he disagreed with any reduction, and he knew that the changes had been agreed before the meeting had taken place. This effectively undermined the value attributed to the opinions of any non- VICAP advisors and cast doubts about what the FBI was really interested in monitoring. Brooks felt that the FBI was only using him and Keppel for support and if the form was a failure it could be said that it was their fault.[195] Somewhat ironically Keppel believed that Pierce Brooks had originally contacted him about VICAP to associate the eventually successful and high profile Bundy case with the need for a national crime centre to collate information. Keppel believed he could have identified Bundy much sooner if VICAP had then existed; but Keppel realized he would be held responsible if the system did not live up to expectations.

In July 1986 the shortened form, the 'VICAP Crime Analysis Report' was released. For such an important document it is little more than a multiple choice checklist, and the FBI boasted that it "can be answered in fifteen-twenty minutes." For the authors, "the relative simplicity of the information, a brief narrative of the case, and the amenability of the data to analytical manipulation will all serve to enhance effectiveness."[196] In Keppel's opinion, reductions in the VICAP crime report showed that the VICAP analysts were eager to deal with a form suited to crime analysis, not for the greater understanding of all murder investigations. He was also left wondering if the trimmed form would be effective in 'connecting' murder cases. Was enough information being submitted? The VICAP staff wanted to remove what they saw as redundancies from the original proposal: "We were obliging and went along with their proposal."[197]

The omission of questions from the reports would restrict the information given by police agencies to the NCAVC and therefore limit their ability to make effective comparisons between cases. The paperwork was more than many police agencies wanted, but according to Robert Keppel this problem could have been foreseen, and "[t]he fact that the form was created without securing local law-enforcement agencies, full commitment created some doubt about their ultimate participation."[198] Local police cooperation was vital to the success of VICAP; without their submissions on unsolved cases there would be no database. By the end of 1989 the VICAP database contained information on 3,700 cases,[199] the vast majority of which had been recorded on the shorter VICAP form.

Interagency cooperation and the information which it would supply would enable the FBI to cross-reference and match cases. The VICAP investigators were not looking for an exact match in *modus operandi* between crime reports, as detectives had done in the past. This was because the killer would learn from previous experience and develop his method of operation to make his actions comfortable and convenient for him. Instead the investigators would look for the 'signature' of the crime. The signature, "consists of acts performed that reach beyond what is necessary to commit the murder." They must be acted out each time in the same manner. In keeping with the New Right who asserted that criminals were motivated by personal 'evil,' the acts were compelled by something "deep within the criminal's mind and psyche," they contained a set of elements that represented what the killer was.[200] Even the signature could evolve over time. For example, "in cases where a sexually sadistic killer performs more post mortem mutilation from one murder to the next. The FBI's behavioral scientists have said that the elements of the original have become more fully developed."[201]

Information submitted to VICAP was confidential with the NCAVC acting as an intermediary who contacted a submitting law enforcement agency if a similar crime was identified. Upon receiving approval VICAP would put the relevant local law enforcement agencies in touch with each other. Initially the forms were in short supply, and this meant that they were to be limited to jurisdictions with populations greater than 50,000,[202] focusing the serial sex murder panic on the anonymity of large city populations. Everyone became a potential serial killer to the increasingly insecure suburban middle class across America. With the forms distributed to city police departments, it is not surprising that the killers were being found there.

Funds had been allocated to several different areas of VICAP to allow the system to operate effectively, but Robert Ressler's superiors channeled money which had been earmarked for junior analysts and data enterers into purchasing computer equipment, high level managers and senior crime analysts. There was little data entered into the system, which left the senior staff with little to manage or analyze, giving the appearance that the program was not living up to its potential.[203] Despite publicizing information on the

Founding the Behavioral Sciences Unit

development and structure of the VICAP system the FBI provided no statistical analysis of their success rate in identifying patterns of crime. There is no mention of clearance rates, and no evidence of cases where the VICAP system has proved to be of use, apart from inadequate anecdotal accounts. According to Arthur Meister VICAP's goal is simply to "match cases," sending out about seventy leads each month to local and state police agencies.[204] It would seem that the system operates solely to ensure increased financing for the FBI and to enhance its role in state crime.

It is common in the United States to have a certain amount of animosity between local and federal investigative agencies. Local agencies object to the FBI appropriating locally-solved cases to boost their own clearance rates, and taking control of investigations when it suits them. This is an important factor in promoting a 'my case' mentality towards crime investigation and in previous years had undoubtedly hindered many investigations. According to Egger the development of the database would develop the ability of agencies to identify crime and "stimulate the necessary interagency communication and sharing of information which is currently almost nonexistent."[205] This appears to be a Catch 22 situation, with the need for interagency cooperation to facilitate interagency cooperation. There are still some cities and states which will not fully participate in VICAP.[206]

Other regional tracking programs were set up but could not submit information to the VICAP databases because their information was gathered and stored differently. The difference between systems is wasteful, since the information being widely reported to one system could be put to good advantage in another, but the widely differing formats preclude the convenient transfer of data from one system to another.[207] This limits the ability of the NCAVC to claim that it is a national database: rather, it is a selective database, and the regional programs are tied rigidly to the boundaries that they set for themselves. Organizational limitations undermine the ability of VICAP to provide a comprehensive source of information for the profilers to use to detect 'patterns' of crime. Without a suitable supply of information, the effectiveness of the profiling system and any claims of scientific validity are let down by the structure of the NCAVC.

Of the multiplicity of definitions of serial murder, the FBI's was the most vague and simplistic, mainly for the benefit of their system. Exaggerating the existence of sex killers, the definition was tailored to focus on a relatively rare crime and exaggerate its occurrence out of proportion. Of the variety of tracking systems the NCAVC was the most ambitious and the least efficient in its execution, not living up to its claims as a national centre. The target of the predatory killers was obviously white, middle class, tax paying America, and the perceived existence of serial sex killers suited the political rhetoric of Ronald Reagan. Reagan's career had been composed of exploiting societal insecurities, even before he became a politician, and the serial killer panic presented itself as an opportunity for him to show his administration was defending America from domestic menaces as well as foreign ones. Once identified by the FBI the news media focused on the sensational stories of sex and violence.

All The News That's Fit To Print
Sensational Sex Crimes and Serial Killers in the News

REPORTING OF VIOLENT SEX CRIME IS A LONG ESTABLISHED staple of news reporting, and newspapers were not slow to recognize the public's interest in eagerly seeking out stories to satisfy this demand, and thereby increase the circulation of their papers. Huge amounts of media attention were directed at serial sex killers, exploiting the most sensational aspects of any case. Privileged in popular culture "[t]hey are the subject of articles and books, radio and television shows—for the remainder of their lives—and they thus attain immortality denied the unenterprizing common man."[1] In this way serial killers are mass culture products, produced by a 'culture industry' and supported by economic and political powers. The culture industry functions to legitimize and perpetuate the existing social order and to persuade individuals passively to accept the values of society.[2] In his influential "Crime Waves as Ideology" essay, Mark Fishman argues that "news plays a crucial role in formulating public issues and events, and in directing their subsequent course."[3]

Sensational Sex Crimes and Serial Killers in the News

Fishman adds that interplay between national elites and media organizations could have been responsible for certain social issues becoming widely accepted as serious problems.[4] Fishman's thesis can be applied to the New Right and FBI promotion of random, motiveless sex crimes as a threat to the security of American society. Ironically, the creation of 'crime waves' or 'moral panics' by the media was exactly what the FBI Crime Index promised to reduce by compiling authoritative statistics. However, exaggerated reporting by both the FBI and the crime press continued.[5] In the process, the rest of the population is a spectator.

Conventional news reporting individualizes crime and removes it from its social context; thus it not only fails to address the wider issues but also only offers a limited range of responses to crime and ignores structural problems in society.[6] Exposed to distorted crime reporting, the public forms "inaccurate estimates to the relative distribution of crimes, overestimating of the likelihood of becoming a victim of violent crime, and perceives that the sentencing of criminals is too lenient."[7] Misinformed, the public misunderstands the crime problem and therefore cannot make reasoned judgments on how to address it. Coverage of sensational and violent crime is easily understood in a competitive commercial environment and reporters' judgments of a story's newsworthiness is based on its ability to attract readers.[8] News reporting's main contribution to 'ideologies' of crime is primarily in establishing what is *unusual* and therefore newsworthy.[9]

Murder has always ranked as one of the most important crimes in the criminal justice system in terms of severity of punishment, but it is also a crime which arouses great public interest and, "[i]f this is true for individual crimes of murder it is even more so for cases of multiple murder,"[10] especially those with a sexual aspect which are committed over an extended period of time. In choosing what, and how, crime is reported, the media helps to construct the social reality of crime; "in amplifying some voices and muting others, in distorting some messages and letting others come through loud and clear, [the press] affects the nature of opposition and hence governance."[11]

At the end of their study Barlow *et al* conclude that criminal justice policy in the US and the media response to it has "a lot to do with creating a stable political economy and little to do with solving the problem of crime,"[12] and it was the former that was a major concern for Reagan's New Right in the 1980s. Numerous studies found that the media misrepresents the true volume of crime, probably due to reliance on police and other official sources for information, sources which seek to reinforce official definitions and political agendas.[13] Mark Fishman observes that the media can create enormous public concern out of "matters unworthy of such elevated attention,"[14] and the effect of heightening public concern increases the readers' fear that they are vulnerable to violent crime. Consequently the media and politicians overemphasize violent offences and ignore white-collar crime.

Serial murder, as defined by the FBI, with its gruesome details of sexual torture and mutilation, satisfied the public appetite. The mix of sex and violence was a familiar one, dating back over a hundred years to the news story which created the stereotype exploited by the FBI, the case of Jack the Ripper. The details of murder cases, especially sex murder cases, lend themselves to sensational news reporting. When the murders are extended into a series the effect is magnified. When a serial sex killer is claimed to be operating, and bodies are being found, police reports provide the main source of information for all forms of media. Eye-catching headlines are crucial to a newspaper to attract its readership and sensational stories about sex scandals and murder are always a popular choice. The FBI's regular reference to the notorious Jack the Ripper murders associated serial killers with a familiar, if mythical, crime mystery. The press identified the famous Ripper murders in London in 1888 and the associated myth established as a panic. The story was reported worldwide, but had a special resonance in America.

Sensational news reporting was a long-established feature of American journalism, but as technology developed so did the style of news reporting. Some of the factors that appealed to the public's tastes were quickly identified and exploited by nineteenth century journals, such as the *National Police Gazette*, which was established in 1845 as a chronicle of crime. Noted for its graphic illustrations of sex and violence which "far outstripped any other publication," the paper's entire reason for existence was to "display spectacles, to appeal to individuals' lusts, fears, hatreds, fantasies and desires with visceral moving images that transformed the world's utter incomprehensibility into readily consumable visual information." Illegal bloodsports such as boxing and cockfighting were regular features along with vaudeville gossip and sex scandals, especially if prominent members of society were involved.[15] The glorious age of enterprise, with the moralistic supremacy of the Horatio Alger ideal, later promoted so vigorously by Reagan and other nostalgic conservatives, was little more than "posturing, role-playing, and false appearances."[27]

At the same time as Anthony Comstock's crusade against vice in America, on the other side of the Atlantic the infamous Jack the Ripper murders, which provided the FBI with a serial sex killer archetype, took place in the Whitechapel district of London's East End. However, at the time the murders were originally viewed as unrelated prostitute killings. Once connected by the news media, the murders transcended fact to become "a mythic representation of the darkest and most bestial aspect of the human condition."[17] The Ripper murders occurred during a period of social conflict, both between the middle and working classes, and between women's rights advocates asserting themselves and conservatives resisting any change in their social position. Sex scandals regularly shocked London society in the 1870s and 1880s, with feminists mobilizing against state regulation of prostitution, and again in 1885 to oppose white slavery and child prostitution. The sex scandals that were revealed by feminist agitation linked the rich and the poor of London.

Symbolizing social unrest and urban degeneracy, Whitechapel became familiar to the middle classes who were obsessed with class conflict and social disintegration, and philanthropic organizations were formed to quell their guilty consciences. The guilt was replaced by fear with riots and looting in the West End of London in 1886 and "Bloody Sunday" in 1887. Following shortly

Sensational Sex Crimes and Serial Killers in the News

after, the Ripper murders fueled the fires of class hatred for both the rich and the poor.[18] It was out of these tensions, along with existing ethnic tensions, that the Ripper myth was constructed, making him "the first major figure to offer himself to, and become, a creation of journalism."[19] Publications such as W T Stead's *Pall Mall Gazette* had previously used sex scandals to sell newspapers to a wide audience, establishing "cross-class prurience."[20] Coverage of the Ripper murders amplified public fear of the unknown killer, and journalists employed sensational melodrama, elaborating on details and adding their own interpretation of events when conveying the story to their readers.

The "Jack" murders were not the only killings in Whitechapel at the time. Eight occurred in twelve months, but what distinguished the perceived series of Ripper murders was the progressive mutilation of successive corpses.[21] The reporting of 'grisly details,' even citing coroner's reports, escalated as the crimes progressed, and for the final murder attributed to "Jack" (that of Mary Jane Kelly), the *Pall Mall Gazette*, unable to suitably depict the mutilations described the victim as "hacked to pieces." In the aftermath of the murder, one journalist observed that "Short of absolutely skinning the next victim from head to heel, it is difficult to see what fresh horror is left to him to commit."[22] Any advance beyond the graphic depictions and excited text seemed incomprehensible.

Commentators were unable to find historical precedent for the Ripper crimes; instead, their theories resembled the literature of the fantastic, and narrative themes and motifs of contemporary literature were incorporated. The sadistic mutilations of the victims brought to mind the writings of Edgar Allen Poe and Robert Louis Stevenson.[23] At the time of the Ripper crimes, Richard Mansfield's dramatization of *The Strange Case of Dr Jekyll and Mr. Hyde* was, ironically, running in the West End Lyceum theatre. A contemporary theory speculated that the real murders reflected the fictional events in Mansfield's play, giving rise to the Ripper myth that "Jack" was a reputable doctor who became a prostitute killer by night.[24] Despite the parallels in fiction "Jack" was seen as a product of the real world, not a literary imagination, and the fictional villains paled in comparison.[25] As a result of the confusion between the real and fictional characteristics of the killer the search for "Jack" was focused on finding an "appropriate" killer who could represent the image of a "distorted and frightening" sexuality, far removed from conventional morality.[26] "Jack" was described by the *Star*, a radical evening newspaper, as "Some nameless reprobate, half-beast, half-man," at large in the East End, "daily gratifying his murderous instincts on the most miserable and defenseless class of the community."[27] Seizing on public interest, newspapers had a considerable stake in perpetuating the story, and published "ghastly details" and outlandish theories to explain the crimes.[28]

Fanning the flames of public insecurity and controversy newspapers did all they could to keep public interest alive, to the extent that they may have gone beyond reporting the news and begun to manufacture it.[29] After reporting the crimes journalists often give nicknames to the unknown perpetrators making them easier for the public to recognize, especially for the duration of a series of crimes. The identity of the mysterious killer was made even more compelling when a note was sent to the police, the author of which identified himself as Jack The Ripper, claimed responsibility for the murders and warned that there were more to come. The note created a persona for the unknown killer, one that was never compromised by the identification and capture of a perpetrator. In a very real sense, the letters became more important than the crimes in explaining the killer's motivation, and set an example that later killers would emulate. While police authorities considered the two communications from "Jack" to be the work of an enterprising journalist, they did help to establish the murders as a media event by "focusing social anxieties and fantasies on a single, elusive, alienated figure who communicated to a 'mass' public through the newspapers."[30] Newspapers published the note and a later postcard, adding to the case's notoriety.

"Jack's" allegation in one of his letters that he was "down on whores" reflected conservative middle-class morality which perceived prostitutes as disease carriers.[31] It was a morality that would continue to be found in many serial killers around the world in the twentieth century, who believed that by murdering prostitutes or 'promiscuous' women they were protecting the social values of society. Richard von Krafft-Ebing's *Psychopathia Sexualis* (1904) had not been published in English at the time of the Ripper murders, nor had Sigmund Freud's theories on sex been published or popularized. Although it was only in retrospect that the mutilations were perceived as sexual, contemporary commentators and the public were fascinated by the removal of the victims' organs, and these reports gave later authors a graphic example of the association of sex and violence influencing the interpretation of the crimes. The association of sex and violence provided the basic elements for a sexual script, which the FBI later picked up on, exemplifying a fantasy of a dominant male figure crossing class boundaries to find the object of his desire, a passive female.[32]

While the identity of the killer was unknown, the social history of the five victims was unpleasantly similar in all cases. They were all middle-aged women who were married but lived separate from their spouses, and economic need forced them into prostitution. Similarly, many of the victims of serial sex killers in the 1970s and eighties, if not the majority, were prostitutes or those living close to the poverty line and forced into transient lifestyles by persistent economic conditions. Diverse interest groups took the victim's characteristics and shaped the Ripper murders to suit their own ideological agenda. To more conservative readers of papers such as *The Times* or *Morning Post* in 1888, just as with the serial sex killer reports in the *New York Times* in the 1980s, the "Jack" case was a morality tale where the wages of sin were death. Suspects in the cases represented the prejudices of police and local residents as well as the local economy of the East End.[33] George Bernard Shaw mocked the Ripper theories of his contemporaries; instead he speculated, with a wry sense of humor, that the killer may be a reformer intent on drawing attention to the squalor of London's East End, saying that "whilst we conventional Social Democrats were wasting our time on education, agitation, and organization, some independent genius has taken the matter in hand."[34]

Official responses to the Ripper murders revealed significant class divisions and sexual antagonisms, and the *Star* asserted that the murders were a class issue. Newspaper coverage intensified the terror felt by women as a result of the sensational stories and the *Police Illustrated News* proposed that the Ripper might move to more respectable areas of London if Whitechapel became too dangerous. Widespread hysteria among women surprised the police as it was only prostitutes who had been victims,[35] but in wider society the Ripper murders,

> Covertly sanctioned male antagonism towards women and buttressed male authority over them. It established a common vocabulary and iconography of male violence that permeated the whole society, papering over class differences and obscuring the different material conditions that provoked sexual antagonism in different classes.[36]

When discussing the murders male professional experts were in a position to shape and dominate the media reports, but when a similar murder occurred in July 1889, the media coverage was not so hysterical. Judith Walkowitz attributes the relaxation of reporting to an orderly dock strike in the East End, which had reassured the middle class and eased class antagonism.[37]

In America, *The National Police Gazette* reported each of the "Jack" murders with "perverse enthusiasm" and the name "Jack" was ascribed to other killers of the time. To maintain public interest Fox published a pamphlet "The History of the Whitechapel Murders" (1889) accusing Scotland Yard of incompetence, but after a few years interest in the "Jack" story began to decline, being replaced by the Lizzie Borden murder case. However, at the end of 1888, the *Pall Mall Gazette* reported that Inspector Andrews from Scotland Yard traveled to New York pursuing a man who was suspected of knowing about the Ripper murders, effectively shifting the geographical focus of "Jack's" future crimes to America. A series of murders in New York in 1895 renewed interest in the Ripper and prompted the *National Police Gazette* to ask "Is Jack The Ripper In New York?"[38]

After the notorious crimes in Whitechapel and the perpetrator's alleged emigration to America, news stories regularly referred to Jack The Ripper crimes when dealing with cases of a specific type of murder. By 1903 the "Jack" crimes were synonymous in popular language with mutilation murders and the term was applied liberally adding to the myth of the "Ripper."[39] In the following years an Atlanta Ripper was believed to be killing black women in the city on a weekly basis during 1911—12, claiming more than twenty victims.[40] Cincinnati's series of five murders in 1913 were also attributed to their own Ripper whom the Burns agency detectives believed they identified as a former car conductor who was committed to a sanitarium.[41]

The public awareness of sensational crimes coincided with other developments in journalism and politics that further shaped the content of news reporting. In mainstream news reporting Michael Schudson finds journalists in the early twentieth century resented the new public relations industry because "news appeared to become less the reporting of events in the world than the *reprinting* of those facts which appealed to special interests who could afford to hire public relations counsel."[42] As early as 1930 it was estimated that fifty per cent of news originated in press releases. After the enormous growth in government bureaucracy during the New Deal and after several wars, there was increasingly pervasive public relations involvement in virtually all public spheres and there is little doubt that the amount of information from press releases being reported as news has increased considerably since then.[43]

Public relations information, however, is not sensational or attention grabbing, and newspapers need stories dealing with elements of life and death, which are essential in attracting the public's attention to a story. Sensational violent crime attracts readers, especially when sexual motives are present and suspense builds in serial crimes as the offender's body count increases. Once a suspect is identified, tried, and found guilty, "if conviction carries with it a term of imprisonment rather than the death penalty, he fizzles out as a monster after a few days or weeks." Caryl Chessman, who was executed in California after more than a decade on death row, referred to reporters who created 'monsters' as "journalistic mythologists" always looking for new inspiration. He observed that, "Whenever the current crop runs low, or the public tires of being horrified and outraged by the monsters currently on display, the monster-makers invariably can be depended upon to bring forth a new one." Exploiting any obvious physical differences, or inventing them, the journalists manipulate superstitious minds to create a cultural product that "would make Hell blush with shame." When newspapers report on crimes they chillingly reconstruct events stressing the inhumanity of the perpetrator. Readers are drawn into an "emotional vortex,"[44] especially when confronted with sex crimes beyond their comprehension and which inflame moral outrage.

Tabloid newspaper reports of Grace Budd's abduction and murder in 1928, by Albert Fish, were the epitome of "cheap melodrama." According to Harold Schechter, the family's tragedy was "a tabloid editor's dream, since few things sold more than the heart-rending spectacle of a sorrowing mother praying for the safe return of her kidnapped daughter." The abduction of Grace Budd was notably different from the other kidnaps reported by the press: no ransom money was ever asked for. The Budd kidnapping escalated parental concern for the safety of their children, and "Of all the evils that plagued the modern world, none is more nightmarish from a parent's point of view than the crime we now call 'stranger abduction.'"[45]

The kidnapping of the Lindbergh baby in March 1932 captured public attention and relegated all other stories to the background. On one day the *New York Times* (March 6, 1932) devoted half of the front page and two further interior pages to coverage of the investigation. Radio networks also kept their "anxious" listeners updated with twenty-four hour bulletins. The Lindbergh kidnapping investigation involved numerous police departments nationwide as well as the Treasury Department and FBI, even though the FBI had no jurisdiction in the case, because there was no evidence that the baby had been transported across state lines. They were attracted by the publicity.

From its inception the FBI made use of the media, and their operations "evolved into an ongoing and highly orchestrated campaign that went into high gear whenever developments threatened to undermine public support or, by raising questions about FBI operations, to precipitate an inquiry into Hoover's leadership of the Bureau."[46] In the wake of the Kansas City massacre (1933), it is alleged that Hoover decided someone had to become a symbol in the war against crime, and it was up to him to lead the crusade.

During the Lindbergh investigation, local police warned local newspapers not to publish any confidential information that had been given to them concerning the appearance of the gold bank note, as such information might alert the kidnappers. Journalist Walter Winchell received information about the bank note a few days after the local press, possibly from Hoover, and did not feel that the police warning applied to him, so he broadcast the information on his radio show. Many police officials, newspaper editors and federal agents were angry, feeling that Winchell could have jeopardized the entire case. The only law enforcement official who did not criticize him was Hoover. Fortunately for the investigators the criminals did not hear the radio show, and when Bruno Hauptmann was arrested two days later Winchell claimed credit for the capture. John Crosby, one of Winchell's critics, described him as a "14-carat sonofabitch," and a devoted right-wing extremist who was dedicated in his loyalty to the bigots among his circle of friends. However his influence on American popular culture should not be underestimated and, in Crosby's opinion, Winchell invented "keyhole journalism" and made use of all the unsavory power that came with it. A single mention in Winchell's column could sell 40,000 copies of "some awful book," and an actor's career could be ruined by an accusation of communist sympathies. In Winchell's moralistic reporting of American degeneracy, Hoover always stood above everyone as a noble and heroic patriot, protecting traditional values.

Winchell, a close friend of J Edgar Hoover and with close connections to organized crime figures in New York, was unquestionably the most influential newspaperman of his time with his widely read syndicated column of society gossip. In the mid-30s his columns were printed in more than 450 newspapers, and in addition he had one of the largest audiences in radio history. Franklin Roosevelt planted ideas in Winchell's columns to test public response to potential policies, and it was customary for him to remain behind after White House press conferences where he was given additional information, further enhancing his journalistic reputation. With praise from Broadway columnists such as Winchell, Ed Sullivan and Louis Sobol, Hoover "cornered the crime-fighting market." The gossip that Hoover picked up through his friendship with the columnists proved useful to him in Washington, where he could use the more damaging information to influence members of Congress.[47]

While Hoover was eagerly chasing publicity and gossip to advance his bureaucratic reputation, other police departments investigated contemporary sex killers. Detective William King, who had doggedly pursued the Budd kidnapping case, approached Winchell to ask him to plant stories in his *New York Daily Mirror* tabloid column, and one such story provoked Albert Fish to write to the Budd family confessing his crime.[48] When caught in December 1934, Fish's arrest made front-page news. The *New York Times* even published Fish's confession that a "lust for blood" had made him murder the girl, the seven previous arrests on his police record, and a detailed explanation of how he had been identified by the police.[49] In the weeks that followed the New York daily papers covered the unfolding story in lavish detail. The *Daily Mirror* and *Daily News* provided a "nonstop feast of juicy revelations, seasoned with the tabloid's own special blend of prurience and moral indignation." The stories were accompanied by graphic speculative illustrations, and often facts were spiced up with colorful names being created for Fish. The *Daily Mirror* tried to take credit for the capture because of Winchell's column as well as making up stories about Fish's life and exaggerating his crimes to suggest he was an unprecedented killer, thus fuelling the paper's own reputation at the same time. Speculations ran wild as to the extent of the crimes and reporters were rarely hindered by facts or official statements. Numerous other murders were attributed to Fish without any real evidence. The *Daily News* also printed stories comparing Fish to Bluebeard and Jack The Ripper. Jack Alexander of the *Daily News* compared Fish to Fritz Haarman, a much more contemporary killer from Weimar Germany.[50] The Fish trial, and that of Bruno Hauptmann, ran concurrently, again relegating the Budd murder to the shadows in favor of the celebrity story. For the first time, still and moving picture cameras were present at a trial, and Walter Winchell's reporting of Hauptmann's proceedings proved to be a high point in establishing his credentials as a serious journalist.[51]

Lessons were learned by the Bureau from the news media response to Lindbergh as well as the shooting of John Dillinger. They came to understand that the press will make a hero out of whoever they see as being in charge of a case, so Hoover saw to it that he was seen publicly as being in charge of every important case. It was also noted that reporters would base their stories on the statement given by the first high-ranking official to comment to the press. After every major arrest a press release was supplied to Hoover for immediate dissemination to the waiting journalists. He particularly favored papers whose editorial policy he admired: his favorites were the *Chicago Tribune*, *New York Daily News*, and the *Washington Star*. Raids were even timed to meet the deadlines of the *Chicago Tribune*. Most newspapers were friendly to the FBI, but the *Washington Post*, *New York Post*, *Denver Post*, and the *St Louis Post Dispatch* were seen as enemies and the *New York Times* was considered the most anti-Bureau paper in the country.[52]

Winchell's influence permeated into American culture, and persisted even when his own career was in decline. 1950s America is generally thought of as a conservative era, mainly remembered with nostalgic fondness as a moral and peaceful time. Suburbs began to be developed and images of the all-American nuclear family permeated the television screen in sit-coms such as *Leave it to Beaver*. There was, however, another side to the idealized notion of middle

Sensational Sex Crimes and Serial Killers in the News

class America, an "unseen America"[53] of sex, drugs, crime, and gossip that conservatives of the 1980s chose to ignore.

The appearance, in quantity, of exploitation magazines was due to several factors. When publishers sensed that soldiers who had gone to the war as boys were returning as men they realized that there was a new market for magazines. Women and blacks who had moved to urban centers to work in the war effort had developed a sense of independence and financial strength, and they too provided a commercial market for publishers. The opening of such markets coincided with a flood of cheap newsprint which became available after 1950 when paper rationing was ended. Alongside these changes, Alan Betrock believes, it was perhaps the rise of television which was the major catalyst in the growth of the exploitation magazine business.[54]

Magazines and cinema were the major leisure pursuits for Americans, but the meteoric rise of television put both on the defensive. In retaliation, magazine publishers fought back against the threat posed by television by incorporating sex, violence, and scandal into their stories, creating the most "sensationalistic" period in American journalism. Styles and conventions used in exploitation magazines were effective and "they paved the way for the use of innuendo, doctored photographs, and journalistic styles that are used today in the modern tabloids."[55]

Numerous magazines during the 1950s and 1960s had promised their readers true crime stories, and with around 100 titles being published, each competed for the honor of being the most "sensationalistic, gruesome and violent," and their titles left little to the imagination. Some, like *Official Police Cases*, carried a sense of authenticity in their titles, an impression which was more obvious in *The FBI: A Pictorial Report* (1957). This was an illustrated one-shot covering thirty Bureau investigations with such traditional criminals as spies, gangsters, bank robbers, kidnappers, saboteurs and the Ku Klux Klan. *The FBI: A Pictorial Report* strongly supported the Bureau, and other true crime magazines generally applauded law enforcement officers. Others, such as *True Crime Expose, Wanted!* (a photo-magazine) and *Women in Crime*, relied on graphic pictures to announce themselves. They covered a variety of approaches but all relied on sensational headlines to attract potential readers. The tone of such magazines was conservative and moralizing, and special one-shot magazines were devoted to pertinent threats said to be facing American society—for example, *USA Inside Report: Menace of the Sex Deviate* (1961), which alleged that 'sexual deviants' were a danger to American society because they were liable to become communist spies, and presumably because communists were also condemned by J Edgar Hoover as 'sexual deviants.' A few years later *Uncensored* (December 1964) reported hundreds of sex killers were at large in several major US cities and in a number of other countries around the world. Described as the "most horrible of all crimes" the offenders randomly prey on "defenseless" women and "normal police procedures are virtually useless in trying to stop them."[56] Sex exposes and drug scandals were both prominent, and the exploitation magazines kept the public informed of the latest subcultural fads. While generally considered 'lowbrow' the magazines had a wide circulation and many famous authors started their careers writing for them. Similarly, it was common for fledgling actors and actresses to pay their bills posing as cover models while waiting for their 'big break' in film.[57]

The ethics of tabloid magazines influenced mainstream reporting, especially in unusual murders and sex crime cases. In the late 1950s, the discovery of Ed Gein's crimes received intense media coverage. Gein lived in the small farming community of Plainfield, Wisconsin and quickly became the prime suspect in the murder of a local woman. When police searched his farm they found the missing woman's body along with parts of numerous other bodies which Gein had stolen from local graveyards. The bodies were cut up and parts used to make home furnishings such as skin lampshades, and skull bowls. The local community in Plainfield was wracked by fear and suspicion, and Gein was mythologized as a bogeyman used to frighten naughty children. 'Big city' newspapers did not hesitate to print exaggerated reports to make the story *more* sensational, often based on erroneous information. A wide circle of people claiming to be long-time close personal friends of Gein's appeared and enthusiastically shared their knowledge. A few people who did know Gein were also interviewed but their stories were often exaggerated or misrepresented, further distorting Gein's popular persona. News media coverage turned Gein into a celebrity, and *Life* magazine (December 2, 1957) led with the Gein case, giving it national prominence. In the same week, *Time* magazine also covered the case, describing Gein as a middle-aged "momma's boy" and an extreme case of "arrested development."[58]

Gein's mother was a zealous Lutheran and a "domestic tyrant" who regarded most of contemporary society as a latter day Sodom, and read to her children biblical passages from Proverbs or the Book of Revelation. Ed Gein, like his mother, had a rigid and self-righteous attitude and saw other women as tainted and fallen creatures. Gein blamed his crimes on the wickedness of women, who he believed were all 'evil' and should be shunned, and he admitted that he shot one of his victims because she was "a rather poor representative of womankind." Both of the women he killed were, in his eyes, the antithesis of his mother, whom he regarded as saintly. Gein claimed to be averse to bloodshed but his favorite topic of conversation, to anyone who would listen, was violence, especially lust murder stories which he read about in true crime magazines like *Startling Detective* or *Inside Crime*, which typically featured half-naked girls on their lurid covers.[59]

Press accounts oversimplified their explanations of Gein's mental condition, and their reporting fuelled the same popular misconceptions of mental illness which were the basis of Robert Bloch's novel *Psycho* (1959). Bloch was intrigued by Gein's case and the idea "that a ghoulish killer with perverted appetites could flourish almost openly in a small rural community where everybody prides himself on knowing everybody's business."[60] At a hearing in 1958, the prosecution argued that Gein was medically insane but legally sane, highlighting the confusion and complexity of the insanity defense. After spending ten years in a hospital for the criminally insane, Gein was finally sent for trial in 1968 (almost a decade after Robert Bloch and Alfred Hitchcock had immortalized him in book and film), only to be found not guilty by reason of insanity.[61]

Lois Higgins, president of the International Association of Police Women, warned that highly publicized killings are likely to set off a cycle of 'copycat' crimes, and she further predicted that Gein's example would lead to "a rampage of bizarre crimes" across the nation.[62] In later years, as news reporting became more international, theoretically the influence of a series of crimes would

potentially become international. Prominent reporting of a crime may serve as inspiration for suitably predisposed individuals. According to William Turner, after the FBI assumed the investigation of Jack Gilbert Graham's bombing of a plane in the 1950s the case was given considerable publicity in various articles and Don Whitehead's book *The FBI Story*. Subsequently a chain of bombings on planes ensued, as well as more than 2,000 false reports of bombs being planted on planes.[63] James Brussel noted a similar flood of copycat crimes after his profile of the "Mad Bomber" was publicized in late December 1956. Due to the media coverage the police received innumerable hoax phone calls and for the next month more than fifty bomb reports each day, sometimes as many as 100.[64]

Between 1962 and 1964 what was claimed to be a series of murders terrified the population of Boston. Young and old women, especially those living alone, were terrified by the Strangler killings, and insecurity increased when it became obvious that the victims, according to the media, did not fall into any particular age group. Repeated warnings were issued by officials and the media adding to public fear, and in response sales of dogs, guns and household locks skyrocketed. Public suspicion and distrust also grew, creating a climate of paranoia.[65] Joseph Fisher believes that no murder investigation, before or after, took on the size and scope of the "Boston Strangler" task force. During the hunt for the killer, the FBI gave a special seminar to local police on fifty varieties of sexual perversion and the personality of sex offenders,[66] reflecting the Bureau's interest in sexual deviance more than a decade before the 'new' post-Hoover FBI publicly began studying sex criminals.

Massachusetts attorney general Edward Brooke issued a report on August 18, 1964, which stated that the murders of older women were "dissimilar in important respects" to those of the younger women, nor where they considered to have been committed by one person.[67] In at least one case an individual identified as a Strangler victim was stabbed to death and a ligature added afterwards to mimic reports in the press of the Boston Strangler's *modus operandi*.[68] Other crimes were thought to have been committed by 'copycats' intentionally imitating the news coverage.[69] Of the panel of legal and medical experts convened to find a pattern in the slayings, only Dr James Brussel maintained that a single killer was responsible for all the murders.[70]

One survivor of a Strangler attack and another potential witness were taken to Bridgewater after DeSalvo began to confess, and while they claimed they had never seen DeSalvo before they did notice that George Nassar, another inmate who exerted considerable influence over DeSalvo, looked familiar.[71] The press reporting of the case was phenomenal and as a precaution DeSalvo was placed under heavy guard in case of attempts to escape or to assassinate him.[72] After researching the case with members of the Boston police forces, Susan Kelly concluded that the Boston Stranglings "were not eleven serial killings—at least six of them were one-on-one murders committed for motives as individual as were the killers."[73]

In June 1966 Albert DeSalvo signed a release granting Gerold Frank "in perpetuity, throughout the world in all languages, the exclusive rights to publish, sell, distribute, perform, or otherwise disseminate all my literary properties and rights to biographical material concerning me." In return, DeSalvo was to receive a percentage of the royalties earned by Frank's book *The Boston Strangler*. Frank denies any such release was ever signed, but Susan Kelly found a copy on file at the US District Court in Boston witnessed by DeSalvo's attorney F Lee Bailey and former guardian Charles McGrath. Frank did believe that DeSalvo was supposed to get some of the release money for the rights, but DeSalvo never received it, although a check for $15,000 was sent by the William Morris Agency in August 1966 and cashed by Bailey.[74] Authorized or not, Frank's book shocked and angered DeSalvo because it reproduced intimate family correspondence.[75]

The *Ladies Home Journal* ran excerpts from Frank's book before it was

Sensational Sex Crimes and Serial Killers in the News

published in November 1966, becoming an immediate bestseller. A few months before DeSalvo's trial for the Green Man sex attacks, Frank's book identified DeSalvo as the Boston Strangler and as a rapist who had attacked over 2,000 women and sexually assaulted them. By the time his case came to trial the months of sensational news reporting convicted DeSalvo in worldwide public opinion, the "most high and merciless of all courts." The *Record-American* also published extracts of the book in January 1967, along with a series of articles on F Lee Bailey and his wife.[76] Accounts of the Strangler murders in newspapers and magazines were "extraordinarily detailed," especially in the *Traveler*, *Globe*, *Herald*, *Record-American* and *Sunday Advertiser*, all printing information related to the condition in which the bodies were found and what had been done to them. Descriptions of the victims' homes were common and one report published a step-by-step account of how the killer had rummaged through their apartments. The influence of the detailed reporting, especially the publication of victims' photographs and comparisons between cases, was evident in DeSalvo's confessions as he regurgitated some pieces of misinformation, as well as true facts, that were identified as having been printed in the *Record-American*.[77]

In the Green Man trial Dr James Brussell, who later assisted the FBI in the profiling research, testified for the defense but did not conduct any physical or neurological tests or interview any of the Bridgewater guards as to whether DeSalvo showed any signs of violent behavior.[78] In his testimony Brussel stated that DeSalvo had not mentioned any desire to profit from confessing to the stranglings, and he did not consider him a compulsive confessor, a highly unusual statement to make since DeSalvo had stated his intention to anyone within earshot to profit from his confessions.[79] After less than four hours of deliberation in the trial for the Green Man sexual assaults, the jury returned a verdict of guilty on all counts and a life sentence was passed by the judge who felt it was clear that DeSalvo was also the Boston Strangler.[80]

The public's understanding of the Boston Strangler case is heavily influenced by Frank's book and the subsequent, and even more distorted, film. After reviewing DeSalvo's full confession—only abbreviated versions were ever publicly released—Susan Kelly said that the transcript "virtually exonerates" DeSalvo.[81] Many details were "wildly inaccurate" and DeSalvo was ignorant of many details that the actual killer would have known. She contends that the police official taking his confession, John Bottomly, was well aware that DeSalvo's confessions were "phony," and that he later profited from the film rights for the story.[82]

Technological advances throughout the twentieth century broadened the definition of the media to include radio, television, newspapers, cinema, the internet and video, among others. Even within the individual media, advances such as computer technology have made for faster and more efficient productions and "[i]n modern, advanced, industrialized societies with strong popular cultures, the mass media have emerged as a main engine in the social construction of reality process."[83] With big corporations acquiring assets in television stations, newspapers, and radio, competitive diversity was lost only to be quickly replaced by a "suffocating tyranny of the middle, silencing disputation and dissent."[84] The social influence of the media is focused on their role of shaping their audience's perception of the surrounding world. Echoing George Orwell, Ron Powers writes, "the advent of vast technocratic political bureaucracies had resulted in a new use for language: an instrument for concealing or preventing thought."[85] This manipulation of language reached its logical apex in the New Right's 'politics of euphemism' to reshape public perceptions.[86] What the media reports and the way in which it is presented provides the information which the public uses to view the world. The use of euphemism and statistics in sound bites simplifies the public's understanding of political and social issues until the world the media conveys to the audience and they believe exists bears little relation to reality.

The media panic over serial sex killers began during the 1970s with high profile 'lurid' newspaper reports'[87] about 'multiple murderers' whose ghoulish activities shocked and alarmed the public. At the time of the reporting none, of the criminals were referred to as 'serial killers,' but in the middle of the next decade the term would be applied to them. Tabloid reporting had exerted a noticeable influence on mainstream journalism and since rape, torture, cannibalism and necrophilia disgusted and fascinated, such stories boosted newspaper circulations and television ratings in a culture looking for a new thrill. The killers were reported as human animals, 'predators,' for whom homicide was the *raison d'être*.[88] They were savage animals who hunted humans as their prey.

The .44 Caliber Murders in New York City (later known as the Son of Sam murders) were the subject of worldwide media attention. During the series of murders, the killer sent letters to Jimmy Breslin at the New York *Daily News* where they were sure to get published and, once received, the paper began "a masterfully conceived, coordinated campaign to wring every ounce of circulation out of the bequest."[89] Beginning on a Sunday (the week's most expensive edition) the paper stage-managed the release of information over a five-day period, building suspense. As the *New York Daily News* and *New York Post* competed for readers, they created public and official hysteria, ensuring that rational debate, and a fair trial for the killer, would be virtually impossible. An angry editorial in the *New Yorker* accused the news press of transforming the murders from a police operation into a political issue, forcing the Mayor and Police Commissioner to "reduce the day-to-day protection provided by police around the city, in order to concentrate on the search for the murderer—a search that, given the lack of clues, is unlikely to be aided by the assignment of more officers." The first Sunday edition of the *Daily News* sold out in one hour, selling over a million copies in total, a figure the paper's circulation only surpassed when David Berkowitz was arrested. The *New Yorker* continued to criticize the tabloid press for publishing more 'non-news' items in regard to the case than in any story since the Mad Bomber in 1957 and noted that, "The Son of Sam has killed six people and wounded seven, and he has sold a lot of newspapers." Jimmy Breslin's commemoration of the anniversary of the first murder was a blatant publicity stunt, and condemned as an example of "journalistic irresponsibility."[90] Two days after the anniversary, when the killer struck again, the *Post* and *Daily News* exploited the grief of the victim's families and recounted in graphic detail the injuries suffered. When Berkowitz was captured, news reports flashed around the world. "The media storm was inescapable. The public was buried under an avalanche of facts, the arrest, and the emerging details of the killer."[91] A letter to the *New York Times* commented that, "Promoters, publishers and authors of print and media, lawyers, businessmen of all kinds are sadly racing to scoop up their share."[92] Jimmy Breslin, Sam's media pen pal, was reported to have been paid an advance of over $150,000 to write a book on the case.[93]

In the wake of the Sam case, legislation was passed in New York State preventing criminals from profiting from their crimes, but ensuring that everyone else could. Although Berkowitz was not originally subject to the Son of Sam law, repeated attempts were eventually successful, and in September 1987 a judge ordered Berkowitz's conservator to pay $118,500 from book and film deals to the victims' families. The decision was hailed as "a major victory for victims" by the Crime Victims Compensation Board who had been trying since 1979 to get the money.[94]

The popular version of the 'Sam' crimes which identified a single killer as responsible for all the murders was convincingly discredited by Maury Terry in *The Ultimate Evil* (1987). Terry identified several men operating in a syndicate who were responsible for the Sam murders, undermining the safe stereotype of the dangerous individual who willingly flaunts society's values. The traditional investigative assumption of looking for a single killer was a major shortcoming of the Hillside Strangler murders in Los Angeles, which sought a single offender for a considerable period of the investigation before it was accepted that at least two killers were working in conjunction. LAPD chief Daryl Gates felt that intrusive media reporting hindered the Hillside Strangler investigation. Each time a body was found the police would routinely examine the location, but after they left reporters would swarm into the area talking to anyone available. The reporters' questions along with news coverage of the case meant that the police had "no way of knowing how much information was legitimate and how much had been distorted by the media."[95] Eventually Gates chose to give regular press conferences to update the media, but it amused him to turn up to the briefings with no information and then try to "give the media something they can write about without giving them anything at all."[96]

Pat Leeds, a "friendly reporter," became interested in the BSU's work after meeting Robert Ressler and wanted to visit Quantico to interview the profilers. The end product, an article in the *Chicago Tribune*, "They Study the Strangest Slayings" (February 15, 1980), met with Bureau approval. Ressler described the article as being as "accurate and flattering as anybody could have wished."[97] However, the Leeds article simply retold the FBI's distorted version of the Vampire Of Sacramento investigation, ignoring the role of local police and crediting the Bureau's profile for the arrest of Richard Chase. Leeds also emphasized the BSU agents' advanced training in behavioral and social sciences without pointing out that the agents, by their own admission, had no interest in why serial killers committed their crimes and that they intentionally simplified their descriptions of the killer's mental state for the benefit of the local police.

Wire services picked up the Leeds article, and the interest it generated led to numerous other articles in *Psychology Today*, *People* magazine and the *New York Times*. Subsequent invitations for Ressler to appear on television and radio programs reflected public interest and helped to promote the BSU as a unique innovation in law enforcement.[98] Later Ann Rule, a close associate of the FBI, wrote a guest editorial in *True Detective* (October 1982) referring to some of the serial killer cases, outlining the VICAP proposals, and calling for a response from the magazines readers.[99]

Able to claim considerable authority, because of their interviews with criminals in jail, it was not reported that the BSU agents had not actively investigated any of the crimes which they cited in their case studies. FBI estimates of the scale of the problem were widely publicized in newspaper accounts publicly defining the threat and, coming from an authoritative source, the statistics carried considerable weight. Without examination the statistics appeared plausible and were taken up by other groups who embellished them further to suit their own ends. Most publications uncritically reproduced the Bureau's theories, using the simplistic terminology developed by the BSU, and cited profilers' opinions as fact. Individuals associated with the FBI, such as Ann Rule, no matter how dubious their credentials, were also cited as 'experts.'[100]

Presenting themselves as authorities on serial murder, the BSU experts assisted a number of journalists and writers who, in the tradition established by Hoover, reciprocated with favorable depictions of the Bureau. More likely to consult with journalists or academics sympathetic to the Bureau, the FBI had considerable discretion over the access it could provide and anyone able to look at BSU materials would have newsworthy or publishable material. Robert Ressler noted the "feeding frenzy" in the media around the time of the formation of VICAP. "In the frenzy, we were using an old tactic in Washington, playing up the problem as a way of getting Congress and the higher-ups in the executive branch to pay attention to it."[101] Put simply, the FBI intentionally exaggerated the threat serial killers posed to society in order to advance their own bureaucratic interests.

A public relations exercise in October 1988 had the FBI profilers give their opinion on the identity of Jack The Ripper to celebrate the 100th anniversary of the Whitechapel murders. Both the original and the centenary of the Jack The Ripper murders were media events[102] and the FBI profilers only added to the superficial authority with which Jack was discussed, lending a legitimacy to the commercialism that exploited the event, as well as reassuring the public of the scientific validity of profiling. Referring to the FBI opinion in a supposedly investigative documentary helped to popularize their ideas and make terms such as 'psychological profiling' more widely known.

The role of the media in reporting serial crime stories raised questions about

Sensational Sex Crimes and Serial Killers in the News

journalistic ethics and practices. Fritz Lang explored the relationship between the news media and a sex killer at large in *While the City Sleeps* (1956), a film which concerned the news media's attempt to exploit the crimes of a sex killer. Notably, it was *not* popular with film critics.[103] After the murder of a young woman the killer writes the message "ask mother" on the wall in lipstick. On hearing the report, media magnate Amos Kyne wants every woman in America "scared silly" every time they put on lipstick. Hypocritically, he then begins eulogizing about the media's responsibility to inform the public of all the facts so they can make informed decisions, a performance which glosses over his obvious desire to exploit public fear of violent crime. The "Lipstick Killer" is a predecessor of what the FBI would later call a serial killer. The killer in Lang's film is connected to a string of unsolved burglaries where "women's things" are stolen, and it is obvious a Freudian sexual motive is being implied, similar to the FBI's Freudian interpretation of crimes. He randomly attacks young, white females, 'nice' girls with respectable jobs such as teachers and librarians. When Amos Kyne suddenly dies, his son Walter (Vincent Price) takes over the family business and escalates the situation by staging a competition to promote whichever of his respective managing editors unmasks the "Lipstick Killer." The result is an escalation in media reporting of the case, distorting its importance and misleading the public.

In the race for promotion, the lack of ethics among the executives becomes obvious as they all strive to advance their own interests before they consider the public interest. Coverage of the story incites public interest and raises the paper's circulation figures, but also puts pressure on the police to find a suspect quickly. Even if they know their suspect is not the killer, they have to be seen to be doing something. The protagonist, Edward Mobley (Dana Andrews), a Pulitzer Prize winning journalist, employs the traditional methods of a crime reporter cultivating contacts in police departments. Through his contacts Mobley receives privileged information, increasing his status as a journalist with exclusive scoops. In conjunction with the police he makes a TV broadcast taunting the Lipstick Killer with claims about how much the police know about him and insulting him to try to draw him out. Mobley, during the same broadcast, announces his own engagement, hoping that the killer will be angry enough to attack his fiancé Nancy (Sally Forrest), but he neglects to discuss it with her in advance.

The nondescript Robert Manners (John Drew Barrymore), the Lipstick Killer, lives with his mother, and in one scene he rants at her that the family he knows is not his real family, and that they wanted a girl instead. Apparently unsure about his personal and gender identity, Manners epitomizes the confusion later attributed by the New Right to the breakdown of traditional family values which was exacerbated by 1960s liberalism, giving rise to the serial killer. The Lipstick Killer bears a considerable resemblance to the real case of William Heirens, who also progressed from burglary to murder, stole women's undergarments and became famous for writing, "For God's sake, catch me before I kill more," on a bedroom wall after committing one of his murders.[104] At one point in the film, Mobley and his police contact even make a vague reference to the case. After a failed murder attempt and a dramatic chase, Manners is captured and confesses to four murders. For his part in the investigation, Mobley is repaid by the police with an exclusive copy of the full text of the killer's confession, and a promotion from his employer.

In the 1980s, the connection between the media and criminals was exploited to its fullest dramatic potential in *The Mean Season* (Phillip Borsos, 1985) with the objective of projecting a more sympathetic image of journalists. Reporter Malcolm Anderson (Kurt Russell) is a "gritty and ambitious" reporter for the *Miami Journal*, but he feels burnt out and is being urged by his girlfriend Christine (Mariel Hemmingway) to leave and go to work for a small weekly paper in Colorado. Anderson's life is suddenly changed when a killer wanting "recognition" contacts him, to use him as a conduit to the public. Cooperating with the police in return for access to exclusive information and functioning as a conduit for the "Numbers Killer," Anderson himself becomes the focus of other newspaper stories and his involvement risks his professional objectivity, safety, and his relationship with Christine. Unlike Mobley in *While the City Sleeps*, he has not yet won a Pulitzer Prize, but he is determined to, whatever the cost.

Almost from the film's outset it is made clear to the audience that newspapers have limited responsibility when Anderson's editor says, "[r]eporters report... we're not the manufacturer [of news], we retail. News gets made somewhere else, we just sell it." He seeks to deny any complicity the media may have in public agenda setting. After a while the killer becomes jealous at the attention Anderson is receiving; the murders are making him too important, allowing him to take credit for the crimes, and the Numbers Killer wants to come forward and speak for himself. He is motivated by a fear of becoming insignificant, reminding him of his childhood when he felt significant knowing everybody on the city block where he lived, but as he grew up he realized he was not important. Using very confused logic, the killer initially claims he wants to be recognized for his crimes. Later he says good behavior goes unnoticed, and he is not responsible for anything he has done.

The film was adapted from *In The Heat Of The Summer* (1982) by John Katzenbach, himself a veteran crime reporter with the *Miami Herald*. When writing the novel Katzenbach claimed he wanted to address philosophical questions facing journalists covering crime stories—namely, what happens when a journalist's work affects the course of a story, and how does a journalist respond to the constant necessity of invading people's privacy at times of great emotional turmoil? For Katzenbach, "What I was driving at was the nature of reporting and the ambivalence of the job." For each journalist, "[t]hat's the argument you in effect go through with yourself over and over and if you don't question that ambiguity you won't be a sensitive reporter."[105] When beginning to research his role at the *Herald*, Kurt Russell said he felt that the reporters and photographers were excessively intrusive but, in traditional public relations style, he claimed he eventually came to believe that they were "very caring people," and although "they may be very callous about how they do their jobs... they're not callous about people."[106] However, Anderson's style

144

of reporting is intrusive rather than investigative, putting himself and the investigation in danger for the sake of his own professional vanity. Katzenbach knew that it was "extremely important not to cut corners when presenting the journalistic aspects." If they were unrealistic then journalists would "jump all over it," and so would he because he did not want his contemporaries criticizing the film en masse.[107] During the shooting of the film, *Herald* staff participated as consultants and extras, adding to the film's credibility and ensuring a favorable representation of the media.

Changes made by Reagan's economic policies helped to create an exaggerated climate of competition in business, making the situation depicted by Lang in *While the City Sleeps* more believable than that in *The Mean Season*. Drawing a large proportion of their revenue from advertising, newspapers divided their readership into demographic sections so they could concentrate on making themselves indispensable to consumers. "Newspapers seek to grasp and hold on to coherent sections of the population," according to Anthony Smith, "growing up with them, growing old with them until their spending power withers away."[108] The papers distribute large amounts of non-political information, but reports became less investigative because of budget cutbacks, and crime reporting was presented in more sensational ways to attract readers and viewers. Artist Gahan Wilson reminisced that when Ed Gein's crimes were first discovered in the late 1950s the newspapers reported in great detail. "Then suddenly this kind of detail stopped, and we got very circumspect announcements." The return to journalistic standards added to public curiosity, and encouraged the subculture of the scandal magazine. However, journalistic standards went full circle, and by the late 1980s commercial competition meant "you have a quickly published pocket book that lovingly retells all."[109]

Media overkill at the time of the events was followed by a second wave of publicity in the form of true crime books and magazines, documentaries, and made for television movies claiming to tell the 'true' stories. By the 1980s these killers were being credited with a prominence that was not a reflection of reality. After the killers' existence and activities were established in the public mind, their threat had to be addressed. Media coverage of the FBI 'Mindhunters' made the public aware of the 'supercops' who, it was claimed, could catch these killers, whoever and whatever they may be.

The influence of tabloid journalism, with similar sensibilities to true crime accounts on mainstream news reporting, continued throughout the 1970s and into the eighties encouraged by the competition of deregulation of the different media. By the end of the decade extreme sensationalism was the accepted practice to attract readers. Anne Schwartz, the first reporter on the scene of the Dahmer murders in 1992, explained her journalistic understanding of what the public wants from a story; "we want to know as much as we can stand, and then we need an explanation, a way of separating ourselves from our curiosity."[110] However, after Dahmer's arrest his neighbors were offered $50 by TV networks for interviews, only to be surpassed by tabloid papers offering $300.[111] The intensive reporting of the case turned the killer into a celebrity.

Schwartz described the opening day of the Dahmer trial as having the "air of a movie premiere, complete with local celebrities, groupies who hounded for autographs, and a full scale media onslaught."[112] According to Jerry Berger, by the mid 1990s, there was nothing to separate tabloid and mainstream journalism, and accuracy in reporting was sacrificed to the need to 'break' a story.[113] Berger blamed the loss of journalistic integrity on the information explosion launched by cable TV in the early 1980s, and continued with online computer services.[114] The result of commentary on criminal justice issues had considerable influence on public opinion, and mainstream news "stimulated fear of crime and shaped it in a very special sense to mean people out there who are the wrong color and have the wrong genes."[115]

Crime magazines began to appear in 1924, but the true crime reportage has a long history in western culture. The detective magazine is "the narrative presentation of real-life criminal cases for mass entertainment,"[116] and according to Dr Park Elliot Dietz they are "always openly displayed, unlike magazines showing nonviolent nudity, and there is no effort to discourage sales to minors."[117] He finds this troubling because, in his opinion, they are "pornography for sexual sadists,"[118] pairing conventionally erotic images with violent and sadistic images. Killers Ed Gein, Harvey Glatman and Ted Bundy's fondness for reading the grisly details offered in such magazines supports Dietz's theory to some degree, although it is important to bear in mind that as avid readers of true crime material, serial killers are consuming a more intensive intake of the conservative moralizing than that traditionally accompanying newspaper crime stories to fuel their fantasies. Exaggerated a step further than the sensational newspaper reports to attract readers, true crime borders on the fictional.

The stories are "fairly explicit," describing the acts of violence in a crime, what was done and how.[119] While claiming to be compiled from police files, they are usually derived from newspaper reports, with stories being intensively recycled from one title to another, and between British and American publications.[120] The magazines focus disproportionately on violent crime, especially murder where sexual violence and torture are involved. Along with detailed descriptions of violent acts the readers are also informed about "methods of investigation, investigative reconstruction of events, and crime laboratory work," providing an "unsurpassed source of public information on techniques for committing crimes, or the errors of unsuccessful offenders, and on methods available to law enforcement agencies for preventing crimes and apprehending offenders."[121] Atmospheric descriptions, quick cutting between scenes, and the use of dialogue are means to advance the plot and add an air of authenticity, "but in fact it is the least authentic feature of true crime writing."[122] Promoting themselves as being of educational value and taking a high moral tone, true crime magazines, and their readers, can avoid allegations of prurience.

The magazines deliver a conservative message, 'crime does not pay,' and they do so in a way which claims to be "exciting and educational, sexually exciting and moralistic." The conservative ideology of the magazines consistently allies the readers with the law enforcement agency perspective in a narrative. Most articles detail "rapid and overpowering" arrests of the culprits and end by reporting the criminal being sentenced to a long prison term, or even the death penalty. However, the audience is also often reminded that there are potentially more similar offenders still at large. Crime is not addressed as a social problem, rather explanations tend to suggest archaic and pre-scientific 'bad blood' or 'original sin' as a cause, reasoning that some people are just born to live a life of crime. On occasion social factors influencing crime are specifically denied.[123]

The popular detective magazines often feature 'sleazy' cover photographs of scantily clad women bound and gagged, or posing with weapons, to attract potential readers. Harvey Glatman posed as a professional photographer to attract young models whom he persuaded to pose for him. After tying and gagging the models he raped them and took his victims into the California deserts where he killed them. Dietz is careful to point out that, "[t]he cases we have described do not prove that detective magazines 'cause' sexual sadism or sadistic offenses," but that they are a "rich source of sexually sadistic imagery."[124] However, the role of pornography in sex crimes during the 1980s was largely anecdotal. The FBI's interviews with criminals focused on sexual aspects of the crimes and specifically asked them what role pornography or detective magazines played in their crimes,[125] reflecting the profiler's main interests and the interests of the Reagan administration.

The true crime magazine, once established, gave rise to the sub-genre of the 'factual' crime novel. Books claiming to be factual accounts of true crime stories have existed for many years but after 1970 there was a marked increase. A relatively recent creation, during the early 1980s 'factual' books on crime were interspersed on shop shelves with biographies of famous Hollywood film stars, but by the end of the decade they had become one of the largest areas of publishing activity, with obscure murder cases being found alongside the most famous accounts of Charles Manson, Ted Bundy and John Wayne Gacy. 'True crime' writers tend to be an assortment of journalists and professionals associated with a particular case who predictably thank numerous police officers for assistance in their acknowledgements. Art Crockett wrote several true crime books in the 1980s about sensational types of crimes and Clifford Linedecker, a "true crime hack,"[126] was one of the most prolific authors, among his books *Night Stalker* (1991) about the Ramirez murders. He was also a former associate editor of tabloid newspapers at the *National Examiner* and later *The Sun* (US).

Perhaps the best-known true crime writer associated with serial murder is Ann Rule, a former policewoman who turned writer initially for a host of true crime magazines. Several of Rule's books focus on serial killers. *The Stranger Beside Me* (1981) is her famous account of her personal involvement in the Ted Bundy case, but she has also written about Jerry Brudos in *The Lust Killer* (1988), and Randall Woodfield in *The I-5 Killer* (1984). She also lectured widely to law-enforcement agencies, including the FBI at Quantico as an expert on serial murder, and to children in schools. In her books Rule regularly thanks law-enforcement officers from relevant jurisdictions and prominent FBI profilers. For example, in the *Lust Killer* she thanks John Douglas, Robert Ressler and Roy Hazelwood for information and assistance they provided her during her research. Ressler's own *Whoever Fights Monsters* (1992) and *I Have Lived in the Monster* (1997), John Douglas's *Mindhunters* (1996), and Roy Hazelwood in *The Evil That Men Do* (1999) are little more than true crime books using dates sparsely so the killers tend to blur into a dense continuum confusing the reader's perspective of the time span involved. Despite his books glorifying the work of the FBI Robert Ressler was sued by the Bureau as he had not had his manuscript approved by them and he was forced to pay a substantial amount.[127]

Commonalities exist in the presentation of the genre. According to James Alan Fox and Jack Levin, "[w]hether written by a journalist, psychologist, or criminologist, virtually all true crime books... tend not to spare the reader the most upsetting and graphic details."[128] Without such details, it is alleged, the killers could give "false and misleading" impressions to the reading audience, possibly presenting themselves as master criminals of some description, or rebellious antiheroes, as opposed to the "ghouls and fiends" they really are.[129] According to Joseph Grixti, writers in the genre "simply appeal to a stock of prejudices and associations based on our familiarity with fictional accounts" from the fantasy and horror genres.[130]

Showing sympathy for criminals is unthinkable for authors in the genre, and stories are invariably recounted from a law-enforcement point of view. The approach allows the readers "to enjoy the display of crime, detection, retribution, while refusing to be drawn into a steady contemplation of themselves as audience, and the subterranean echoes which the case disturbs, would be fruitless and arid."[131] The books are speculative history, told with retrospective clarity. Limited references to dates are given in the books, often backed up with fabricated dialogue and vague explanations of the criminal's actions, but as in true crime magazines rarely are any attempts made to identify the social causes of a crime. All of the notable sex killers of the 1970s have books devoted to their crimes, along with chapters devoted to them in general books on crime. Public interest was acknowledged when *Time-Life* published a twenty volume set of books focusing on accounts of real crimes, and in 1992 Doubleday established the first book club devoted to the genre, reflecting its growing popularity and influence as a source of information.

While recounting the graphic details of crimes, the reactionary subtext of such books deny the reader the view of theories which see crime as a phenomenon produced by society. In Clifford Linedecker's *The Man Who Killed Boys* (1980), the author states that blaming society "can make reformers feel very good, but it is counter productive because it merely provides the lawless with ready-made excuses for their actions by tracing the genesis of their criminality to fathers, mothers, broken homes, poverty, or some other individual condition." He chooses to believe that some people become criminals because they chose to live that lifestyle. Echoing Reagan and the 'paranoid' ideology of his appointees, Linedecker exaggerates, adding, "There is so much concern for the civil liberties of sex criminals that it is almost illegal to try to protect women or children from them." Inciting insecurity in his readers by exaggerating the justice system's potential shortcomings, Linedecker claims that each year thousands of sex offenders walk out of prisons and mental hospitals with their behavior uncorrected to look for new victims.[132]

One true crime book does offer an insight into possible reasons for no affluent serial killers ever being caught. Dr Martin Obler and Thomas Calvin's *Fatal Analysis* (1997) recounts the story of a New York serial killer called the Soda Pop Slasher. To preserve client confidentiality, Obler's patient is referred to as Devon Cardou, a student with a 154 IQ studying for a psychology doctorate at a New York University, and thought to be destined for a brilliant career. Cardou is referred by an associate of Obler's for counseling as a deviant whose sexuality is causing problems among other students. Where most serial killers who have been caught come from, at best, lower middle-class families, it is noted that Cardou's family is wealthy, but still dysfunctional. Obler quickly concludes that Cardou is a psychopath, and through the patient's insinuations, that he is the killer in question but, rather than inform the police, Obler continues counseling his patient, eventually claiming credit for redirecting his interests away from murder and into law, and later politics. At the end of the book Obler notes that many psychopaths, because of their desire for power and instinct for survival at other people's expense, enter politics, employing their desire for domination and control to further their ruthless and self-serving careers.[133]

Criminals are rarely happy about the books portraying them. The style of the writing often simplifies the case, presenting the reader with a distorted version of reality. Dennis Nilsen, himself a convicted serial killer, recognized the phenomena which attracted the audience, saying, "The population at large is neither 'normal' or 'average.' They seem to be bound together by a collective ignorance of themselves and what they are. They have, every one of them, got their deep dark thoughts with many a skeleton rattling in their secret cupboard."[134] The initial response to a sensational crime is "a flood of popular self-righteous condemnation but a willingness to, with friends and acquaintances, talk over and over again the appropriate bits of the case."[135] In May 1993 Randy Kraft, one of California's Freeway Killers, sued Dennis McDougal and Warner Books for $60 million, claiming that the book *Angel of Darkness* was an unfair portrayal of him as sick and twisted.[136] Tim Cahill's *Buried Dreams* claimed to be based on the investigative reporting of Russ Ewing and hours of interviews with John Wayne Gacy, something which Gacy denied, calling the book "pure fantasy." Prison records showed that Ewing had only talked to Gacy on one occasion for less than an hour in April 1980 before he was barred from the prison. The animosity between Gacy and Ewing was evident when Gacy wrote, "Russ Ewing would prostitute his own mother for a dollar."[137] Gacy sent a copy of a manuscript called *A Question of Doubt*, through a third party, to Doubleday for consideration, but the script was read and returned by James Moser who rejected it because Gacy's "version of the details of his arrest, arraignment, trial and conviction is not compelling or convincing enough to create a sympathetic portrait." After Gacy's treatment by conventional news media, it would be difficult to say what could reverse the negative image the public had of him. Moser concluded, "I'm afraid that in the light of his guilt the question of a fair shake will be an academic one in the minds of most readers."[138] Eventually, Gacy's own company did publish *A Question of Doubt* (1993) and two volumes of selected correspondence, but coming from a small company with limited distribution his books are a minor curiosity and not widely read.

Brian Masters, who admits his own interest in "extreme exemplars of human weakness,"[139] was commissioned by a New York publisher to write a book about the Jeffrey Dahmer case after the success of his account of Dennis Nilsen's crimes, *Killing For Company* (1986). However, when presented with a draft of *The Shrine of Jeffrey Dahmer* the company rejected it. In Masters' opinion, "pity, dismay and anguish" were not enough for his publishers, who wanted "loud overt disapproval." The New York publisher "seemed to think that to try to understand depravity was itself a sin, certainly one which the American public, otherwise greedy for narratives of serial murder, would be unwilling to accept. I was obliged to withdraw the book, which will now be published only in Britain."[140] Masters' book was later published in America by another company.

Increasingly graphic news reporting, and the need for sensational stories to attract an audience in a competitive market, distorted the public's understanding of crime problems and divorced them from other social issues. 'True crime' books recycled original, but speculative, news reports, usually mixed with a conservative moral tone, keeping especially shocking crime stories in the public eye. The emphasis on 'official' versions of cases gave authenticity to crime reporting and continued into later television docudramas which further distorted facts, justified by dramatic license and the requirements of the medium in an increasingly competitive market.

Belief Is A Poor Substitute For Thought
Serial Killers and Law & Order Issues as Entertainment

MORE INFLUENTIALLY THAN NEWSPAPERS, CINEMA AND television conveyed to a mass audience a sensational and dramatic representation of contemporary society. Ever vigilant to the potential of new technology, beginning in 1947, J Edgar Hoover began sending memos to the fledgling Federal Communications Commission (FCC), warning that members of the Communist Party, or sympathizers, might apply for television station licenses, a recognition of the propaganda potential of television. As a result some license applications were rejected and shortly after, the Hollywood blacklist spread from the cinema industry to television broadcasting. Hollywood film executives dropped writers who were considered 'unfriendly' to the House Un-American Activities Committee (HUAC), and lists of questionable names were distributed to television executives and sponsors. Erik Barnouw observed that, "Evolving from a radio industry born under military influence and reared by big business, [television] now entered an adolescence traumatized by phobias. It would learn caution and cowardice."[1]

The pervasive HUAC ideology ensured that television programming would be 'friendly' to conservative spectators, and following the accepted formula; TV quickly rose in popularity at the expense of cinema and radio.[2] The meteoric rise in the popularity of television created a new generation of media celebrities, among them Ronald Reagan, and ensured news reporting would have a more graphic and immediate impact on the American public. It was Reagan's confidence in front of the camera throughout his career, which made him seem more relaxed and affable than his rivals, consolidating his popularity despite his extreme views. As a commercial and political tool, television's influence is difficult to overestimate, selling as it does products, political candidates and lifestyles to a vast audience worldwide. By the end of the New Right's occupation of the White House anyone who appeared on television was considered a 'celebrity.' According to David Litwinsky, of ALL Direct Mail Inc., "Jeffrey Dahmer is a celebrity. His name draws attention, positive or negative, but celebrity is celebrity regardless."[3]

The dominance of television, reached in the 1980s, had been building for some time. During the 1960s and 1970s, television news reporting became more graphic with the unrest in American cities, civil rights protests and antiwar demonstrations. The Zapruder film of president John F Kennedy's assassination, possibly the most shocking film footage of all time, was finally aired in full in March 1975, fuelling innumerable 'conspiracy theories.' News programs had to compete with other primetime television shows and other news stations, and began to broadcast more graphic and sensational footage. In July 1974 Chris Chubbuck, the anchorwoman for the *Suncoast Digest* TV show, killed herself on camera. Her last words acknowledged the direction taken by television, when she said, "In keeping with Channel 40's policy of bringing you the latest in blood and guts and in living color, you are going to see another first—attempted suicide." She then drew a revolver and shot herself in the head, dying fourteen hours later.[4]

Comparably, in January 1987 Pennsylvania state treasurer R Budd Dwyer called a press conference. The reporters attending the conference expected they were going to witness his resignation, after he was convicted of bribery the previous month and faced a possible fifty-five years in prison. After protesting his innocence for thirty minutes Dwyer handed sealed envelopes to three of his former colleagues, then he pulled a .357 magnum from another envelope and killed himself. Local TV stations broadcast the events live, even taking the time to have camera close-ups of Dwyer's corpse. CBS and ABC used still photographs instead of video footage, and news agencies carried a series of photographs, but only tabloid newspapers used the most explicit.[5] Richard Tithecott astutely observed that, "Perversion has become less that which civilization defines itself against and more of an event at which civilization cheers and feigns horror,"[6] and in the race for ratings anything could be justified if accompanied by a moralizing speech. From the conduct of the Reagan administration's political activities it was clear that the New Right ideology took precedence over the law. New Right administrative policies, which cut social spending in favor of military expenditure, also favored deregulation of business over public-interest considerations, increasing competition in the

Serial Killers and Law & Order Issues as Entertainment

television industry. Quality of programming suffered as stations competed more aggressively for viewing figures and the advertising figures, and hence profits, which they brought.

By appointing Mark S Fowler to head the FCC, Reagan fundamentally changed the way in which the FCC operated, and the way in which television broadcasters viewed their audiences. According to Fowler television was "just another appliance...a toaster with pictures." In his opinion, "[i]t was time to move away from thinking about broadcasters as trustees. It was time to treat them the way almost everyone else does—that is, as business."[7] The system of public licensing, which had been in effect since 1934, was discarded, giving existing stations permanent access to publicly owned airwaves. Broadcasting authority requirements setting minimum levels of airtime to be devoted to news and public service programs were abandoned, affecting the quality of those programs, as well as the quality of public affairs, religious and children's programming scheduled by television stations.[8]

Along with the removal of public service programming regulations, the FCC expanded the amount of time a TV station could devote to advertisements per hour. Reagan also wanted new technologies such as cable television to be opened up to free competition, meaning more television, and more advertisers competing for the attention of a finite audience. The removal of regulations and a relaxation by Congress of limits on the number of stations a company could own expanded the potential for profit for television stations. In response to this, the average price of a TV station doubled between 1982 and 1984,[9] and competition for viewing figures intensified. The profit motive was exemplified by the rise of television soap operas with their low costs but, if popular, high advertising revenue. *Dallas* and *Dynasty* were readily identified in households across America, if not the world.

The unreality of the 1980s cannot solely be blamed on the Reagan administration, but the President's "persistent and repeated" disdain for facts, and rhetoric idealizing an American past that never existed, did not help.[10] As President, Reagan offered only slogans and simplifications to the public. His personality suited television's passive audience of spectators rather than participants. The emphasis on the criminal as an isolated individual, rather than highlighting systematic flaws in society, made it easier for sections of the American population to "disconnect from unwelcome intrusions and search for new rituals to fill their daily lives."[11]

In the late 1970s made-for-television films, wryly called 'trauma dramas,' appeared as an equivalent of the 'public service dramas' of previous decades. They also bore a considerable similarity to the "Timely Topic" quickies made in the 1940s and fifties by specialist independent filmmakers on nickel-and-dime budgets to exploit widespread public concerns with drugs and sexual morality.[12] Invoking traditional American populism, which coincided with Reagan's family values rhetoric, the 'docudrama' was always 'based on a true story,' and mixed documentary and dramatic styles in an attempt to exploit public concerns, but which also reflected public disillusionment with government institutions.[13]

The makers preferred prominent newspaper stories, usually the most sensational cases, which involved "everyday people, somebody like your neighbor doing something unexpected."[14] Often films of 'true crimes' were themselves subject to follow-up news reporting when broadcast, but were "sanitized" by network TV broadcast standards, removing most of the horrific violence.[15] The boy-next-door stereotype of the serial killer combined with the sensational nature (and number) of their sex crimes made them a financially desirable property for film producers. However, Ruth Slawson of NBC said she declined numerous pitches for the rights to the Jeffrey Dahmer case because, in her opinion, it was "much too weird and repulsive for television."[16]

The 'trauma dramas' began by focusing on unexpected diseases or family traumas. The case of the Walsh family was prime material for adaptation in light of the national media coverage, and the film *Adam* (1983) reassures the audience with its authenticity, opening with the warning, "The story you are about to see is true. The names of the principal characters and government officials have not been changed." In reaction to an unresponsive system parents take matters into their own hands, and in the case of John Walsh his legislative crusade identifies him as a 'citizen politician,' cast from the same mould as Reagan, and implies that any parent facing a trauma could also become a populist political activist. Walsh's character, in real life and in the film, epitomized Reagan's individualistic populism, and *Adam*, like almost all of the 'trauma dramas,' was characterized by parental fanaticism.[17] *Adam* and other 'trauma dramas' emphasized 'normal' family life and reinforced Reagan's idealized 'family values.'[18]

When production agencies began competing for the rights to stories in the 1980s, "It became a shark feed."[19] One commentator described the change in television movies' subject matter as away from "disease-of-the-week movies to victim pictures," especially to criminals with dangerous obsessions and sociopathic behavior."[20] The component parts of serial killer cases, sexual homicides, kidnap, rape and murder, were traditional features of network films and mini-series, but the explosion in popularity of tabloid television, local newscasts, video cameras and satellite feeds made the incidents more readily available to producers who knew the sensational stories' potential to attract ratings.[21] One observer commented, "No network has yet gone broke *overestimating* its audience's appetite for sleaze."[22]

The true crime genre of made-for-TV movies produced 'real story' accounts of the most notable serial sex killer cases, *The Deliberate Stranger* (Marvin J. Chomsky, 1986), *Out of the Darkness* (Jud Taylor, 1985), *To Catch A Killer* (Eric Till, 1991), and *Overkill: The Aileen Wournos Story* (Peter Levin, 1993), to name only a few. These reflected more about tabloid journalism reporting, and true crime magazine stories, than they did about the reality of an investigation, and added to the credibility of 'official' verdicts by making the viewer omniscient and providing unchallenging narratives. In doing so they reinforced the public perception of guilt.

The TV networks openly acknowledged their motives for broadcasting crime stories as simply to "get ratings." Eventually 'true story' films became an important part of network TV programming. Crime films accounted for thirty-five to forty per cent of the total made-for- TV film market by the early 1990s. Also to their advantage, docudrama's can construct a simple narrative to present the events of a case in a way that can have far more emotional impact than disjointed news reports, which are spaced out over days, weeks or months.[23] While the 'Son of Sam' laws, passed in the aftermath of the Berkowitz trial, prevented criminals from profiting from their crimes, it did not stop victims, lawyers and law-enforcement officials from profiting from headline crimes. The commercial potential for story rights was recognized, sometimes by more than one person associated with a case.

As an integral part of cinema and TV, crime dramas were common, but dramas 'based' on real cases carried a greater sense of urgency. One of the most highly praised true crime dramas, *The Boston Strangler* (Richard Fleischer, 1968), was based on Gerold Frank's dubious bestseller of the same name and highlights many of the legal problems presented by later docudramas. In September 1967, Gerold Frank notified Fox that he was granting them permission for a film version of his *Boston Strangler* book, after they bought the property for $200,000.[24] John Bottomly, assistant Attorney General during the Boston Strangler investigation, went to work for Twentieth Century Fox as a consultant on the film, in which Henry Fonda portrays Bottomly as the hero of the investigation and Tony Curtis plays Albert DeSalvo. Bottomly also tried to recruit other consultants from the Boston police departments to work as technical advisors but no one agreed.[25]

The film explicitly names DeSalvo as the Boston Strangler, as Frank had done in his book, even though up to that time DeSalvo had not even been charged with any of the crimes attributed to the Boston Strangler. Richard Fleischer and Edward Anhalt, who wrote the screenplay of *The Boston Strangler*, were faced with the dilemma of writing about crimes for mass entertainment which no-one was ever charged with, and identifying a criminal responsible for those crimes, effectively reversing the traditional legal assumption of 'innocent until proven guilty.' The Attorney General's office turned down requests for assistance from the filmmakers, citing their fears that a film naming DeSalvo as the Strangler could jeopardize his trial, or any future prosecutions. However, Fleischer described the film as "the story of a fragmented personality" and asserted that, "If anything, [it] would help DeSalvo if he ever came to trial."[26] Edward Brooke turned down a five-figure, and then a six-figure, sum to portray himself in the film. His reason for declining was his concern over the number of factual distortions in the script and he hinted that he would consider legal action if the portrayal of his character was not changed to reflect reality. Later he threatened to sue if the film mentioned him at all.[27]

Henry Fonda's portrayal of Bottomly contrasts sharply, and ironically, with the opinions of people who worked on the task force. On screen Fonda plays Bottomly as a sympathetic and dynamic character leading the investigation, not surprising bearing in mind that Bottomly was the film's main technical advisor. Author and journalist George Higgins said that during the investigation he never heard anyone talk about Bottomly without using the word 'asshole' as "either a suffix or a prefix. I started to think maybe it was part of the guy's name." Another retired police officer remembered Bottomly as someone who "had to get permission from his mom to swat a fly."[28]

When the film premiered in Fall 1968, it bore little resemblance to Gerold Frank's book, and even less to the truth. One Cambridge police officer who worked on the investigation described the film as a "crock of shit."[29] The murders are out of sequence and in the wrong cities, the task force is formed much later in the killings than it was in reality, giving the impression that it is the focusing of police resources which brings a speedy resolution. Notably F Lee Bailey, possibly the most important character in the story, is not mentioned at all because he did not like the script or the payment he was offered for the use of his name. DeSalvo wanted to sue Twentieth Century Fox but the rules of Bridgewater hospital, where he was being held, would not permit that. A federal court judge refused DeSalvo's request to issue an injunction against *The Boston Strangler*, describing the film as a "responsible treatment of a theme much broader than the fate of its central character."[30]

When the film premiered the debate about its ethics resumed and Kevin Thomas of the *LA Times* questioned the premise of the film asking, "Should a film label a man a mass murderer, even though he has confessed to the crimes, when he has yet to come to trial?" In *Esquire* magazine, Wilfrid Sheed had no doubts saying, *"The Boston Strangler* is dirty pool... movies should not bring in convictions before courts do, and... a man with a living wife and children should be left to molder quietly in his asylum. I would not care to have been in their particular playground the day the film hit Boston."[31] *The Boston Strangler* supported the politically motivated resolution to a media-created crime panic. The film never questions DeSalvo's guilt, even though the Boston police were very skeptical whether the murders really were a series committed by a single offender. There was considerable evidence implicating a number of suspects in separate cases. Reassuring the public that justice had been done by simplifying reality and ignoring any information which might cast doubt upon the comfortable resolution, *The Boston Strangler* set the standard which subsequent films emulated.

The only notable exception from the convention is the *Atlanta Child Murders* (John Erman, 1985), a five hour TV mini-series which was later edited down into a film, and which cast "serious doubt on Wayne Williams' guilt and implicitly suggests that he may have been a scapegoat for public officials to calm public hysteria."[32] The Atlanta murders were, however, the pivotal case in establishing the BSU profiles as a valuable investigative tool. Local newspapers, the *Atlanta Journal* and the *Atlanta Constitution*, sought to discredit the film in their reporting for almost a year before the film was broadcast, and ridiculed any idea that it could present the case fairly. After Williams' conviction in 1982 the news media reported that the entire population in Atlanta, most specifically black children and their parents, could look forward to resuming a normal life since the killer had been caught. By raising questions about the investigation the *Atlanta Child Murders* was accused of reawakening public fear, and that 'distortions' and 'errors' within the film would do grievous injury to the whole city of Atlanta.[33]

Prominent figures in the making of the film were portrayed by the press as being motivated by antagonism toward the system, desire for notoriety, racism and greed. For these reasons, it was claimed, it was impossible for the film to be objective. Chet Dettlinger, author of *The List* (1984), criticized the Atlanta police department and judicial system for the way in which the Williams case was handled, and was hired as a consultant. Dettlinger felt anxious about the film's chances, "If it's anything like my book they will probably try to ban it.... The Chamber of Commerce wants to sweep the killings under the rug." Reporters continually pointed out Dettlinger's direct involvement in the script and implied that he was a "malcontent who was making money by calling into question the guilt of Wayne Williams." Another consultant was Camille Bell, mother of one of the murdered children and a controversial figure during the investigation. She had been particularly vocal in calling for a task force to be set up, but made numerous appearances on the *Phil Donahue Show* criticizing the investigation and Williams' trial, which she referred to as a "fiasco." Eventually she even aided Williams' defense lawyers.[34]

Abby Mann, who wrote the five-hour mini-series, was well known for previous work including *Judgment at Nuremberg* (1961), *The Marcus-Nelson Murders* (1973), and *King* (1978), the television biography of Martin Luther King Jr. When researching the story, Mann interviewed officers from the Atlanta police department, defense and prosecution attorneys, the mothers of some of the murdered children, and Wayne Williams.[35] He was skeptical about the term 'docudrama,' defining it as bad drama and adding that television hardly ever does anything courageous, or says anything new. A story as sensational and widely publicized as the Atlanta Child Murders was almost bound to be used as the basis for a TV film. However, Mann sought to break with the traditional approach to docudramas and questioned the official version of events, raising questions about the crimes and the investigations.[36] The narrator in the film, Chet Dettlinger (Martin Sheen), sums up the importance of the case when he says, "That splash was to change the course of Atlanta and perhaps American justice."[37]

The reason for Mann's interest was that he had long been distressed at the use of unsupported fiber evidence in criminal trials. He pointed out, "Usually, you should only use fiber evidence to support or direct evidence like eyewitness testimony... But if police are going to use fiber evidence without other corroborating evidence, we ought to know about it, because the same thing could be used against us." Mann was also concerned with the legal precedent of allowing the prosecution to link Williams to eleven other cases with which he was never formally charged. He believed that the prosecution "did not have the responsibility of proving his guilt in those cases, but those other cases were constantly mentioned in order to influence the jury." In the screenplay he sought to make the audience question whether that should be acceptable as legal practice.[38]

The Williams case had, for Mann, "all the trappings of what disturbs me about urban justice and the way the criminal justice system treats poor black defendants differently from defendants who are white and middle class."[39] The civil rights movement had made changes in society but, in Mann's opinion, "The blacks who had been fighting the establishment suddenly became the establishment." Adopting a conservative ideology once incorporated into the existing political and economic power structure, black politicians continued to ignore what Mann identified as the real murderers, the "greed and indifference, which still rule the streets."[40] The *Atlanta Child Murders* appealed to a wider range of social ills than just racism. In the film Dettlinger says, "This was the case of the black, mad homosexual killer, with elements that appealed to every prejudice, superstition and hang up in our contemporary society."[41]

In the days leading up to the film's broadcast CBS met with an Atlanta Task Force of seventy-five civic, political and religious leaders from Atlanta to discuss criticism of the film. CBS maintained that the film was "accurate, balanced and fair,"[42] but the task force alleged that it was inaccurate, and unfairly depicted Atlanta as a city torn by crime and racial divisions.[43] Before broadcast, Mayor Andrew Young sent telegrams to the 100 leading corporate advertisers in America expressing his "deep concern" about the *Atlanta Child Murders* film.[44] Former governor George Busbee was "not satisfied," asserting that, "There is no way for the viewers to know what is and is not fiction."[45] Along with others such as Mayor Young, Busbee wanted airtime to discuss what they saw as the distortions in the facts. Mann defended his work saying that, "If anything we bent over backwards to strengthen the prosecution's case."[46] Despite the discussions between CBS and the 'Atlanta Task Force,' newspapers reported that city officials, child psychologists, teachers, ministers, police chiefs and parents were concerned that questions raised in the film could have harmful effects on children in the city. A group of psychologists and counselors was reported as setting up a hotline on nights that *Atlanta Child Murders* was broadcast,[47] a considerably more swift response than officials had paid to the original murders.

An advisory message, written on screen as well as narrated, warned viewers that the film is "not a documentary, but a drama based on certain facts surrounding the murder and disappearances of children in Atlanta between 1979 and 1981. Some of the events and characters are fictionalized for dramatic purposes." Also there was a warning that it contained scenes which might be disturbing for young viewers. When the film was shown to the mothers and relatives of ten of the murdered children they saw some inaccuracies, but shared many of the producer's suspicions about Williams' complicity in the crimes. One of the relatives felt: "No one wanted to know what happened to those kids… They just wanted a scapegoat, and if this will help reopen the case, then the film is a blessing." Williams' father was pleased with the film, believing that, "Now the whole world can see why my boy should be turned loose."[48] The *New York Times* followed the Atlanta papers in its review, and while praising the film for fine performances, to the reviewer it still remained an "irresponsible piece of work."[49] Critics outside America were more complimentary. One reviewer, noticing the number of "loose threads" running through the screenplay, commented that Mann had related the case to the audience with "admirable clarity and complexity."[50]

During the court scene Williams' attorney, Al Binder (Jason Robards), challenges witnesses who claim to have seen some of the victims in Williams' company. He points out their own criminal histories and suggests they might have been promised some reward for their testimony. Several years after the film was released it was revealed that financial gain had motivated Bobby Toland, a key prosecution witness. The two prosecuting attorneys were played by veteran actors Rip Torn and Andrew Robinson, the "two craziest actors traditionally associated with maniac roles."[51] By the end of the trial DA Slaton (Rip Torn) confesses, "This is the first case I ever tried where I didn't know the where, the when, the why or even the how." An apt summary of the prosecution's case. The screenplay by Abby Mann contended that the political and economic power structure in Atlanta decided: "We gotta find someone to hang this on. We don't care who it is."[52] He theorized that, just like the conviction of Bruno Hauptman for the Lindbergh kidnapping, city officials wanted any conviction to close the case. Mann's uneasiness with the conviction is reflected in the last lines spoken by the narrator, when he says, "This case won't be closed for me until I open a door that says once and for all Wayne Williams was guilty or he was a sacrificial lamb on the altar of the good name of Atlanta." John Erman, the film's director, believed that the *Atlanta Child Murders* would justifiably disturb viewers, "We all like to think that the police and the government are there to protect us, and that we are living in a safe society. I think that one of these things that this film says is that we are living in an unsafe society."[53] City officials were not happy at being tried on television and found guilty. Numerous influential figures (many of whom complained about their own portrayal in the film), civic groups and even some of the victims' families were quoted by the Atlanta press condemning the film's negative portrayal of Atlanta's leaders. Falling back on traditional animosity, Jim Minter of the Atlanta *Journal* attacked the film as being "an old story with a new locale. The usual indictment of the rural south set among the glittering skyscrapers of Atlanta, where we thought, mistakenly, we were beyond all that."[54]

Receiving high "but not extraordinary" nationwide ratings[55] of fifty million viewers,[56] the *Atlanta Child Murders* fueled controversy over television's use of 'docudramas.' Increasingly popular as a form of TV programming, the docudrama became important to network television in its attempts to attract larger audiences for the potential advertising revenue they would bring.[57] In the market created by Reagan's deregulation policies the competition for audiences became more intense. While television has always been a "continuum of fact and fiction," the problem with docudramas and their claim to authenticity was, according to Richard Salant of CBS, that "people just don't know where docu ends and drama begins." This was a charge which could be laid at much of television, especially in the 1980s. The volume of information passed on to a viewer means that, "People can't remember something on the news or elsewhere."[58]

The unusual feature of the *Atlanta Child Murders* and the resulting criticism directed at it by the news media is that it is the only serial killer docudrama which questions the outcome of an official police investigation. The effect of this on the audience is uncertain. It is possible that the film was less effective because it contradicted media coverage of the case; on the other hand William Adams, of George Washington University, contended that criticizing the investigation may have reinforced a public tendency to believe that authority "fouled up." Either way it raised several issues about the validity of docudramas as a source of public information. As a partial remedy, Richard Salant suggested that docudramas which involved current issues, as most of them do, should, when broadcast, be followed by a scheduled discussion to examine the film from a journalistic point of view, in much the same way as political events are analyzed in special programs which offer different points of view. Salant concluded, "Why should entertainment be immune from an effort to let the public make up their own mind?"[59] While the suggestion was interesting and might help inform the public, it is one which is rarely implemented.

Subsequent dramatizations did not ask questions about the efficiency of the police investigation, raise doubts about the guilt of those convicted, or question the politicization of crime policy. *Out of the Darkness* (Jud Taylor, 1985) retold the Son of Sam story. Only one killer is ever shown in the film despite allegations by Berkowitz that others had been involved in the killing with him, and doubts among police investigators that a single killer could fit the variety of photofits constructed by survivors and witnesses of the attacks attributed to the '.44 Caliber Killer.' Later the New York police acknowledged Maury Terry's work in *The Ultimate Evil* (1987), investigating the finer points of numerous discrepancies in the case and developing evidence against two of Berkowitz's associates who died in mysterious circumstances. In *Out of the Darkness* the compression of characters and simplification of events reflects the limitations of docudramas as a storytelling medium, especially in depicting complex serial investigations. However, it also creates more singular and dynamic investigative law officers.

As public interest in crime issues escalated and the media competition demanded higher viewing figures, the time between the events occurring and their dramatization diminished. Official law and order co-operation in production enhanced a docudrama's authenticity and commercial viability. Even before the opening of *Easy Prey* (Sandor Stern, 1986), which recounts the story of Christopher Wilder's murder spree, an on-screen message informs viewers that, "The following dramatization is based on personal interviews, press announcements and published accounts. The FBI personnel depicted in this movie are representative of those involved in the case." Viewers are assured that they are about to see as close to a 'true' retelling of events as possible.

Posing as a fashion photographer, Christopher Wilder (Gerald McRaney) lures attractive, but naive, young women to his car and then abducts them. While Wilder is usually described as a 'spree killer' in newspapers and true crime books, for this TV film he is called a serial killer, tapping into the contemporary concern generated by politicians and the media. Wilder made a highly publicized dash across America, kidnapping, torturing, raping and finally killing a string of young women while law enforcement agencies, including the FBI, frantically tried to catch him. The story begins halfway through Wilder's crimes and is recounted from the point of view of Tina Marie Risico (Shawnee Smith) whom Wilder kidnaps and rapes but does not kill because he wants to use her to lure more victims. Initially Wilder's stated intention is to take Tina to Mexico and trade her for drugs (cocaine), and he taunts her, asking if she knows what happens to girls who are sold into white slavery. His plans are halted when he hears a news report on his car radio of a police raid arresting his drug-dealing associates across the border.[60] Tina is obviously very naive, at one point explaining to Wilder that she got into the car with him because she is sixteen and wanted to be noticed. She rationalizes that being told she was pretty would draw attention to who she was and give her value in the world. From earlier references to Tina's father, it is obvious she is from a dysfunctional family and the lack of attention in her upbringing appears, superficially, to be what made her vulnerable to Wilder.[61]

Tina's narration begins with her own abduction in Torrence (California). She is unaware of Wilder's previous crimes until she sees a news report naming him as the suspect in the murders of three women and the abduction of six others. She describes Wilder as "normal" when she is trying to explain to the police why she went with him at first, and she adds that Wilder did not look like a TV criminal or like Jack The Ripper, reflecting the negative effects of criminal stereotypes and emphasizing the FBI's assertion in their generic serial killer profile that the offenders are abnormally normal. The superficial normality of serial killers is returned to later in the film, when FBI agent Paul Worthy (Sean McCann) scolds his daughter for being home forty minutes late. Worthy's fear for his family's security is heightened by his job. His daughter reassures him that, unlike Tina, she would not get into a car with a "jerk," but her father retorts, "What if he's not a jerk? What if he's good-looking? What if he flatters you? What if he charms you?" Again this emphasizes the normality of serial killers on which the FBI focused. Worthy later blames Wilder's crime spree on judges who released him back into society after he had been arrested for raping a girl but plea-bargained down to a lesser charge.

Fran Alton (Kate Lynch), a female FBI agent from the Behavioral Sciences Support Unit (BSSU), appears in the film and describes Wilder as being on a "feeding frenzy," but because he is using his own credit cards she believes he wants to be caught. When briefing local police on her theory, which eventually proves to be completely correct, according to the film's narrative, she is greeted with absolutely no skepticism or dissent. The FBI are fully in charge of the investigation, and are portrayed in a very flattering light. They are active in investigating Wilder's crimes, connecting abductions, finding witnesses and tracing the path he has taken and devoting 500 agents nationwide to the case. Uncharacteristically they even go out of their way to make sure they do not offend local police or encroach on their jurisdiction. In contrast, the local Torrence police initially assume that Tina is a runaway and are disinterested until their detectives hear from the FBI about the *modus operandi* Wilder is using. Once they realize that Tina's disappearance from the mall matches Wilder's other crimes they rush to notify the Bureau. It is the involvement of the dynamic FBI agents which appears to focus the investigation by bringing their expertise and resources to bear, but the case is never truly solved because Wilder is killed in an accidental shooting. After the scandals of the 1970s, *Easy Prey* is unusually uncritical of the Bureau's intentions and attempts to establish the professionalism emphasized by Clarence Kelley and William Webster, who sought to create a 'new' identity for the FBI.

Many docudramas are based on true crime speculative history books and do not involve the FBI at all. Perhaps the most famous is *The Deliberate Stranger* (Marvin J Chomsky, 1986), based on Ann Rule's bestseller of the same name. While not overtly spreading the myth of the 'new' Bureau, both narratives do rely on the serial killer stereotype to construct the character of the sex criminal. In *Overkill*, Fox and Levin noted that glamorous actors portraying vicious killers unfortunately infuse the criminals with the glamour associated with

Serial Killers and Law & Order Issues as Entertainment

Hollywood.[62] Nowhere is that more obvious than in *The Deliberate Stranger* where Mark Harmon, who had recently been voted sexiest man in the world by *People* magazine, portrays Ted Bundy. Robert Keppel, who investigated Bundy's crimes and interviewed him, thought that Harmon was a good choice to play Bundy because of their resemblance, but conceded that Harmon did not capture accurately the sinister side of Bundy's character.[63] However, the docudramatist is not interested in relating to the audience the true horror of the crimes; instead, the focus is on the certainty of the offender's guilt, reassuring the audience that 'crime does not pay.'

Prominent crimes from the 1970s continued to provide subject matter for docu-dramas, exploiting and increasing public fear. The Hillside Stranglers provided obvious material in the paranoid climate of the 1980s, and Darcy O'Brien's *Two Of A Kind* (1985) was adapted for a television audience in *The Case of The Hillside Stranglers* (Steve Gethers, 1989). Apart from one brief appearance on a news broadcast, Daryl Gates was missing from *The Case of The Hillside Stranglers* entirely, despite being Chief of the LAPD and conducting press conferences. One highly embarrassing incident involving Gates which occurred during the case is therefore completely ignored.

A recaptured felon named George Shawshank told Boston police that during the time he was loose he had hid out in Beverly Hills with his friend Peter Mark Jones, who was the Hillside Strangler. Bob Grogan who headed the investigation immediately went to Boston to check out Shawshank's story, and shortly afterwards Jones was arrested, suspected of committing two murders. Gates announced the arrest before it could be established whether there was evidence to support Shawshank's claim. Unfortunately there was none. Angry with Grogan for making such a foolish mistake, Gates had to formally apologize to Jones and take the blame.[64] Not surprisingly, the incident was absent from the film. Like most docudramas, *The Case of the Hillside Stranglers* presents viewers with simplified versions of an extremely complex investigation where the first suspects identified are the guilty offenders. The crimes are eventually solved by chance, when a former LAPD officer who moves to Washington state notices similarities between the Hillside Strangler murders and the murders of two young women in Bellingham.

Manhunt: Search For The Night Stalker (Bruce Seth Green, 1989), a reconstruction of the investigation of a series of brutal murders and rapes in Los Angeles during the summer of 1985, is notable both for portraying a non-white serial killer, and for the reappearance of Frank Salerno who also investigated the Hillside Stranglers. The Night Stalker crimes were widely reported in the press as grotesque and sadistic, but the film does not describe them explicitly. Without such a description, the audience has no way to gauge just how grotesque and unusual the crimes were. While the sexual brutality is minimized, the film does make a point of mentioning that the Night Stalker cut out the eyes of one of his victims and took them away. Also in the film there is some discussion of the Satanic symbols found in the apartments of some victims.

Technology is the way to catch serial killers according to the film.

Better To Reign In Hell

Fingerprints are found in a stolen car used by the Night Stalker and by using the $25 million Cal-ID computer he is identified as Richard Munoz Ramirez, because of his history of petty crimes. Phillip Carlo, in his book *The Night Stalker* (1996), reveals that this 'official' version of the story is not true. The police had already identified a 'Rick,' 'Ricardo' or 'Richard Ramirez' as a suspect in the case, and when the print was found, it was taken to Sacramento and all of the Ramirez files were *manually* searched.[65] Again, like most crime dramas, the film simplifies a complicated investigation to provide an unquestionable resolution and concludes the story at the arrest of the criminal rather than at the end of the trial. The simplification of investigative procedures tends to reinforce conservative ideologies supporting increased police budgets, because it is the focusing of police resources which appears to solve cases.

To Catch A Killer (Eric Till, 1991) is based on the investigation in Chicago in the late 1970s of John Wayne Gacy, the Killer Clown, and highlights the idea that a single dedicated police officer can bring a criminal to justice through his own efforts, despite bureaucratic restraints. It also underlines the point made in many 'trauma dramas' that any problem can be solved by focusing bureaucratic resources. Gacy himself was offended by the production of a TV docu-drama about him. He wrote to Fox Broadcasting, the director Eric Till, and actor Brian Dennehy, who was to play Gacy, protesting that the film was a "fraud"[66] and "fantasy garbage."[67] Dennehy took Gacy's alarm as an endorsement of the film's accuracy, stating "This picture must work."[68] As with *Out of the Darkness*, there is no mention of the other people who were implicated as being involved in the murders. There is only Gacy, the criminal mastermind behind the murders of thirty-three young men in a respectable suburban community. However, Detective Joe Kozenczak who took most of the credit in the film for capturing Gacy openly admitted that he believed others had been involved in the murders.[69]

The film was littered with inaccuracies and inconsistencies, and a newspaper column in Chicago asked readers to write in with errors they noticed in *To Catch A Killer*. Viewers observed cars appeared in the film that did not exist in the 1970s, as did cell phones and police officers with Canadian accents (the film was shot in Ontario). As the film nears its conclusion and Gacy feels the evidence building against him, and responds by drinking heavily and using drugs. His arrest is preceded by a car chase, no doubt added to introduce some dynamism into a tedious script, but this ending distorts reality. When Gacy was actually arrested, he was sitting at a stop light in a car that was being driven by one of his employees.

One of the most interesting inaccuracies, which carries a great deal of cinematic effect, was simply in the selection of actors to play the main roles. Brian Dennehy, who was cast to play Gacy, is 6' 4" while the real Gacy is only 5' 9," and Michael Riley who played Kozenczak is 5' 8" and the real Kozenczak is 6' 5" tall. This subtly alters the viewers' perception of the confrontations between the two characters, making Kozenczak seem more vulnerable, and therefore heroic, in his determination to catch the killer, and Gacy seem like a bully, and more cowardly as he picks on those around him who are smaller.

Serial Killers and Law & Order Issues as Entertainment

Peter Maiken, who had co-authored *Killer Clown* (1983) about the Gacy crimes, even wrote to one newspaper agreeing with Gacy that the film was a "fantasy." While researching his book Maiken interviewed nearly 200 people, among them virtually every police officer involved in the case—except Kozenczak, who declined. Their collective accounts led Maiken to see a very different series of events, and in his opinion Joe Kozenczak did not deserve credit for solving the crimes.[70] Despite this the film closes with an on-screen message that the methods used by detective Kozenczak to catch Gacy became the textbook case study used by the FBI agents which they in turn taught to state and local police.

To coincide with the broadcast, Gacy agreed to break his twelve-year silence and to be interviewed by Walter Jacobson for CBS, and Mike Harvey of CBS assured Gacy that the interviews would put forward his side of the story.[71] Evidently Gacy trusted Harvey and two-and-a-half hours of interview material was recorded. After seeing the TV broadcast of the film and the interview Gacy was incensed. Less than eighteen minutes of the interview was used, and Gacy felt it had been cut in such a way as to change the context of his answers and all of the information and discussion of the inconsistencies of the case were omitted. Writing to Harvey, Gacy accused him of making promises which were "a lot of bullshit."[72] Using simplification and avoiding any doubts about the investigation, the film reassures the public that justice was done. However, it is at the expense of a fuller understanding of the case.

The distortions in docudramas reached a peak with William Friedkin's film *Rampage*, based on the Richard Chase Vampire of Sacramento killings. The film was originally made for release in 1987, but the De Laurentis Entertainment Group's bankruptcy meant that *Rampage* remained unseen in the US until it was recut and released in 1992. The original 1987 version of the film, never shown in the US, was, however, released on video in Europe. The European video release did not promote the film as having been based on a 'true story,' but when released in the US in 1992 an added on-screen message informs viewers that the story they are about to see is "*inspired* by true events" (emphasis added). In reality, neither version of Friedkin's film reflects the investigation of the Chase murders with any degree of accuracy.

A comparison between the limited video release in Europe and the US-released version in 1992 shows a number of substantial and important changes made to the film, to make the film more palatable to the audience, not to make it a more realistic or honest account of a murder investigation. The 1987 version of *Rampage* was, according to the director, a "very ambivalent" film, setting the scene for "an energetic debate in which issues of sanity and personal responsibility are dramatically discussed,"[73] but the 1992 version was a reactionary and paranoid attack on the insanity defense. Friedkin believed the screenplay he initially proposed was a "very risky, very uncommercial subject," and that very few studios would have considered financing it. However, for someone who appeared genuinely to want to make his screenplay into a film, Friedkin's vision went astray somewhere. He commented, "I did know when I started to make it, but as I see it [now] I'm not sure it's clear at all."[74]

Better To Reign In Hell

Early in his life Friedkin had been an idealistic opponent of capital punishment, beginning his filmmaking career with the documentary *The People Versus Paul Crump* (1962) which saved Paul Crump from the electric chair. But with age, he obviously became more uncertain. By the time he came to make *Rampage*, Friedkin said, "I think the notion of the insanity plea has gotten way out of hand,"[75] and his feeling toward capital punishment became more ambivalent as a result. Where the 1987 cut was uncertain in its focus, the 1992 version presents a "chillingly effective" and "horrifyingly matter-of-fact"[76] account of an unforgiving retributionist justice system. Michael Biehn, who played assistant District Attorney Anthony Fraser, claimed that initially William Friedkin did not want to make a statement with *Rampage*, "But he found out that audiences didn't want to come out of the movie saying 'Jesus, was he right? Was he wrong?' They wanted to be told that the system is fucked up! And once they were told that, the movie started to get very good test scores in previews."[77] Evidently, the story 'inspired' by Richard Chase was subsequently shaped by existing audience prejudices and a decade of paranoid political rhetoric amplifying fear of crime. It was this New Right vision of crime that was more evident than the director's vision in an attempt to make an artistic or commercial product. The most obvious difference between the two versions of the same film, by the same director, is in their resolutions; in the 1987 version (only released in Europe) Fraser is ultimately opposed to the death penalty, but in the 1992 version of *Rampage* the case convinces Fraser that the death penalty is a justified punishment.

Richard Chase, when portrayed in *Rampage*, is renamed Charlie Reece (Alex McArthur), and is said to be a sexually-motivated killer, although it is never graphically shown or made clear why he is labeled such. This reflects the same Freudian interpretation of crimes as that promoted by the FBI in their serial sex killer study—which included Richard Chase. The idea of 'random' and 'stranger' violence is also emphasized when it is asserted that Reece picks his victims by "accident." Numerous basic factual inconsistencies exist in both versions of the film, such as Reece's identification by the husband of one of his victims, when Chase was actually identified by a woman, with whom he had gone to high school, who chanced to see him behaving very strangely a few days before the murders. For dramatic effect, a fictional pursuit is introduced into the film where police officers pursue the suspect from the garage where he works, and the chase eventually ends in a children's' playground, where Reece is arrested. After his arrest the police search his mother's house, where he lives. Richard Chase, however, lived alone, a fact which was vital to his mental degeneration resulting in the crimes he committed. Building on Reece living at home, the narrative goes on to paint a picture of a dysfunctional family where he witnessed his father abusing his mother, and after his father died he was smothered by his domineering, and mentally unstable, mother. The powerful mother image was a prominent feature of Reagan's rhetoric in the 1960s when he claimed that 'momism' was undermining American values. An earlier extreme version of the image was sensationalized by Robert Bloch in his novel *Psycho* (1959), which permanently changed the popular conception of mentally disturbed sex killers. In the film the basement of Reece's mother's house, where he lives, is littered with Nazi regalia and an assortment of human and animal organs, as was the home of Ed Gein, upon whom Bloch based his Norman Bates character. The police discovery of his hoard simultaneously alienates the audience from any feelings of sympathy for Reece and emphasizes his guilt.

In one scene the defense attorney is trying to plea-bargain with Fraser, offering a guilty plea in return for a life sentence in prison or a hospital, pointing out that accepting the plea would save the state a lot of money by avoiding the expense of further investigation and the cost of the trial. In response Fraser angrily cites an extreme case of a man who was released from hospital in 1980 (by that time, Richard Chase was actually dead) and then raped a twelve year-old girl, cutting off her arms and leaving her to die. The type of example cited by Fraser is exactly the sort of atypical case used by victims' rights groups to support their claims and provoke public reaction, even though such grotesque mutilation murders are obviously shocking because they happen so rarely. Symbolically representing the rights of the victim, Fraser encourages Mr Tippet (Royce D Applegate) to testify so the jury can see the pain he suffered because of the murder of his wife and child. To force Tippet's decision, he threatens that if he does not testify, Reece could be acquitted or found not guilty by reason of insanity and released someday from hospital. Fraser's threat devalues the investigative procedures of law enforcement, which had been very effective and efficient in the Chase investigation, and the criminal justice system which Fraser represents. Fraser's threat exaggerates the value of victim testimony, and reflects the shift in emphasis in criminal proceedings to that advocated by Reagan and numerous conservative interest groups. Reece's escape from custody by killing two of his guards emphasizes how dangerous he is, and his subsequent sacrilegious murder of a priest, whose blood he virtually bathes in, underlines the lack of remorse for his crimes and the complete absence of respect for society's values. This was an outrage to many following a decade of fundamentalist religious fervor. When he is recaptured, the judge rules that information about his escape is not relevant in the current trial, outraging viewers and bolstering Fraser's depiction of the legal system as unresponsive to victims. Unfortunately, Friedkin's work is only 'inspired' by the Vampire of Sacramento case and in reality Chase never escaped, nor even tried to. He never killed any guards or priests, and he was considered a relatively docile prisoner.

Reece's mental state is a central feature of his crimes and of the way in which his case is argued at trial. Medical experts are enlisted by defense and prosecution in the trial to argue over Reece's life. Their medical diagnosis of Reece's illness will only be used to determine whether he was, at the time of his crimes, capable of understanding that his actions were wrong but, before the trial, it is made clear to the audience that the psychiatrists are motivated by self-interest and personal ideology, not by concern for the criminal justice system.

The expert for the prosecution, Dr Paul Rudin (Roy London), is visited at

his offices at Sunnyslopes hospital by the defense expert, Dr Benjamin Keddie (John Harkins). Rudin admits that the hospital is operating "well beyond capacity," treating fifty or sixty patients, and that it is difficult for the hospital to maintain a suitable standard of care. The conversation soon turns to the subject of Charlie Reece who had been a patient in Rudin's hospital up until less than six months before the killings began. He was released by a staff doctor who did not see the potential for violence in Reece's behavior, undermining the audience's faith in medical expert opinion. The script refers to budget cuts which made it preferable for the hospital to release Reece, rather than continue treatment. No attempt is made to consider political accountability. Keddie pressures Rudin into altering his diagnosis of Reece, to take some time and go over his files again and look for indications of his persecution delusions and paranoid schizophrenia so they could co-ordinate their presentation. If it is known that Reece was certified and then released from the hospital, Rudin would be sued. At this point, *Rampage* again obviously deviates from the facts of the case. Richard Chase committed his murders in 1977—78, but *Rampage* is set in 1987, almost a decade later. The time difference permits Keddie to cite John Hinckley's assassination attempt on Reagan, and the following lawsuit against Hinckley's psychiatrist as a precedent. The psychiatrist, who was sued for being unable to predict Hinckley's future violent behavior, was, according to Keddie, something to which Rudin should pay attention. The film's concern with the insanity defense was brought about by the director's interest in the trials of John Wayne Gacy and John Hinckley. Friedkin felt that Gacy being found sane, despite being convicted of thirty-three murders, whereas Hinckley was declared insane for failing to commit a murder, was "a serious blip in the system."[78] Keddie, the defense expert, makes clear his intentions when he tells Rudin that they are the only thing that stands between Reece and death and under those circumstances, "We have every right to stretch the truth if necessary to save his life." This is an example of Ronald Markman's point that "a lot of psychiatrists and psychologists allow their personal, social, or political opinions to color their evaluations." But the same could obviously be said of the FBI experts from the BSU and the 'experts' they consult within the mental health profession. Markman also believes that, "generally speaking competent psychiatrists avoid the courtroom"; it is only "marginal players" who are called upon to give evaluations, casting doubts about the credentials of Dr Joel Norris and Dr Park Elliot Dietz. Unfortunately, for Markman, the court assumes the opinions of the marginal 'expert' are just as authoritative as that of a competent psychiatrist.[79] The attack on the legal system in *Rampage* as unresponsive and the depiction of liberal psychologists as scheming ideologues reflects the rightward political shift encouraged by the New Right, but it does nothing to depict the complexities of the insanity defense and only encourages partisan political ignorance.

The most significant change in the film's narrative is the close of the trial. In the original 1987 version of Friedkin's film, the trial gives a glimpse of Reece's frailties when he makes an emotional outburst in court asking for mercy. He acknowledges the terrible things that he has done and that he must be punished, but he ends his plea saying, "If I die now, all I ever did with my life was kill people." It is obvious the Reece *wants* to be something other than a murderer, he wants to try to pay back the families for some of the suffering he caused them. The scene then shifts to Fraser in a helicopter dictating a letter to his superior, district attorney Spencer Whalen (Andy Romano), who advocated seeking the death penalty for Reece. His dictation shows that Fraser is not happy with his role in the prosecution of the case or the charges made. He says:

> After I saw the Ellis house and the Tippetts house, I *wanted* to believe that Reece was legally sane. I came to understand that he understood every atrocity he had committed. I agreed with you that we owed something to the legal system, to the victims. So I set myself up as the avenger of suffering. [emphasis added]

This is the same symbolic role adopted by John Walsh and Ronald Reagan when championing victims' rights. After Reece's medical examination Fraser does not believe Reece is legally sane. Cutting to Reece's cell, just as his lawyer arrives to tell him the results, Fraser's narration continues and the story takes its final turn. Reece lies dead on his bunk, in a pose which Friedkin's shooting script describes as "Christ-like,"[80] and Fraser concludes his dictated message, "I don't believe execution is the answer. I don't know what the answer is... I don't want to kill this man." Ultimately Reece overdosed on his medication just as Richard Chase had done, one of the few factually correct aspects of the film, probably having saved his medicine in a desperate attempt to stop the voices in his head. All of this is removed from the recut *Rampage*, presenting the audience with a radically different message.

In the 1992 version of *Rampage*, Fraser shouts his closing statement, which focuses on the same victims' rights which the New Right emphasized. He asserts that, "The life of an innocent human being is worth more than the life of a murderer." Reece is found guilty on all counts but his lawyer whispers to him, "It isn't over yet. It's only the first part of the trial. We still have a shot at saving your life. We can show them that you weren't responsible." This scene is *not* in the 1987 version. A medical examination is ordered for Reece to look for chemical abnormalities in his brain, and the result of the test shows "a picture of madness" and as a consequence he is admitted to a mental hospital. The recut version removed Reece's courtroom speech, Fraser's narrated memo, and Reece's overdose and death. In their place is a scene of Reece writing a letter to Mr Tippett telling him that he did not kill his wife out of malice, and she is now in a better place. Ending the letter, he invites Mr Tippetts to visit him so they can discuss things further. Closing with an on-screen message, the 1992 version ominously informs the audience that: "Charles Reece has served four years in a state mental health facility. He has had one hearing to determine his eligibility for release. His next is due in six months." This implies that Reece, despite obviously being guilty and having shown no remorse for his action, by claiming insanity could be released back into society after only a few years in a mental hospital. The audience is left in no doubt that there are serious flaws in the American legal system. However, Ronald Markman believes that, "in highly political cases, the system finds the will to keep dangerous people behind bars."[81]

In his study of Friedkin's career, Thomas Clagett concludes, "In *Rampage* [1987] Friedkin raises important, volatile issues and resolves them timidly."[82] The film fails to involve or engage the audience. The 1992 recut version of the film is more determined to direct the viewers, pointing out the scheming of psychologists and the devious nature of criminals. The original *Rampage* had shown "not a fucked-up legal system but a terminally fucked-up world."[83] However, when recut, *Rampage* "becomes a tirade against a judicial system that would spare someone like Reece by deeming him criminally insane." Associating the film's fictional storyline, no matter how loosely, with real events undermines confidence in the judicial system and in the motivation of expert medical testimony. In her review for the *New York Times*, Jane Maslin describes the re-edited version as a "polemical attack on the insanity defense," powerful enough to present a "cogent and disturbing case even to those who did not share the film's political views."[84] By distorting reality until the only thing identifiable is a vague series of crimes, and Friedkin presents an essentially fictional story which supports the New Right and FBI crime agenda.

The crimes exploited by Friedkin in *Rampage* had occurred several years before he began making his film, but as market competition increased, the time taken for a story to move from headline to primetime decreased. In 1992 Jeffrey Dahmer was arrested and Donald Evans began confessing to dozens

Serial Killers and Law & Order Issues as Entertainment

of murders, but it was the case of Aileen Wournos, falsely described by FBI spokespersons and the media as the first female serial killer, which was quickly turned into a docudrama and released the following year. *Overkill: The Aileen Wuornos Story* (Peter Levin, 1993) leaves the audience in no doubt that the film is based on an already-familiar case, but John O'Connor in his *New York Times* review concludes that the film offers the viewer "fudged details and standard banalities."[85] The police pursuing her are sympathetic and patient, unlike the real investigating officers. The familiar idea of a cycle of abuse, where the abused becomes the abuser, is presented to the audience by the wife of one of the detectives when she says, "It's ironic, now the biggest case of your life comes along and you're hunting down a victim of child abuse." Loaded with clichés and speculation, the film adequately reflected newspaper reporting of the Wuornos case describing her as a serial killer, a label which even the FBI attributed to Wuornos. This shows either a serious misunderstanding of their own definition or a desire to attract the public's attention.

In his comedy *Serial Mom* (1994), John Waters lampoons the conventions of the true crime film and challenges their authenticity from the opening on-screen message: "This film is a true story. The screenplay is based on court testimony, sworn declarations, and hundreds of interviews conducted by the film makers." A complete fabrication, but the film is no less factual than many docudramas, and there is the usual artificial concern for innocent individuals whose names are changed "in the interests of a larger truth." The message continues, "No-one involved in the crimes has received any form of financial compensation," recognizing the profit motive inherent in the genre. The film subverts American ideals of family, suburban lifestyles and public interest in legal issues. Inverting the FBI serial killer stereotype beyond recognition, Waters depicts a glamorous all-American suburban mother, Beverly Sutphin (Kathleen Turner), as a loveable psychopath who commits murder to avenge transgressions of family values or her conservative sense of social etiquette. Paradoxically, she is prepared to make obscene phone-calls, sends anonymous hate mail to her neighbor, and sings Barry Manilow love songs as she drives to kill someone, but she will not read about current films because they are too violent. Peter Travers, a critic for *Rolling Stone*, found that *Serial Mom* evoked the same atmosphere as David Lynch's *Blue Velvet* (1986), "in the way darkness lurks just below the surface of sunny suburbia."[86]

Alongside the proliferation of 'true story' films of dubious documentary authenticity were Reality TV shows, promoted as a new type of program, using real video news footage and dramatic reconstructions of shocking and sensational crimes to lure viewers. Reality TV was a hybrid program format. Once restricted to the fringes of syndicated television as the worst excess of the schedules, it was adopted by shows such as *America's Most Wanted*, and *Unsolved Mysteries*. It took the news, or public service format, and on top of that the producers superimposed entertainment elements, effectively creating the "televisual equivalent of the wanted poster."[87] They updated a familiar cultural artifact from the wild west for the 1980s. More importantly, they were cheap and easy to make and attracted young "viewers reared on the jump-cut style of MTV."[88] Thomas Herwitz, the Fox executive in charge of *America's Most Wanted*, boasted, "we're adding millions of eyes and ears to the law-enforcement efforts in this country."[89] Those in charge of the Fox Network's news stations were not happy with the new series and distanced themselves from it, and one news executive said, "listening to those West Coast guys saying things like, 'We're creating brutal video'—it's not the way we cover news... News is not 'brutal video.'"[90]

There are obvious differences, however. The 'reality' shows are, "a made for the masses infomercial whose makers cleanse their conscience with thoughts of do-gooding while turning personal tragedy into a ratings puller."[91] John Walsh, the show's host, called it "television with a social purpose," a way for the public to get involved in crime fighting "without resorting to vigilantism,"[92] and Robert Ressler thought the program was "often helpful to law enforcement."[93] However, it was also one of the most controversial programs on TV.[94] While wanted posters simply distributed information, 'reality' shows re-enacted social transgression for peak time audiences' viewing pleasure, sensationalizing the crimes to attract the largest audience possible in a highly competitive, deregulated industry. The Fox network was delighted with the audience figures for *America's Most Wanted*, even though a similar audience share on any other network would have meant the programs' cancellation.[95]

John Walsh saw things in more populist terms saying, "I think people are eager to watch and call us with information because they are feeling helpless. There are 280,000 felons out there, and this program gives the audience the sense that they can do something about [it]."[96] This might have been good for getting audience ratings but the distinction between fact and fiction was blurred for the viewer. Actors depicted actual crimes in conjunction with film news footage, photographs, and interviews with police or participants. Audiences were encouraged to participate in the show by making telephone calls to special television studio numbers with information related to the crime reconstruction. According to Jack Breslin, *America's Most Wanted* was "a chance to explore the human passions and emotions of crime and its victims while helping police capture the fugitives involved."[97]

The pilot of *America's Most Wanted* was aired on the Fox network on February 5, 1988. Two days before, William Sessions, the new Director of the FBI, had appeared in a press conference at the FBI headquarters with John Walsh, the show's host, and Michael Linder, the show's producer. Sessions endorsed the citizen co-operation aspect of *America's Most Wanted* and stressed the show's potential benefit to the public. The show would also help viewers see an accurate portrayal of how the FBI worked and reassure them about the Bureau's role in law enforcement. Bureau opinion was divided, with some agents being in favor of using the media to help catch fugitives, especially those "making a trail of terror across several states." In the end, it was the belief that public support was needed which won out. FBI Chief of Operations, Buck Revell, asserted, "if this show could inform, not inflame, public sentiment against crime, it could help all law enforcement."[98] Wiley Thompson, a Bureau spokesman, made it clear that the FBI viewed the show as an extension of their own publicity campaigns and that, "The FBI is not in the entertainment business. Our cooperation is based on the fact that we would like to solicit citizen cooperation in trying to apprehend fugitives. Thus far, we are very pleased with the program and the results."[99] However, Thompson also reported that the FBI would evaluate the program from week to week to ensure it met with the appropriate standards for the Bureau's continued co-operation.[100] In 1991, the *Los Angeles Daily News* reported that the FBI had an exclusive, unpublicized deal with the producers of *America's Most Wanted* and *Unsolved Mysteries*, which meant that those shows would be the first to announce additions to the FBI Ten Most Wanted list. An LA spokeswoman for the Bureau, Karen Gardner, told *Daily News* reporters that, "The day you guys can deliver up sixty million households, we'll work exclusively with you." Swanson Carter, FBI Chief of Special Productions added, "The element of surprise is exactly how we capture them.... We go where we think we have the best shot." Broadcast nationally, the show provided an efficient way for the Bureau to publicize its fugitives.[101]

Bureau involvement in the show had presented "severe ethical and legal problems" for John Otto, who was acting FBI Director in the time between William Webster's resignation and Sessions' appointment. It was noted that the Bureau's desire to "make desperately sure" that it was accurately represented took precedence for them, but to *America's Most Wanted*, "Some producers and programmers would call that censorship; others consider it the price of cooperation."[102] An FBI public affairs officer acted as a liaison between the Bureau and the show's producers. Once a fugitive had been selected, the liaison would put the producers in contact with the appropriate FBI agent who was assigned to the case. The agent would provide all of the information, pictures, and public records necessary for the filming, as well as acting as advisor. On the night of the broadcast, the agent would attend the show to follow up on information phoned in by viewers. A seven-city promotional tour was organized for the program, along with a $100,000 print advertising campaign. The tour covered as many talk shows and radio interviews as could be arranged, along with evening news features and a series of photo sessions.[103]

However, whatever benefit the FBI association might offer television producers, both *America's Most Wanted* and *Unsolved Mysteries* were "powerful tools used by the FBI press office for finding fugitives." Between the two shows, they located about fifty fugitives per year.[104] Crime coverage in Reality TV, like that of newspapers, "reinforces the symbolism of the dominant social order."[105] John Walsh was seen by the public as a victim's advocate, and an advocate of children's rights. After his initial disagreements with the FBI and Justice Department for their unwillingness to become involved in his son's abduction, Walsh gained an air of authority by serving as a consultant to the Justice Department.[106]

The criminals on *America's Most Wanted* exemplified human viciousness, they threatened the collective integrity of whole communities, and they violated the moral boundaries set by common consent. It was usually 'high status' criminals who were involved, the violent crimes they committed were against people, not property, and neither *America's Most Wanted* or *Unsolved Mysteries* dealt with corporate or political crimes. While the vignettes presented the victims in a sympathetic way, the social histories of the criminals were caricatures of existing stereotypes.[107] Walsh's rhetoric endorsing victims' rights was exactly the same as Reagan's. He saw the criminal justice system as being in chaos, with victims occupying the lowest priority and the rights of the accused being emphasized, ensuring repeat offenders were treated too lightly. In his view, "Too often, the more violent a crime the more the defendant's rights are protected, in contrast to the needs of the victim." Rehabilitation for him was "sometimes [an] impossible endeavor," which outweighed the victim's need for "fairness and retribution."[108] Like Reagan, Walsh's concern was not with justice, it was with revenge. Acting as contemporary morality plays, the crimes *America's Most Wanted* presented symbolized the dangers which threatened the established social order, and underlined a sense of modern danger, in a world where anyone could be a victim or a criminal.[109]

Good ratings and "substantial, prestigious media coverage" helped to sell *America's Most Wanted* to the public, but more importantly to advertisers, who had initially seen it as controversial. Fox Network were delighted with the show's performance and its budget of $125,000 to $140,000 made it a "bargain by network standards."[110] Initial successes of video *vérité* shows put competitive pressures on other networks to introduce tabloid sensationalism into their own magazine shows, largely replacing documentary programming.[111]

America's Most Wanted received many endorsements, mainly from newspapers and right-wing politicians, but it also had a considerable number of critics. James Fox, a criminal justice expert at North Eastern University, focused his criticism on the effect that the fear and suspicion generated by the show caused people to suspect each other as well as strangers.[112] Reality television shows confused their audiences about whether they were news or entertainment. In a Times-Mirror Interest Index in 1989, it was found that half of those surveyed believed *America's Most Wanted* was a news program, with similar results for *Inside Edition* and *A Current Affair*. Younger people, who tend to be lighter consumers of news, approved of the 'reality' television shows as re-enacted events. Older viewers did not have such a broad definition of news and were more skeptical of the fabricated re-enacted events.[113]

Reality TV was criticized by many people. Jonathan Turley, of George Washington University Law School, was not enthusiastic about the new programming format: "All of a sudden we're deputizing millions of people to become police officers, people who have no training, or telling them to become reporters... play Deputy Dawg and maybe you'll get on *I Witness Video*. Or better yet, you'll get on *A Current Affair*, a dead person who filmed his own shooting. But you know, no one's concerned with that because it's good *entertainment*."[114] Journalist Ron Powers, on ABC's *Nightline*, said he saw the show as a new kind of pornography which did not serve any useful purpose,[115] a "noxious" series which "contributed to the cultural acceptance of gunplay as a spectator sport."[116]

However the most serious criticism, in terms of the show's legal consequences, came from Colleen O'Conner of the ACLU. She pointed to the *America's Most Wanted* vignettes which usually depicted crimes which people were suspected of, not convicted. A nationally televised dramatic re-enactment of a crime could seriously undermine the ability of a defendant to get a fair trial. The profiles of criminals on *America's Most Wanted*, like the FBI psychological profiles, gave the appearance of scientific authority without necessarily being correct.[117] O'Connor also believed that the program highlighted the danger of journalism becoming too comfortable in its connection with police agencies.[118] Robin Andersen noted that the police increasingly defined crime and identified issues in law enforcement through the media and in consequence, "Constitutional assumptions about due process and civil liberties, such as protection against unwarranted search and seizure and the presumption of innocence, are antithetical to the crime tabloid formula, which does not conceal its approval of the abuse of police power."[119] In their quest for cheap entertainment, television producers helped to increase the public's misunderstanding of the criminal justice system. In the mutually convenient arrangement between the FBI, the police and the media, producers coached the police in what to say, what lines to repeat for dramatic effect, and how to play to the camera. *America's Most Wanted* also had the dubious honor of being listed by the National Coalition of Television Violence as the most violent primetime television show.[120]

The popularity of reality programs dwindled, and in 1996 Fox claimed that low audience ratings for *America's Most Wanted*, combined with a need to schedule comedies in the Saturday evening timeslot meant the series was to be cancelled. The final episode, a special about the still-unsolved murder of John Walsh's own son Adam, was scheduled for September 21, 1996, with subsequent specials and a film of the program being planned. Walsh accepted the network's decision to cancel the program saying bitterly, "Hollywood's not about public service, it's about making money."[121] In response to the announcement that the show was to be cancelled, Fox received 185,000 letters of protest from the public, fifty-five from members of Congress, thirty-seven from state governors and one from each of the fifty state Attorney Generals.[122] Thomas Constantine, head of the DEA, wrote to Rupert Murdoch claiming that: "The loss of *America's Most Wanted* will be devastating to American law-enforcement efforts and the safety of our communities."[123] They vastly exaggerated the importance of the program. The FBI also released a statement praising the series for "enabling millions of Americans to learn firsthand the nature and terrible consequences of crime in this country."[124] Reprieved from permanent cancellation, after six weeks off the air, *America's Most Wanted* returned on November 9, 1996.[125]

In the competitive market Geraldo Rivera, the 'King of Trash,' attempted a live satellite link with Charles Manson for his *Geraldo* show, and Tribune Entertainment Group (TEG), Rivera's company, approached Robert Ressler to participate. Unable to convince the California Department of Corrections to allow the satellite link, they instead recorded an "extensive" interview with Manson which was broadcast in several parts. Robert Ressler and Jack Levin appeared in the studio to critique what Manson said in the interviews,[126] but Manson had no chance to respond to their comments. TEG also wrote to John Wayne Gacy in February 1988 trying to encourage him to participate in a similar live satellite link-up. Peter Simmons, a representative of TEG, tried to assure Gacy that his company was "not trying to exploit or overly dramatize anything, not you, not your situation, and not society."[127] If that were true it would have been a first for Rivera, and Gacy declined the offer.

Tabloid television thrived on sensational stories, and the crime panics during the 1980s provided a constant stream of allegations of child abuse, 'Satanic' cults, sex crime, and drugs. Often all were rolled together in one episode. Charles Manson was interviewed by Diane Sawyer for *Turning Point* (ABC) along with some of the other Family members, a "ghoulish display" which was considered to be something of a watershed, even for the tabloid shows. An 18.1 per cent rating was enough to place it in the top ten. Choosing Manson as the first feature was seen as a clever ploy by ABC news president Roone Arledge, as a way to immediately draw viewers to the show. The first weekly episode of *Dateline* (NBC) brought serial killer Jeffrey Dahmer and his father together. Previously Dahmer had talked to *Inside Edition* and *Day One*, and *Sally Jesse Raphael* was lined up to be next before the warden at the Columbia Correctional Institute banned future interviews. However, despite the grotesque subject matter, Dahmer's episode of *Dateline* got a 15.3 rating, the show's highest-ever.[128] Frustrated by the mainstream media's 'scrupulous' avoidance of glorifying murderers or understanding them, author Poppy Z Brite criticized *Inside Edition* for the moralizing and unrevealing questions they asked Jeffrey Dahmer.[129]

Despite television companies' attempts to justify the shows and demonstrate their social merit, the American Psychotherapy Association called on its members to boycott appearing on tabloid programs as they promoted the worst elements of popular psychology. Further criticism came from former Secretary of Education, William Bennett, who described the afternoon talk show genre as the "moral equivalent of watching a train wreck."[130] But the programs' ability to attract large audiences and appeal to advertisers meant that they would continue to preach their conservative philosophy, justified by a stream of extreme crimes symbolically undermining traditional social values.

After coverage on TV news programs and tabloid shows (*Inside Edition* and *Hard Copy*), the trial of Aileen Wuornos in 1993 was broadcast on the cable channel Court TV, and later footage from one of her murder trials was condensed, and simplified, into the *Aileen Wournos: Serial Killer or Victim* video. Nick Broomfield's documentary, *Aileen Wuornos: The Selling of a Serial Killer* (1993), importantly highlights the media's role in creating serial killers as a product for the entertainment industry. The traditional joke that a serial killer appoints a lawyer after they find a literary agent is reversed by Broomfield when he suggests that it was the Florida police investigators who were involved with Hollywood producers negotiating for film rights before Wuornos' conviction. In that light, it is obviously advantageous for the police and the entertainment industry to maximize the publicity surrounding the case and the number of victims attributed to Wuornos.

Nick Bougas' documentary *Serial Killers* (1994) shows very graphic pictures of crime victims, sure to cause controversy, but also enabling the audience to see the reality of the crimes, stripped down, without any Hollywood glitz or dramatic reconstructions of reality television. During the narration, Bougas points to some of the ironies of the sensational crimes: Gary Heidnik was receiving 100 per cent disability payments from the military but was still found competent to stand trial and be sentenced to death; Wayne Henley, although still a minor at the time of the 'Candy Man' killings, was sentenced to death as an adult; and Jeffery Dahmer who, despite admitting to his crimes and co-operating fully with the investigation, could only be given consecutive life sentences because Wisconsin has no capital punishment. While Bougas hints at the arbitrariness and politicization of the criminal justice system, the idea is never explicitly discussed.

After Court TV broadcast Jeffrey Dahmer's trial, the 'highlights' were collected and produced as a video, *The Trial of Jeffrey Dahmer* (1992). The documentary shows excerpts from the hearings to determine Dahmer's competency to stand trial for the sixteen murders to which he confessed. Testifying for the prosecution was Dr Park Elliot Dietz, a long time associate of the FBI who collaborated with BSU personnel to write articles for professional journals. The only defense expert shown on the video is Dr Dorothy Otnow Lewis. Robert Ressler, who had recently retired from the FBI, is not shown in the documentary but he also testified for the defense stating that he did not believe that Dahmer was responsible for his actions. The judge ruled that Ressler did not have the required expertise to make such an assertion. The idea that an associate of the Bureau and an FBI 'expert' can both work from the same theories but develop completely opposite opinions raises questions about the authority of the experts and the basis of their theories. Ressler was viewed by the trial judge as being an expert in the psychology of killers at large, but he was not capable of presenting an authoritative opinion of a captured offender. Another documentary which attempts to examine the conventional media and political versions of a serial killer story is *Confessions of a Serial Killer* (1993), focusing on Henry Lee Lucas, who enjoyed his time in the media spotlight. To Lucas,

> It's like being a movie star. You're just playing the part... Make out you're the worst serial killer in the history of the United States and that's what I did... The news media would come running. Interview after interview... I started staying on television twenty-four hours a day. I mean it changed me and it got so that I thought I was the biggest movie star in this country.[131]

The documentary examines Lucas' confessions and his attorney's detailed catalogue of discrepancies in the case, including the Texas Rangers ignoring evidence that showed Lucas was innocent of certain crimes. Lucas' attorney, Viz Feazell, was also indicted on various charges, including murder, but in court he was acquitted and found to have been framed by the Rangers. In a subsequent lawsuit against a Dallas TV station Feazell was awarded damages of $58 million.

While Bundy's final confession supported the arguments of anti-pornography Christian groups, another serial sex killer inadvertently provided advocates of increasingly punitive punishments with a focus for their crusade. A major embarrassment occurred for the Illinois correctional authorities when parts of a video tape which had been made secretly in Stateville maximum security prison was broadcast, initially by local TV stations, but later on network news. The tape was two hours long and had been made over a two-day period in 1988 by Richard Speck and two other inmates using video equipment reserved for staff training. Speck, who became notorious for raping and murdering eight nurses in Chicago one night in July 1966, had a prison job as a painter which allowed him to move more freely than other prisoners. Although constant supervision was still required, the existence of the video proved that his supervision by prison authorities was lax. The least shocking part of the video was Speck's admission that he had committed the Chicago murders, for the first time dropping his claims that he had suffered from drug-induced amnesia. He showed no remorse or contrition for the crimes and, as if that was not bad enough for the authorities, Speck strips off his work jumpsuit to reveal his blue female underwear. In the video he also snorts cocaine and engages in sex with another prisoner while telling the camera that he has had the time of his life in prison. He says, "If only they knew how much fun I was having in here they would turn me loose." He continues to boast about the number of lovers he has had, but he could not count high enough to be sure of the exact number. The sudden appearance of the tape raised questions about the prison's security and supervision of inmates, and Republican representative Peter Roskam was suitably outraged, declaring it a "disaster," and not what the taxpayers were bargaining for.[132] The video was more shocking than anything a tabloid show could possibly have staged, and provided advocates of a more punitive prison system with propaganda for their cause as well as boosting viewing figures of news stations broadcasting segments of the video.

The connection between law-enforcement and the entertainment industry was evident initially in newspaper crime reporting and developed alongside technological advances. Given the media's reliance on the police for factual information and its dependence on rare and sensational cases to sell papers, it is not surprising that a conservative and moralizing tone was adopted, especially in regard to crimes which symbolically challenged America social values. While docudramas, Reality TV and tabloid chat shows continued in the tradition of print reporting, they attempt to claim authenticity by enlisting the assistance of law-enforcement agencies in various capacities. With increased competition, news programs also incorporated dramatic elements of crime drama until the boundary between fact and fiction became blurred. Similarly, in an increasingly competitive market for fictional works, some authors sought out the FBI's assistance to boost the credibility of their work, and this provided the Bureau with an opportunity to draw on familiar elements of the Jack The Ripper case, the myth of the G-Man action detective, and the serial killer interviews which they conducted to produce a potent 'new' image for the FBI.

Not So Much *Apocalypse Now,* as Apocalypse From Now On

Law & Order in the 1990s

GEORGE BUSH, REAGAN'S VICE-PRESIDENT, WAS ELECTED president in 1989 with no obvious attempt to build a political persona of his own. He continued implementing the New Right agenda, and exploited the crime issue and the 'Dirty Harry' Callahan cliché established by his predecessor in his campaign against Michael Dukakis saying, "Clint Eastwood's answer to violent crime is 'Go ahead, make my day.' My opponent's answer is slightly different. His motto is, 'Go ahead, have a nice weekend.'"[1] Bush was referring to Willie Horton, a black man serving life without parole who was included on a furlough program in Massachusetts where Dukakis was governor. While on a weekend release, Horton burglarized the home of a white couple in Maryland, assaulting a man and raping his fiancée, whom politicians and the media depicted as "decent, middle-class people, randomly victimized."[2] After a decade of serial sex killers, child abductions and increasing fear of random crime, Horton's case seemed all too preventable.

Numerous lurid reports of random crimes involving rape, murder and serious injury were publicized by the media, provoking emotional rather than rational debate, "absorbing attention, energy, and funds" which could have been used more effectively to support serious methods of crime prevention. David Anderson refers to laws, policies and practices designed to vent communal outrage rather than reduce crime as "expressive justice," which was reflected in the Calvinist idea of 'evil' promoted in the 1980s by the New Right. While reinforcing traditional religious and social values, "expressive justice" denied any possibility of rehabilitation and the rhetoric focused on punishing and confining deviants. The crimes, which were often perpetrated by black repeat offenders on innocent middle-class white victims, added an ugly racial slant. Random crimes against middle-class whites did not constitute a majority of crimes, but news reports ignited a public outcry that could not be ignored by city officials.[3]

Lee Atwater, Bush's 1988 campaign manager, wanted to isolate a few issues to identify Dukakis as a "liberal weirdo," out of step with mainstream American thought. As governor, Dukakis vetoed a law that required teachers to lead students in the Pledge of Allegiance, and even members of Bush's campaign team admitted that in doing so Dukakis was technically right. But Roger Ailes, one of Bush's advisors, also knew that the American public would react instinctively to the issue and the Republican strategists used it to stigmatize Dukakis as unpatriotic. In June 1988, the July issue of *Reader's Digest* was distributed, featuring a provocatively titled article by Robert James Bidinotto. The article, "Getting away with murder," focused on the Horton case, exaggerating the facts for "lurid" effect, but also giving the case legitimacy as a political campaign issue. News reporters and Democrats suspected high-level co-ordination between Republicans and executives in the traditionally conservative magazine. Defending the article Kenneth Tomlinson, executive editor at *Reader's Digest*, said the article was rushed into the July issue to avoid publishing it when the election campaign was underway. Despite Republican denials, Lee Atwater boasted that Bidinotto's article would spread the story nationwide and lead voters to believe that Horton really was Dukakis's running mate.[4]

Bush exploited the Horton case at every opportunity, most memorably in a thirty second TV commercial, which broadcast a picture of Horton taken after a highway chase and shootout. In the picture Horton was unshaven, slack-jawed and had one eye closed, all of which combined to make him look subhuman, and even Horton had to admit he looked "incredibly wicked."[5] The voice-over accompanying the advert announced, "Bush supports the death penalty for first-degree murderers. Dukakis not only opposes the death penalty, he allowed first-degree murderers to have weekend passes from prison."[6] The Republican strategy was to personalize the issue. A fundraising letter sent to Maryland Republicans went so far as to print pictures of Horton and Dukakis and posed the question: "Is this your pro-family team for 1988?"[7] At the Illinois Republican State Convention, Bush continued his exaggerated onslaught, claiming that Dukakis had let "Murderers out on vacation to terrorize innocent people.... Democrats can't find it in their hearts to get tough on criminals... I think Governor Dukakis owes the American people an explanation of why he supports this outrageous program."[8] Also a flyer was circulated in Illinois by a Republican group, which read: "All the murderers and rapists and drug pushers and child molesters in Massachusetts vote for Michael Dukakis. We in Illinois can vote against him."[9]

In Illinois convicted serial sex killer John Wayne Gacy complained that Bush was making use of his name in campaigns and filed a suit for $2 million accusing Bush, Associated Press and several other organizations for using his name in campaign literature. Bush's campaign literature wrongly suggested that Gacy, who had been convicted of more murders than anyone else in American history, would be eligible for weekend passes under a work-release program, the same as that which permitted Willie Horton to be freed in Massachusetts, if Dukakis was elected[10]—although this was an absurd claim. Gacy faced twelve death penalties and twenty-one life sentences, but the Bush rhetoric raised questions about the so-called 'revolving door' criminal justice system.

Eventually Dukakis responded to the allegations of Republicans with his own adverts highlighting the distortion of facts and pointing out that in the 1960s, while Reagan was Governor, the state of California operated a furlough program and some prisoners committed crimes while on release. Also, during

Law & Order in the 1990s

Reagan's presidency, federal prisons operated a similar system. Mimicking the Republican tactics, Dukakis found equivalent criminals to Horton with which to embarrass Bush, the most notable being a resident in a federally funded halfway house in Texas who raped and murdered a minister's wife. Ironically, Bush, then Vice-President, visited the house to present a presidential award.[11] Although the Democrats attempted to fight back by seizing the crime issue early in the campaign, the Republicans took control, exploiting public fear and increasing anger. Because of public fear created by Reagan's apocalyptic rhetoric, crime proposals had been adopted which were enormously expensive and affected already limited budgets for schools, health care, education and future economic development.[12]

Public fear of crime was manipulated nationwide to endorse legislation advocating harsher penalties against sexually violent offenders. Stuart Scheingold notes that victim advocacy is rooted in and dependent on "an overheated and fear-ridden political climate" where "sporadic outbursts of public anger" receive unrepresentative attention and at such times, "recourse to simplistic solutions and scapegoating thrives and enlightened political leadership falters."[13] The 1980s were such an overheated political and emotional climate and the legislation produced showed just how limited the solutions being offered were. The 1989 Community Protection Act (CPA) in Washington State drew support from Republicans and feminist criminologists sympathetic to victim advocacy, but the legislation was criticized by a variety of civil liberties groups for introducing preventative detention and for being likely to encourage vigilante violence when residents were notified that convicted violent sex offenders had been released into communities.

Media reporting of predatory sex offenders and serial sex killers was virtually identical. It was claimed both shared the same dysfunctional family histories and uncontrollable deviant urges, and would continue to reoffend, amassing a large number of innocent victims. Rather than allow the sex offenders, potential serial sex killers, the freedom and opportunity to commit more crimes, indefinite detention for offenders who refused treatment seemed a reasonable course of action to many. As with John Walsh's missing children crusade in the 1980s, in Washington State "there is reason to believe that the influence of victim advocacy groups was rooted in the horror of a particularly appalling crime." Scheingold's study concluded that in Washington state, the "legislative success of victim advocacy was closely associated with the male organ," specifically the sexual mutilation of a Tacoma boy, which provided conservative legislators with a perfect opportunity to push through their policies. Libertarians viewed the CPA as a threat to the criminal justice system and the attention paid to victim advocacy groups as responding to victims' punitive impulses rather than preventative justice. Furthermore the CPA ensures that reintegration of sex offenders into society after they have served their sentences will be virtually impossible, excluding them from ever becoming productive members of society, a factor that was acknowledged by some advocates.[14]

The lifetime registration requirement of the CPA made sure society never forgave or forgot the offence. Families of sex offenders were frightened about what would happen if the public learned a relative of theirs had been convicted. The potential backlash against them, and the disgrace, led some to commit suicide.[15] John Reinstein, legal director of the Massachusetts ACLU, says sex offender registration laws are unconstitutional and are a "facile and largely ineffectual attempt to deal with a complex problem, that seems likely in the long run to do little good and much harm—not just to sex offenders, but to their families and their victims as well."[16]

Another consequence of the registration laws has been the expansion of 'rehab ghettoes,' similar to the 'psychiatric ghettoes' of the 1960s and 1970s, areas of cheap housing where drug addicts, alcoholics and ex-convicts live and which have expanded to include sex offenders. Robert Shilling, a detective with the Seattle Police Department special assault team, noted that many criminals were released from prison with nothing more than "a bus ticket and thirty-five dollars,"[17] and as their victims are often relatives, their crimes alienate family members, leaving them isolated. Tim Baker, president of the Capitol Hill Community Council in Seattle, reported that new residents arriving in the area think, "Oh my God, I'm living next to eight sex offenders. As soon as my lease is up, I'm out of here," making it harder to build communities and increasing transience. Often the sex offenders will find themselves in homeless shelters or houses run by social service agencies, meaning poorer neighborhoods will become the focus of higher concentrations of deviants, adding to the transient nature of the neighborhoods.[18]

The Los Angeles riots in 1992 forced urban issues back onto the national political agenda and, predictably, Republicans blamed the riots on the failure of Great Society programs; in contrast the Democrats blamed them on twelve years of Republican denial and neglect. Nationwide the adverse effects of New Right social and economic policies were felt, and had been for some time. In April 1990 the conservative Business Roundtable released a statement saying that:

> In the brief period of the past decade, we have amassed trillions of dollars in debt; we have regressed from being the largest creditor nation in the world to the biggest debtor; we have witnessed the federal deficit absorb over half our net savings; we have become increasingly dependent on foreign capital, inexorably ceding our influence over both our domestic and international policies. And we have embarked upon a course, which cannot be sustained without high cost—economic and social and human.[19]

Their statement does not, however, acknowledge how corporate America encouraged and benefited from the same New Right programs which caused the nation's economic decline. Even long-time Republican strategist Kevin Phillips acknowledged that twelve years of New Right politics had failed to deal with the major issues of law enforcement, race, taxation, fiscal management, and the role of government. Reagan's 'revitalization' of America, like his policies, was short-term and symbolic. Despite New Right promises to reinvigorate

Law & Order in the 1990s

America and vocal boasts of success during the twelve years of the Reagan-Bush era, there was no 'morning in America.'

During the preparations for the 1992 elections, Republicans sought a criminal equivalent of the Willie Horton case to use in Bush's campaign to retain the presidency. Opposition researchers for the Republican Party identified Mario Cuomo, Governor of New York, as the strongest Democratic challenger, and in their investigations they developed information about Arthur Shawcross, the Genese River Killer, a convicted child murderer paroled in 1987 only to kill again in the Rochester area of New York City. Some of the Bush campaign members relished the opportunity to exploit Shawcross, a white serial sex killer, in their rhetoric to demonstrate that the Horton case was not a race issue, but a crime issue. Shawcross had been convicted of manslaughter of a child in 1972 and paroled in 1987 after serving fifteen years of a twenty-five year sentence. Upon release, Shawcross was alleged to have begun killing again until his capture in 1989 but, unlike Horton's attack on innocent middle-class white victims, Shawcross's victims were usually prostitutes, and therefore carried less weight in a symbolic law-and-order debate. Republican researchers noted that Shawcross had been given early release, a fact that they intended to exploit, but with time off for good behavior he was only paroled two years before his full sentence was complete. The real issue in the case was the plea bargain negotiated by the prosecution during Shawcross's trial in 1972, which reduced a murder charge to manslaughter. It was felt by many that the bargain was excessively lenient, and the official who negotiated it incompetent—but he was a Republican.[20]

When Bill Clinton was recognized as the strongest Democratic contender, the Republican opposition researchers again set about finding a suitably embarrassing case to use against him to show he was 'soft on crime.' Initially Charles Lloyd Patterson looked likely to be the Arkansas equivalent of Willie Horton. Patterson was convicted of several charges, including hiring someone to kill his ex-wife's divorce lawyer, and sentenced to forty years, but still qualified for a state furlough program, and while on release he absconded but was recaptured in Texas after commandeering two planes. When his case came to trial, Patterson surprised the court by claiming that Arkansas Republicans had encouraged him to escape, assuring Patterson that if he did he would be "taken care of" by their party. Patterson's allegations were denied by Republican officials, and the jury did not believe him,[21] but his claims made him unsuitable as a symbol of liberal leniency.

Seeking to distance himself from earlier 'liberal' Democratic party policies, Bill Clinton described himself as a "third way" Democrat, a new-styled centrist.[22] His campaign focused on middle class issues, and an editorial in *The Progressive* (December 1992) attacked him for behaving as though there were no poor or homeless people in the country. The editorial went further, predicting that, "Since he knows he'll be hit from the right, it is to his right he will move. And since he, his advisers, and the pundits are interpreting his victory as a vindication of his rightward strategy, there is no reason to expect he will abandon it."[23]

185

Better To Reign In Hell

Seeing the danger of being seen as 'soft on crime,' it has been claimed that Clinton used the execution of Ricky Ray Rector to emphasize his toughness. Merle Black, of Emory University, noted that in southern states the death penalty was used as a litmus test for executive leadership, especially for Democratic candidates, to the extent that he could not think of a Southern politician elected Governor since 1976 who had not been in favor of capital punishment.[24] Rector shot three men in an argument in 1981 and later killed a police officer. While attempting to commit suicide, he inflicted massive amounts of brain damage on himself but still survived. Despite having an IQ in the sixties, erratic behavior, and childlike comprehension of his situation, Rector was tried as a normal person and sentenced to death.[25] To many commentators it seemed incomprehensible that Rector's execution would be carried out, but when his appeals ran out only governor Clinton could spare his life. In an election year, political posturing to deprive the Bush campaign of a powerful issue decided Clinton's response. Carl Stern, Janet Reno's former public affairs director, said Clinton and his aides were determined they would usurp the Republican's lead in law-and-order issues, and he refused to issue an order of clemency.[26] It was immediately obvious to anyone concerned that you cannot get much tougher on crime than executing someone in Rector's condition.[27] Jeff Rosenzweig, Rector's lawyer, believed that the execution would be remembered as a "disgrace to the state," and wondered, "At what level of disability do you kill people?"[28] Jay Jacobson, head of the Arkansas ACLU, summed up the symbolic value of the execution when he declared, "If you can kill Rector, you can kill anybody."[29] Because of Clinton's draconian stance on the death penalty, the crime issue was relegated to the background in the 1992 election, and family values and economic issues came to the forefront. Without the crime issue Bush's campaign had no focus, and it was hoped that Clinton's victory would change policy direction.

Clinton's 1994 Anti-Crime Bill was the most extensive legislation of its kind in American history, allocating $30 billion, but no new ideas were put forward to change the economic or social structures that generate crime and violence. Instead the policies and media response remained within the conventional parameters to 'get tough' on crime.[30] The federal death penalty was expanded, with a further fifty additional offences being included and sound bites dominated the public discourse. The Anti-Crime Bill also gave the FBI authority to operate their Combined DNA Index System (CODIS) and set national standards for forensic DNA testing, the latest scientific advance being promoted by the Bureau. The anti-crime bill also required every state to establish a register of sex offenders and a mechanism for alerting the public to their whereabouts, and any state failing to comply risked losing their share of the federal crime budget.[31] Congress passed Clinton's crime bill, to be funded by savings made from reducing the federal workforce, but Clinton's budget called for the same savings to be used to reduce the federal deficit.[32] Reflecting the continuing fear of crime and influence of accusations of leniency, during the 1994 state political campaigns, Howard Kurtz observes that, "although other traditional hot-button issues—welfare, taxes, immigration, personal ethics also are prominent, crime remains the thirty second weapon of choice, and the charge most often is that an incumbent is responsible for turning inmates loose."[33] Also in 1994 crime fever swept through California, with 240 new crime laws being passed and 100 statutes enacted increasing penalties.[34]

In California the 'Three Strikes' habitual offender statute was passed into law, and was seen as the latest in a long line of attempts to find quick-fix solutions. The Three Strikes legislation was drafted by Mike Reynolds, whose eighteen year old daughter Kimber was murdered in 1992 during a failed robbery, along with Justice James Ardaiz. Reynolds' proposal received support from a variety of interest groups, among them the California Corrections and Peace Officers Association, the largest prison officers' union in the country, which would obviously benefit from the expansion of the prison system, and the National Rifle Association, a traditionally conservative group who were thought to support the legislation because it distracted public attention from proposed strict gun legislation. Although the Three Strikes law attracted considerable financial backing and media coverage, no credible justice organization advanced an endorsement.[35]

Although other states adopted similar laws, California's was the most draconian. Habitual offender statutes varied in significant ways; some gave judges and prosecutors discretion in invoking harsher sentences, others varied in what constituted a prior 'Strike' and how many were required to invoke enhanced sentences. Even the sentence imposed on the habitual offender was not consistent, and in some instances it could mean life without parole.[36] In his extensive study of the Three Strikes legislation Michael Vitiello concludes that governor Pete Wilson's support for the legislation provides a case study of "sound bite electioneering substituting for careful analysis of frustratingly complex social and penelogical problems."[37] The Sentencing Project concluded in its 1994 report that "there is no reason to believe that continuing to increase the severity of penalties will have any significant impact on crime," and Robert Gangi, executive director of the Correctional Association of New York, remarked that the policy was an "extension of a policy that has proven a failure."[38]

Mike Reynolds' efforts to enact the Three Strikes legislation met with little success until the kidnapping and murder of Polly Klaas in October 1993. The Klaas family, like the Walsh family in the 1980s, went to great efforts to locate their missing child and attracted nationwide publicity and support before their daughter's death was discovered. Richard Allen Davis, a repeat offender, was arrested and confessed to raping and murdering the girl, and the FBI were credited with providing the technical assistance that resolved the case.[39] In light of the contemporary political climate and public awareness of random sex crimes, Davis symbolized the failure of the criminal justice system. The Klaas murder and a general perception of rising crime focused public opinion, and when Reynolds secured Marc Klaas's signature on his petition supporting 'Three Strikes,' it became the fastest-qualifying voter initiative in California's history[40] and the two fathers gained "virtually invincible credibility."[41] Marc Klaas initially backed the Three Strikes but he later withdrew his support, saying the legislation was "too hard on soft crime and too soft on hard crime."[42] His criticism, although specifically directed at the California legislation, could be applied to many multiple offender statutes which focus on a number of offences rather than distinguishing between individual offenders. Despite losing Marc Klaas's support and facing criticism, the legislation was still passed. Before the Three Strikes law was enacted, the Governor and legislators were aware of the bill's weaknesses but ignored alternative, less severe, legislation. The public panic surrounding sex crimes overshadowed rational debate, and Three Strikes sailed through the legislature, despite its acknowledged flaws.[43]

After the introduction of the Three Strikes law in 1994, thirty other states adopted similar legislation, and ten introduced tougher sentencing laws. Politicians, eager to win votes, embraced a "get even tougher" attitude towards criminal sentencing.[44] Under the Florida habitual offender statute, passed in a climate of panic, only twenty per cent of eligible offenders received increased sentences, but the influx from that small percentage flooded the already overcrowded state prison system. With insufficient funds to construct more prison space, criminal justice officials accelerated the release of inmates not sentenced under the habitual offender statute, meaning that violent offenders were serving shorter sentences and being released to make space for less dangerous repeat offenders. The consequence for the state was a twenty-eight per cent increase in violent crime and eleven per cent increase in other serious crimes. The legislature responded by eliminating the habitual offender statute in 1993.[45]

Ironically, it was defense cutbacks in the 1970s which meant that companies who formerly bid on military contracts turned their attention to the domestic War on Crime. Private prisons became one of the fastest growing sectors in the Prison-Industrial Complex (PIC) that emerged in the 1980s, and consisted of businessmen and organizations who benefited economically from the construction and maintenance of prisons.

In 1992, the Department of Justice published *The Case For More Incarceration* as part of a concerted attempt to encourage states to build more prisons. The report misused data which the researchers involved later retracted, but Attorney General William Barr continued to use the report to convince states to build more prisons. Also in 1992 the Justice Department flew dozens of state officials to Washington DC, at the taxpayer's expense, for a conference energetically encouraging the expansion of prison space. Speakers and topics at the conference were tightly orchestrated to stifle dissent but the plan backfired to some extent when many participants expressed their resentment at federal government attempts to influence state crime policy.[46] Anthony Sciarrino reported that an internal Federal Prison Industries (FPI) document, "A Vision for the Future" (June 30, 1993), asserted that, "the time has come to modify its [FPI] internal functions to operate successfully in any market, and with any partner, and with any business... the new marketplace has a requirement that mandates truly competitive requirements for price, quality and customer service."[47] Private corporations and federal bureaucrats both sought to profit from increased incarceration rates.

The appointment of Louis J Freeh as director of the FBI in 1993 was intended to symbolize a new era for the Bureau. According to President Clinton, Louis Freeh was a "law enforcement legend" and under his influence it was hoped that the FBI would "recapture the imagination of the American people."[48] Freeh was a former FBI agent, prosecutor in the US Attorney's Office, and federal judge. His credentials as a "moral touchstone" were emphasized, as was his determination for thorough police work, which earned him the reputation of not knowing what the word 'quit' meant.[49]

Continuing the 1980s call to arms, Freeh encouraged citizens to "take back the streets, their neighborhoods, their towns, their cities." His words reassured the public that the FBI would continue its role in making America a good place to live in, but there was no mention in his speeches of the overburdened local and state police who deal with most crime, and who received little recognition. After Freeh took his position as director, he returned to a familiar 'paranoid' style of crime fighting, giving speeches reporting homicide rates tripling since 1960, robberies and forcible rapes increasing by 500 per cent and aggravated assault increasing by 600 per cent. Citing a study by the International Association of Chiefs of Police (April 1993), he stated that crime increased by 371 per cent, nine times faster than the population growth, raising public fears further.[50] However, burdened by the past Freeh inherited the controversy surrounding the FBI shootouts at Ruby Ridge (1992) and Waco (1993), where the reliance on military tactics caused disastrous results.

During the siege at the Waco settlement, the media reported allegations of child sex abuse within the Davidian community, exploiting public awareness of sex crimes to generate support for the heavy handed FBI tactics. However, the Bureau of Alcohol Tobacco and Firearms (BATF), who conducted the initial raid which led to the siege, have no jurisdiction over sex crimes. The standoff was resolved abruptly when a fire swept through the settlement killing eighty-six men, women and children. In the aftermath Bill Clinton and Janet Reno took full responsibility for the FBI actions and a number of explanations were offered as to the origin of the fire, the most popular being a mass suicide by what the media had portrayed as a 'cult' of religious fanatics which reflected the news media depictions of the Davidians[51]—eerily reminiscent of the media reporting of Charles Manson and The Family, and the official report on the Waco siege absolved the FBI and Reno of any blame. Revelations in 1999 that the FBI had used flammable tear gas during the siege, something which they had consistently denied undermined the Bureau's public image. Mark Potock of the Southern Poverty Law Center ominously, but accurately, observed that doubts raised gave credence "to the wildest and most controversial views of what happened at Waco. It makes it difficult to believe what the government says."[52]

With the end of the Cold War and the breakup of the Soviet Union, Freeh raised the specter of international organized crime gangs. In response to the threat he said, "We must provide greater and greater international assistance in order to minimize the threat posed by these criminal elements."[53] International police officials already attended Quantico at that time, but that was not enough, because, "criminals once confined within a country's borders now operate on a global scale, and law enforcement must adjust to this new playing field."[54] In response, the International Law Enforcement Academy (ILEA) was set up in Budapest, and began accepting students in April 1995 from former communist countries, to be trained to fight rising crime. The University of Virginia, the FBI's partner in increasing police professionalization, through their Department of Continuing Education, played a "vital role" in developing the educational syllabus for the ILEA. This was something which Freeh wanted to replicate in other parts of the world, expanding FBI influence.

Despite initial praise, it was soon noted that Freeh had adopted some of Hoover's practices. Removing the last remnants of Hoover's old guard, Freeh transferred senior agents at the "whim of his displeasure" to remote outposts. In their place, the Friends of Louie (FOL) received appointments and, in time, preferential treatment. In the *Sunday Times* Paul Eddy pointed out the almost constant criticism of the FBI in the 1990s for "sloppiness, incompetence, arrogance [and] even corruption." Due to the series of crises even the Bureau's motto of 'Fidelity, Bravery, Integrity' was transformed into "Fumbling, Bumbling, Idiots."[55]

Despite academic investigations by James Fox and Jack Levin, Phillip Jenkins and Joel Best of the serial murder and child abduction panics, further Congressional hearings were scheduled for September 1995, a forum which, for the first time, explicitly connected serial murder and the panic over child abductions. Shortly before the hearings, the FBI reshuffled their internal departments and created the Child Abduction and Serial Killer Unit as part of the Critical Incident Response Group (CIRG) to confront "two of the most critical threats to our citizens." Claims were made that the unit's research *could* lead to the earlier resolution of future cases, but no predictions were made that the CIRG could prevent murders. Virtually every expert called to testify at the hearings argued, as usual, for an increased Bureau role in the investigation, because local law enforcement is ill equipped to deal with the problem. Representative Bill McCollum said: "The early entry of the FBI can ensure that the best investigative resource, and the highest level of coordination can be brought to bear immediately in a given case," and that the FBI, who could link crimes and track missing children, was hindered by jurisdictional confusion, enabling criminals to remain active.[56] The FBI's role as mythical 'supercops' was reaffirmed, once more making them superior to local and state police. But the Bureau's results still fall short of their boast about their investigative abilities and forensic standards.

In the course of the hearings John Walsh reaffirmed the distinction between the 'old' and the 'new' FBI. Using the example of the Bureau's reluctance to get involved in the hunt for his missing son in the early 1980s, which he identified with the 'old' FBI dominated by priorities set by Hoover, he implied that the 'new' FBI, after having its priorities superficially redirected during the Reagan era, would be eager to get involved in the hunt for missing children. Profiles were said to be "extremely important" in the War on Crime against serial sex killers and child abductors, despite dissatisfaction in the police community, and no proven display of their value. Walsh testified that he wanted to dispel the myths surrounding serial sex killers, before going on to restate the FBI stereotype which had been largely discredited. Walsh did not inform the subcommittee that, when investigated, the vast majority of Henry Lee Lucas' confessions could not be substantiated, and many had been prompted by over-eager police officers, an idea vaguely hinted at later by Ken Lanning.[57] Ignoring widespread criticism of FBI statistics in general and the academic investigations of their serial sex killer statistics, agent Bill Hagmaier claimed that figures cited by the FBI were "considered conservative at best."[58]

Like the earlier hearings on serial murder in the 1980s, testimony focused on the sexual aspects of murder and child abduction. Supporting the New Right crime agenda, continued by Clinton, FBI agent Ken Lanning denied that missing children cases were a race issue, with white families receiving preference, and Robin Montgomery, head of the CIRG, concurred stating, "a child is simply a child" to the investigators. However, Lanning did admit that investigations could be based on socioeconomic considerations, undermining the equality of investigation and implicitly acknowledging a racist bent.

Representative Bill McCollum acknowledged during the hearings that the subcommittee were "very sympathetic" to Walsh's ideas and continued that "Democrats and Republicans may have our disputes over the details, but in principle we generally agree on the direction in which we need to go."[59] This consensus reflected the general movement in the US towards a conservative political centre. Calling for drastic action, Representative Fred Heineman added, "I have to admit that across this country for so many years we have been swatting mosquitoes and perhaps it is time to drain the swamp."[60]

A further attack on the credibility of the FBI came in 1997 when a report examining allegations by agent Frederic Whitehurst that the Bureau's laboratory was operating improperly was published. The Justice Department's own forensic report on the claims was described as a "devastating official undermining"[61] of the Bureau's abilities, especially in light of their own exaggerated claims of professionalism and scientific pre-eminence.

The Nation (August 11—18, 1997) featured a special report on the 'new' post-Hoover FBI by David Burnham, a crime reporter for the *New York Times*. Analyzing the Bureau's prosecution rate in comparison to other agencies, and interviewing a variety of people involved in the criminal justice system, Burnham's report painted a bleak picture, concluding that the FBI was more politically powerful in the mid 1990s than at any other time, and that, "the FBI today is a sloppy, unresponsive, badly managed, uncooperative and out of touch agency that is aggressively trying to expand its control over the American people."[62] In his report Burnham cites the opinion of a Republican former assistant Attorney General saying,

> Unfortunately, the ghost of Hoover still stalks the hallways. As in the
> past, the challenge of trying to protect the FBI against all kinds of criticism

remains the most important single task of the FBI officials. As in the past, the FBI often does not cooperate with other enforcement agencies. As in the past, the FBI mostly sets the Justice Department's agenda.[63]

Little has changed in the priorities of the FBI or in crime policy because the limited debate is dominated by conservative ideologues. The use of crime as a political weapon by the New Right shifted the political debate far to the right, and to be elected it is necessary for politicians to show they are 'tough' on crime, curtailing discussion of any policies focusing on rehabilitation. The serial sex killer provided conservative moralists with a symbolic figure to support their arguments of moral decay. Consistent with the tradition of American criminal justice policy the Three Strikes legislation and sex offender laws avoided confronting domestic family violence, gun availability and drug-use prevention which would be more effective long term measures to lower crime rates.[64] The 'hell' created by the New Right and FBI is a 'paranoid' society devoid of trust, and one of scapegoating in order to avoid social issues. The use of the threat of random violent crimes legitimized harsh legislation which affected mainly non-violent offenders, thus increasing America's prison population. The crime policies to thwart the Nietzschian 'monsters' offered by Reagan's administration (and later that of Clinton) were self-fulfilling and self-defeating, creating more crimes and a larger criminal class which superficially endorsed their apocalyptic claims about an ever-rising tide of crime. Keith Geiger reported that seventy per cent of American prison space was built after 1985, while during the 1980s only eleven per cent of the nation's classrooms were constructed,[65] and the expense of habitual offender statutes meant that education budgets would suffer because of crime hysteria. Barry Krisberg suggested, with more than a little irony, that maybe the university campuses of UCLA and Berkeley, pride of the state and symbols which Reagan defended as governor of California, could be refitted as prisons.[66]

The image of the serial sex killer was created by the FBI in the media during the 1980s and perpetuated in popular culture even after Bill Clinton came to office. Advances in technology and media deregulation in the 1980s created numerous television channels with program schedules to be filled, but with limited budgets. Documentaries, docudramas and films about fictional serial killers are regularly shown, keeping the public aware of their 'crimes.' In fiction serial killers continue to flourish, and Thomas Harris' third serial killer novel, *Hannibal* (1999) was published amid considerable engineered media publicity and speculation about who would play Clarice Starling and Hannibal Lecter in the film adaptation, again projecting the FBI stereotype into the mainstream.

In the 1990s the BSU was incorporated into the CIRG, but their role as educators of local and state police officers continued to shape the priorities, assumptions, and techniques of local police departments, in America and around the world. This scientific analysis of crime was institutionalized and emphasized the absence of individual responsibility rather than social factors as the cause of crime, thus perpetuating the Bureau's conservative ideology.

Law & Order in the 1990s

Like the mythical serial sex killer who continues his career in crime until captured or killed, the FBI will continue to perpetuate their crime myths until exposed.

Notes

1. Introduction Evil is a Medieval Superstition

1. C A MacDonald, "The Politics of Paranoia," *History Today* (July 1984): 6.

2. Reagan quoted in Gregory Krupey, "The Christian Right, Zionism, and the Coming of the Penteholocaust," in Adam Parfrey (ed) *Apocalypse Culture* (expanded and revised edition), Feral House, Los Angeles, 1990: 289.

3. Stanley Cohen, *Folk Devils and Moral Panics*, Basil Blackwell, 1980: 9.

4. Richard Sparks, "Masculinity and Heroism in the Hollywood 'Blockbuster,'" *British Journal of Criminology* (v.36 No.3, 1996): 349.

5. Joel Achenbach, "Serial Killers: Shattering the Myth," *Washington Post* (14 April 1991): F1.

6. Isidore Silver, "Introduction," in Isidore Silver (ed), *The Crime Control Establishment*, Spectrum Books, Prentice-Hall Inc., New Jersey, 1974: 2.

7. Steven R. Donziger (ed), *The Real War On Crime: The Report of the National Criminal Justice Commission,* Harper Perennial, New York, 1995: 63.

8. Walter Lippman, *Drift and Mastery: An Attempt To Diagnose The Current Unrest,* Prentice-Hall Inc., New Jersey, 1961: 15–16.

9. Roosevelt quoted in Brian MacArthur (ed), *The Penguin Book of Twentieth Century Speeches,* Penguin Books, London, 1993: 125.

10. Emil Durkheim, *The Division of Labor in Society*, The Free Press, Glencoe, Illinois, 1964: 102.

11. Cohen, *Folk Devils and Moral Panics*: 10.

12. Jon Christensen et al, "The Selling of the Police," *Contemporary Crises* (v.6): 238–39.

13. Joseph C. Fisher, *Killer Among Us: Public Reactions To Serial Murder*, Praeger, Westport, Connecticut, 1997: 18. See also James Brown, "Historical Similarity of Twentieth Century Serial Sexual Homicide to Pre-Twentieth Century Occurrence of Vampirism," *American Journal of Forensic Psychiatry* (v.12 No.2, 1991).

14. Caryl Chessman, *Trial By Ordeal*, Longmans, London, 1956: 132.

15. Hoffer quoted in Haynes Johnson, *Sleepwalking Through History*, Anchor Books, New York, 1992: 206.

16. Ibid

17. "The Federal Role in Investigation of Serial Violent Crime," Hearings before a Subcommittee on Government Operations, House of Representatives 99 Congress, 2 Session, 9 April and 21 May 1986: 53. Hereafter "The Federal Role in Investigation of Serial Violent Crime" (April 9 and May 21, 1986).

18. Silver, Introduction, Silver (ed), *The Crime Control Establishment*: 1.

19. Richard Hofstader, *Paranoid Style of American Politics*, Jonathon Cape, London, 1966: 4.

20. Ibid: 29

194

Notes

21 Joel Norris, *Jeffrey Dahmer*, Pinnacle Books, New York, 1992: 264.

22 James A. Brussel, *Casebook of a Crime Psychiatrist*, Mayflower, London, 1970: 37–38.

23 Ibid: 38.

24 Schecter quoted in Richard Tithecott, *Of Men and Monsters: Jeffrey Dahmer and theConstruction of the Serial Killer*, Wisconsin, London, 1997: 53.

25 Richard Maxwell Brown, "Historical Patterns of Violence in America," in Hugh Davis Graham and Ted Robert Gurr (ed), *History of Violence in America*, Bantam Books, New York, 1969: 76.

26 Elliot Leyton, *Hunting Humans*, Penguin, London, 1989: 364.

27 Elayne Rapping, "The Uses of Violence," Progressive (August1991): 36.

2. Fidelity, Bravery and Integrity
The Rise and Fall of the FBI Myth

1   Silver, "Federal Crime-Control Establishment," in Isidore Silver (ed), *The Crime Control Establishment*: 17, 19.

2   Joel Kovel, *Red Hunting in the Promised Land*, Cassell, London, 1997: 90.

3   Richard Gid Powers, "J Edgar Hoover and The Detective Hero," *Journal of Popular Culture* (Fall 1975): 258.

4   Don Whitehead, *The FBI Story*, Pocket Books Inc., New York, 1956: 18. In 1963 Random House published a 'young readers' edition of *The FBI Story*.

5   Frank Pearce, "Crime, Corporations and American Social Order," in Ian Taylor and Laurie Taylor (ed), *Politics and Deviance: Papers From The National Deviancy Conference*, Penguin, London, 1973: 23.

6   Powers, "J Edgar Hoover and the Detective Hero," *Journal of Popular Culture* (Fall 1975): 259.

7   Ibid: 260–61.

8   Edelman, *The Symbolic Use of Politics*: 13.

9   William Turner cited in Dirk C Gibson, "Quantative Description of FBI Public Relations," *Public Relations Review* (Spring 1997): 17. It was reported that Hoover tried to discredit Turner after his book was published. In 1968 information was released from the Bureau's LA office to Joe Pyne before Turner appeared on Pyne's talk show. Whitehead was an Associated Press reporter in whose "integrity, ability, and objectivity" Hoover had "complete confidence." Turner, *Hoover's FBI*: 113.

10 Powers, "J Edgar Hoover and the Detective Hero," *Journal of Popular Culture* (Fall 1975): 262.

11 Whitehead, *The FBI Story*: 26.

12 Powers, "J Edgar Hoover and the Detective Hero," *Journal of Popular Culture* (Fall 1975): 262.

13 David J Langum, *Crossing Over The Line: Legislating Morality and the Mann Act*, U Chicago P, Chicago and London, 1994: 3.

14 Ibid: 258.

15 Ibid: 4.

16 Ibid: 259. Langum documents many

of the Mann Act prosecutions that did not involve commercial prostitution, and dedicates his book to "the victims of the Department of Justice."

17   Lowenthal, "The Beginning of the Crime-Control Bureaucracy," in Isidore Silver (ed), *The Crime-Control Establishment*: 24.

18   Roberta Strauss Feuerlicht, *America's Reign of Terror*, Random House, New York, 1971: 16–17.

19   Archibald Stevenson, a former New York lawyer and later an FBI agent, cited in Lowenthal, "The Beginning of the Crime-Control Bureaucracy": 26.

20   Feuerlicht, *America's Reign of Terror*: 60, 79–80.

21   Ibid: 85–87.

22   Lowenthal, "The Beginning of the Crime-Control Bureaucracy," in Silver (ed), *The Crime-Control Establishment*: 28.

23   Feuerlicht, *America's Reign of Terror*: 93, 95, 100.

24   Ibid: 96–102, 104.

25   Lowenthal, "The Beginning of the Crime-Control Bureaucracy," in Silver (ed), *The Crime-Control Establishment*: 30.

26   Robert Lindsey, "Thefts of Autos Go Down, The First Drop in History," *New York Times* (March 11, 1973): A1.

27   Lowenthal, "The Beginning of the Crime-Control Bureaucracy," in Silver (ed), *The Crime-Control Establishment*: 24, 31, 43, 45. Sponsors of the Dyer Act were interested in prosecuting full-time professional car thieves, but the FBI concentrated on casual car thieves and by 1964 those prosecuted under the Dyer Act, the largest single category of all federal convictions, accounted for one quarter of all inmates in federal prisons. In a 1964 review of the Dyer Act, Harry Subins found that the FBI prosecutions were primarily to

enhance evaluations of its achievements; he further recommended cutting back on such prosecutions. In June 1970 the Justice Department ordered the FBI to stop presenting Dyer Act cases to federal prosecutors. Burnham, *Above the Law*: 88.

28   Peter M Blau and Marshall W Meyer, *Bureaucracy in Modern Society*, Random House, New York, 1971: 25.

29   Carlos Clarens, *Crime Movies: From Griffith To The Godfather And Beyond*, W W Norton and Co. New York, 1980: 117.

30   Adams quoted in Whitehead, *The FBI Story*: 76.

31   Gibson, "Quantative Description," *Public Relations Review* (Spring 1997): 14, 11.

32   Kenneth O'Reilly, "A New Deal For The FBI: The Roosevelt Administration, Crime Control, and National Security," *Journal of American History* (December 1982): 641.

33   Ibid: 642.

34   Turner, *Hoover's FBI*: 226.

35   Hoover quoted in Gibson, "Quantative Description," *Public Relations Review* (Spring 1997): 13.

36   Whitehead, *The FBI Story*: 17.

37   Turner, *Hoover's FBI*: 227.

38   Clarens, *Crime Movies*: 117.

39   Anthony Summer, *Official and Confidential: The Secret Life of J Edgar Hoover*, Corgi, London, 1994: 84.

40   Ibid: 84–85.

41   Milton S Mayer, "The Myth Of The G-Man," *Forum* (September 1935): 145.

42   Whitehead, *The FBI Story*: 17. See also Turner, *Hoover's FBI*: 240.

43   Christopher Lydon, "J Edgar Hoover Made FBI Formidable With Politics, Publicity and Results," *New York Times* (May 3, 1972)

44   Turner, *Hoover's FBI*: 242-44

45   Ibid: 229.

Notes

46 Ibid: 226.

47 Paul A Zolbe, "The Uniform Crime: 50 Years Of Progress," *FBI Law Enforcement Bulletin* (September 1980): 2.

48 Kessler, *The FBI*: 39.

49 Zolbe, "The Uniform Crime," *FBI Law Enforcement Bulletin* (September 1980): 2.

50 Gresham M Sykes, "Critical Criminology," *Journal of Criminal Law and Criminology* (v.65 No.2, 1974), 209.

51 Leyton, *Hunting Humans*: 20 (note).

52 Sykes, "Critical Criminology," *Journal of Criminal Law and Criminology* (v.65 No.2, 1974): 209.

53 Turner, *Hoover's FBI*: 229.

54 J Edgar Hoover, "Organized Protection Against Organized Predatory Crimes," *Journal of Criminal Law and Criminology* (July/August 1933): 479.

55 Ibid.

56 Ibid: 482.

57 G Russell Girardin and William J Helmer, *Dillinger: The Untold Story*, Indiana UP, Bloomington and Indianapolis, 1994: 263. For an example of FBI self-promotion see "G-Men Wage Unending War," *Literary Digest* (August 3, 1935): 18–19; J Edgar Hoover. "Science at the scene of the crime," *Scientific American* (July 1936): 12–14.

58 Turner, *Hoover's FBI*: 113.

59 Kessler, *The FBI*: 26.

60 Fred Cook, *The FBI Nobody Knows*, Pyramid Books, New York, 1964: 164.

61 Jack Alexander, "The Director," *New Yorker* (1 September 1937): 24.

62 Norris quoted in Max Lowenthal, *The Federal Bureau of Investigation*, William Sloane and Associates, New York, 1950: 393.

63 Eugene Lewis quoted in Lowenthal, *The Federal Bureau of Investigation*: 390.

64 Richard Gid Powers, *Secrecy and Power: The Life of J Edgar Hoover*, Free Press, New York, 1987: 489.

65 Mayer, "The Myth Of The G-Man," *Forum* (September 1935): 146.

66 Ernest Kahlar Alix notes that after the death sentence was passed on Hauptmann editorials in the *New York Times* endorsed the verdict and the investigation as an example of efficient criminal justice. However, they also acknowledged that Hauptmann's exact role in the crime was not clear, and that some people would dissent from the final verdict. Ernest K. Alix, *Ransom Kidnapping in America, 1874–1974: The Creation of a Capitol Crime*, Southern Illinois UP, Carbondale and Edwardsville, 1974: 110. A decade later Ludovic Kennedy claimed, in *The Airman and the Carpenter* (1985), that Hauptmann was framed by the police, who faked evidence and intimidated witnesses to provide a scapegoat for the crime. Kennedy concluded that, "Hauptmann was guilty of nothing more than dishonesty." He had been involved in a shady business deal where he received money from a character closely associated with the crime.

67 Clarens, *Crime Movies*: 117.

68 Mayer, "The Myth Of The G-Man," *Forum* (September 1935): 146–47. For an examination of the press coverage of kidnapping crimes and federal involvement in their investigation see Alix, *Ransom Kidnapping in America, 1874–1974*: 74–124.

69 Ibid: 144–45.

70 Powers, "J Edgar Hoover and the Detective Hero," *Journal of Popular Culture* (Fall 1975): 266.

71 Mayer, "The Myth Of The G-Man," *Forum* (September 1935): 145.

72 Peter Arnold, *Great Crimes and Trials of the 20th Century*, BCA, London, 1995: 33–35.

73 Clarens, *Crime Movies*: 117. Kelly spent the rest of his life in prison. For a time he was shipped to the maximum security Alcatraz prison where he was a model prisoner, behaving so well that he was transferred back to the mainland where he died of a heart attack in 1954.

74 Powers, "J Edgar Hoover and the Detective Hero," *Journal of Popular Culture* (Fall 1975): 267, 263.

75 Clarens, *Crime Movies*: 120. This was later taken over by Violent Criminal Apprehension Program (VICAP) as the 'VICAP Ten Most Wanted List.'

76 Michael Benton, *The Illustrated History of Crime Comics*, Taylor Publishing Company, Dallas, Texas, 1993: 9. 85

77 Ibid: 3, 8, 9.

78 Clarens, *Crime Movies*: 117. The cases of Charles Urschel's kidnapping and 'Machine-Gun' Kelly's arrest are prime examples of the exaggeration of the facts to manipulate public perception of the FBI's work.

79 Howard McLellan, "Shoot to kill? A Note on the G-Men's methods," *Harpers* (January 1936): 236.

80 Clarens, *Crime Movies*: 121.

81 Powers, *Secrecy and Power*: 189.

82 Keenan quoted in McLellan, "Shoot to Kill?," *Harpers* (January 1936): 236–37.

83 Powers, *Secrecy and Power*: 190. Despite the impressive label of Public Enemy attributed to Dillinger there is no proof that he ever killed anyone.

84 O'Reilly, "A New Deal For The FBI," *Journal of American History* (December 1982): 642.

85 Girardin and Helmer, *Dillinger: The Untold Story*: 263–64.

86 O'Reilly, "A New Deal For The FBI," *Journal of American History* (December 1982): 643.

87 Mayer, "The Myth Of The G-Man,"

Forum (September 1935): 145.

88 Clarens, *Crime Movies*: 121.

89 The details of the discrepancies were originally stated in Jay Robert Nash and Ron Offen's *Dillinger: Dead or Alive* (1970), and are subsequently found in many popular true crime books such as Ian Schott, *World Famous Gangsters*, Paragon, London, 1996: 91–92; and on various internet sites such as "John Dillinger: Controversial Death," *Crime Library* online at [w] www.crimelibrary.com/americana/dillinger/12.htm; and "Did John Dillinger really die," *Altered Dimensions* online at [w] www.spartechsoftware.com/dimensions/crime/johndillenger.htm. The discrepancies in the autopsy report have given rise to a number of theories about what happened that night, however FBI denies the discrepancies claiming that they were mistakes made at the coroner's office. Claims that Dillinger had undergone plastic surgery do not account for his change in appearance because it did not prevent some of Dillinger's contemporaries from being recognized. The uncertainty undermined the Bureau's reputation, and the only way to be sure who died that night in Chicago would be to exhume the body for scientific testing.

90 Cummings quoted in McLellan, "Shoot to kill?," *Harpers* (January 1936): 237.

91 Ibid: 241. Other examples cited of cases cleared by death include 'Babyface' Nelson, Legs Diamond, and the partnership of Bonnie Parker and Clyde Barrow. More contemporary examples would be the case of Andrew Cunanan, the suspected murderer of Gianni Versace, who was credited with several other killings.

92 Stephen Early quoted in O'Reilly, "A New Deal For The FBI," *Journal of*

Notes

American History (December 1982): 643.

93   Ibid: 644.

94   Powers, *Secrecy and Power*: 197.

95   O'Reilly, "A New Deal For The FBI," *Journal of American History* (December 1982): 644.

96   Powers, *Secrecy And Power*: 198.

97   O'Reilly, "A New Deal For The FBI," *Journal of American History* (December 1982): 645.

98   Hays cited in Clarens, *Crime Movies*: 121.

99   Michael Murphy and Cherly Murphy, "The Devil Thumbs His Nose!," *Psychotronic* (No.8, Winter 1990): 21–28.

100   Stephen D Gladis, "The FBI National Academy's First 50 Years," *FBI Law Enforcement Bulletin* (July 1985): 2.

101   Gladis, "The FBI National Academy's First 50 Years," *FBI Law Enforcement Bulletin* (July 1985): 3–4.

102   O'Reilly, "A New Deal For The FBI," *Journal of American History* (December 1982): 645.

103   Kovel, *Red Hunting in the Promised Land*: 93.

104   "Why Tap Wires," *The Nation* (March 8, 1941): 258.

105   Cook, *The FBI Nobody Knows*: 422-23.

106   Ibid: 422–23.

107   Newton, *Serial Slaughter*: 110.

108   Dempsey quoted in Harold Schechter, *Deranged*, Pocket Books, New York, 1990: 300.

109   "Kansas Building Scaffolding Since 1870," *New York Times* (September 3, 1930): A12. Panzram's story was filmed as *Killer: a Journal of Murder* (Tim Metcalfe, 1996).

110   Hoover quoted in Richard Kyle-Kieth, *The High Price of Pornography*, Public Affairs Press, Washington DC, 1961: 55.

111   Hoover quoted in Alan Betrock, *Unseen America*, Shake Books, New York, 1990: 6.

112   Hoover quoted in Richard H Kuh, *Foolish Figleaves? Pornography in- and out-of Court*, Macmillan, New York, 1967: 6.

113   Kyle-Kieth, *The High Price of Pornography*: 55–56.

114   Kyle-Kieth, *The High Price of Pornography*: 57.

115   Hoover quoted in Ibid: 55.

116   Roberts, *The Smut Rakers*: 80, 82.

117   Powers, "J Edgar Hoover and the Detective Hero," *Journal of Popular Culture* (Fall 1975): 259.

118   Historian Alpheus T Mason cited in Lydon, "J Edgar Hoover Made FBI Formidable With Politics, Publicity and Results," *New York Times* (May 3, 1972): A52.

119   Kessler, *The FBI*: 27.

120   Ibid: 26.

121   Keller, *The Liberals And J Edgar Hoover*: 3, 191.

122   John Ellif quoted in Arlie Schardt, "Civil Rights: Too Much, Too Late," in Pat Watter and Stephen Gillers (ed), *Investigating the FBI*, Ballantine, New York, 1973: 169.

123   Hoover quoted in Ibid: 167–68.

124   Gladis, "The FBI National Academy's First 50 Years," *FBI Law Enforcement Bulletin* (July 1995): 7.

125   Gary Groth, "Paul Mavrides Interview," *Comics Journal* (April 1994): 48. Mavrides later became an important figure in the California counterculture, most notably as a comics artist.

126   Powers, *Secrecy and Power*, 405. *Escobedo* invalidated confessions when the accused was denied access to a lawyer, while *Miranda* required police to inform suspects of their Constitutional rights.

127   Keller, *The Liberals and J Edgar Hoover*: 194.

128   Katzenbach quoted in Graham, "A

Contemporary History": 488, 491, 494.

129   Gladis, "The FBI National Academy's First 50 Years," *FBI Law Enforcement Bulletin* (July 1995): 7.

130   Lydon, "J Edgar Hoover Made FBI Formidable with Politics, Publicity and Results," *New York Times* (May 3, 1972): A52

131   Hoover cited in Frank Pearce, "Crime, Corporations and the American Social Order": 13. One of the fundamental problems with the 'crime clock' method of presenting statistics is that as the population increases it is inevitable that the interval between crimes will decrease, even if the reported crime rate remains constant.

132   Hoover cited in Committee on the Judiciary, US Senate, "Capital Punishment as a Matter of Legislative Policy," in Hugo Bedau (ed) *The Death Penalty in America*, Oxford, New York, 1982: 312.

133   Graham, "A Contemporary History": 487.

134   Ohlin quoted in ibid, "A Contemporary History": 487.

135   Clark quoted in ibid: 486.

136   Graham, "A Contemporary History": 486–87, 494–99.

137   Professor Wilson quoted in ibid: 504.

138   Kovel, *Red Hunting in the Promised Land*: 97–98.

139   Nixon quoted in Russell Miller, *Bunny: The Real Story Of Playboy*, Corgi Books, London, 1985: 214.

140   Powers, *Secrecy and Power*: 486.

141   Douglas and Olshaker, *Mindhunters*: 65.

142   Reagan quoted in Anthony Summers, "Hidden Hoover," *Vanity Fair* (March 1993): 135.

143   Burger quoted in Nan Robertson, "Hoover Lies in State Capitol," *New York Times* (May 4, 1972): A18.

144   Spock quoted in Graham, "J Edgar

Hoover, 77, Dies; Will Lie In State In Capitol," *New York Times* (May 3, 1972): A53.

145   Ibid. Tributes to Hoover were led by President Nixon, and followed by vice-president Spiro Agnew, John Mitchell, Governor George Wallace, and Chief Justice Warren Burger among others. Governor Ronald Reagan of California attended the funeral, and he took his place at the back of the procession. Former agent Hank Messick claimed that the greatest public service Hoover ever performed was when he died. As far as Messick could see Hoover had been a law enforcement disaster.

146   Kessler, *The FBI*: 500. Ironically, the monument Hoover planned for himself, the J Edgar Hoover building in Washington DC was not completed during his lifetime. It was finally opened in 1975.

147   Smith, "After Almost a Half a Century, the Process of Selecting a Director of the FBI Begins," *New York Times* (May 3, 1972): A53.

148   Ibid: A53.

149   Ibid: 185, 36.

150   Powers, *Secrecy and Power*: 486, 488. In the aftermath of the Watergate revelations, applications to join the CIA actually tripled, and many of the prospective agents were from America's best schools. It was suggested that a poor job market and feelings of patriotism had directed their choice of career. Hougan, *Spooks*: 58.

151   McCrystal et al, *Watergate: The Full Inside Story*: 233.

152   Silver, "Federal Crime-Control Establishment": 20.

153   Ellif, *The Reform Of The FBI*: 189.

154   Ibid: 4, 189.

155   Phillip Taubman, "New Charter For FBI Won't Have Easy Sailing," *New York Times* (August 5, 1979): IV 2.

Notes

156 Smith, "After Almost a Half a Century, the Process of Selecting a Director of the FBI Begins," *New York Times* (May 3, 1973): A53.

157 Kelly quoted in Paul Eddy, "True Defective Stories," *Sunday Times Magazine* (August 10, 1997): 33.

158 Webster quoted in Mel Gussow, "The Seberg Tragedy," *New York Times Magazine* (November 30, 1980): 51.

159 Kessler, *The FBI*: 27.

160 Dr John Money, professor of Medical Psychology at Johns Hopkins University, quoted in Summers, *Official and Confidential*: 542–43.

161 Smith, "After Almost a Half a Century, the Process of Selecting a Director of the FBI Begins," *New York Times* (May 3, 1973): A53.

162 Oliver Revell cited in Kessler, *The FBI*: 71. Revell was then the Special Agent in charge of the Dallas field office, he had formerly been associate deputy FBI director for investigations.

163 Phillip Taubman, "Top FBI Structure Revised By Webster; 3 Chief Aides Named," *New York Times* (August 8, 1979): A1, A13.

164 "FBI is liberalizing discipline of Agents," *New York Times* (October 11, 1979): A14. It was never made clear why homosexuality would make agents ineffective where extra-marital affairs would not.

165 John M Crewdson, "Former FBI Agent Tells Investigators of Widespread Abuse and Corruption," *New York*

Times (January 20, 1979): A8. See also M Wesley Swearingen, *FBI Secrets: An Agents Expose*, South End Press, Boston, Mass, 1995.

166 Warren Weaver Jr, "Mondale Disloses Program to Tighten FBI and CIA Curbs," *New York Times* (August 9, 1977): A1, A20.

167 Taubman, "Carter Administration Unveils Proposed FBI Charter," *New York Times* (August 1, 1979): A8.

168 "Federal Bureau of Investigation," in *Public Papers of the President: Jimmy Carter 1979, Volume 2*, US Government Printing Office, Washington DC, 1980: 1334–36.

169 Phillip Taubman, "New Charter For FBI Won't Have Easy Sailing," *New York Times* (August 5, 1979) IV: 2.

170 Kessler, *The FBI*: 72–73.

171 John M Crewdson, "Former FBI Agent Tells Investigators of Widespread Abuses and Corruption," *New York Times* (January 20, 1979): A8.

172 "Official Finds FBI Discriminate in Hiring," *New York Times* (August 1, 1981): A26.

173 Nicholas M Horrock, "Trial of Ex-FBI Official Raises Fears Of National Security Data," *New York Times* (February 6, 1979): B6.

174 Gladis, "The FBI National Academy's First 50 Years," *FBI Law Enforcement Bulletin* (July 1985): 9.

175 "In FBI Agent's Novel, its 'Humps' vs. 'Suits,'" *New York Times* (November 20, 1992): A16.

3. Contagious, But Fortunately Not Hereditary
Origins of the New Right

1   James Ridgeway, *Blood in the Face*, Thunders Mouth Press, New York, 1990: 186.

2   Robert Dallek, *Ronald Reagan: The Politics of Symbolism*, Harvard UP, Cambridge, MA, 1984: 194.

3   M J Heale, "Red Scare Politics," *Journal of American Studies* (v.20, 1986): 32.

4   Irving Kristol, "American Conservatism 1945–1995," *Public Interest* (Fall 1995): 84, 87. Kristol was an influential character in the formulation of the New Right 'ideology', and the *New York Times* referred to him as their 'patron saint'. William Rusher, publisher of the *National Review*, was a supporter of Goldwater and helped plot the coup by which the conservative element of the Republican party became dominant.

5   Ibid: 15–16. See also Kristol, "American Conservatism 1945-1995," *Public Interest* (Fall 1995): 87.

6   Ibid: 15.

7   Ridgeway, *Blood in the Face*: 16.

8   James Q. Wilson, "A Guide to Reagan Country," *Commentary* (No.43, 1967): 45.

9   Wills, *Nixon Agonistes*: 75. For a New Right appraisal of California's culture and relevance see Wilson, "A Guide to Reagan Country," *Commentary* (No.43, 1967): 37–45.

10 Wilson, "A Guide to Reagan Country," *Commentary* (No.43, 1967): 45.

11 Wills, *Nixon Agonistes*: 76.

12 Wilson, "A Guide to Reagan Country," *Commentary* (No.43, 1967): 44.

13 Stephen E Ambrose, *Nixon: The Educa-* *tion of a Politician, Volume 1*, Simon and Schuster, London, 1987: 545. Mervyn LeRoy, the director of *The FBI Story* (1959), was the co-chairman of the Celebrities for Nixon Committee in 1960 which tried to attract the support of Ronald Reagan.

14 David Steigerwald, *The Sixties and the End of Modern America*, St Martin Press, New York, 1995: 280.

15 Wills, *Nixon Agonistes*: 250..

16 Kristol, "American Conservatism 1945-1995," *Public Interest* (Fall 1995): 81, 84. See also Wills, *Nixon Agonistes*: 250.

17 Hofstadter, "The Goldwater Debacle," *Encounter* (January 1965): 69.

18 Garry Wills, *Reagan's America: Innocents At Home*, Doubleday and Co, New York, 1987: 308. One of Goldwater's other financial supporters was Ralph Cordiner, Chief of General Electric, who employed Ronald Reagan as a spokesman for his company.

19 Hofstadter, "The Goldwater Debacle," *Encounter* (January 1965): 66–69.

20 Peter J Benekos and Alida V Merlo, "Three Strikes and You're Out!," *Federal Probation* (March 1995): 3.

21 Johnson, *Sleepwalking Through History*: 66.

22 William Miller, *A New History of the United States* [revised edition], Paladin Books, London, 1970: 433.

23 Commission report quoted in Tony G Poveda, "The Image of the Criminal," *Issues in Criminology* (v.5 No.1, 1970): 80.

24 Powers, *Secrecy and Power*: 395.

25 Steigerwald, *The Sixties and the End of*

Notes

Modern America: 188.

26　Wills, *Nixon Agonistes*: 267.

27　Bill Boyarsky, *Ronald Reagan: His Life and Rise to the Presidency*, Random House, New York, 1981: 103.

28　Steigerwald, *The Sixties and the End of Modern America*: 189.

29　Reagan quoted in Dallek, *Ronald Reagan: The Politics of Symbolism*: 4.

30　Wills, *Reagan's America*: 76–77.

31　Ibid: 165.

32　Dallek, *Ronald Reagan: The Politics of Symbolism*: 23.

33　Wills, *Reagan's America*: 166, 178–79.

34　Johnson, *Sleepwalking Through History*: 47.

35　Johnson, *Sleepwalking Through History*: 57.

36　Edwards, *Early Reagan*: 455–57.

37　Ibid: 457, 462–63.

38　Ambrose, *Nixon, Volume 1*: 546, 563.

39　Kenneth Anger, *Hollywood Babylon II*, Arrow Books, London, 1986: 306.

40　Ambrose, *Nixon, Volume 1*: 645, 542.

41　Boyarsky, *Ronald Reagan: His Life and Rise to the Presidency*: 83.

42　Bill Boyarsky, *The Rise of Ronald Reagan*, Random House, New York, 1968: 20, 26.

43　Ibid: 40.

44　Gerard De Groot, "Reagan's Rise," *History Today* (February 1990): 31. While a student at Eureka college Reagan also participated in a strike. He differentiated this from the Berkley protests by saying the strike in Eureka was supported by nearly all of the faculty, which, in his opinion, legitimized it. When faculty members at Berkeley had supported the strike Reagan attacked them for "inciting students to intemperate acts with inflammatory charges." Boyarsky, *The Rise of Ronald Reagan*: 47.

45　Turner, *Hoover's FBI*: 228.

46　Hoover quoted in Norman Ollestad, *Inside The FBI*, Lyle Stuart, New York, 1967: 6.

47　De Groot, "Reagan's Rise," *History Today* (February 1990): 31–32. Reagan never did understand the purpose of college, the encouragement of debate and dissent, to challenge what was wrong or endorse what was of value in the course of academic education. For Reagan it was a place for personal advancement. Dallek, *Ronald Reagan: The Politics of Symbolism*: 5.

48　Calabrese, "Reagan, Examined," *New York Times* (March 23, 1980): E21.

49　Reagan quoted in Boyarsky, *Ronald Reagan: His Life and Rise to the Presidency*: 186.

50　Milton R Machlin, "The Chessman Case," *New York Times Book Review* (July 16, 1961): 26. Chief William Henry Parker was a career police officer credited with reorganising the Los Angeles police department along military lines and reforming its discipline after 1950, when widespread corruption and abuses of power were public knowledge. After Parker's appointment he quickly became the second most famous law enforcement agent in America after Hoover, and conflicts between the two were the reason that Hoover ceased to vacation in California. Parker was a staunch moralist and blatant racist (white supremacist), one of his most notable actions being to close jazz clubs to prevent race mixing. His paramilitary policing tactics saw black and Latino neighbourhoods treated like occupied territories in need of strict, almost martial, law enforcement. Police treatment of ethnic minorities added to discontent which exploded in the 1965 Watts riots. Parker retired the following year. Daryl Gates, Parker's driver during the 1960s and later LAPD chief learned much of his trademark racial insensitivity and draconian police tactics from Parker.

51 Boyarsky, *Ronald Reagan: His Life and Rise to the Presidency*: 186.

52 Wills, *Nixon Agonistes*: 247.

53 Wills, *Reagan's America*: 308.

54 Boyarsky, *The Rise of Ronald Reagan*: 5.

55 Ibid: 41, 7.

56 Boyarsky, *Ronald Reagan: His Life and Rise to the Presidency*: 9.

57 Boyarsky, *The Rise of Ronald Reagan*: 24–25.

58 Jessica Mitford, *The American Prison Business*, Penguin, London, 1977: 174–76.

59 Michael Calabrese, "Reagan, Examined," *New York Times* (March 23, 1980): E21. Most of the welfare recipients were genuinely needy. Dallek, *Ronald Reagan: The Politics of Symbolism*: 41.

60 Boyarsky, *Ronald Reagan: His Life and Rise to the Presidency*: 178, 186.

61 Ibid: 187, 189, 185. Mitchell was a black laundry worker with a criminal record spanning twenty years. In May 1963 he had been convicted of killing a white police officer during the robbery of a restaurant and sentenced to death. Mitchell had to be dragged into the gas chamber screaming and prison records show that it was twelve minutes before he was officially pronounced dead. Stephen Trombley, *The Execution Protocol*, Arrow Books, London, 1993: 15. The next case for Reagan's consideration was that of Calvin Thomas, convicted of throwing a firebomb into the home of a woman acquaintance, killing her baby.

62 Nathaniel Sheppard Jr, "Community Mental Health Care Getting Second Thoughts," *New York Times* (July 23, 1979): A13.

63 Robert D Miller, "The Criminalization Of The Mentally Ill," *Criminal Behaviour and Mental Health* (v.3, 1993): 242. The brutal conditions in some mental hospitals were the subject of the *Titicut Follies* (Frederick Wiseman, 1967) documentary made concerning the Bridgewater State Hospital which was banned from public screening for decades after its release. State officials contended the film invaded the privacy of the inmates; however, Wiseman cited an obvious conflict of interest in that the state was trying to prevent the public from knowing about hospital conditions. Eventually the documentary was given a formal release in August 1991. William H. Hanan, "Judge Ends Ban On Film Of Asylum," *New York Times* (August 3, 1991): A12. Tom Ryan's *Screw: A Guard's View of Bridgewater State Hospital* (South End Press, Boston, 1981) chronicled his experiences as a guard at the hospital during an eighteen month period in the mid 1970s. Ryan reported violent beatings of inmates and numerous rapes. The patients were given heavy dosages of psychoactive drugs to keep them 'under control'.

64 Miller, "The Criminalization Of The Mentally ill," *Criminal Behaviour and Mental Health* (v.3, 1993): 242–44.

65 "Debate Set Off By Mass Killings," *New York Times* (11 November 1973): A31.

66 Abrahamson, "The Criminalization of Mentally Disordered Behaviour," *Hospital and Community Psychiatry* (April 1972): 15.

67 Sheppard, "Community Mental Health Care Getting Second Thoughts," *New York Times* (July 23, 1979): A13.

68 Lunde, *Murder and Madness*: 74–75.

69 Ibid: 81.

70 Ressler and Schactman, *Whoever Fights Monsters*: 1–2.

Notes

71   Low quoted in ibid: 7.

72   Ibid. During the investigation of the 'Vampire' murders, investigators were aware that some fringe associates of Charles Manson were living in Sacramento when the killings occurred. A number of "concerned citizens" saw similarities between the 'Vampire' killings and the Manson Family murders a decade earlier, but Ray Biondi was convinced that the killings were the work of a single killer. Ted Bundy, who had escaped from jail in Colorado, was also named as a suspect, distracting police attention until it became clear that his *modus operandi* was noticeably different. Biondi and Hecox, *The Dracula Killer*: 94–96.

73   Ressler and Schactman, *Whoever Fights Monsters*: 3–4, 7, 9, 46. John Lindley Frazier and Herb Mullin were also described by Ressler as 'disorganised' murderers.

74   Morton Birnbaum, "Care for Mentally Ill," *New York Times* (January 30, 1972): IV12. See also "A Plea For the Mentally Retarded," *New York Times* (June 25, 1972) IV: 3.

75   Boyarsky, *Ronald Reagan: His Life and Rise to the Presidency*: 182. In 1965 the legislature confined the death penalty to those who were convicted of killing a police officer in the line of duty or those who murdered fellow inmates in prison. Restricted executions continued until June 1967, after which time no further executions took place.

76   "Coast Man Guilty in 8 Murders," *New York Times* (November 9, 1973): 5.

77   "Debate Set Off By Mass Killings," *New York Times* (November 11, 1973): 31.

78   Ibid. From his study, Larry Sosowsky agrees that a knowledge of diagnostic factors alone does not allow professionals in the field of mental health to make reliable predictions concerning recidivism. Larry Sosowsky, "Explaining The Increased Arrest Rate Among Mental Patients: A Cautionary Note," *American Journal of Psychiatry* (December 1980): 1604.

79   Martin A Lee and Bruce Shlain, *Acid Dreams*, Grove Press, New York, 1992: 189–90.

80   Miller, "The Criminalization Of The Mentally Ill," *Criminal Behaviour and Mental Health* (v.3, 1993): 244.

81   Dolby quoted in Sheppard, "Community Mental Health Care Getting Second Thoughts," *New York Times* (July 23, 1979): A13.

82   Stiegerwald, *The Sixties and the End of Modern America*: 272.

83   Wills, *Nixon Agonistes*: 256, 77–78.

84   Les Evans, "Watergate and the White House: From Kennedy to Nixon and Beyond," in Les Evans and Allan Myers (ed), *Watergate and the Myth of American Democracy*, Pathfinder Press, New York, 1974: 28–30.

85   Wills, *Nixon Agonistes*: 254, 257. He kept this promise when he selected Spiro Agnew, Governor of Maryland, as his running mate.

86   Nixon, *The Memoirs of Richard Nixon: Volume 1*, Warner Books, New York, 1978: 26.

87   Ibid: 443, 79, 261.

88   Thomas T Noguchi and Joseph Di Mona, *Coroner To The Stars*, Guild Publishing, London, 1986: 129.

89   Denise Noe, "Charles Manson: The Myth And The Reality," *Gauntlet* (No.1, 1995): 66.

90   Jock Young, "The Hippie Solution: An Essay In The Politics Of Leisure," in Ian Taylor and Laurie Taylor (ed), *Politics and Deviance*, Pelican, London, 1973: 200.

91   Nuel Eummons, *Manson In His Own Words*, Grove Press, New York, 1986: 149.

92   Susan Atkins, *Child of Satan, Child of God*, Hodder and Stoughton, London, 1977: 75–81, 103, 106.

93   Robert J Semple Jr, "Nixon Calls Manson Guilty, Later Withdraws Remark," *New York Times* (August 4, 1970), A1.

94   "Manson Calls Nixon Key to Conviction," *New York Times* (August 13, 1975): A13.

95   Peter Ross Range, "Who Will Be The First?," *New York Times Magazine* (March 11, 1979): 75.

96   Range, "Who Will Be The First?," *New York Times Magazine* (March 11, 1979): 76.

97   Wicker, "Playing to the Fear of Crime," *New York Times* (March 13, 1973): 39.

98   Duffy quoted in Range, "Who Will Be The First?," *New York Times Magazine* (March 11, 1979): 78.

99   Bremer quoted in James W Clarke, *American Assassins: The Darker Side of Politics*, Princeton University Press, Princeton, New Jersey, 1982: 188.

100   Cal McCrystal et al, *Watergate: The Full Inside Story*, Andre Deutsch Ltd., London, 1973: 128-29. Charles Colson was also given the task of compiling the White House enemies list which included 200 Democrats, journalists and academics. Little is really known about Bremer. He was reported to be obsessed with the character of Alex from *A Clockwork Orange* (Stanley Kubrick, 1971), and that he had read about John Wilkes Booth, Lee Harvey Oswald and Sirhan Sirhan. Bremer never explained his motives and declined to give interviews in prison. The FBI did interview him for their serial killer study, and he provided a basis for the character of Travis Bickle in *Taxi Driver* (Martin Scorsese, 1976). Several years after the shooting Wallace, being interviewed by Barbara Walters, raised a pertinent question about the incident. How did anyone know where Bremer, who was usually reported to be a drifter, lived less than an hour after the attempt on his life? It has also never been established where Bremer got the money to pay the large bills he ran up while stalking Nixon and Wallace. Reports that he had been seen with Anthony Ulasewicz, a White House operative, also faded into the background. Carl Sifakis, *Encyclopaedia of Assassins*, Facts On File, New York, 1991: 199–200.

101   William W Shannon, "To Save America's Lost Children," *New York Times* (August 8, 1972): A33.

102   Shannon, "To Save America's Lost Children," *New York Times* (August 8, 1972): A33.

103   Nixon quoted in "Nixon Terms Hoover a Giant of America," *New York Times* (May 5, 1972): A15.

104   Robert M Smith, "New Director Says Nixon Wants Nonpolitical FBI: Gray Discusses Agency," *New York Times* (May 5, 1972): A1, 14.

105   Theodore White quoted in Richard Reeves, *A Ford Not A Lincoln*, Hutchinson and Co Ltd, London, 1976: 171–72.

106   Reeves, *A Ford Not A Lincoln*: 29.

107   Ibid.

108   Ibid: 41–43, 54, 68.

109   Fromme was a member of Manson's Family. However, Moore was a former FBI informer who had been on the periphery of a number of radical movements in the Bay Area. Jesse Bravin, *Squeaky: The Life and Times of Lynette Alice Fromme*, St Martin's Griffin, New York, 1997: 284.

110   David Von Drehle, *Among the Lowest of the Dead*, Fawcett Crest, New York, 1995: 127. Spenkelink was seen as a career criminal progressing from juvenile deliquency as a teenage

'pot head' to serious felonies (multiple counts of armed robbery and escaping from prison), and finally to murder. He pleaded self-defence but the prosecution argued that the victim had been sleeping when shot, and then bludgeoned. The prosecution portrayed Spenkelink as a ruthless criminal who showed no signs of rehabilitation. It was suggested by a Florida supreme court justice that he had been discriminated against by the police because he was an underprivileged drifter. After Spenkelink's execution, Governor Graham signed an execution warrant for Howard V Douglas who had been convicted of murdering his former lover's husband (Jesse Atkins Jr.) after abducting them both. After forcing them to have sex while he watched, Douglas killed the husband, and then raped Mrs Atkins and held her and her children prisoner for nine days.

111 Range, "Who Will Be The First?," *New York Times Magazine* (March 11, 1979): 82.

112 Ibid: 78. Killing a black person, even by another black person, was only one tenth as likely to be punished with a death sentence as taking a white life. A black person convicted of killing a white person was five times as likely to receive capital punishment than a white doing the same thing. A similar study by researchers from the University of Iowa had similar findings. Leslie Maitland Werner, "Federal Study Finds Rate Of Executions Rising," *New York Times* (July 9, 1984): A8. This was the very practice which *Furman vs. Georgia* was supposed to strike down.

113 Jenkins, *Using Murder*: 131.

114 Palmer quoted in Range, "Who Will Be The First?," *New York Times Magazine* (March 11, 1979): 72.

4. Walt Disney's Last Wish
The New Right and Ronald Reagan

1 Robin Williams described Ronald Reagan as 'Walt Disney's Last Wish' in his comedy routines, suggesting that Reagan was an animatronic puppet. Disney's close public association with wholesome American values and his ideology of extreme right-wing politics was what Williams' joke was trying to highlight. Walt Disney Studios had also designed the inaugural program when Reagan became governor of California in 1967. Bill Boyarsky, *The Rise of Ronald Reagan*, Random House, New York, 1968: 164.

2 Frank Van Der Linder cited in Dallek, *Ronald Reagan: The Politics of Symbolism*: 7.

3 "Remarks in New Orleans, Louisiana, at the Annual Meeting of the International Association of Chiefs of Police (September 28, 1981)," in *The Public Papers of the Presidents: Ronald Reagan 1981, Volume 1*, United States Government Printing Office, Washington DC, 1982: 840–41, 844.

4 Gillian Peele, "The Agenda of the

New Right," in Dilys Hill et al. (ed), *The Reagan Presidency. An Incompetent Revolution?*, MacMillan, London, 1990: 40.

5   Kristol, "American Conservatism 1945–1995," *Public Interest* (Fall 1995): 88–89.

6   Krauthammer, "A Social Conservative Credo," *Public Interest* (Fall 1995): 18–21.

7   Kristol, "American Conservatism 1945–1995," *Public Interest* (Fall 1995): 89–90. 'Welfare' served as a euphemism for a variety of ethnic groups, all of whom were members of the 'underclass'. Unskilled, poorly educated, and unemployed they had no economic influence, and therefore no political power.

8   Ridgeway, *Blood in the Face*: 186.

9   Dorothy Wickenden, "Abandoned Americans," *New Republic* (March 18, 1985): 24.

10   John Herbers, "Nation's Crime Rate Is Up Again, With Smaller Cities Leading Rise," *New York Times* (October 28, 1979): A64.

11   Boyarsky, *Ronald Reagan: His Life and Rise to the Presidency*: 185.

12   Cannon quoted in Barber, "Candidate Reagan and the 'sucker generation'," *Columbia Journalism Review* (November/December 1987): 34. William Bagley was a former Republican state senate leader who had worked closely with Reagan's gubernatorial administration in Sacramento. Gore Vidal noted that Democratic speaker Bob Moretti effectively ran California during Reagan's time as governor. Aside from announcing policies Reagan spent most of his time travelling around the nation giving speeches on Communism. Gore Vidal, *Armageddon? Essays 1983–87*, Andre Deutsch Limited, London, 1987: 86.

13   Johnson, *Sleepwalking Through History*: 13–14.

14   Evan Thomas, "Yankee Doodle Candidate," *Time* (June 25, 1984): 23.

15   Johnson, *Sleepwalking Through History*: 139.

16   Edwards, *Early Reagan*: 457.

17   Dallek, *Ronald Reagan: The Politics of Symbolism*: 194. The low turnout of eligible voters could be applied to any presidential election, but few candidates have trumpeted such a minimal success into a grand mandate for changes as Reagan did. Political commentator Norman Solomon observed that in late twentieth century politics, "The ability to numb and delude is the ability to control." Norman Solomon, *False Hope: The Politics of Illusion in the Clinton Era*, Common Courage, Monroe, Maine, 1994: 112.

18   David Mervin, "Ronald Reagan's Place in History," *Journal of American Studies* (v.23, 1989): 275. See also King and Schudson, "The Myth of the Great Communicator," *Columbia Journalism Review* (November/December 1987): 39.

19   Johnson, *Sleepwalking Through History*: 20, 19.

20   Joseph Lanza, *The Cocktail: The Influence of Spirits on the American Psyche*, St Martins Press, New York, 1995: 147–48. In 1981 Nancy Reagan proudly announced that hard liquor would once more be served in the White House.

21   Johnson, *Sleepwalking Through History*: 20.

22   Anger, *Hollywood Babylon II*: 312.

23   Johnson, *Sleepwalking Through History*: 14.

24   Barber, "Candidate Reagan and the 'sucker generation'," *Columbia Journalism Review* (November/December 1987): 33.

Notes

25   Dallek, *Ronald Reagan: The Politics of Symbolism*: 67.

26   King and Schudson, "The Myth of the Great Communicator," *Columbia Journalism Review* (November/December 1987): 37, 39.

27   "Disapproval of Reagan Up Sharply in New Poll," *New York Times* (March 18, 1981): A22.

28   Hugh Sidey, "Scripture for a New Religion," *Time* (March 2, 1981): 29.

29   Elizabeth A Stanko, "Women, Crime and Fear," *The Annals of the American Academy of Politics and Social Sciences* (May 1995): 51. Released in 1980, The Figgie Report on Fear of Crime found that public fear of crime, especially among women, increased in the late 1960s throught to the mid 1970s, declining towards the end of the decade. The report also discovered that two-fifths of Americans were "highly fearful" of becoming victims of violent crime, a finding which was reflected in numerous opinion polls during the 1970s. Mark H Moore and Robert C Trojanowicz, "Policing and the fear of crime," *Perspectives on Policing* (June 1988): 2.

30   Dan Moldea, *Dark Victory*, Viking, New York, 1986: 319–320.

31   Pear, "Reagan's Advisers Giving Priority to Street Crime and Victims Aid," *New York Times* (November 15, 1980): A9.

32   "Cheap Talk About Crime," *New York Times* (September 30, 1981): A30.

33   Stuart Taylor Jr, "New Attack On Crime," *New York Times* (September 30, 1981): A28.

34   Glasser quoted in Moldea, *Dark Victory*: 321.

35   Unnamed agent quoted in ibid: 324.

36   Bertram Gross, "Reagan's Criminal 'Anti-Crime' Fix," in Alan Gartner et al. (ed), *What Reagan Is Doing To Us*, Perennial Library, New York, 1982: 89.

37   Taylor Jr, "New Attack On Crime," *New York Times* (September 30, 1981): A28.

38   "Cheap Talk About Crime," *New York Times* (September 30, 1981): A30.

39   Platt, "US Criminal Justice In The Reagan Administration," *Crime and Social Justice* (No.29): 59.

40   Douglas and Olshaker, *Mindhunters*: 331. Foster had starred as a teenage prostitute in *Taxi Driver* (Martin Scorcese, 1976) a film loosely based on Arthur Bremer's attempt to kill George Wallace in 1972, which Hinckley repeatedly watched. Hinckley was also a member of the National Socialist Party of America (Nazi Party), but an application to have his membership renewed was refused by the party after the assassination attempt. Carl Sifakis, *Encyclopedia of Assassination*, Facts on File, New York, 1991: 159–60.

41   Johnson, *Sleepwalking Through History*: 160.

42   Ibid.

43   Samuel C Patterson, "Political Leaders and the Assassination of President Kennedy," in William J Crotty (ed), *Assassinations and the Political Order*, Torchlight Books, New York, 1971: 269, 272.

44   Johnson, *Sleepwalking Through History*: 162.

45   Ibid: 153–154.

46   Hugh Sidey, "Scripture for a New Religion," *Time* (March 2, 1981): 29.

47   "Remarks at the Annual Conference of the National Sheriff's Association in Hartford Connecticut. June 20, 1984", in *The Public Papers of the Presidents: Ronald Reagan, 1984*, United States Government Printing Office, Washington, 1985: 884–886.

48   Leslie Maitland Werner, "Federal Study Finds Rate Of Executions Rising," *New York Times* (July 9, 1984): A8. Along with

the Manson Family, associations would be made in the media to the crimes of Herb Mullins, John Lindley Frazier and Ed Kemper.

49 Gest et al., "Justice Under Reagan," *US News and World Report* (October 14, 1985): 59.

50 "Reagan, On Radio, Urges Passage of Crime Bill," *New York Times* (February 19, 1984): A34.

51 Vossler quoted in "High Court Curbs Right of Suspects," *New York Times* (June 13, 1984): A1, B13. See also "Excerpts From Supreme Court Decision On Rights Of Suspects," *New York Times* (June 13, 1984): B13.

52 Linda Greenhouse, "A New Angrier Mood On Death Penalty Appeals," *New York Times* (November 11, 1983): A22.

53 Rehnquist quoted in ibid.

54 "No 'Games' On Death Row," *New York Times* (December 1, 1993): A26.

55 *Habeas Corpus* comes from the Latin meaning 'you have the body'. A writ of *Habeas Corpus* is a check on the manner in which state courts respect the consitutional rights of the accused. In *Brown v. Vasquez* (1991, 1992) the Supreme Court recognised that the writ of *Habeas Corpus* "is the fundamental instrument for safeguarding individual freedom against arbitrary and lawless state action." The writ is a judicial order to a prison official ordering that an inmate be brought to court where it can be determined if they are detained legally or should be released.

56 Robert Sherrill, "Death Row On Trial," *New York Times Magazine* (November 13, 1983): 80–83, 98–116.

57 Ibid: 60.

58 Platt, "US Criminal Justice In The Reagan Administration," *Crime and Social Justice* (No.29): 61.

59 Gest et al, "Justice Under Reagan," *US News and World Report* (October 14, 1985): 58–59.

60 Finn-DeLuca, "Victim Participation At Sentencing," *Criminal Law Bulletin* (v.30, 1994): 424.

61 Robert Pear, "FBI Chief Forsees Little Change Under Reagan," *New York Times* (November 21, 1980): A23.

62 Gest et al, "Justice Under Reagan," *US News and World Report* (October 14, 1985): 60.

63 Platt, "US Criminal Justice In The Reagan Administration," *Crime and Social Justice* (No.29): 59.

64 Dairmuid Jeffreys, *The Bureau: Inside Today's FBI*, Pan Books, London, 1995: 267, 191–92. For a full transcript of Executive Order 12333 see Scott D Beckinridge, *The CIA and the US Intelligence System*, Westview Press, Boulder, Co, 1986: 330–347.

65 Etan Patz was six years old when he disappeared on May 25, 1979, after leaving home in lower Manhattan to go to school. By the time of the missing children panic he had not been found. In 1984 James Slaughter was charged with attempted grand larceny and aggravated harassment for attempting to extort $2,500 from Patz's father, implying that he could guarantee the child's safety. "Extortion Bid Charged In The Patz Boy's Case," *New York Times* (May 22, 1984): B2. See also Selwyn Raab, "The Unrelenting Search For Etan Patz," *New York Times* (July 26, 1979): B1.

66 Adam Walsh had been abducted from a department store on July 27, 1981. A man was reported dragging a child into a blue van, but despite this information, a $5,000 reward, and a massive police ground search he was not found. The FBI refused to enter the case because there was

Notes

no ransom note nor any evidence of interstate transportation (there was no evidence of interstate transportation in the Atlanta Child Murders but the FBI used it anyway as an excuse to join the investigation). John Walsh appeared on local and national TV to try to find his son but his efforts were unsuccessful. Adam's severed head was found in a swamp canal in Vero Beach, Florida. The rest of his body was never located.

67   Neal Karlen et al., "How Many Missing Kids," *Newsweek* (October 7, 1985): 30–31.

68   "A Plea For Missing Children," *New York Times* (October 28, 1983): A18.

69   Joel Best, "Missing Children, Misleading Statistics," *Public Interest* (Summer 1988): 85. In 1982 an article in the *New York Times* also put the figure at 50,000. "Child Abductions A Rising Concern," *New York Times* (December 5, 1982): A77.

70   "Child Abductions A Rising Concern," *New York Times* (December 5, 1982): A77.

71   Karlen et al, "How Many Missing Kids," *Newsweek* (October 7, 1985): 30–31.

72   Jack Breslin, *America's Most Wanted: How Television Catches Crooks*, Harper and Row, New York, 1990: 80.

73   "Reason To Care," *New York Times* (February 7, 1988): B33.

74   Breslin, *America's Most Wanted*: 80, 82–83. Originally the show was called *Most Wanted* but copyright problems forced the producers to change the programme's name. *Most Wanted* was a late 1970s TV crime drama about a special police unit headed by Robert Stack. In the pilot episode, a made-for-TV film, a psychopath rapes a series of nuns while collecting crucifixes as trophies.

75   Weiss, "Where Have All the Children Gone," *The Sunday Correspondent* (April 22, 1990): 45.

76   Karlen et al, "How many Missing Kids," *Newsweek* (October 7, 1985): 30–31.

77   Spock quoted in Weiss, "Where Have All the Children Gone," *The Sunday Correspondent* (April 22, 1990): 45.

78   "Loss Of Evidence Impeded Inquiry Into Boy's Death," *New York Times* (February 18, 1996): A30. Eventually police interviewed Jeffrey Dahmer in a Wisconsin prison about the murder of Adam Walsh when they found information that Dahmer had been in the Hollywood, Fl, area at the time. "Suspect Scrutinized in Slaying of Adam Walsh," *New York Times* (June 15, 1995): A15.

79   Agopian quoted in Best, "Missing children, misleading statistics," *Public Interest* (Summer 1988): 85.

80   Bell quoted in Nathaniel Sheppard Jr, "Atlanta Marking Halloween Carefully," *New York Times* (November 1, 1980): A12.

81   Ibid.

82   Wayne King, "Trade is Giving Atlanta International Status," *New York Times* (June 26, 1979): A14.

83   Jackson quoted in Reginald Stuart, "Tension over Atlanta Killing Tests Racial Harmony," *New York Times* (March 24, 1981): A16.

84   M A Farber, "Investigators Feel Many Killers, Seperatly, Slew Atlanta Children," *New York Times* (March 15, 1981): A32.

85   Bernard D Headley, "Ideological Constructions Of Race And The 'Atlanta Tragedy'," *Contemporary Crises* (No.10, 1986): 183–89, 193.

86   Douglas and Olshaker, *Mindhunters*: 199.

87   Wendell Rawls Jr, "4 Children Hunted By 1,000 In Atlanta," *New York Times* (November 2, 1980): A28. One of the

strangest volunteers in the searches was Mitch Werbel and his group of trainees. Werbel trained bodyguards and foreign anti-terrorist squads at a private training ground in Georgia. He offered his help to try to organize "well meaning amateurs." "5th Atlanta Weekend Hunt Ends Without New Clues," New York Times (November 16, 1980): A28.

88 Nathaniel Sheppard Jr, "US Officials Work To Calm Racial Fears in Atlanta," New York Times (October 30, 1980): A21. Newspapers reported a variety of violent Klan related crimes across the South. In one instance the FBI began a manhunt for James Vaughn, who was suspected of murdering blacks in five Southern cities. Headley, "Ideological Constructions of Race and the 'Atlanta Tregedy'," Contemporary Crises (No.10, 1986): 197, 193. See also Shields, "The Atlanta Story," Columbia Journalism Review (September/October 1981): 33; Wayne King, "The Violent Rebirth of the Klan," New York Times Magazine (December 7, 1980).

89 Wendell Rawls Jr, "Body of Black Boy Found In Atlanta," New York Times (November 3, 1980): A20.

90 Sheppard Jr, "US Officials Work To Calm Racial Fears in Atlanta," New York Times (October 30, 1980): A21.

91 Pear, "FBI Chief Forsees Little Change Under Reagan," New York Times (November 21, 1980): A23.

92 Jackson quoted in M A Farber, "Investigators Feel Many Killers, Seperately, Slew Atlanta Children," New York Times (March 15, 1981): A32.

93 Burton quoted in ibid.

94 Ibid.

95 "Jersey 'Psychic' Searches Atlanta For Killer Of Children," New York Times (October 23, 1980): A21.

96 John M. Crewdson, "Hundreds Search in Atlanta After Discovery of Skeleton," New York Times (January 11, 1981): A20. Pierce Brooks worked on the notorious Black Dahlia case in LA in the 1940 but came to prominence as the investigating detective in the Onion Field Murders which was immortalized in a book by Joseph Wambaugh and a film of the same name by Harold Becker in 1979. Brooks also investigated the murders committed by Harvey Glatman, a 1950s serial sex killer.

97 Glover quoted in "Murdered Children Honoured in Atlanta," New York Times (November 6, 1980): A21.

98 Wendell Rawls Jr, "5 Outside detectives to aid Atlanta's hunt for Children," New York Times (November 7, 1980): A12.

99 Brown quoted in "5 Visiting detectives begin work on murders of children in Atlanta," New York Times (November 12, 1980): A19.

100 Ibid.

101 Wendall Rawls Jr, "Body of Black Boy is found in Atlanta," New York Times (November 3, 1980): A20. The first victims five were found in wooded areas buried in shallow graves, later ones were easily found in uncovered locations. Five had been strangled, one had been shot, two stabbed, one beaten to death, and one was so badly decomposed that the cause of death could not be determined. To November 1980 twelve victims were male and two were female, and only one of the female victims had been sexually assaulted. The only consistent feature was that they were all black.

102 Reginald Stuart, "Atlanta Deaths: Fear Felt By the Young," New York Times (January 26, 1981): A12.

103 Reginald Stuart, "Reagan Agrees to Meeting on Child Slayings in At-

Notes

lanta," *New York Times* (January 30, 1981): A8.

104 Bush quoted in Wendell Rawls Jr, "Atlanta Labors To Find Who Is Killing Its Children," *New York Times* (February 22, 1981): A1.

105 "FBI ordered to assist in Atlanta child Slaying," *New York Times* (February 8, 1981): A24.

106 Adam Clymer, "Bush Visits Families of Murdered Children in Atlanta," *New York Times* (March 15, 1981): A31.

107 Douglas and Olshaker, *Mindhunters*: 374.

108 Ibid: 202, 204. One of the main reasons behind Douglas and Hazelwood's rejection of racial motivation, despite strong information provided to the contrary by informants to the Bureau's Georgia field office, was that the crimes were not public enough, and that the bodies were not displayed blatantly enough.

109 Keppel and Birnes, *The Riverman*: 94.

110 Jackson quoted in Wendell Rawls Jr, "Atlanta Officials In A Rift With The FBI," *New York Times* (April 15, 1981): A15.

111 Ibid.

112 Rawls Jr, "Atlanta Labors To Find Who Is Killing Its Children," *New York Times* (February 22, 1981): A1.

113 Keppel and Birnes, *The Riverman*: 98–99, 101.

114 Ibid: 101.

115 Interview with Robert Keppel August 28, 1998.

116 Wendell Rawls Jr, "Officials in Atlanta Suggest FBI Mishandled Key Lead in Slayings," *New York Times* (June 14, 1981): A1, A34.

117 Interview with Robert Keppel by the author, August 26, 1998.

118 Keppel and Birnes, *The Riverman*: 112.

119 Interview with Robert Keppel by the author, August 26, 1998.

120 Wendell Rawls Jr, "Atlanta Man, Detained 12 Hours, Denies Role in Any of 28 Killings," *New York Times* (June 5, 1981): A12.

121 Young quoted in "Man Questioned In Atlanta Killings," *New York Times* (June 4, 1981): A20.

122 David B Hilder "2d Defense Expert Views Williams Fiber Expert," *Washington Post* (February 18, 1982): A11. Even the origin of the carpet fibres was in doubt when the FBI dated them to being produced in 1970–71 and Williams' father claimed his carpet had been bought in 1968. Art Harris, "Father Disputes Experts On Carpet Data," *Washington Post* (February 20, 1982): A1.

123 Rawls Jr, "Officials in Atlanta Suggest FBI Mishandled Key Lead in Slayings," *New York Times* (June 14, 1981): A34.

124 Divan quoted in"FBI Starts To Withdraw Agents Assigned To Atlanta," *New York Times* (June 25, 1981): A14.

125 Slaton quoted in Art Harris, "Atlanta Doubts," *Washington Post* (March 1, 1982): A8. Roy Innis, head of the Congress On Racial Equality (CORE), asked Maury Terry, an acknowledged authority on the Son of Sam murders, for assistance during the Atlanta Child Murders investigation. Innis and CORE unearthed information which suggested that Williams had been acting in conjunction with others, but the state and federal authorities chose to ignore the information. Maury Terry, *The Ultimate Evil*, Paragon/ Diamond, London, 1993: 613–614.

126 Douglas and Olshaker, *Mindhunters*: 222.

127 Harris, "Atlanta Doubts," *Washington Post* (March 1, 1982): A1, A8.

128 Art Harris,"Families of Atlanta Victims Make Own Judgements on Williams," *Washington Post* (February 7, 1982),

A5.

129   Bell quoted in Harris, "Atlanta Doubts," *Washington Post* (March 1, 1982): A1.

130   Michael Newton, *Raising Hell*, Warner Books, New York, 1994: 30.

131   Diane E H Russell and Candida Ellis, "Annihilation By Murder and By the Media: The Other Atlanta Femicides," in Radford and Russell (ed), *Femicide*: 161–62.

132   Williams quoted in Art Harris, "Williams Reveals a New Image As Defense Ends," *Washington Post* (February 25, 1982): A2.

133   "Lawyer Sees Hope For Retrial In Atlanta Murders," *New York Times* (August 30, 1987): A26.

134   Jeffers, *Profiles in Evil*: 133.

135   Reagan quoted in "Bill on Missing Children Signed By President," *New York Times* (October 13, 1982): A23.

136   Breslin, *America's Most Wanted*: 331.

137   Jeffers, *Profiles in Evil*: 134.

138   "Bill On Missing Children Signed By President," *New York Times* (October 13, 1982): A23.

139   Jeffers, *Profiles in Evil*: 138.

140   Reagan quoted in "Reagan, On Radio, Urges Passage of Crime Bill," *New York Times* (February 19, 1984): A34.

141   "Mary Thornton, "Photographer Sought in Manhunt," *Washington Post* (April 6, 1984): A2; Ronald Kessler, "Object of Manhunt Fatally Shoots Self," *Washington Post* (April 14, 1984): A1. According to Robert Ressler, the reason Christopher Wilder was originally classified as a serial killer by the FBI and later redesignated a 'spree' killer was because he did not have a cooling off period between his crimes. Ressler et al, *Sexual Homicide*: 140.

142   For example Michaud, "The FBI's Psyche Squad," *New York Times Magazine* (October 26, 1986): 40; Robert Ressler et al, "Sexual Killers And Their Victims: Identifying Patterns Through Crime Scene Analysis," *Journal of Interpersonal Violence* (September 1986): 306.

143   Douglas and Olshaker, *Mindhunters*: 30.

144   Wilson and Seaman, *Serial Killers*: 32, 186.

145   Elliot Leyton cited in Wilson and Seaman, *Serial Killers*: 297.

146   Hoffman, *A Venom In The Blood*: ix.

147   Douglas and Olshaker, *Mindhunters*: 356.

148   Harold Schechter and David Everitt, *The A–Z Encyclopaedia of Serial Killers*, Pocket Books, New York, 1996: 294.

149   Daniel S Hellman and Nathan Blackman, "Enuresis, Firesetting, and Cruelty to Animals: A Triad Predictive of Adult Crime," *American Journal of Psychiatry* (June 1966): 1431–35. See also Curt Suplee, "Serial Killers: Frighteningly Close To Normal," *Washington Post* (August 5, 1991): A3.

150   Robert Fieldmore Lewis, "Alone on Death Row with Ted Bundy," in Sondra London (ed), *Knockin' On Joe*, Nemesis Books, London, 1993: 66.

151   Schechter and Everitt, *The A–Z Encyclopaedia of Serial Killers*: 320–22.

152   Otto, "Statement of John Otto", in "Serial Murders: hearing before the Subcommittee on Juvenile Justice of the Committe on the Judiciary, United States Senate, Ninety Eighth Congress, first session, on patterns of murders committed by one person, in large numbers with no apparent rhyme, reason or motivation, (July 12, 1983): 56. Hereafter "Serial Murder" (July 12, 1983).

153   David Shribman, "$10.3 Billion In Spending Cuts Passed By House To Shave Deficit," *New York Times* (October 26, 1983): B7.

154   Reagan quoted in "Reagan Asks For A

Notes

Return To Traditional Values," *New York Times* (June 17, 1983): A18.

155 Burnham, "From G-Man To Cursor Man," *New York Times* (October 22, 1984): A16.

156 Drehle, *Among The Lowest Of The Dead*: 285, 283.

157 Jenkins, *Using Murder*: 130. Thomas was Vice-President for Communications with the 'Moral Majority'. His philosophy led him to denounce secular humanism, homosexuals, and the gay rights movement.

158 Drehle, *Among The Lowest Of The Dead*: 297–301.

159 Ibid: 301–03.

160 Fox and Levin, *Overkill*: 11.

161 Jacob V Lamar, "I Deserve To Die," *Time* (February 6, 1989): 34. Dobson was a psychologist who heads a $50 million non-profit corporation based in southern California which publishes *Focus on the Family* magazine, distributing 1.9 million copies of each issue. Dobson has his own radio show and has published several books, among them *Dare to Discipline* (1970), which advocated corporal punishment and condemned the new morality of the 1960s. Susan Garrett Baker, wife of the US sectretary of state was on the board of directors of Focus, and Gary Bauer, who had served for eight years as a domestic advisor to Reagan, headed the Council on Family Research which it bought in 1988. Within two years it became the biggest Evangelical Christian lobbying group in Washington. Dobson urged his supporters to protect the family from pornography, feminism, homosexual rights, day care centres, abortion, and rock music lyrics. He also opposed the Civil Rights Restoration Act and supported Bush in his presidential election campaign. Laura Sessions Stepp, "The Empire Built on Family and Faith," *Washington Post* (August 8, 1990): C1, C2, C3.

162 Dirk Johnson, "For Families, Killer's Death Eases Doubts But Not Pain," *New York Times* (February 13, 1989): A1.

163 Jon Nordheimer, "Bundy Is Put To Death In Florida After Admitting Trail Of Killings," *New York Times* (January 25, 1989): A1, A20.

164 "Bundy Toll May Be More Than 50, Prosecutor In Case Says," *New York Times* (January 26, 1989): A21.

165 Johnson, "For Families, Killer's Death Eases Doubts But Not Pain," *New York Times* (February 13, 1989): A1.

166 Dodd quoted in Lane and Gregg, *The New Encyclopaedia of Serial Killers*: 126.

167 John Kifner, "Man Who Killed 33 Is Executed In Illinois," *New York Times* (May 10, 1994): A12.

168 Carey Goldberg, "Families Hope Freeway Killer's Execution Ends Their Years of Pain," *New York Times* (February 22, 1996): A14. See also, "Man Known as Freeway Killer Is Executed," *New York Times* (February 24, 1996): A7.

169 Waxman quoted in Ibid: A14.

170 "Federal District Court Bans San Quentin's Secret Execution Procedures," ACLU online at [w] www.aclu.org/news/n031397b.html

171 Andrew Vachss, "Sex Predators Can't Be Saved," *New York Times* (January 5, 1993): A15.

172 Anthony M Platt, "The Politics of Law and Order," *Social Justice* (v.21, No.3): 5.

173 Ibid.

5. Plague-Rats
Founding the Behavioral Sciences Unit

1   "Statement of panel," in "The Federal Role In The Investigation Of Violent Crime," (April 9 and May 21, 1986): 10.

2   Turner, Hoover's FBI: 3.

3   Powers, Secrecy And Power: 486.

4   English quoted in "The Federal Role In The Investigation Of Violent Crime," (April 9 and May 21, 1986): 1.

5   Lois H Herrington cited in Jeffers, Profiles In Evil: 32.

6   Steven A Egger, "Toward A Working Definition Of Serial Murder," Journal of Police Science and Administration (v.12 No.3, 1984): 353.

7   Stephen G Michaud, "The FBI's Psyche Squad," New York Times Magazine (October 26, 1986): 40.

8   Egger, "Toward A Working Definition Of Serial Murder," Journal of Police Science and Administration (v.12 No.3, 1984): 353, 351.

9   Keppel and Birnes, The Riverman: 119, 349.

10   J J Nordby, "Boostrapping While Barefoot," Synthese (December 1989): 377. See also Keppel and Birnes, The Riverman: 119.

11   Keppel and Birnes, The Riverman: 119–20.

12   Ann Rule in "Statements of panel," in "Serial Murder" (July 12, 1983): 18.

13   Lucinda Franks, "Don't Shoot: In the New FBI Patience Come First," New Yorker (July 22, 1996): 27.

14   Julie R Linkins, "FBI Academy: 25 Years of Law Enforcement Leadership," FBI Law Enforcement Bulletin (May 1997): 2, 5.

15   Michaud, "The FBI's Psyche Squad," New York Times Magazine (October 26, 1986): 42. Prior to Ressler the term "serial murderer" was used by John Brophy in The Meaning of Murder (1966) to identify murders that were linked by a 'repetition of effect' that would, by their nature, draw attention to themselves. Donald Lunde also used the term in Murder and Madness (1975): 47. Ressler acknowledges that he picked up the idea of serial crime at an international training session in England from British police instructors and felt it was apt; it was only later that he reflected upon his childhood memories. Ressler and Schachtman, Whoever Fights Monsters: 35.

16   Richard G Rappaport, "The Serial And Mass Murderer: Patterns, Differentiation, Pathology," American Journal Of Forensic Psychiatry (v.9 No.1, 1988): 42.

17   Arlen Specter, "Opening Statement of Hon. Arlen Specter," in "Serial Murder" (July 12, 1983): 1.

18   Newton, Serial Slaughter: 1.

19   "Statement of John Otto," (April 9 and May 21, 1986): 4, 1.

20   Henry P Lundesguarde quoted in Egger, "Toward A Working Definition Of Serial Murder," Journal of Police Science and Administration (v.12 No.3, 1984): 352.

21   Wilson and Seaman, Serial Killers: 32.

22   Robert Ressler et al, Sexual Homicide, Lexington Books, New York, 1995: 139.

23   Wilson and Seaman, Serial Killers: 62.

24   Egger, "Toward A Working Definition

Notes

Of Serial Murder," *Journal of Police Science and Administration* (v.12 No.3, 1984): 352.

25 Roger Depue quoted in Michaud, "The FBI's Psyche Squad," *New York Times Magazine* (October 26, 1986): 40.

26 Rule, "Statements of panel," in "Serial Murder" (July 12, 1983): 14. Ann Rule flatteringly describes herself as a 'fact-detective writer', the majority of her 'true crime' style books deal with sex killers.

27 Lindsey, "Officials Cite A Rise In Killers Who Roam U.S. For Victims," *New York Times* (January 21, 1984): A1.

28 Darrach and Norris, "American Tragedy," *Life* (August 1984): 60.

29 Tannahill, *Flesh And Blood*: 260.

30 Rule, "Statements of panel," in "Serial Murder"(July 12, 1983): 14.

31 Robert Brittain, "The Sadistic Murderer," *Medicine Science and Law* (No.10, 1970): 198–207.

32 Harold Schechter, "A Movie Made Me Do It," *New York Times* (December 3, 1995): D15.

33 Cited in David Gresswell and Clive Hollin, "Multiple Murder," *British Journal of Criminology* (Winter 1994): 2. In an example of the Bureau's blatant self-promotion the front cover of Robert K. Ressler et al, *Sexual Homicide* (1988) quoted the *FBI Law Enforcement Bulletin* which praised the book, substantially written by its own agents, for offering "an enlightening and practical, yet academically sound, view from the law enforcement investigators viewpoint—a powerful tool for identifying and apprehending sexual killers."

34 The killers are regularly referred to as 'predators'. For example "Statement of John Otto in The Federal Role In The Investigation Of Violent Crime," (April 9 and May 21, 1986): 4; "Statement Of John Walsh," in "Serial Killers and Child Abductions: Hearing before the Subcommittee on Juvenile Justice of the committee on the Judiciary," House of Representatives, 104th Congress, 1st session, September 14, 1995: 11. [Hereafter "Serial Killers And Child Abductions," (September 14, 1995)].

35 Douglas quoted in Brooks, "The Federal Role In Investigation Of Serial Violent Crime: 45th Report" (September 25, 1986): 3.

36 Rule in "Statements of panel," in "Serial Murder" (July 12, 1983): 14.

37 Phillip Jenkins, "African Americans and Serial Homicide," *American Journal of Criminal Homicide* (v.17 No.2, 1993): 47–60.

38 Belea T Keeney and Kathleen M Heide, "Gender Differences and Serial Murderers," *Journal of Interpersonal Violence* (September 1994): 383, 392. Justice Department list thirty-six known female serial killers in this century, but the exact definition used to identify them is not stated.

39 Chibulas quoted in Michael Reynolds, *Dead Ends*, Warner Books, New York, 1992: 238.

40 Hazelwood quoted in Patricia Pearson, *When She Was Bad*, Penguin, New York, 1998: 157. Emphasis added.

41 Gresswell and Hollin, "Multiple Murder," *British Journal of Criminology* (Winter 1994): 4.

42 DeSalvo's confessions were all that linked him with the 'Boston Strangler' murders, there were no witnesses or forensic evidence. In Lucas's case it was again the confessions that implicated him in virtually all of the crimes, and investigators prompted many of those confessions. In the Dahmer case there was plenty of physical evidence to implicate Dahmer in the murders which took place in his apartment, but his

claims to be a cannibal could not be verified and Dennis Nielsen, the English killer who had eaten parts of his victims, dismissed Dahmer's allegations as being concocted to get attention. Phillip Arreola, Milwaukee police chief, said that Dahmer's claims to be a cannibal were probably "wishful thinking" and the evidence was not consistent with his confessions. Arreola quoted in Tithecott, *Of Men and Monsters*: 66.

43   Jeffers, *Profiles in Evil*: 32.

44   The real targets for serial killers were the most vulnerable in society, most commonly male and female prostitutes, homeless people and drifters.

45   William Webster, "Letter," in "Serial Murder (July 12, 1983): 9.

46   Bruce Porter, "Mindhunters," *Psychology Today* (April 1983): 46. See also Egger, "Toward A Working Definition Of Serial Murder," *Journal of Police Science and Administration* (v.12 No.3, 1984): 352.

47   Webster in "Serial Murder" (July 12, 1983): 7. See also Walsh in "Serial Murder" (July 12, 1983): 26.

48   Hawkins quoted in ibid: 11.

49   Hawkins quoted in ibid: 10.

50   Rule in "Serial Murder" (1983): 11.

51   Robert Lindsey, "Officials Cite A Rise In Killers Who Roam U.S. For Victims," *New York Times* (January 21, 1984): A7.

52   Ibid: A17.

53   Jenkins, *Using Murder*: 66.

54   Mark Starr et al, "The Random Killers," *Newsweek* (November 26, 1984): 100.

55   "Statement of John Otto," in "The Federal Role In The Investigation Of Violent Crime," (April 9 and May 21, 1986): 5.

56   Darrach and Norris, "American Tragedy," *Life* (August 1984): 60.

57   Leyton, *Hunting Humans*: 12. Mark Starr reports an estimate by William Webster that there were thirty active serial kill-

ers, and alleges other local police felt this estimate was too conservative. Mark Starr et al, "The Random Killers," *Newsweek* (November 26, 1984): 100.

58   R Conrath, "Guys Who Shoot To Thrill," *Revue Francaise D'etitude Americaines* (No.60, 1994): 145.

59   Wilson and Seaman, *Serial Killers*: 2.

60   J A Fox, "Murder They Wrote," *Contemporary Psychology* (v.35 No.9, 1990): 891.

61   James P Scanlan, "The Perils of Provocative Statistics," *Public Interest* (Winter 1991): 14.

62   Dietz, "Mass, Serial And Sensational Homicides," *Bulletin of the New York Academy of Medicine* (June 1986): 478–479.

63   Pierce Brooks, "The Federal Role In Investigation Of Serial Violent Crime: 45th Report," (September 25, 1986): 10. Writer and journalist H. Paul Jeffers credits the initial BSU estimates to Roger Depue, then chief of the BSU. Jeffers, *Profiles in Evil*: 93.

64   T Gest, "On the Trail of America's Serial Killers," *US News and World Report* (April 30, 1984): 53.

65   Egger, "Toward A Working Definition Of Serial Murder," *Journal of Police Science and Administration* (v.12 No.3, 1984): 355. See also Newton, *Serial Slaughter*: 5.

66   Davis quoted in Donziger serial, *The Real War On Crime*: 68.

67   Robert O Heck of the Justice Department was quoted as saying that 4,000 people were killed by at least thirty-five roaming serial killers in one year. This appears to be the initial source for many inflated statistics, and this in itself is a very dubious statistic. Robert Lindsey. "Officials Cite A Rise In Killers Who Roam U.S. For Victims," *New York Times* (January 21, 1984): A7. By 1994 the FBI estimated that there might be

Notes

"only dozens" of serial killers active in the United States. Tannahill, *Flesh And Blood*: 254.

68   The same conclusion is also reached by Egger, "Toward A Working Definition Of Serial Murder," *Journal of Police Science and Administration* (v.12 No.3, 1984): 355–356.

69   Leyton, *Hunting Humans*: 20.

70   Gresswell and Hollin, "Multiple Murder," *British Journal of Criminology* (Winter 1994): 5.

71   Pierce Brooks et al, "Serial Murder: A Criminal Justice Response," *Police Chief* (June 1987): 39.

72   Interview with Robert Keppel by the author, August 26, 1998.

73   Ann Rule, "Proposal: VICAP The Violent Criminal Apprehension Program," in "Serial Murder" (July 12, 1983): 25. Ironically her statement was originally published in *True Detective* (October 1982).

74   "Statement of John Otto," in "The Federal Role In The Investigation Of Violent Crime," (April 9 and May 21, 1986): 6.

75   Keppel and Birnes, *The Riverman*: 327.

76   "Statement of John Otto," in "The Federal Role In The Investigation Of Violent Crime" (April 9 and May 21, 1986): 7.

77   Examples of the appropriation of the term are found in, Brad Darrach and Joel Norris "An American Tragedy," *Life* (August 1984): 58–74; Kagan, "Serial Murderers," *Omni* (June 1984): 20, 120; Michaud, "The FBI's Psyche Squad," *New York Times* (October 26, 1986): 40–42; "Experts Say Mass Murderers are rare but on the Rise," *New York Times* (January 3, 1988): A16.

78   Joseph Berger, "Traits Shared By Mass Killers Remains Unknown To Experts," *New York Times* (August 27, 1984):

A13.

79   Patricia Leeds, "They Study The Strangest Slayings," *Chicago Tribune* (February 15, 1980): 1, 4.

80   Brooks et al, "Serial Murder," *Police Chief* (June 1987): 39–41.

81   Michaud, "The FBI's Psyche Squad," *New York Times Magazine* (October 26, 1986): 40.

82   Letter from Arthur P Meister to the author dated March 24, 1998. Emphasis added.

83   "The Federal Role In The Investigation Of Violent Crime," (April 9 and May 21, 1986): 22.

84   Brooks et al, "Serial Murder," *Police Chief* (June 1987): 41.

85   "Crime Scene and Profile Characteristics of Organized And Disorganized Murderers," *FBI Law Enforcement Bulletin* (August 1985): 18.

86   Krist Boardman, "Sadists Who Used Tools To Torture Hookers!," in Rose G Mandelsberg serial, *Torture Killers*, Pinnacle, New York, 1991: 399.

87   "The Federal Role In The Investigation Of Violent Crime," (April 9 and May 21, 1986): 22.

88   Douglas and Olshaker, *Mindhunters*: 112–113.

89   Interview with Robert Keppel August 26, 1998. Keppel noted that he had seen two separate interviews where Kemper talked about the same double murder, and on both occasions his explanations were different and at odds with the physical evidence. After studying the crimes and confessions Keppel concluded that Kemper was telling his audience what they wanted to hear.

90   Goldman, *The X-Files Book of the Unexplained: Volume Two*: 65.

91   Interview with Robert Keppel August 26, 1998. In his writing Robert Ressler claims to have interviewed Ted Bundy

but Keppel, who spent a considerable time interviewing Bundy, says Ressler only got as far asking Bundy for an interview and was refused.

92   Letter to Garland E of Springfield, Illinois from John Wayne Gacy dated April 28, 1992, in Gacy, *More Letters To Mr Gacy*: np.

93   Robert K Ressler and Tom Schachtman, *Whoever Fights Monsters*: 46. Referring to the interviews with Juan Corona, Herb Mullin, and John Lindley Frazier.

94   Rosenbaum, "FBI's Agent Provocateur," *Vanity Fair* (April 1993): 41.

95   Keppel and Birnes, The Riverman: 342.

96   "Serial killer who didn't fit profile convicted," *Houston Chronicle* [w] www.chron.com/content/chronicle/metropolitan/97/01/08/serial.html. The focus on motiveless crimes committed by strangers also distracted the investigation into crimes to which Robert Berdella eventually confessed.

97   Rosenbaum, "FBI's Agent Provocateur," *Vanity Fair* (April 1993): 41.

98   Maury Terry, *The Ultimate Evil*, Bantam Books, 1989: 40, 77.

99   Robert Ressler and Tom Schachtman, *I Have Lived In The Monster*, Simon and Schuster, New York, 1997: 67.

100   *United States of America ex-rel John Gacy N00921 v Gerorge Wellburn and Roland Burris* entered on August 19, 1992. Reprinted in *More Letters to Mr Gacy*: np. In *I Have Lived In The Monster*, Ressler quotes Gacy identifying employees Baker, Chandler and Sandler as having committed the murders. Another former Gacy employee, Robin Gecht, was convicted for his part in the 'Chicago Rippers' murders. In that case four men, in a group, were convicted of a series of prostitute rape/murders that took place between May 1981 and Sep-

tember 1982. Gecht had previously been convicted of violent sex offences but he was not implicated in the Gacy investigation. While Gacy delighted in relating his sexual adventures it should be noted that he claimed he was born with an "enlarged bottleneck heart" and could therefore not participate in any strenuous activities calling into question how he could have disposed of the victims' bodies alone. Donald J. Sears, *To Kill Again: The Motivation and Development of Serial Murder*, Scholarly Resources Inc., Wilmington, Delaware, 1991: 21–22.

101   Newton, *Serial Slaughter*: 110.

102   Brooks, "The Federal Role In Investigation Of Serial Violent Crime: 45th Report," (September 25, 1986): 6.

103   Douglas quoted in ibid: 5.

104   Kessler, *The FBI*: 27.

105   Ibid: 98.

106   Keppel and Birnes, *The Riverman*: 228.

107   Berger, "Traits Shared By Mass Killers Remain Unknown To Experts," *New York Times* (August 27, 1984): A13.

108   John McNaughton, director of *Henry: Portrait of a Serial Killer* (1986) quoted in John Martin, "John McNaughton: Portrait of a Serious Conspirator," in Chas Balun (ed), *Deep Red* (Special Edition), Fantaco Enterprises, Inc, New York, 1991: 86. Attention seekers who confess to crimes they did not commit are said to have a 'delusional criminality complex.'

109   Whitlock quoted in Fay S. Joyce, "2 Suspects Stories Of Killings Culled," *New York Times* (November 4, 1983): A20. The exaggerated estimates reach as high as 2,000 dead according to one source. Dr Joel Norris, *Henry Lee Lucas*, Zebra Books, New York, 1991: 7. A time line of Lucas's movements placed him in Florida picking up welfare checks on

Notes

the same day he confessed to committing a murder several hundred miles away.

110 Ressler and Schachtman, *Whoever Fights Monsters*: 238.

111 Jeffers, *Profiles in Evil*: 42.

112 Jacqueline Boles and Phillip W. Davis, "Defending Atlanta," *Journal of American Culture* (v.11, 1988), 61. Robert Keppel, one of the investigative consultants with the Atlanta Task Force, writes that in his trial Williams was only linked to ten of the other murders. Robert D Keppel, *Serial Murder: Future Implications For Police Investigations*, Anderson Publishing Company, 1989: 23–24.

113 Jon Nordheimer, "Bundy Is Executed In Florida Murder," *New York Times* (January 25, 1989): A12. Similarly the number of murders attributed to the Manson Family fluctuates from eight to more than forty. See Bugliosi and Gentry, *Helter Skelter*: 585–588.

114 Brooks et al, "Serial Murder," *Police Chief* (June 1987): 41.

115 Keppel and Birnes, *The Riverman*: 119.

116 Hazelwood, "The NCAVC Training Program," *FBI Law Enforcement Bulletin* (December 1986): 26.

117 Gresswell and Hollin, "Multiple Murder," *British Journal of Criminology* (Winter 1994): 2.

118 Robert Hazelwood and John Douglas, "The Lust Murderer," *FBI Law Enforcement Bulletin* (April 1980): 22. Emphasis added.

119 Porter, "Mindhunters," *Psychology Today* (April 1983): 50.

120 William Webster cited in "Serial Murder" (July 12, 1983): 5.

121 "Federal Program Is Launched To Catch Serial Murderers," *Criminal Justice Newsletter* (August 1, 1984): 1.

122 Brown, "Historical Similarity Of Twentieth Century Serial Sexual Homicide to Pre-Twentieth Century Occurrences of Vampirism," *American Journal of Forensic Psychiatry* (v. 12 No.2, 1991): 13.

123 Michaud, "The FBI's Psyche Squad," *New York Times Magazine* (October 26, 1986): 75.

124 Leeds, "They Study the Strangest Slayings," *Chicago Tribune* (February 15, 1980): 4.

125 Campbell, "Portrait Of A Mass Killer," *Psychology Today* (May 1976): 112.

126 Douglas in "The Federal Role In The Investigation Of Violent Crime," (April 9 and May 21, 1986): 15–16.

127 Porter, "Mindhunters," *Psychology Today* (April 1983): 50.

128 Ressler et al, "Sexual Killers And Their Victims: Identifying Patterns Through Crime Scene Analysis," *Journal of Interpersonal Violence* (September 1986): 290–91, 293. Emphasis added.

129 Sondra London (ed), *Knockin' On Joe: Voices From Death Row*, Nemesis Books, London, 1993: 234.

130 Kessler, *The FBI*: 310.

131 Wilson and Seaman, *Serial Killers*: 89.

132 Douglas and Olshaker, *Mindhunters*: 32.

133 Ressler quoted in Goldman, *The X-Files Book of the Unexplained: Volume Two*: 63.

134 Park Elliot Dietz, "Sex Offender Profiling By The FBI: A Preliminary Conceptual Model," *Proceedings of a Forensic Science Symposium on the Analysis of Sexual Assault Evidence* (July 1983): 180.

135 Interview with Robert Keppel by the author August 26, 1998.

136 Carlo Ginzberg quoted in Nordby, "Bootstrapping While Barefoot," *Synthese* (December 1989): 386.

137 For example Douglas and Olshaker, *Mindhunters*: 31. See also Leeds, "They

study the strangest slayings," *Chicago Tribune* (February 15, 1980): 4.

138   Douglas and Olshaker, *Mindhunters*: 31.

139   Park Elliot Dietz, "Sex Offender Profiling By The FBI," *Proceedings of a Forensic Science Symposium on the Analysis of Sexual Assault Evidence* (July 1983): 179.

140   Ibid.

141   Dietz, "Sex Offender Profiling By The FBI," *Proceedings of a Forensic Science Symposium on the Analysis of Sexual Assault Evidence* (July 1983):179.

142   Brussel, *Casebook Of A Crime Psychiatrist*: 50–51, 64–65, 15. When confronted by the police at home Metesky was not actually dressed in a suit because it was late at night and he had been in bed.

143   Susan Kelly, *The Boston Stranglers: The Public Conviction of Albert DeSalvo and the True Story of Eleven Shocking Murders*, Birch Lane Press, Madison Avenue, New York, 1995. In *Casebook Of A Crime Psychiatrist*, Brussel stated that he believed Bailey had read the report of the Medical-Psychiatric Committee, paying special attention to Brussel's dubious single killer theory, and tailored DeSalvo's defense strategy from that. By using Brussel's theory, Bailey legitimized the idea of a lone sex killer and ensured DeSalvo would be recognized as the Boston Strangler despite the obvious contradictions in his confessions.

144   Brussel, *Casebook Of A Crime Psychiatrist*: 135.

145   Ibid: 138.

146   Ibid: 140, 143.

147   Ibid: 162, 168, 171.

148   Douglas and Olshaker, *Mindhunters*: 34, 89.

149   Ault and Hazelwood in Jeffers, *Profiles In Evil*: 6. The American military, where Douglas, Hazelwood, and Ressler had come to the FBI from, discovered the potential of psychology during WWII and invested considerable amounts of money on behavioral research.

150   Dietz, "Sex Offender Profiling By The FBI," *Proceedings of a Forensic Science Symposium on the Analysis of Sexual Assault Evidence* (July 1983)" 180.

151   Campbell, "Portrait Of A Mass Killer," *Psychology Today* (May 1976): 111.

152   Jeffers, *Profiles in Evil*: 42.

153   Peter J Neufeld and Neville Colman, "When Science Takes The Witness Stand," *Scientific American* (May 1990): 25.

154   Goad, "Night Of A Hundred Mass-Murdering/Serial Killing Stars," *ANSWER Me!* (No.2, 1992): 84.

155   Alex Duval Smith, "CIA and FBI Reputations In Tatters," *Guardian* (April 19, 1997): 15.

156   Binder quoted in Stephen Farber, "A Docudrama Aims To Reopen A Case," *New York Times* (September 2, 1984): B17.

157   Headley, "Ideological Constructions Of Race And The 'Atlanta Tragedy'," *Contemporary Crises* (No.10, 1986): 193. Shields also points out that there was 'no center' to the crimes, just a 'string of corpses'. Initially the killings were seen as nothing more than an upswing in the number of homicides. The string of 'related' killings did not appear until a conservative press picked up on the story. Shields. "The Atlanta Story," *Columbia Journalism Review* (September–October 1981): 30, 33–34.

158   Douglas and Olshaker, *Mindhunters*: 215.

159   Rosenbaum, "The FBI's Agent Provocateur," *Vanity Fair* (April 1993): 41.

Notes

160   Wilson and Seaman, *Serial Killers*: 132.

161   "U.S.S. Iowa Tragedy: An Investigative Failure: Report Of The Investigations Subcommittee And Defense Policy Panel Of The Committee On Armed Services," House of Representatives, 101 Congress, 2nd session, March 5, 1990: 43. Hereafter "USS Iowa Tragedy: An Investigative Failure" (March 5, 1990).

162   Woody Haut, *Neon Noir*, Serpents Tail, London, 1999: 216.

163   Brooks, "The Federal Role In Investigation Of Serial Violent Crime'" (September 25, 1986): 8.

164   Opinion of the experts quoted in "USS Iowa Tragedy: An Investigative Failure" (March 5, 1990): 43.

165   Ibid: 43–45. The team of experts was professionally trained in psychological evaluation.

166   Campbell, "Portrait of a Mass Killer," *Psychology Today* (May 1976): 110.

167   Interview with Robert Keppel by the author August 26, 1998.

168   Ressler and Schactman, *Whoever Fights Monsters*: 11.

169   Keppel was a friend of Biondi's and was aware of his feelings on the subject. In an attempt to set the record straight Biondi wrote *The Vampire of Killer* (1992). Interview with Robert Keppel by the author August 26, 1998.

170   Ray Biondi and Walt Hecox, *The Dracula Killer*, Mondo Books London, 1992: np ('Authors Note'): 149–50.

171   Campbell, "Portrait of a Mass Killer," *Psychology Today* (May 1976): 119.

172   Jeffers, *Profiles in Evil*: 42.

173   Bob Graham, "The Fall Guy," *Sunday Times Magazine* (April 20, 1997): 16–19.

174   Campbell, "Portrait of a Mass Killer," *Psychology Today* (May 1976): 116.

175   Lindsay quoted in Ron Rosenbaum, "The FBI's Agent Provocateur," *Vanity Fair* (April 1993): 40.

176   Schlossberg and Reiser cited in Campbell, "Portrait of a Mass Killer," *Psychology Today* (May 1976): 116.

177   Nordby, "Boostrapping While Barefoot," *Synthese* (December 1989): 379.

178   Lindsay cited in Rosenbaum, "The FBI's Agent Provocateur," *Vanity Fair* (April 1993): 41.

179   Wilson and Seaman, *Serial Killers*: 86.

180   Campbell, "Portrait of a Mass Killer," *Psychology Today* (May 1976): 112.

181   Ibid: 119.

182   Boxley quoted in ibid: 119.

183   Lindsay quoted in Rosenbaum, "The FBI's Agent Provocateur," *Vanity Fair* (April 1993): 41.

184   Brooks et al, "Serial Murder," *Police Chief* (June 1987): 39.

185   Ressler quoted in Michaud, "The FBI's Psyche Squad," *New York Times Magazine* (October 26, 1986): 42.

186   Keppel and Birnes, *The Riverman*: 328.

187   Jeffers, *Profiles in Evil*: 29.

188   Michaud, "The FBI's Psyche Squad," *New York Times Magazine* (October 26, 1986): 75. See also Jeffers, *Profiles in Evil*: 29; Egger, "Toward A Working Definition Of Serial Murder," *Journal of Police Science and Administration* (v.12 No.3, 1984): 349.

189   Keppel and Birnes, *The Riverman*: 328.

190   Jeffers, *Profiles in Evil*: 93.

191   Kessler, *The FBI*: 320.

192   David Icove, "Automated Crime Profiling," *FBI Law Enforcement Bulletin* (December 1986): 29.

193   Keppel and Birnes, *The Riverman*: 122.

194   Icove, "Automated Crime Profiling," *FBI Law Enforcement Bulletin* (December 1986): 28.

195   Keppel and Birnes, *The Riverman*: 125,

327–28.

196   Howlett et al, "The Violent Criminal Ap-
       prehension Program," *FBI Law Enforce-
       ment Bulletin* (December 1986): 18.

197   Keppel and Birnes, *The Riverman*:
       328–29.

198   Ibid: 327–29.

199   Jeffers, *Profiles in Evil*: 16.

200   Douglas and Olshaker, *Mindhunt-
       ers*: 69.

201   Keppel and Birnes, *The Riverman*:
       341.

202   Howlett, et al, "The Violent Criminal Ap-
       prehension Program," *FBI Law Enforce-
       ment Bulletin* (December 1986): 18.

203   Ressler and Schachtman, *Whoever
       Fights Monsters*: 242–43.

204   Letter from Arthur P Meister to the
       author March 24, 1998.

205   Egger, "Toward A Working Definition
       Of Serial Murder," Journal of Police
       Science and Administration (v.12
       No.3, 1984): 355. See also Kessler,
       The FBI: 98.

206   Ressler and Schachtman, *Whoever
       Fights Monsters*: 243.

207   Brooks, "The Federal Role In Investiga-
       tion Of Serial Violent Crime: 45th Re-
       port," (25 September 1986): 8–10.

6. All The News That's Fit To Print
Sensational Sex Crimes &
Serial Killers in the News

1   Leyton, *Hunting Humans*: 22.

2   Hanna Adoni and Sherrill Mane, "Me-
     dia and the Social Construction of
     Reality," *Communication Research*
     (July 1984): 332–33.

3   Mark Fishman, "Crime Waves As
     Ideology," *Social Problems* (v.25,
     1978): 542.

4   Ibid.

5   Drew Humphries, "Serious Crime, News
     Coverage, and Ideology," *Crime and
     Delinquency* (April 1981): 196.

6   Barlow et al, "Mobilizing Support for
     Social Control in a Declining Econo-
     my," *Crime and Delinquency* (April
     1995): 201.

7   Alexis M Durham III, et al, "Images of
     Crime and Justice," *Journal of Criminal*

     Justice (v.23 No.2, 1995): 150–151; See
     also G Gerbner and L Gross, "Living
     With Television," *Journal of Commu-
     nication Inquiry* (v.26, 1976): 173–199;
     J. Roberts and A Doob, "News Media
     Influences on Public Views of Sentenc-
     ing," *Law and Human Behavior* (v.14
     No.5, 1990): 451–468; T.J. Flanagan et
     al, "Public Perceptions of the Criminal
     Courts," *Journal of Research in Crime
     and Delinquency* (v.22, 1985): 66–82.

8   Humphries, "Serious Crime, News
     Coverage, and Ideology," *Crime
     and Delinquency* (April 1981): 196. See
     also Steven M Chermak, "Body Count
     News," *Justice Quarterly* (December
     1994): 567.

9   Barlow et al, "Mobilizing Support for

Notes

Social Control in a Declining Economy," *Crime and Delinquency* (April 1995): 196.

10 D J Gee, "A Pathologists View of Multiple Murder," *Forensic Science International* (No.38, 1988): 56.

11 Leon V Sigal, "Sources Make The News," in Robert Karl Manhoff and Michael Schudson (eds), *Reading The News*, Pantheon Books, New York, 1987: 37.

12 Barlow et al, "Mobilizing Support for Social Control in a Declining Economy," *Crime and Delinquency* (April 1995): 201.

13 Gorelick, "'Join Our War'," *Crime and Delinquency* (July 1989): 421–422.

14 Fishman, "Crime waves as Ideology," *Social Problems* (v.25, 1978): 531–543.

15 Elliot J Gorn, "The Wicked World: The National Police Gazette and Gilded-Age America," *Media Studies Journal* (No.6, 1991): 5–6.

16 Ibid: 1, 15.

17 Gary Colville and Patrick Luciano, "Jack The Ripper: His Life and Crimes in Popular Entertainment," *Filmfax* (February/March 1992): 66.

18 Judith Walkowitz, "Jack the Ripper and the Myth of Male Violence," *Feminist Studies* (Fall 1982): 545–546.

19 Clive Bloom, "The House That Jack Built: The Jack The Ripper Legend and the Power of the Unknown," in Clive Bloom (ed), *Nineteenth Century Suspense*, St Martins Press, New York, 1988: 123.

20 Walkowitz, "Jack the Ripper and the Myth of Male Violence," *Feminist Studies* (Fall 1982): 545.

21 Fisher, *Killer Among Us*: 200.

22 Journalist quoted in ibid: 202, 215.

23 Walkowitz, "Jack the Ripper and the Myth of Male Violence," *Feminist Studies* (Fall 1982): 550.

24 John McCarty, *Movie Psychos and Madmen: Film Psychopaths from Jekyll and Hyde to Hannibal Lecter*, Citadel Books, New York, 1993: 21.

25 Colville and Luciano, "Jack The Ripper," *Filmfax* (February/March 1992): 66.

26 Sander L Gilman, "I'm Down on Whores: Race and Gender in Victorian London," in David Theo Goldberg (ed), *Anatomy of Racism*, U Minnesota P, Minneapolis, 1990: 160.

27 *The Star* quoted in Walkowitz, "Jack the Ripper and the Myth of Male Violence," *Feminist Studies* (Fall 1982): 550.

28 Fisher, *Killer Among Us*: 209.

29 Ibid: 209.

30 Walkowitz, "Jack the Ripper and the Myth of Male Violence," *Feminist Studies* (Fall 1982): 551. See also Clive Bloom, "The House That Jack Built." The police received 350 messages in all, from different people, all claiming to be the murderer.

31 Gilman, "I'm Down on Whores": 150–51.

32 Walkowitz, "Jack the Ripper and the Myth of Male Violence," *Feminist Studies* (Fall 1982): 550, 546. Originally published in German in 1886 the work was expanded and Krafft-Ebing actually uses Jack in his study (case 17) with the assumption that a single killer committed nine murders. Alongside 'Jack', Krafft-Ebing reports several other "lustmurderers", "necrophiliacs" and numerous other criminal sexual deviants similar to those later reported to the FBI.

33 Ibid: 554.

34 Shaw quoted in Fisher, *Killer Among Us*: 200.

35 Walkowitz, "Jack the Ripper and the Myth of Male Violence," *Feminist Studies* (Fall 1982): 567, 560, 566.

36 Ibid: 563.

37   Ibid: 568–569.

38   Colville and Luciano "Jack The Ripper: His Life and Crimes in Popular Entertainment," *Filmfax* (No.32, February/March 1992): 67.

39   "Woman Slain By A Jack The Ripper," *New York Times* (December 21, 1903): 2.

40   "Eight Victims Now Of Atlanta Ripper," *New York Times* (July 3, 1911): 3. See also "Another Ripper Murder," *New York Times* (May 12, 1912): 6.

41   "Trace Slayer of 5 Women," *New York Times* (December 19, 1913): 2.

42   Michael Schudson quoted in Carlin Romano, "The Grisly Truth About The Bare Facts," in Robert K. Manhoff and Michael Schudson (eds), *Reading The News*, Pantheon Books, New York, 1987: 50–51.

43   Romano, "The Grisly Truth About The Bare Facts": 51.

44   Chessman, *Trial By Ordeal*: 130–132.

45   Harold Schechter, *Deranged*, Pocket Books, New York, 1990, : 59, 68, 3, 101.

46   Athan Theoharris and John Stuart Cox, *The Boss*: 203.

47   Machlin, *The Gossip Wars*: 116, 128, 132–134.

48   Schechter, *Deranged*: 115.

49   "Budd Girl's Body Found; Killed By Painter in 1928," *New York Times* (December 14, 1934): A1.

50   Schechter, *Deranged*, 168, 175–179, 169–170. Haarman was charged with twenty-seven murders but suspected of twenty more. He and his partner Hans Gans preyed on young refugees who were flooding into Hanover at the end of WWI. Ironically Haarman ran a detective bureau called the Lasso agency in partnership with a local police official and was commonly called 'detective Haarman'. Gans and Haarman would sell their victims' clothes at a local market, they would also cut up the bodies and sell steaks of human meat at the market to dispose of the bodies. Gans received a life sentence for his crimes which was later commuted to twelve years. Haarman was sentenced to death. While waiting for his execution Haarman wrote a detailed confession describing the delight he got from killing. At his request he was beheaded in the marketplace where he had sold the human meat and his brain was shipped to Goettingen University to be studied.

51   Machlin, *The Gossip Wars*: 123–124.

52   Gibson, "Quantative Description," *Public Relations Review* (Spring 1997): 16.

53   Alan Betrock, *The 100 Greatest Cult Exploitation Magazines*, Shake Books, New York, 1987: np.

54   Ibid.

55   Ibid

56   Joe Chibit, "Why The Epidemic of Sex Murders?," *Uncensored* (December 1964): 26.

57   Ibid.

58   Schecter, *Deviant*: 95, 119, 112, 139, 180.

59   Ibid: 11, 17, 22, 162, 188–89, 67, 38–39.

60   Ibid: 141.

61   Ibid: 201.

62   Ibid: 165.

63   Turner, *Hoover's FBI*: 127–127.

64   Brussel, *Casebook Of A Crime Psychiatrist*: 52.

65   Fisher, *Killer Among Us*: 38–39.

66   Ibid: 44.

67   Kelly, *The Boston Stranglers*: 26–27.

68   Ibid: 27.

69   Ibid: 28.

70   Fisher, *Killer Among Us*: 45.

71   Kelly, *The Boston Stranglers*: 163–64.

72   Ibid: 87.

73   Ibid: x, 161. See Also Fisher, *Killer Among Us*: 31. Because of Kelly's book

Notes

the 'cold case' squad of the Boston police department reopened the Boston Strangler case in 1999 hoping to compare DNA samples from De-Salvo with those taken from Strangler victims. The only sample from a victim that could be found was degraded too badly to be used, and plans to get DeSalvo's DNA from the knife that killed him floundered as it has been lost. Detectives plan to exhume his body to get a DNA sample. James Bone, "Detectives Check Mystery of the Boston Strangler," *The Times* (July 10, 1999): 7.

74   Ibid: 77.

75   Ibid: 117.

76   Ibid: 78–79, 161, 88. The Green Man sexual assaults took place after the Boston Strangler series of murders had apparently ceased in mid 1964. The crimes were *never* seen as being related. DeSalvo, based on his earlier conviction for sexual assault as the Measuring Man, became a suspect in the Green Man crimes. While being held in Bridgewater for psychological evaluation before standing trial for the Green Man assaults DeSalvo began hinting that he possessed significant information concerning the Boston Strangler. Gerold Frank's book and the subsequent film, and testimony at the Green Man trial, identified DeSalvo as the Strangler but no witnesses or physical evidence ever substanti-ated DeSalvo's claims, and much contradicted his confessions.

77   Ibid: 170–71. Susan Kelly noted that DeSalvo had at least six sources of information available to him when making his confession, and his photo-graphic memory enabled him to retain varied and detailed information. Kelly, *The Boston Stranglers*: 173–175.

78   Ibid: 85.

79   Ibid: 85.

80   Ibid: 90. No physical evidence or eye-witnesses ever connected DeSalvo to any of the 'Boston Strangler' killings.

81   Ibid: 175.

82   Ibid: ix.

83   Ray Surette, *Media, Crime, and Criminal Justice: Images and Realities*, Wadsworth, London, 1998: 7.

84   Powers, *The Beast, the Eunuch and the Glass-Eyed Child*: xiii.

85   Ibid: xxii.

86   William T Martin Riches, *The Civil Rights Movement: Struggle and Resistance*, Macmillan Press Ltd., London, 1997: 109.

87   Keppel and Birnes, *The Riverman*: 119.

88   Wilson and Seaman, *Serial Killers*: 72.

89   Fisher, *Killer Among Us*: 106.

90   "Talk of the Town," *New Yorker* (August 15, 1977): 21.

91   Fisher, *Killer Among Us*: 115.

92   Letter from Ronald Neuwirth in "Son of Sam," *New York Times* (August 18, 1977): A20.

93   "Talk of the Town," *New Yorker* (August 15, 1977): 22.

94   "The 'Son of Sam' Killer is Told To Pay Victims," *New York Times* (September 2, 1987): A3. As an alternative to rights of the accused Reagan's administra-tion promoted the rights of crime vic-tims. The 1977 New York State 'Son of Sam' law, and similar legislation which followed in forty-one other states, au-thorized the confiscation of earnings by a criminal which were received as a result of written or spoken accounts of crimes. The laws were never ap-plied to David Berkowitz, the Son of Sam killer, because he was found to be mentally incompetent to stand trial, and they were rarely invoked after. When used the laws placed the criminal's assets in an escrow account

for five years. Any funds not claimed by the victim's relatives after that time would be returned to the criminal. Later legislation expanded the scope of the Son of Sam laws and a 1984 federal law permitted judges, as part of sentencing proceedings, to order forfeiture of defendants' assets from book or film rights. Victims' families also participated at parole hearings, allowing them to have the last word.

95 Daryl F Gates and Diane K Shah, *Chief: My Life in the LAPD*, Bantam Books, New York, 1992: 168.

96 Ibid: 168.

97 Ressler and Schactman, *Whoever Fights Monsters*: 276.

98 Ibid: 276–277.

99 The editorial is reprinted in "Serial Murder" (July 12, 1983): 25.

100 "Are Serial Killers On The Rise," *US News and World Report* (September 9, 1985): 14.

101 Ressler and Schactman, *Whoever Fights Monsters*: 241.

102 Jane Caputi, "The New Founding Fathers," *Journal of American Culture* (v.13, 1990): 3.

103 McCarty, *Madmen*: 76.

104 William Heirens was a seventeen year old who got sexual satisfaction from burglary. He killed two women and an eight year old girl, and mutilated two of the bodies. In the course of his crimes he made no attempt to conceal his identity, and once caught was sentenced to life in prison. Douglas and Ressler interviewed Heirens as part of the BSU serial killer study.

105 Katzenbach quoted in Jane Gross, "An Actor Explores the Fourth Estate," *New York Times* (February 10, 1985), B19.

106 Russell quoted in ibid: B19.

107 Katzenbach quoted in ibid.

108 Anthony Smith, *The Newspapers: An International History*, Thames and Hudson, London, 1979: 147.

109 Wilson quoted in Jack Hitt, "In Pursuit of Pure Horror," *Harpers* (October 1989): 48.

110 Schwartz quoted in "Murder By Homophobia," *The Advocate* (July 30, 1992): 81.

111 Tithecott, *Of Men and Monsters*: 101.

112 Ruth E Schwartz, *The Man Who Could Not Kill Enough*, Mondo Books London, 1992: 186.

113 Jerry Berger, "Damn the Facts—Roll the Presses," *Editor and Publisher* (May 14, 1994): 56, 46.

114 Berger, "Damn the Facts—Roll the Presses," *Editor and Publisher* (May 14, 1994): 56, 46.

115 Noam Chomsky, *Class Warfare*, Common Courage Press, Monroe, Mn, 1996: 82.

116 Deborah Cameron, "Pleasure and Danger, Sex and Death" in Gary Day (ed), *Readings in Popular Culture*, St Martins, New York, 1990: 131.

117 Park Elliot Dietz et al, "Detective Magazines: Pornography for the Sexual Sadist," *Journal of Forensic Sciences* (January 1986): 207.

118 Ibid: 197.

119 Dietz et al, "Detective Magazines," *Journal of Forensic Sciences* (January 1986): 198.

120 Cameron, "Pleasure and Danger, Sex and Death": 132.

121 Dietz et al, "Detective Magazines," *Journal of Forensic Sciences* (January 1986): 201–202, 208.

122 Cameron, "Pleasure and Danger, Sex and Death": 133.

123 Ibid: 137.

124 Dietz et al, "Detective Magazines," *Journal of Forensic Sciences* (January 1986): 208–09.

125 "The Federal Role In The Investigation Of Violent Crime," (April 9 and May 21, 1986): 36.

Notes

126 Dan Kelly, "The Sad Last Testament of Chester Rose," *Book Happy* (No.4, Summer 1999): 11.

127 Interview with Robert Keppel by the author, August 26, 1998.

128 Fox and Levin, *Overkill*: 5–6.

129 Ibid: 6–7.

130 Joseph Grixti, "Consuming Cannibals," *Journal of America Culture* (Spring 1995): 89.

131 Brian Masters, *Killing For Company*, Coronet, London, 1986: 26.

132 Clifford Linedecker, *The Man Who Killed Boys*, St Martins Press, New York, 1980: 244–245.

133 Dr Martin Obler and Thomas Calvin, *Fatal Analysis*, St Martins, New York, 1997: 348.

134 Masters, *Killing For Company*: 25.

135 Ibid: 26.

136 "Sidelines," *Fortean Times* (December 1993–January 1994): 11.

137 "Buried Dreams is a Fraud and a Hoax" dated 11 March 1986 in Gacy, *More Letters To Mr Gacy*: np.

138 Letter from James G Moser to Mychaljlo Kusma dated August 22, 1986, in ibid: np.

139 Brian Masters, "Marks of the Beast," *Times Sunday Review* (February 6, 1993): 10.

140 Ibid: 11.

7. Belief Is A Poor Substitute For Thought
Serial Killers and Law & Order Issues as Entertainment

1 Barnouw quoted in Gini Graham Scott, *Can We Talk: The Power and Influence of Talk Shows*, Insight Books, New York, 1996: 191.

2 Ibid.

3 Litwinsky quoted in Michael Moore and Kathleen Glynn, *Adventures in a TV Nation*, Harper Perennial, New York, 1998: 110.

4 David Kerekes and David Slater, *Killing For Culture: An Illustrated History of Death From Mondo to Snuff*, Annihilation Books, London, 1993: 269.

5 Ibid: 266–268.

6 Tithecott, *Of Men and Monsters*: 129.

7 Fowler quoted in Johnson, *Sleepwalking Through History*: 141.

8 Ibid.

9 Johnson, *Sleepwalking Through History*: 141–142. See also Dan Moldea, *Dark Victory*: 307.

10 Ian I Mitroff and Warren Bennis, *The Unreality Industry*, Oxford UP, Oxford, 1993: 9.

11 Johnson, *Sleepwalking Through History*: 141, 140.

12 David F Friedman, *A Youth In Babylon*, Prometheus Books, New York, 1990: 51.

13 Linda Feuer, *Seeing Through the Eighties: Television and Reaganism*, Duke UP, Durham, 1995: 19.

14 Slawson quoted in Carter, "Story Rights For Crimes Certainly Pay," *New York Times* (June 15, 1992): D7.

15 Fox and Levin, *Overkill*: 9.

16 Carter, "Story Rights For Crimes Certainly Pay," *New York Times* (June 15, 1992): D7.

17 Feuer, *Seeing Through the Eighties*: 22, 24.

18 Ibid: 22.

19 Carter, "Story Rights For Crimes Certainly Pay," *New York Times* (June 15, 1992): D7.

20 Jeff Silverman, "Murder, Mayhem Stalk", *New York Times* (November 22, 1992): B28, B1.

21 Ibid: B28.

22 John J O'Connor, "The line Between Drama and Lies," *New York Times* (December 31, 1992): C11. Emphasis added.

23 Smith, "'Child Murders' Sparks Debate On Docudramas," *New York Times* (February 4, 1985): C17.

24 Kelly, *The Boston Stranglers*: 147. $15,000 was paid to 'Robert McKay', a mysterious character whom DeSalvo claims was his lawyer F Lee Bailey, and Bailey claims was DeSalvo. An investigation by the Bar Association found that a substantial amount of money was owed to DeSalvo and his claim that Bailey was acting in his own interest had merit.

25 Ibid: 106. One officer, Phillip DiNatale, did become a consultant, reportedly being paid $60,000 for his assistance, but the other officers, and even ex-officers, would not cooperate in making the film. The police department would only provide a minimal number of officers to divert traffic from areas where scenes for the film were being shot. Kelley, *The Boston Stranglers*: 108.

26 Fleischer quoted in McCarty, *Movie Psychos and Madmen*: 144.

27 Kelley, *The Boston Stranglers*: 108–109. Other individuals refused to give permission to Fox to use their names so their character's names were changed for the film.

28 Ibid: 21–22, 119–120.

29 Ibid: 110.

30 McCarty, *Movie Psychos and Madmen*, 144. DeSalvo's Lawyer, by that time Thomas C Troy, argued that the film would prejudice his client's ability to get a fair trial, but later he admitted that the real purpose was to get a full accounting from F Lee Bailey with regard to the financial arrangements made, while he was DeSalvo's representative, for book and film rights.

31 Ibid: 144.

32 William E Schmidt, "TV Movie On Atlanta Child Killings Stirs Debate And Casts Doubt On Guilt," *New York Times* (February 1, 1985): A12.

33 Jacqueline Boles and Phillip W Davis, "Defending Atlanta: Press Reaction to a Movie on the Missing and Murdered Children," *Journal of American Culture* (v.11, 1988): 61, 64.

34 Ibid: 62, 63. Camille Bell moved to Florida in 1982 to escape persecution in Atlanta for her outspoken beliefs that Williams was innocent. In 1985, prominent lawyers William Kunstler and Alan Dershowitz assisted Williams' lawyer Lynn Whatley in trying to reopen the case.

35 Stephen Farber, "A Docudrama Aims To Reopen A Case," *New York Times* (September 2, 1984): B17.

36 Ibid: B17.

37 Richard Combs, "The Atlanta Child Murders," *Monthly Film Bulletin* (June 1985): 196.

38 Farber, "A Docudrama Aims To Reopen A Case," *New York Times* (September 2, 1984): B17.

39 Mann quoted in Boles and Davis, "Defending Atlanta," *Journal of American Culture* (v.11, 1988): 62.

40 Mann quoted in Farber, "A Docudrama Aims To Reopen A Case," *New*

Notes

York Times (September 2, 1984): B17.

41   Dettlinger quoted in John Corry, "'The Atlanta Child Murders': Trial By TV," *New York Times* (February 10, 1985): B29.

42   Sally Bedell Smith, "Atlanta Task Force and CBS Discuss Child Murder Film," *New York Times* (February 5, 1985): C18.

43   Schmidt, "TV Movie On Atlanta Child Killings Stirs Debate And Casts Doubt On Guilt," *New York Times* (February 1, 1985): A12.

44   Young quoted in "Atlanta Mayor Sends Protest To Advertisers," *New York Times* (February 11, 1985): A10.

45   Busbee quoted in Sally Bedell Smith, "Atlanta Murder Film To Get CBS Advisory," *New York Times* (February 6, 1985): C22.

46   Busbee quoted in Schmidt, "TV Movie On Atlanta Child Killings Stirs Debate And Casts Doubt On Guilt," *New York Times* (February 1, 1985): A12.

47   Boles and Davis, "Defending Atlanta," *Journal of American Culture* (v.11, 1988): 64.

48   Schmidt, "TV Movie On Atlanta Child Killings Stirs Debate And Casts Doubt On Guilt," *New York Times* (February 1, 1985): A12.

49   Corry, "'The Atlanta Child Murders': Trial By TV," *New York Times* (February 10, 1985): B29.

50   Combs, "The Atlanta Child Murders," *Monthly Film Bulletin* (June 1985): 196.

51   Anthony Petkovich, "Wrestling Scorpio: An Interview With Andrew Robinson," *Psychotronic* (No.23, 1996): 55.

52   Ibid: 55.

53   Erman quoted in Farber, "A Docudrama Aims To Reopen A Case," *New York Times* (September 2, 1984), B17.

54   Minter quoted in Boles and Davis, "Defending Atlanta," *Journal of American Culture* (v.11, 1988): 64, 65.

55   "'Atlanta Child Murders' Draws Strong Ratings," *New York Times* (February 13, 1985): C25.

56   Sally Bedell Smith, "TV Docudrama: A Question of Ethics," *New York Times* (February 14, 1985): C30.

57   Smith, "'Child Murders' Sparks Debate On Docudramas," *New York Times* (February 4, 1985): C17.

58   Smith, "TV Docudrama: A Question of Ethics," *New York Times* (February 14, 1985): C30.

59   Salant quoted in ibid.

60   According to Wilder's sex therapist he enjoyed dominating women and fantasizing about white slavery, a crime to which the FBI were inextricably linked in their own G-Man myth. John Fowles' book *The Collector* (1963) was said to have affected Wilder and his fantasies but he had a long history of involvement in sex crimes beginning with his participation in a gang rape when he was a fifteen year old schoolboy in Australia and, as a consequence, he was given electro-shock therapy to curb his sex drive. Julie Malear, "Chris Wilder's Sadistic Sex-Slaying Spree!," in Rose G Mandelsberg (ed), *Torture Killers*, Pinnacle, New York, 1991: 33, 39.

61   Paradoxically Fran Altman, an FBI profiler, also suggests that it is because Tina had previously been raped (aged thirteen) and did not respond to the ordeal in the same way as Wilder's other victims, who came from 'normal' backgrounds, that he let her live. Her theory led her to believe that Wilder viewed Tina as the one woman who would not reject him.

62   Fox and Levin, *Overkill*: 8–9.

63   Interview with Robert Keppel by the author, August 26, 1998.

64   Gates and Shah, *Chief*: 172–173.

65   Phillip Carlo, *The Night Stalker*, Pinnacle Books, New York, 1996: 172.

66   John Wayne Gacy, *More Letters To Mr Gacy: Selected Correspondence of John Wayne Gacy*, MYCO Associates, Baton Rouge, Louisiana, 1992: np.

67   Letter from John Wayne Gacy to Steve Saunders of WGN-TV Chicago dated April 14, 1992, in ibid: np.

68   Dennehy quoted in Peter Johnson "Pot/Kettle," *USA Today* (January 22, 1992): 3D.

69   Letter from John Wayne Gacy to Fox Broadcasting dated 17 June 1991, in Gacy, *More Letters To Mr Gacy*: np.

70   Ibid, np. Maiken felt Sheriff's Policeman Greg Bedoe had played an important role, but his character was completely omitted from the film.

71   Letter from Mike Harvey to John Wayne Gacy dated April 15, 1992, in ibid: np.

72   Letter from John Wayne Gacy to Mike Harvey dated May 21, 1992, in ibid: np.

73   Friedkin quoted in Mark Kermode, "Friedkin vs. Friedkin: Rampage Revisited," *Video Watchdog* (September/October 1992): 37.

74   Friedkin quoted in Thomas D Clagett, *William Friedkin: Films of Aberration and Obsession*, McFarland and Co. Inc, Jefferson, North Carolina, 1990: 248, 249.

75   Friedkin quoted in ibid: 248. Friedkin witnessed the execution of Vincent Ciucci, Paul Crump's cellmate, at the request of the condemned, but even the impact of that experience faded with time.

76   Jane Maslin, "Random Murder Spree In A Friedkin Thriller," *New York Times* (October 30, 1992): C27.

77   Biehn quoted in Kermode, "Friedkin vs. Friedkin," *Video Watchdog* (September/October 1992): 37.

78   Friedkin quoted in Clagett, *William Friedkin*: 248.

79   Markman and Bosco, *Alone With The Devil*: 273, 272.

80   Friedkin quoted in Kermode, "Friedkin vs. Friedkin," *Video Watchdog* (September/October 1992): 42.

81   Markman and Bosco, *Alone With The Devil*: 274.

82   Clagett, *William Friedkin*: 253.

83   Kermode, "Friedkin vs. Friedkin," *Video Watchdog* (September–October 1992): 42.

84   Janet Maslin, "Random Murder Spree In A Friedkin Thriller," *New York Times* (October 30, 1992): C27.

85   O'Connor, "With a Nip and a Tuck TV Imitates Life," *New York Times* (November 17, 1992): C15.

86   Peter Travers, "Serial Mom," *Rolling Stone* (May 5, 1994): 100–102.

87   Alison Jones, "George Sluizer: He's Got Time For Crime Time," *Crime Time* (No.6, 1996): 21.

88   Robin Andersen, "'Reality' TV and Criminal Injustice," *The Humanist* (September/October 1994): 8.

89   Herwitz quoted in Steven Weinstein, "No Place To Hide," *LA Times* (April 13, 1988): D12.

90   Steve Erlanger, "Criminal Pursuit, From An Armchair," *New York Times* (February 7, 1988): B33.

91   Jones, "George Sluizer: He's Got Time For Crime Time," *Crime Time* (No.6, 1996): 21. 'Infomercial' is technical jargon for 'information-commercial.'

92   Walsh quoted in Weinstein, "No Place To Hide," *LA Times* (April 13, 1988): D12.

93   Ressler and Schachtman, *Whoever Fights Monsters*: 288.

94   Prial, "Freeze! You're On TV," *New York Times Magazine* (September 25, 1988): 56.

95   Aljean Harmetz, "Fugitives Drawing Viewers," *New York Times* (April 20, 1988): C22.

Notes

96 Walsh quoted in Weinstein, "No Place To Hide," *LA Times* (April 13, 1988): D12.

97 Breslin, *America's Most Wanted*: 12.

98 Revell quoted in ibid: 15.

99 Thompson quoted in Weinstein, "No Place To Hide," *LA Times* (April 13, 1988): D12.

100 Erlanger, "Criminal Pursuit, From An Armchair," *New York Times* (February 7, 1988): B33.

101 Carter quoted in "FBI Gives Television Programs Exclusives On New Fugitives," *New York Times* (September 15, 1991): A25.

102 Breslin, *America's Most Wanted*: 15.

103 Ibid: 95–96, 115.

104 Kessler, *The FBI*: 495.

105 Cavender and Bon-Mauphin, "Fear and Loathing on Reality Television," *Sociological Inquiry* (v63, No3, 1993): 306.

106 Breslin, *America's Most Wanted*: 85. Walsh served for three years, alongside people like the true crime writer Ann Rule, as one of five civilian advisors to VICAP. He testified before congressional committees seventeen times and before law makers in forty-seven states. In the course of his crusade he was awarded various accolades adding to his status, among them, 'Man of the Year 1982' from the National District Attorney's Association, 'Outstanding Citizen' award in 1984 from the Association of Federal Investigators, and his appointment as 'Presidential Advisor on Child Advocacy.'

107 Cavender and Bon-Mauphin, "Fear and Loathing on Reality Television," *Sociological Inquiry* (v.63, No.3, 1993): 306–08.

108 Walsh quoted in Breslin, *America's Most Wanted*: 340.

109 Cavender and Bon-Mauphin, "Fear and Loathing on Reality Television," *Sociological Inquiry* (v.63, No.3, 1993): 311.

110 Breslin, *America's Most Wanted*: 174, 180–181.

111 Lichter, Lichter and Rothman, *Prime Time*: 5.

112 Breslin, *America's Most Wanted*: 298.

113 Thomas B Rosensteil, "Viewers Found To Confuse TV Entertainment With News," *LA Times* (August 17, 1989): A17.

114 Turley quoted in Kerekes and Slater, *Killing For Culture*: 280.

115 Powers quoted in Breslin, *America's Most Wanted*: 298.

116 Powers, *The Beast, The Eunuch, and the Glass-Eyed Child*: 90.

117 Breslin, *America's Most Wanted*: 299.

118 Ibid: 300.

119 Andersen, "'Reality' TV and Criminal Injustice," *The Humanist* (September/October 1994): 8, 12.

120 Breslin, *America's Most Wanted*: 292.

121 Walsh quoted in Lawrie Mifflin, "Officials Try To Save TV Crime Show," *New York Times* (September 7, 1996): A8.

122 John Walsh and Susan Schindehette, *Tears of Rage*, Pocket Books, New York, 1997: 272.

123 Constantine quoted in Mifflin, "Officials Try To Save TV Crime Show," *New York Times* (September 7, 1996): A8.

124 Ibid: A8.

125 Walsh and Schindehette, *Tears of Rage*: 274.

126 Ressler and Schactman, *Whoever Fights Monsters*: 246.

127 Letter from Pet Simmons to John Wayne Gacy dated February 14, 1988, in Gacy, *More Letters To Mr. Gacy*: np.

128 Ibid: 77.

129 Poppy Z Brite, "The Poetry of Violence," in Karl French (ed), *Screen Violence*, Bloomsbury Publishing, London, 1996: 64. Brite, author of several violent novels, felt that asking Dahmer ques-

tions such as 'What did it taste like?', among others, would have been more revealing.

130 Bennett quoted in Pietrasik, "Go Ricki, Go!," *Guardian* (November 7, 1997): Friday Review 2.

131 Keith Soothill, "The Serial Killer Industry," *Journal of Forensic Psychiatry* (v.4 No2, 1993): 347.

132 Sandra Skowron, "Videotape of Illinois Serial Killer Puts Prison on the Hot Seat," *Oregonian* (May 13, 1996): A1.

8. Not So Much *Apocalypse Now*, as Apocalypse From Now On
Law & Order in the 1990s

1 George Bush quoted in Michael Rogin, "'Make My Day!' Spectacle as Amnesia in Imperial Politics," *Representations* (Winter 1990): 120.

2 Anderson, *Crime and the Politics of Hysteria*: 3. Horton was initially convicted for the murder of Joey Fournier. False stories circulated during the Bush campaign alleging that the victim had been sexually mutilated loosely identifying Horton with the characteristics usually associated with serial sex killers of the 1970s and eighties.

3 Ibid: 24–25, 15, 5–6, 9.

4 Ibid: 211–212, 221, 223. Tomlinson was a former director of the right-wing conservative Voice of America. Bidinotto's wife was a social acquaintance of Republican Andrew Card who unsuccessfully ran for the Massachusetts legislature. When asked about the article Card denied that Bidinotto had written at the request of the Bush campaign organizers; instead, he described Bidinotto as "a fellow who has political instinct."

5 Horton quoted in ibid: 5, 232–233. The

advert was broadcast on cable TV channels for four weeks in September and early October 1988. Numerous consultants and political action groups ran parallel with the official Bush campaign, and while it was obvious that their efforts were intended to benefit Bush they remained financially independent. Democrats alleged that the commercial, created and financed by the National Security Political Action Committee, was produced in collusion with the Bush campaign and violated public financing laws.

6 Ibid: 231.

7 Ibid: 236–37. Bush campaign officials denied that they had been responsible for the letter but journalists and commentators found the denials, in light of the tight control kept by campaign organizers, difficult to believe.

8 Bush quoted in ibid: 215.

9 Flyer quoted in ibid: 215.

10 "Serial Killer Sues Bush For Campaign Libel," *Detroit Free Press* (March 11, 1989) reprinted in Gacy, *More Letters To Mr Gacy*: np. The Republican

Notes

National Committee, Chicago Tribune, Illinois Republican State Central Committee and Robert Gouty and Co (a Chicago public relations firm) were also cited in the suit filed by Gacy. See also Letter to Ed of Bremerton, Washington, from John Wayne Gacy dated October 31, 1988, in Gacy, *More Letters To Mr Gacy*: np.

11   Anderson, *Crime and the Politics of Hysteria*: 240.

12   Barry Krisberg, "Distorted By Fear: The Make Believe War On Crime," *Social Justice* (v.21 No.3): 38.

13   Stuart A Scheingold et al, "Sexual Violence, Victim Advocacy, and Republican Criminology: Washington State's Community Protection Act," *Law and Society Review* (v.28 No.4, 1994): 743, 760.

14   Ibid: 748, 730–731, 740.

15   "Sex Offender Registration: A New Kind of Scarlet Letter," *ACLU-Massachusetts Newsletter* (April 1997): np. One released offender, Joseph Gallardo was convicted of having uncoerced oral sex with his girlfriend's ten year old daughter, but it was the Washington state attorney general's office which used its discretion and chose to prosecute the case after a significant period of time had elapsed. While in prison Gallardo chose not to participate in a therapy program because it would not have been completed until some time after his release date. He was not eligible to be detained by the CPA but his name was distributed to local residents identifying him as a 'sex predator' and warning that he had moved into the area. Posters put up in his community described him as "an extremely dangerous untreated sex offender with a very high probability of reoffense," an exaggeration of his crime encouraging public fear.

In response cars cruised by his house shouting abuse and his home was burned down. Gallardo moved to New Mexico but the media informed the public there and he was forced to move again. Andriette, "New Predatory Sex Laws," *The Guide* (Seattle) (May 1995): 17; "Burn Thy Neighbor," *Time* (July 26, 1993): 58; "What Fresh Start?," *Economist* (July 24–30, 1993): 26. Another offender lost two jobs, was evicted from apartments twice and was forced to live in his car. Rendered "essentially homeless and unemployed" he was finally rearrested for failing to register his third move of location. Scheingold et al, "Sexual Violence, Victim Advocacy, and Republican Criminology," *Law and Society Review* (v.28 No.4, 1994): 757. An attempt on convicted sex-offender Michael Groff's life in New Jersey was widely publicized. The attack was linked to 'Megan's Law,' the New Jersey sex-offender law, and his two attackers were identified as Kenneth Kerkes, a corrections officer, and his father, but their vigilantism was reckless and risked injuring bystanders. John J O'Reilly, a New Jersey prosecutor, was angered by the attack on Groff saying "we're not going to tolerate this kind of vigilantism. 'Megan's Law' was never intended to permit or condone harassment or intimidation of individuals who have paid their debt to society." Jon Nordheimer, "Vigilante Attack in New Jersey is Linked to Sex-Offenders Law," *New York Times* (January 11, 1995): A1, B5.

16   Reinstein quoted in "Sex Offender Registration: A New Kind of Scarlet Letter," *ACLU-Massachusetts Newsletter* (April 1997): np. See also Todd S. Purdum, "Registry Laws Tar Sex-Crime Convicts Broad Brush," *New York Times* (July 1,

1997): A1, 19.

17 Shilling quoted in Vanessa Ho, "Sex offenders often have no choice but to cluster in neighborhoods," *Seattle Post-Intelligencer* (February 5, 1998): np.

18 Baker quoted in ibid.

19 Berman, *America's Right Turn*: 145.

20 Anderson, *Crime and the Politics of Hysteria*: 251–252. Shawcross confessed to committing eleven murders in twenty-one months, and nine of the victims were prostitutes. Predictably the charges against him were only for second-degree murder and it was noted that the victims' lifestyles made them easy targets for a serial killer. "Rochester Jury Convicts Parolee In Serial Killings," *New York Times* (December 14, 1990): B2. A subsequent string of drug addict and prostitute murders between 1989 and 1992 raised public fears in Rochester that another serial killer was active in the area. The killings came in the midst of a police crackdown on prostitution and newspaper reports fuelled public concern for moral decay. "Series of Rochester Killings Brings up Fearful Memories," *New York Times* (November 15, 1992): A52.

21 Ibid: 253.

22 Berman, *America's Right Turn*: 159.

23 *The Progressive* quoted in Solomon, *False Hope*: 113.

24 Peter Applebone, "Arkansas Execution Raises Questions On Governor's Politics," *New York Times* (January 25, 1992): A8.

25 Anderson, *Crime and the Politics of Hysteria*: 253. In his first term as governor in 1978–82 Clinton commuted seventy sentences, but was attacked for being soft on crime. In response to the accusations between 1983 and 1992 he only commuted seven executions.

26 Mark Johnson, "Wild Thing," *The George* (August 1997): 88.

27 Anderson, *Crime and the Politics of Hysteria*: 255–256.

28 Rosenzweig quoted in Applebone, "Arkansas Execution Raises Questions On Governor's Politics," *New York Times* (January 25, 1992): A8.

29 Anderson, *Crime and the Politics of Hysteria*: 255–256. Rector's ignorance of his circumstances, right up to his execution, was exemplified during his last meal when he kept his dessert to eat before going to bed, in keeping with his usual routine. He did not understand that he was to be executed and would not be back for his pecan pie.

30 Barlow et al, "Mobilizing Support For Social Control in a Declining Economy," *Crime and Delinquency* (April 1995): 201.

31 Andriette, "New Predatory Sex Laws," *The Guide* (Seattle) (May 1995): 17. See also Anderson, *Crime and the Politics of Hysteria*: 16.

32 Krisberg, "Distorted By Fear," *Social Justice* (v.21 No.3): 38–39.

33 Howard Kurtz, "The Campaign Weapon of Choice," *Washington Post National Weekly Edition* (September 19–25, 1994): 12.

34 Andriette, "New Predatory Sex Laws," *The Guide* [Seattle] (May 1995): 18.

35 Krisberg, "Distorted By Fear," *Social Justice* (v.21 No.3): 46.

36 Michael Vitiello, "Three Strikes: Can We Return To Rationality?," *Journal of Criminal Law and Criminology* (Winter 1998): 396–397, 400–401, 402.

37 Vitiello, "Three Strikes," *Journal of Criminal Law and Criminology* (Winter 1998): 399, 396.

38 Benekos and Merlo, "Three Strikes and You're Out!," *Federal Probation* (March 1995): 7.

Notes

39 "Serial Killers And Child Abductions," (September 14, 1995): 80.

40 Vitiello, "Three Strikes," *Journal of Criminal Law and Criminology* (Winter 1998): 412.

41 Anderson, *Crime and the Politics of Hysteria*: 23.

42 Daniel M Weintraub, "Lone Justice," *LA Times* (February 14, 1995): E1.

43 Vitiello, "Three Strikes," *Journal of Criminal Law and Criminology* (Winter 1998): 459, 410.

44 Benekos and Merlo, "Three Strikes and You're Out!," *Federal Probation* (March 1995): 3.

45 Krisberg, "Distorted By Fear," *Social Justice* (v.21 No.3): 45–46. In 1995 Glen Rogers, the Cross Country Killer, was a suspect in a number of murders in Louisiana, Mississippi, Ohio, Florida and California, and he topped the FBI's Ten Most Wanted List. Before the series of murders began Rogers was arrested three times in California, between June and November 1995, for serious violent assaults but served less than fifty days in jail because of overcrowding. Emulating Henry Lee Lucas, Rogers confessed to many crimes, attracting considerable media attention before recanting and professing his innocence. "Overcrowding Freed Suspected Serial Killer in California," *NRA CrimeStrike Bulletin* (November 21, 1995): np; "Drifter Asserts He's Innocent in Killings of 5 People," *New York Times* (November 19, 1995): A38.

46 Donziger (ed), *The Real War On Crime*: 75–76.

47 "A Vision For the Future" quoted in Sciarinno, "Prisoners = Profit," *Z* (October 1993): 16. By 1993 the FPI was a half-billion dollar a year industry manufacturing electronic cables for NASA and office furniture for the Social Security Administration.

48 Eddy, "True Defective Stories," *Sunday Times Magazine* (August 10, 1997): 33.

49 Ibid.

50 Freeh, "Where the FBI Stands Today," *Vital Speeches of the Day* (January 15, 1994): 194.

51 For example "Thy Kingdom Come," *Time* (March 15, 1993): 43–47; Simon Tisdall, "Madmen, Martyrs and Crazy Cults," *Guardian* (March 6–7, 1993): 23.

52 Potock quoted in Elaine Lafferty, "Waco time bomb still ticking," *Irish Times* (September 4, 1999): 14.

53 Ibid: 196.

54 Julie R. Linkins, "FBI Academy: 25 Years of Law Enforcement Leadership," *FBI Law Enforcement Bulletin* (May 1997): 4.

55 Eddy, "True Defective Stories," *Sunday Times Magazine* (August 10, 1997): 33, 38.

56 "Serial Killers And Child Abductions," (September 14, 1995): 23, 1, 3, 2.

57 Ibid: 9, 4, 33.

58 Hagmaier quoted in ibid: 46. Ironically, in 1998 Henry Lee Lucas, who helped to establish the stereotype of the serial sex killer as a traveling killer, had his only death penalty conviction questioned by the Texas Board of Pardons and Paroles. Governor George Bush Jr. publicly requested the review of the Lucas case and in June they recommended that he should not be executed for the Orange Socks murder (of an unidentified female hitchhiker in Texas) because the evidence suggested that he *did not* commit the crime. It was the first time since 1976 that the Board recommended commutation without being prompted by a court decision, but it did not recommend the conviction should be overturned. Victor Rodriguez,

chairman of the Board, commented "I felt that he had raised enough questions. When you're deciding life and death, enough questions is enough." State attorney general Jim Mattox also concluded that there was compelling evidence that Lucas was not guilty. Carol Marie Cropper, "Commute Death Sentence of Multiple Killer, Texas Panel Says," New York Times (June 26, 1998): A10. Ironically, Lucas died in Prison of a heart attack in 2001.

59 McCollum quoted in "Serial Killers And Child Abductions," (September 14, 1995): 13, 14.

60 Heineman quoted in ibid: 22. While the 'expertise' of the FBI in identifying serial sex killers is dubious so is their speed efficiency when assisting other police agencies. An investigation by police in the Central American state of Belize into the murders of seven girls was hindered by FBI delays in carrying out key forensic DNA tests. As a consequence suspects arrested were released due to lack of evidence and the Belize authorities considered approaching Scotland Yard for assistance. Sandra Jordan, "Belize Baffled By Serial Killings," The Observer (October 24, 1999): 28.

61 Ed Vulliamy and Peter Marshall, "FBI in Tainted Evidence Scandal," Observer (February 16, 1997): 10.

62 David Burnham, "The FBI: A Special Report" in The Nation on-line [w] www.thenation.com/issue/970811/ 0811burn.html [downloaded April 6, 1998]

63 Ibid.

64 Benekos and Merlo, "Three Strikes and You're Out!," Federal Probation (March 1995): 8.

65 Keith Geiger, "Upgrading School Buildings," Washington Post National Weekly Edition (September 26–October 2, 1994): 22.

66 Krisberg, "Distorted By Fear," Social Justice (v.21 No.3): 45.

Index

Index

Index

Index

Index

Index

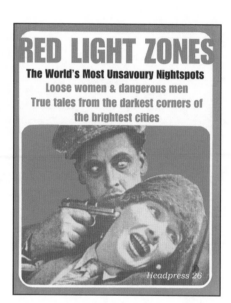

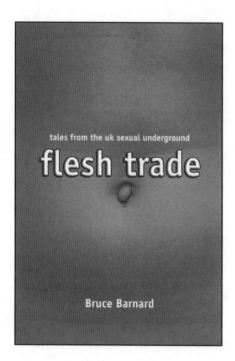

Coming Soon

BAD MAGS

The strangest, sleaziest, and most unusual periodicals ever published!

by Tom Brinkmann

The flip side of popular culture as seen through magazines and tabloids.

Illuminating the darker recesses of "pop lit," *Bad Mags* is packed with in depth information on hundreds of amazing publications and the equally amazing people and publishing houses behind them.

This eye-popping array of way-out titles reflects the mood and fast-changing times of several generations of readers, incorporating subject matter as diverse as outlaw bikers, Satanism, punk rock, Charles Manson, mobs and gangs, sexploitation movies, violence, and drugs.

ISBN **1-900486-423** Pbk **576pp**
Illustrated (with eight
pages of colour)
Price **UK £17.99/US $24.95**

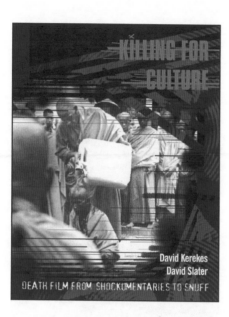

Coming Soon

CHELSEA HOTEL MANHATTAN

by Joe Ambrose

Extreme living in New York's Chelsea Hotel, from the Beats through Punk, and on into the present day.

Joe Ambrose stayed at the Chelsea Hotel, home to many famous authors, artists and outlaws down the years. Andy Warhol shot *Chelsea Girls* there and welsh poet Dylan Thomas died there, having reputedly inspired the young Zimmerman to change his name to Bob Dylan.

This the first factual book on the building and features conversations with William Burroughs, Paul Bowles, Gerard Malanga, Victor Bockris and others.

Every room at the Chelsea tells its own story—not unlike The Overlook in Stephen King's *The Shining*. Sid Vicious met his death in one room, an episode recounted in detail by Rockets Redglare.

ISBN **1-900486-60-1** Pbk **160pp**
Illustrated
Price **UK£10.99/US $19.95**